General Editors:

HOW SCHOOLS IMPROVE

OTHER TITLES IN THE SCHOOL DEVELOPMENT SERIES

R. Bollington, D. Hopkins and M. West:
An Introduction to Teacher Appraisal

P. Dalin:
Changing the School Culture

M. Fullan:
The New Meaning of Educational Change

D. Hargreaves and D. Hopkins:
The Empowered School

D. Hopkins, M. Ainscow and M. West:
School Improvement in an Era of Change

K. S. Louis and M. B. Miles:
Improving the Urban High School

J. Murphy:
Restructuring Education

D. Reynolds and P. Cuttance:
School Effectiveness

P. Ribbins and E. Whale:
Improving Education

F. Scheerens:
Effective Schooling

FORTHCOMING TITLES

J. Chapman, V. Wilkinson and D. Aspin:
Quality Schooling

C. Teddlie and S. Stringfield:
Schools Make a Difference

Dr. Desmond Pearce.

HOW SCHOOLS IMPROVE
An International Report

Per Dalin
with
Tekle Ayono,
Anbesu Biazen,
Birhanu Dibaba,
Mumtaz Jahan,
Matthew B. Miles
and
Carlos Rojas

CASSELL

Cassell
Villiers House   387 Park Avenue South
41/47 Strand   New York
London WC2N 5JE   NY 10016-8810

© IMTEC 1994

All rights reserved. No part of this publication may be reproduced or transmitted in any form or by any means, electronic or mechanical including photocopying, recording or any information storage or retrieval system without prior permission in writing from the publishers.

First published 1994

British Library Cataloguing-in-Publication Data
A catalogue record for this book is available from the British Library.

ISBN 0-304-32744-1 (hardback)
    0-304-32736-0 (paperback)

Typeset by Colset Pte Ltd, Singapore
Printed and bound in Great Britain by Redwood Books, Trowbridge, Wiltshire

Contents

Preface	vii
How Schools Improve: Executive Summary	ix
Part 1 Introduction	1
1 Learning from Success	3
2 Experiences from Field Work in Typically Successful Schools	14
Part 2 The Country Reports	41
3 The Escuela Nueva School Programme in Colombia	43
4 The Primary Education Reform Programme in Ethiopia	66
5 Universal Primary Education in Bangladesh	120
Part 3 International Analysis and Recommendations	153
6 The Success Seen Centrally	155
7 The Outcomes of Educational Reform - Seen Locally	181
8 Explaining Implementation, Impact and Institutionalization	199
9 Findings	223
10 Implications	254
Appendix 1: Research Questions	304
Appendix 2: Local-level Study	310
Appendix 3: Country-level Factors Accounting for Success of the Programme	320

Appendix 4: Worktables	322
Appendix 5: Summary of Factors Accounting for Success of Local Implementation	346
Appendix 6: Operational Definitions	347
Bibliography	364
Index	367

Preface

The HSI project is the combined work of 14 researchers and a number of technical staff in Bangladesh, Colombia and Ethiopia, five international advisors and coaches, three administrative staff in IMTEC and, not least, key persons in both the World Bank and the Norwegian Government who helped to design and supervise the programme and pay the costs.

The idea of conducting such a complex study at 31 different sites in three developing countries was quite a challenge! All the agencies involved: Bangladesh Bureau of Educational Information and Statistics (BANBEIS), Bangladesh; Instituto SER de Investigación, Colombia; Institute for Curriculum Development and Research, Ethiopia; and IMTEC have done a terrific job in getting the work done. It has been a major learning process for everyone involved; thanks go to all the institutions and project leaders for their commitment.

The researchers involved — Anowar-Ul-Aziz, Delwar Hossain, Abdul Jabbar, Mumtaz Jahan and Siddiqur Rahman in Bangladesh; Blanca Lilia Caro, Patricia Rodríguez and Carlos Rojas in Colombia; and Tekle Ayono, Abebe Bekele, Anbesu Biazen, Birhanu Dibaba, Melesse Delelegne and Tassew Zewdie in Ethiopia — have conducted a very complex, qualitative study, and at the same time, have gone through a comprehensive coaching and learning process. They have, at times, worked in difficult conditions, and I am both thankful for and impressed by their motivation and performance. The entire study rested on the care, energy and skill they brought to their work. These three research teams are a valuable resource for governments, donors and universities.

The coaches who worked with me, Ray Chesterfield (Colombia), Styrbjörn Gustafsson and Hallvard Kåre Kuløy (Bangladesh), made it possible to link the international intentions with national and local realities. Our many telefaxes, telephone conversations and meetings made my job much easier. The study was coordinated from IMTEC's side by Hallvard Kåre Kuløy, who helped us to keep order in the very complex files and to administer us as a group through the last four years. Iwo Gajda very ably handled the complex graphic lay-out tasks, and our two excellent colleagues Kari Strøm and Inger Johanne Lange typed and checked hundreds of details. This is probably the most complicated writing job anyone in IMTEC has undertaken in its 20 years of existence, with data submitted by a large number of individuals in forms ranging from handwriting to the most advanced computer lay-outs.

Adriaan Verspoor of the World Bank who initiated the project, and whose report, *Pathways to Educational Change*, is the very basis for this study, has played his usual effective managerial role. He has shown a key interest in the study, always been supportive and fair, and has not forgotten that he is also monitoring our work. He knows that pressure and support go together!

Michael Huberman and Matthew B. Miles, members of the international panel of experts, both made outstanding contributions to the design of the study and the development of the instrumentation. Michael helped with redesign and redevelopment of the study, and played a key role in the redesign meeting in Rome. Matthew worked out the operational definitions and the displays for the study. Matthew also played a unique and key role as my expert advisor and coach during the many months of preparation of this report. He is a critical advisor who discovers and raises the fundamental issues. He is also a colleague and friend who knows when support is needed.

Per Dalin, Oslo, March 1992

How Schools Improve:
Executive Summary

BACKGROUND

Educational reform is a long and complex process involving thousands of individuals at all levels of the system. Research on national reform efforts in the industrialized world shows that the implementation and institutionalization of major reforms often takes as long as 20 years, and that the reform process itself is a critical determinant of outcomes. We have learned a lot about the management of educational change in the western hemisphere over the past 20 to 30 years by studying comprehensive national change programmes. These studies have become guides to policy planning and implementation. While such studies have been rather common in the Western hemisphere, they have been rare in lesser developed countries.

Governments in lesser developed countries, and donor organizations, with an agenda of supporting educational change programme in these countries, have little research to guide their practice. Therefore in the period 1986 to 1989, the World Bank initiated a review of their own experiences from bank lending to education, with the intention of learning more about the management of educational change, relevant to lesser developed countries (Verspoor, 1989). The World Bank study was able to document a number of key variables in policy implementation and provided a number of recommendations to governments and donors. At the same time, the World Bank recommended that more in-depth, field-based studies be conducted to test the findings, and to explore in depth some of the dilemmas in educational change.

THE 'HOW SCHOOLS IMPROVE' STUDY

The main purpose of the HSI study was to describe and analyse the change process at the national and local level in three different national educational reform efforts. Unlike other studies that have documented failures in reaching desired reform goals, the HSI study was set up to learn from success, to provide non-ambiguous advice for policy and practice. The desk review of World Bank study (Verspoor, 1989) identified some 21 countries with 'successful educational reform efforts' and, based on the decision that primary school reforms should be studied, the following countries and projects were selected:

- **Colombia** with the innovative 'Escuela Nueva' programme, initiated locally based on a UNESCO concept, and gradually developed into a national program for rural primary schools over the past 15 to 20 years; a project also partly financed by external donors (including the World Bank).
- **Ethiopia** with a major, nationwide, comprehensive primary education reform under way since 1974, initiated, planned and implemented by the government with external donor support (including the World Bank).
- **Bangladesh** with a large, nationwide 'Universal Primary Education' project,

initiated, planned and implemented by the government, with large scale assistance from IDA. The project has been implemented over a 10- to 15-year period.

The sampling criteria were that the schools should be in rural areas, in communities with average or less than average resources, with a better than average enrolment rate (boys and girls), and located in districts that had given attention to the reform.

The research questions

The study was partly set up to confirm some of the main findings from the World Bank desk study. The main part of the study, however, was exploratory, aiming to discover some of the key factors contributing to successful implementation and institutionalization of educational changes. The main research questions were:

1. What are the outcomes of successful strategies for the implementation of educational change, seen in terms of quality of implementation, institutionalization and student outcomes, as well as in terms of unexpected outcomes?
2. What do successful strategies look like, both at the macro (country) and micro (local school) level?
3. What determines successful strategies? Determinants may include administrative capacity development, teacher training and commitment-building efforts, among others.
4. How are successful strategies at the macro and micro levels linked, seen from the central and school levels?

The answer to these questions was expected to help planners and policy makers in the design of educational reform strategies. The study explored links between key factors in reform processes (e.g. in-service training) on the one hand, and outcomes of the reform on the other. The HSI study was able to demonstrate such relationships, and to learn more about the conditions under which successful outcomes are achieved. Thus the findings are not only valuable to the three countries studied, formulating strategies for school improvements, but they also provide insights into more generic issues in educational reform.

The HSI methodology

The HSI project was a qualitative research project, designed by an international research panel, redesigned by the panel members and representatives of the national HSI Research teams, and implemented by the same teams. The IMTEC organization in Oslo, Norway, has been the executive agency. The Norwegian Ministry for Development Cooperation has financed the study, and the World Bank has been responsible for overall coordination and supervision. The project included a detailed study of 31 rural primary schools in Colombia, Ethiopia and Bangladesh, placed in their regional and national context. The field work, the case descriptions and analyses, and the three national reports were completed by the 14 national HSI researchers. More than 1,000 hours of interviews were conducted in the field. The methodology used in the HSI study, based on earlier work by Matthew B. Miles and A. Michael Huberman, included a detailed coding of field notes, presentation and analysis of findings in structured 'data displays', and a comparison of schools based on a rating of key variables studied.

The sample schools in each country have been compared in terms of their outcomes, defined as:

- degree of implementation of key aspects of the reform;
- degree of impact on students, teachers and the school as an organization;
  degree of institutionalization of the reform, or its 'routinization' of practices.

On the basis of this comparison (completed in a Cross-Site Analysis Matrix), the schools were sorted into three categories: the excellent schools, the very good schools and the good schools. As the process of reform was analysed in each of the 31 schools, it was possible to compare the characteristics of the reform process in the three categories of school, and thereby find which factors discriminate among the three groups of schools. This comparative analysis is the basis for the findings in this study.

What are the outcomes of educational reforms?

The three reforms studied demonstrate clear success in terms of outcomes at different levels in our sample schools.

Implementation The major components of the reforms have been implemented and the classrooms have changed. The very nature of the teaching–learning process has been changed in the Colombian schools, a new curriculum and new methods are used in the Ethiopian schools, and new classrooms and free textbooks have changed the nature of daily instruction in Bangladesh.

Student impact Student attitudes and behaviour have been positively influenced in all three systems. More effective students, such as improved student leadership in Colombia; more regular attendance in Ethiopia; and participation in co-curricular activities are examples of a more active and involved student. The best schools show improved achievement scores, and the enrolment rate is increasing in Ethiopia and Bangladesh.

Teacher impact Teacher motivation shows high to medium impact and discriminates the excellent and very good schools. Teacher classroom behaviour shows high to medium impact in all three countries.

School outcomes All three systems have, to a varied degree, benefitted from improvements of the physical facilities. The relationship between the school and the community shows high to medium impact.

Institutionalization The reforms have been practised for many years in our sample of schools, and have been well 'routinized'.

A preview of the main findings

The findings may be summarized as the essential ingredients of successful educational reform:

1. A national operational commitment to quality improvement that is well planned — and evolving — as experiences from the field provide learning opportunities for regional and central reform planners. A national effort that

is made concrete through systematic management and a professional support structure, and an effort that is sustained over at least ten years.

2. A strong local capacity with a strong emphasis on school and classroom practice. This means local empowerment, room to manage local implementation, latitude for adapting the programme to be maximally effective locally, assistance that enables teacher mastery to develop, and the encouragement to develop local materials.

3. A coherent linkage system between central, district and local school levels via information, assistance, pressure and rewards. The various means of communication in the system must reflect engagement and commitment between levels, not bureaucratic, rule-driven control.

The HSI study demonstrates that reform strategies matter, and that simplistic and 'quick fix' solutions do not work. It also demonstrates that national reform programmes may succeed with very different starting points, i.e. with a local innovation (Colombia), with a national political initiative (Ethiopia) or with an external donor-driven, large-scale, modestly innovative programme (Bangladesh). It is not a question of 'bottom up' versus 'top down', it is a question of meeting the three principles of reform stated above — in whatever mix that works in a given national context.

What 'central factors' make a difference?

The HSI study confirms some of the findings of the World Bank study as far as 'central factors' are concerned:

1. Stable and long term political support is essential for primary education reform to succeed.

2. Successful change strategies strengthen the administrative capacity at both the centre and the periphery of the system. This includes the strengthening of policy and planning institutions, the development of a competent cadre of national staff, clear structural support for coordination, an adequate information and monitoring system, and adequate resources.

3. High outcomes are achieved by programmes adopted on the basis of internally, as well as externally, driven policies. Strong internal forces for reform were apparent in all three countries. Externally, major donors played an active role in all phases of the reform effort.

4. Reforms depend on a permanent and locally available in-service teacher training system and an effective system of supervision and support. All three systems have a combination of training and supervision locally available as a regular part of the school work. The training and supervision system is seen as having 'high impact' in all three countries.

5. Successful reform efforts encourage teacher motivation and commitment. More empowerment through delegation, combined with staff development and support, produces higher commitment among teachers.

6. Commitment is built and maintained through local participation (e.g. parents), external agency support and demonstrated success. Community participation is seen as a high impact factor in both Ethiopia and Colombia. It is a weak factor in

Bangladesh. Agency support has been crucial in all three countries (see above), and demonstrated success has been a particularly important factor in Colombia (see below).

What factors work at the school level?

Some of the factors mentioned above are clearly linked to what happens in the schools. If the factors that are experienced by teachers and local administrators are examined more closely, we find the following:

1. Assistance, usually defined as in-service teacher training, is a key determinant for teacher mastery, and teacher mastery is a key variable for the understanding of improved classroom practice in all three countries. Assistance works best when it is concrete, locally available, regular and on-going, linked to practice, provides opportunities to practice new behaviour and is supported by a climate of cooperation.

2. Supervision is another key element in a successful change strategy, a function usually shared between the headmaster and local inspectors. When it is seen as help, it is timely and relevant, related to practice and readily available, and practised in an atmosphere of trust.

3. 'Pressure', defined as 'pedagogical requirements', or pressure to 'do it right' in Colombia; and as 'control' and pressure to perform in Bangladesh and Ethiopia, is seen as a key factor in Ethiopia and Bangladesh and to some extent also in Colombia.

4. Decentralization and delegation is seen as a key factor. It leads to empowerment and commitment to the reform, to responsive local adaptations and, in some cases, to shared decision-making. In Colombia, empowerment means that the 'headmaster and the teachers decide all important things'. In Ethiopia empowerment means that the headmaster, teachers and parents share power and take responsibility. Empowerment is felt only to a marginal degree in Bangladesh.

5. Teaching-learning materials contribute to teacher mastery and improved classroom practice in all three countries. The more teachers are involved in local development of materials, the more this leads to teacher mastery.

6. Success experience is a high impact factor in Colombia, and is related to the changes teachers and parents see in children. The Ethiopian schools experience success as related to the changes in the school as a whole, in particular in its ability to generate its own income, while success experiences in Bangladesh are associated with increased enrolment and improved achievement, and an increase in scholarships.

7. Community support is a high impact factor in Colombia and Ethiopia, and a discriminating factor in Bangladesh. In Colombia parents will support the school after having seen 'changes in kids'; in Ethiopia parents take a very active role in school management and provide donations to the school.

What makes for success?

What characterizes the excellent and the very good schools? This section summarizes what characterizes them in terms of the factors studied, as compared to the good schools:

- the in-service training process is well implemented, regular, relevant and practical;
- the school works actively on the adaptation of the curriculum and the production of local teaching-learning materials (except for Bangladesh);
- the needed resources (buildings, classrooms, etc.) are available;
- the headmaster is motivated, plays a more active, coordinative and supportive role, is an instructional leader, works closely with teachers, encourages teachers and shares responsibilities;
- there is a team spirit in the school, teachers cooperate, student attitude toward the reform is positive, and teachers help each other with instructional problems;
- supervision is regular, shared between the supervisor and the headmaster (though not in Colombia), and appears as a combination of pressure and support;
- the school experiences more success, more positive students, 'changes in kids' (Colombia), teacher cooperation, professional exchanges and extra resources (e.g. from the community);
- the school gets more support from the community; parents are more interested in the schooling of their children, the community gives material support and financial support (Ethiopia).

There are other country-specific factors that discriminate excellent and very good schools from good schools, including empowerment (Ethiopia), local adaptation of materials (Ethiopia), and pressure (Bangladesh).

The three change strategies

In this section the findings of how success is achieved are summarized (see Figures 8.1–8.3 in Chapter 8, pages 203, 212 and 219). How can the government, local authorities, schools and communities work together so that successful implementation and institutionalization are achieved?

There are some important common elements across all three countries:

1. Rural primary education has been a top political priority, sustained over many years. This is clearly expressed in Bangladesh and Ethiopia from the outset, it has become a policy over time in Colombia, and is presently an established national policy there.

2. The reforms have a base in a strong 'national team' of educational leaders with knowledge, skills and commitment to the cause. The team was originally an independent group in Colombia (the 'EN resource team'), and an official national team in both Ethiopia and Bangladesh. Strong team leadership was sustained over many years.

3. All three reforms aim at changing classroom practice, and therefore attempt to influence teachers, students and the school as an organization.

4. All three systems have tried to 'reach the teacher', to change his/her attitudes, behaviour and role. Teacher mastery is central to all three reform efforts.
5. Various forms of staff development, to include school-based in-service training, local adaptation of the curiculum and materials, pedagogical supervision, as well as national training efforts (e.g. Ethiopia), are a key strategy in all three systems.
6. Assistance is a key strategy in all three reforms. School-based assistance, or at least assistance as close to the school and the classroom as possible, is a common characteristic. Often 'assistance' means in-service training; however, it is also forms of supervision, consultancies, advice-giving and problem-solving. The closer the 'advice-giver' is to the school, the greater the impact.

The three reform strategies also differ considerably:

1. In terms of their degree of 'restructuring' the entire system (as opposed to taking the existing structure for granted and trying to change teacher and classroom practice directly):
   - The Ethiopian reform is the most comprehensive in terms of 'restructuring' the system, changing policies, national institutions, division of labour, roles and relationships, the curriculum and the organization of schooling. As a consequence, it also had a 'longer way' to go to reach the individual teacher and classroom.
   - The Colombian reform is the one with the shortest route from the reform idea to the classroom. It is a fairly straightforward 'package' that could positively influence the daily life of students in a relatively short period of time. At the same time the existing Colombian school system and its structure was left 'untouched'. It may have consequences for dissemination and institutionalization.
   - The Bangladesh reform is closer to the Ethiopian strategy than the Colombian strategy, but still different. It does take restructuring seriously, however, mainly in the area of management. In this area significant innovations are introduced that clearly have had a positive impact on rural primary schools. On the other hand, it gave less emphasis to areas like user involvement, community involvement, and the teaching-learning process was partly 'neglected'.
2. In terms of degree of decentralization, the systems are clearly different. The Colombian reform effort is basically a 'bottom-up' effort that gradually has been given national status and legitimacy. The Ethiopian reform is a centrally managed reform, that has delegated certain functions down the system, and gradually given power to various actors at the local level. The Bangladesh reform effort is clearly the most centralistic effort, and lacks much delegation to the school level, although it does have an aspect of decentralization to the regional supervisory Upazila level.
3. The use of management and systematic monitoring differs in the three systems. This is partly related to the degree of centralization, but it goes beyond this dimension of management. The Colombian system does not use management and monitoring through the hierarchy as an important element of the reform

strategy. It is much more based on collegial interaction and in-service training. The costs are that some schools are not achieving reform and the solutions may be ad hoc. The Ethiopian and the Bangladesh systems use management and monitoring systematically as a communication vehicle, as pressure, and as a feedback mechanism to ensure successful implementation. Also in these systems, though in-service training and collegial supervision are important, the central role of management, particularly through on-going monitoring, plays an important role.

4. Linkage that enables the user to 'connect' with the ideas, policies and norms of the innovation, is common to all three systems, though the 'communication link' differs:

- In Colombia the linkage is mainly the guide combined with training, more or less a self-instructional package that transmits the message. To some extent the external resource persons, through regular supervision and support, also help to 'connect'.

- In Ethiopia, there are many strong linkages. The strongest are probably the regular quarterly reports combined with supervision visits and in-service training. The annual education conference also serves as a 'pep-talk' mechanism and helps to transmit the latest ideas.

- In Bangladesh the 'link' is the AUEO (local supervisory officer). He/she is supported by the UEO and others, but clearly it is through the AUEO person that the messages are carried.

5. The development and use of materials is another key factor that differs in the way it is practised. In Bangladesh the materials are centrally produced, and the teacher is mainly seen as a consumer of this material. The consequences seem to be less commitment, less local adaptation and less enthusiasm. In both Ethiopia and Colombia the teacher is assumed to actively develop materials, locally produced. The *Teachers' guide* gives these possibilities in Colombia, while the School Pedagogical Centres (SPC) gives a similar opportunity in Ethiopia. The implication is that the teacher is seen as a producer, and this does seem to lead to higher commitment, success experiences, and an active role.

6. The roles of parents and the community differ considerably in the three systems. In Ethiopia parents and the community play an important formal role in rural schools, participating in the school management committee, contributing land, labour and cash. In Colombia parents are involved more as a consequence of the success they experience with the EN reform. Parent and community participation may be an official part of the reform in Bangladesh, but are weak in our sample schools. There is some evidence that where parents show an interest in their children's schooling it has positive impact on outcomes; however, the general impression is that 'all comes from above'. The Bangladesh reform is a centralized system that hasn't built enough local capacity, though where we find small signs of local commitment, adaptation, etc., it works.

WHAT HAVE WE LEARNED?

Before the HSI study and other ground-breaking studies many people assumed that there were certain 'obvious truths' about reform:

- reforms should be incremental and gradual rather than wide-ranging;
- tight inspection and control are essential for success;
- the issue is designing a reform and its materials so well that it can be implemented faithfully and well with minimal training and assistance, in other words teachers are 'consumers' of new reform ideas;
- success depends mainly on the quality of the reform ideas;
- schools in general are resistant to reforms;
- either 'top-down' or 'bottom-up' strategies work — depending on the educational context referred to.

All these 'obvious truths' have been shown to be false, both in this study as it relates to developing countries, and in other recent significant studies in industrialized countries.

The HSI study findings on effective reform strategies can be summarized in the following way:

1. Educational reform is a local process. The school is the centre of change, not the ministry or the district administration. Schools determine the degree of success, they can block implementation, enfeeble it, or bring it to effective life. For schools to improve the quality of their programmes effectively, they need to play an active and creative role.

2. Central support is vital. The issue for the central ministry is learning to support local schools in their efforts. In other words, learning how to make demands on, support, encourage, empower, enable, and build a strong local school. More responsibilities to the individual school presupposes a strong support structure from the system at large, one that must be built around the real needs of schools in development. At the central level it implies that a 'system of reform' and a division of labour is needed to support the local level effectively.

3. Effective system linkages are essential. The strategy in complex systems is to identify effective linkages, non-bureaucratic in nature, between the national, district and local levels. For communication within the system to be effective, local empowerment, usually as a consequence of more decentralization, is needed. So is a clear administrative role that combines pressure and support and secures the delivery of needed resources.

4. The reform process is a learning process. The process is evolutionary and developmental in nature; it cannot be blueprinted ahead of time. The key to success is to get good data from all parts of the system on a continuous basis, studied and worked on at the school/district level, and subsequently at the central level. This implies a competent supervision and monitoring system.

5. Think systemic and big. A vision of reform that affects school life substantially will have more effect than a cautious, incremental approach. Any major reform in complex systems needs to build structures and capabilities at all levels. Ad hoc

solutions will not work in the long run, only institution-building based on a sustained commitment works.

6. Focus on classroom practice. The clue is to focus on the dynamics of the classroom and the individual school, since these dynamics to a large extent determine implementation success. It is essential that the supporting materials are of good quality, whether nationally developed and locally adapted, or locally built from the start.

7. See teachers as learners. Good materials and facilities are necessary but insufficient conditions. Teacher mastery is crucial for impact on students, and can best be developed through a systematic local learning process that includes in-service training, supervision and coaching in a collegial atmosphere.

8. Commitment is essential at all levels. Sustained effort and the maintenance of needed support structures are crucial at the central level. Commitment is essential at the district and school level; however, it cannot be transmitted directly to schools. Commitment at the school level results from empowered successful action, personal mastery that starts with good assistance and develops from practice. In effect, local empowerment builds 'emotional' as well as administrative and problem-solving capacity.

9. Both local and central initiatives work. Innovative ideas that start locally (Colombia), nationally (Ethiopia) or with external donors (Bangladesh) can all succeed, if programmes meet the criteria of national commitment, local capacity building and linkage, in a configuration that makes sense for the particular country.

10. Parent and community participation contribute to success. Parent and community participation lead to commitment and have an effect on the outcomes. However, they are also essential for the development and maintenance of primary schools in rural areas. Effective participation includes a real role for parents in school decision making.

These basic findings, seen at a national and local level, echo what has been found in the earlier Verspoor study as well as in major studies of national reform efforts in the industrialized countries (Dalin, 1973; Berman and McLaughlin, 1977; Crandall et al., 1982) and in in-depth studies of smaller-scale innovations (Huberman and Miles, 1984; Louis and Miles, 1990; Fullan and Stiegelbauer, 1991; Dalin and Rolff, 1992). Thus we believe they are generic and quite fundamental.

IMPLICATIONS

Chapter 10 of this report examines the implications of the findings in relationship to each country, and for primary school reform efforts in general in lesser developed countries. The latter is summarized in this section:

1. Decentralization and delegation of responsibilities is a key strategy to develop empowerment, commitment and local development. Headmasters and teachers in schools that have more responsibility work more closely with the supervisor and participate more actively in in-service training programmes. We recommend a systematic process of decentralization, provided that the government actively

supports the initiative, sets standards, provides materials, training and supervision, and carefully monitors the decentralization process over several years. Successful decentralization is dependent on an institution building process that needs to have support from the local office.

2. School-community relations need to be nurtured and further developed. Good relations contribute to student outcomes, school impact and institutionalization. We particularly recommend that:

   - parents are invited to play a more significant role in the schools, and that the schools establish regular procedures to involve parents actively;
   - communities get the responsibility of financing part of the costs of the school of primary education;
   - parents be offered training opportunities for their full involvement as parents in school affairs.

3. School-district relations is another important element in any reform strategy. The district needs to play a leadership role, insisting on performance and standards, and at the same time carefully listening to the users and being prepared to offer assistance. We recommend.

   - training to help districts become more professional in the 'helping relationship', and to develop district inspectors in an instructional leadership function;
   - organizational development training for school staffs to enable them to work actively in an open dialogue with the 'new inspector'-role.

4. The role of government is essential for the necessary mobilization of political support and resources, to give legitimacy to the efforts of reform, and to build a system of reform. In particular, we recommend that:

   - governments invest in staff development of the core national staff;
   - the government is concerned with institution building to develop the capabilities of a range of important institutions, e.g. for curriculum development, materials development, and staff development;
   - the government provides the necessary resources on the basis of reliable mapping of local needs;
   - the government stays close to implementation, e.g. through local inspectors and staff development.

5. The role of donors has been essential in all the three reform efforts studied. Donors play a political, as well as an economic and professional role. We recommend that donors:

   - develop expertise on strategies for educational reform and help governments design a reform plan, be less concerned with content than with the conditions for a plan to be implemented and institutionalized;
   - help the government to evaluate the reform and provide data for decision makers;
   - provide selective financing to encourage innovative work, and plan investments to enable the government to institutionalize the reform;

- enable the system to build capacity, competent staff and a support structure that functions;
- support structural changes to enable a new and relevant infra-structure to develop;
- support research on the change process to give governments a better guide to the management of change.

The HSI study shows that reform strategies matter, that strategic and coordinated efforts do make a difference, and that primary educational reforms in rural areas can succeed. We now know much more clearly how success can be achieved.

Part 1

Introduction

This part introduces the reader to the HSI study, the research questions, the methods of work and the reforms studied (Chapter 1). Chapter 2 takes the reader to one typical school working with the innovations in each of the three countries, Colombia, Ethiopia and Bangladesh.

Readers who want a quick overview of the study are advised to read Chapter 1 and the Executive Summary. Readers who want to understand how the 'reform works' in a school in one of the countries, without going through the school cases in the Country Reports, may choose to read one or more of the three cases in Chapter 2.

Chapter 1

Learning from Success

In recent years there has been increasing concern in the international donor community, including the World Bank, and in many governments, about the mounting evidence documenting the inability of schools in developing countries to provide students with an education, resulting in minimal acceptable standards of learning achievement. A number of projects aimed at quality improvement, several supported by the World Bank, have brought disappointing results. Evaluation reports and other studies conclude that the implementation and institutionalization of educational change programmes is a complex political, social and professional process that is hard to achieve (Lockheed and Verspoor, 1991).

To address these concerns the education department of the World Bank in 1984 started a programme of research and review aimed at the identification of strategies that had been demonstrably effective in bringing about quality improvement in developing countries. In essence this effort was a review of the World Bank experiences on the basis of documentation in the project files (Verspoor, 1989, here called the 'Verspoor study').

While research of the process of educational change has been conducted for more than 30 years in the OECD-countries, (the Western industrialized countries) and a rich literature on the topic exists, such studies are rare in lesser developed countries (LDCs). Policies and strategies for renewal of the educational systems in the OECD-countries have to a large extent learned from the research and experiences of the last 30 years; the same is not true for the LDCs (see the Bibliography). The situation in developing countries calls for well-designed, tailor-made studies that can help us to better understand the dynamics of educational change in these countries. Since we know from many disappointing project accounts what does not work, why not learn from what seems to work? That was the starting point and rationale for the study 'How Schools Improve' (HSI).

THE FINDINGS OF THE VERSPOOR STUDY

As already mentioned HSI was created on the basis of a 'desk-study' in the World Bank that came up with some very important conclusions. However, it was also a study with limitations, as it was not based on actual field work. The study selected 21 projects for a detailed review, from 282 education projects with a total of 296 educational change programmes that cost US$6.4 billion; these represented 60 per cent of the total cost of Bank-supported education projects approved during the period 1962 to 1984. The sample differed somewhat from the typical Bank-supported projects. It did not emphasize curiculum change to the same extent as traditional projects; instead organizational change and administrative development were more common. Also the sample projects were more balanced, employing broader change strategies, and the sample included a higher proportion of elementary education projects.

Findings[1]

The study showed that, broadly speaking, there were two types of initiation processes, one driven largely by external forces (donor agencies) in league with national educators, and a second driven by internal political and ideological considerations. High outcomes were reported for both types of programme. High outcome projects were well prepared, however they also focused on the capacity to manage change and to institutionalize projects following the development and implementation period.

Verspoor found that the design of an implementation strategy appropriate for the situation and the change programme is of vital importance for success. The factors he found to strongly influence the strategy were:

1. Differences in the degree of environmental uncertainties, often created by economic crises, uncertain commitment, or political turbulence.
2. The degree of innovation of the change programme, assessed in the context of the existing level of educational development and teaching practice.

He found four appropriate change strategies, shown in Table 1.1. The 'progressive innovation' strategy aims at the implementation of a number of successive changes, each modest in itself, whose cumulative effect over time can result in considerable change. The 'incremental expansion' intends to implement ambitious innovations in a gradually increasing number of schools, usually through a 'small scale experiment' approach. The 'discrete change', Verspoor sees as the traditional approach, implementing a change programme in a limited number of schools without clearly specified broader policy objectives. The 'permanent pilot' programmes aspire to national coverage, show promising results in a pilot phase, but do not manage to mobilize enough support and resources to make the transition to national application. Verspoor found that programmes aiming at broad national coverage adopted incremental strategies. Second, ambitious change programmes were all implemented under conditions of

Table 1.1 National reform strategies

	Low uncertainty	High uncertainty
Low innovation	Progressive innovation	Discrete change
High innovation	Incremental expansion	Permanent pilot

[1] This section draws heavily on the summary of findings in the Verspoor study (Verspoor, 1989).

reasonable environmental stability. Third, programme transformation nearly always occurs, and fourth, over time, the implementation strategies also change.

Verspoor found that there were three processes that play a key role aiming at institutionalization:

- administrative development
- in-service teacher training
- building and maintaining commitment.

Administrative development was found to be a key factor in success, and included changes in structures, communication and evaluation systems; strengthening institutions; staff training; and increased funding. The common element in success was the strengthening of the administrative capacity at the school and district level. Large scale World Bank projects are also dependent on the development of effective policy, planning and supporting institutions at the central level.

The study found that effectively implemented in-service teacher training was the second most important factor for successful implementation. It was found that to be effective it should be locally available, provided with an effective system of supervision and support, and be based on the teacher's level of knowledge and experience. Finally the building of commitment was seen as crucial for success; broadening the support base, including local implementors and parents, and the provision of opportunities for professional growth for teachers. Consistent external support can salvage a programme to which the government is, often informally, not committed, and the best way to build commitment is through success.

THE STUDY 'HOW SCHOOLS IMPROVE'

This study was based on the Verspoor study, and was partly set up to confirm some of Verspoor's main findings. The factors studied by Verspoor were mainly 'country level factors', and the 'linkages' from the country level to the local level. HSI intended to describe and analyze several of these factors. At the 'country level', therefore, the study is mainly confirmatory in nature. It was also, however, exploratory and intended to discover some of the key factors contributing to successful implementation and institutionalization of educational changes. The study was built around the following research questions (for a detailed review, see Appendix 1, p. 304):

1. What are the outcomes of successful strategies for the implementation of educational change, seen in terms of quality of implementation, institutionalization and student outcomes, as well as in terms of unexpected outcomes?

2. What do successful strategies look like, both at the macro (country) and micro (local school) level?

3. What determines successful strategies? Determinants may include administrative capacity development, teacher training and commitment-building efforts, among others.

4. How are successful strategies at the macro and micro levels linked, seen from the central and school levels?

The study was ambitious. It intended to describe and analyse not only the outcomes and the strategies used in a reform, but also had the ambition of explaining why the schools succeed. This may be done in one cultural context, and with a well-trained team of researchers. HSI worked with three developing countries and with research teams that, at the outset, had limited experience with this kind of study.

The country level study

This part of the study was relatively brief and confirmatory in nature, building mainly on the Verspoor findings. Since the study would deal with reforms that have been underway for a number of years, much of the data would be historical and based on documentation and interviews with key actors. More specifically, this part of the study would be concerned with questions related to the following:

1. Outcomes: how do key actors at the central level perceive the outcomes of the reform? To what extent would the reform elements actually have been implemented? What impact did it have on students and teachers? To what extent is the reform 'built-in' to the system, or has it become a natural part of the primary education system?

2. How was the reform done? What actually took place, centrally and throughout the system in the history of the reform? How was the reform planned, financed and adapted during the long process of implementation? What support strategies (e.g. teacher training, materials) were developed? How was the reform managed, and to what extent did the country build the 'infra-structure' necessary to support and maintain the reform?

3. What determines successful strategies? To what extent were factors in the Verspoor study present, and did they lead to programme success? Did the country strengthen the national organizations, and did it matter? Did the country build and expand commitment to the reform? To what extent did the country build 'a system of reform', with a good division of labour, the needed infra-structure, and a reasonable devolution of decision-making to regional and local levels?

4. How are successful strategies at the central level linked to local school implementation? We are looking at comprehensive, nation-wide efforts over several years, with probably a variety of local and institutional factors that may determine success. To what extent did central strategies 'reach' the school, help the school to master new practice and implement the elements of the reform? Were there unintended linkages? Or would we discover success where no clear linkages exist?

These questions (and more) were raised with key central reform figures, people who had been close to the scene, in a political, administrative or professional role. The intention was to discuss the issues with a variety of informants, including those who fought for the reform and those who hesitated or were negative about the reform from the outset.

The school level sub-study

This sub-study was more extensive, and mostly exploratory, since little was known about how local-level implementation proceeds. The purpose was to understand what the reform looks like from the viewpoints of students, parents, teachers, headmasters and local administrators and support personnel. More precisely the sub-study was concerned with the following issues:

1. Outcomes: how do local actors perceive the outcomes? What is the impact on students? Do they learn more; from a more relevant curriculum? Do changes in student behaviour, e.g. participation and discipline, occur? What about teacher behaviour, do we see a more skilful and professional teacher? To what extent is his/her knowledge base expanded? What happens to the school as an organization? Are procedures, norms, the organizational climate different? Did the relationship to the community improve? To what extent were all the components of the reform implemented, or was something dropped or adapted? And finally, is the reform 'built-in' to the daily life of the school, has it been 'institutionalized'?

2. What do successful strategies look like? First, how do local people assess the reform programme? What is important to them? Did it 'fit' with their needs? How was the reform programme influenced by local contextual factors, e.g. staff and community characteristics and context? How was the implementation process done, how was it experienced, what helped and what hindered the implementation process? What did the school do to cope with the challenges of the reform?

3. What determines successful strategies? By comparing schools with varying amounts of success the study attempts to clarify what factors affect the degree of success. These may be local contextual factors (community, student characteristics, etc.), or they may be related to the administrative capacity (e.g. presence or involvement, monitoring and supervision), the degree of assistance, or the extent to which the school actually experiences success, to mention a few central factors in the study.

4. Are successes at the local level linked, or influenced, by macro-level strategies? These may be intended or unintended links related to received resources, received pressure, assistance, supervision, administrative role, local adaptation or empowerment, to mention a few central factors in the study.

Learning from success

This study would focus on success. The Verspoor study provided an excellent base as a number of projects had been reviewed, and a total of 21 selected for their high achievement in implementing educational change. In the process of identifying countries and projects for the HSI project, the World Bank applied the following criteria:

> In selecting the cases the following criteria will be applied:
> (i) at least moderate implementation success;
> (ii) regional diversity, with at least one African case;
> (iii) potential local research capability.
>
> The case study will focus in particular on:
> (i) a detailed analysis of the change strategy in respect of time horizon, sequencing of actions, planning and adaptation of programme content and implementation strategies, and the role of environmental influences;
> (ii) a detailed review of the design and the contribution to programme success of the key change variables identified in the exploratory review: administrative development, in-service teacher training and commitment building;
> (iii) assessing outcomes in respect of programme application and institutionalization, as well as student learning.
>
> Information would be collected from documentation available from the Bank files and the local project files, through interviews of key participants in the implementation, observation of classroom processes and the testing of students. (Letter from the World Bank to the Norwegian Ministry of Development Cooperation)

The three countries and projects selected were:

1. Colombia with the innovative 'Escuela Nueva' programme, initiated locally based on a UNESCO concept, and gradually developed into a national programme for rural primary schools over the past 15 to 20 years, a project also partly financed by external donors (including the World Bank) (see Chapter 3).
2. Ethiopia with a major nationwide, comprehensive primary education reform under way since 1974, initiated, planned and implemented by the government with external donor support (including the World Bank) (see Chapter 4).
3. Bangladesh with a large nationwide 'universal primary education' project, initiated, planned and implemented by the government, with large scale assistance from IDA. The project has been implemented over a 10 to 15 year period (see Chapter 5).

In spite of turbulence and lack of resources, and with pressing needs in nearly all areas of life, these countries have been able to push consistently for nationwide implementation and institutionalization of primary education reforms, even in the poor rural areas.

The next sampling question was: 'What kind of schools should be selected?' Would we study rural schools, urban schools, large or small schools? Would we study schools with a relatively favourable resource situation? These were some of the first questions we asked ourselves. The following sampling decisions were taken:

1. We would study both small and large primary schools in rural areas or small cities.
2. We would select schools in communities with average or less than average resources.
3. We wanted schools with better than average enrolment rates, i.e. schools that are better than average in attracting and retaining students. We assume that the enrolment rate includes both boys and girls.
4. We wanted schools in districts that, from the point of view of the ministry, had given attention to the reform, worked hard to implement it and really had made an 'above average' effort. These districts should also have a mixture of poor and well-to-do communities, and should be reasonably accessible. Up to one day's travel to visit a school was acceptable. Three districts were selected in each country.

The process of selecting the districts and schools was fairly lengthy. IMTEC (see below) worked with the ministries to clarify the criteria, and the ministries selected the three school districts. Within the district the ministry asked the educational district administration to identify excellent/very good schools in terms of their ability to implement the reform, and to identify individuals who had worked closely with these schools. Interviews were held with several district persons (e.g. teacher trainers, inspectors, etc.) to describe the schools in the initial sample. In some districts the HSI researcher (see below) also visited the schools to get an impression over and above his/her interview data. Finally a total of 12 schools were selected in Colombia, 10 in Bangladesh and 9 in Ethiopia, a total of 31 schools.

Through these criteria and procedures we got an initial sample of excellent rural primary schools, known by several local informants in different types of position to be unusually good schools. These were first nominations. What turned out to be the real group of excellent schools, very good schools and good schools was determined empirically through the research project as the researchers studied the initial sample. In other words, we found that within the group of first nominated schools, there were differences in terms of implementation, impact and institutionalization of the reform. On the basis of our empirical findings we then grouped the original 31 schools into the three groups mentioned.

THE HSI METHODOLOGY

HSI was a qualitative research project, based on a systematic research approach developed by Matthew B. Miles and A. Michael Huberman, both members of the HSI International Research Panel (Miles and Huberman, 1984). IMTEC published in 1992 a separate manual outlining the approach, with the operational definitions and the instrumentation used. A short summary of the methodology is given in this chapter.

Data in a qualitative research project usually appear in words, and seldom in numbers. They often appear in a fairly lengthy narrative text, and a large number of words need to be organized to be 'ready for analysis'. 'Analysis' consists of three types of activities, namely data reduction, data display and conclusion drawing/verification. To get to this point some steps needed to be taken:

1. The research questions were the starting point. HSI was built upon the findings of the Verspoor study, as well as findings from several 'implementation studies' in the OECD-countries. Although the four general research questions are general, the sub-questions are fairly specific and not by chance. They form a systematic entity with both open-ended, exploratory questions, and more confirmatory ones (see Appendix 1).

2. Instrumentation in the form of interview guides and observation instruments (for classroom observation) were then developed, closely connected with the main research questions and the sub-questions (see Appendix 2 for sample interview guide).

3. Data displays: closely tied to the research questions and the interview guides the form of data presentations called *data displays* was developed. A total of 18 central level and school level displays were developed. All critical information was supposed to be reduced to a form that could be presented in these displays and used for analysis. Three 'cross-site displays' were also developed to compare schools within a country (see Chapters 3 to 5 for examples). The research questions, the displays and the instrumentation were revised, following field testing of instruments and the redesign meeting with country representatives organized in Rome early in the project (May, 1988).

4. Data-gathering and coding of data: each country HSI team consisted of four to six researchers, who were responsible for the collection of data, analysis and reporting of two or three schools (in addition to district and country level responsibilities). Each site was visited over several days, in most cases twice during data-gathering. Usually the HSI team worked in the same district at the same time, and had the opportunity to meet regularly to discuss the work. This practice varied considerably from country to country. A total of about 1000 interview-hours have been used in the project, and approximately twice this number for coding, analysis and country reporting.

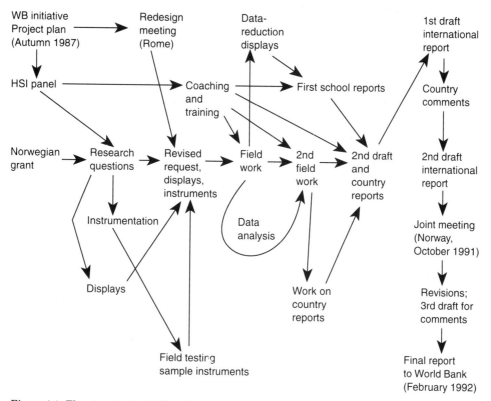

Figure 1.1 *The steps in the HSI-study.*

5. Training and coaching: a coach was assigned to each country to assist the teams with training and problem-solving. Styrbjörn Gustavsson worked with the Bangladesh team, Ray Chesterfield with the Colombia team, and Per Dalin with the Ethiopia team. Each team studied the book, *Qualitative Data Analysis: A Sourcebook of New Methods* (Miles and Huberman, 1984), and the coach provided several days' training, usually spread over the first half year of the project. Further coaching took place for periods of 3 to 7 days; an average of four times per country over an 18-month period of the project [1988-1990].

6. Case writing and analysis: each researcher has been responsible for the final product — the school case. In the process of writing, the team-leader and the entire team has used considerable time to discuss the case, to look at alternative interpretations, to discuss standards, ratings and presentations. Although each case is the responsibility of the individual researcher, it belongs to a country report for which the entire team is responsible.

7. International report: based on the country studies, the cross-site displays (see Chapters 3 to 5), and the participation of all HSI

researchers, this final international report is presented, with conclusions and recommendations to the World Bank (see Chapters 9 and 10).

Figure 1.1 illustrates the steps in the HSI study.

THE ORGANIZATION OF THE HSI STUDY

HSI was a World Bank study financed through a grant from the Norwegian Ministry for Development Cooperation. It was managed by the Population and Human Resource Department (HPR), and the supervision was assigned to Adriaan M. Verspoor. An international research panel (Mathew B. Miles, A. Michael Huberman and Per Dalin) was appointed to give the Bank advice on the design and development of the study.

IMTEC, the international learning cooperative in Norway, was sub-contracted to implement the study, assign responsibilities to national research teams, conduct training and supervision, arrange for a 'redesign meeting' and a final international meeting, and be responsible for the completion of the country reports and the international report. Hallvard K. Kuløy of IMTEC was the project coordinator. Per Dalin is responsible for this international report, and cooperated with Anbesu Biazen, Tekle Ayano, Mamtaj Jahan and Carlos Rojas (see chapters 2-5); Per Dalin was also responsible for the international analysis and wrote Chapters 1, 6, 7, 8 and 9.

IMTEC initially sub-contracted the work in the three countries to the following institutions:

- **Bangladesh:** Bangladesh Bureau of Educational Information and Statistics (BANBEIS), Government of Bangladesh, Dhaka
- **Colombia:** Instituto SER de Investigación, Bogotá
- **Ethiopia:** Institute for Curriculum Development and Research, Ministry of Education, Addis Ababa.

Participation of the HSI members in the design and development of the project was a major concern, and the World Bank and the international panel had a strong influence from the outset. It was decided to involve all HSI members in a critical review of the project. All available documentation was therefore sent for review, and a meeting was held in Rome in May 1989, to 'redesign' the project. Based on a number of comments the project was improved in several aspects. Through on-going supervision, coach reports and written communication, the project has also been 'formed' during the implementation period.

HSI was completed by the following researchers:

- **Bangladesh:** Anowar-Ul-Aziz, Delwar Hossain, Abdul Jabbar, Mamtaj Jahan and Siddiqur Rahman;
- **Colombia:** Blanca Lilia Caro, Patricia Rodríguez, Carlos Rojas and Zoriada Castillo;
- **Ethiopia:** Abebe Bekele, Anbesu Biazen, Berhanu Dibaba, Melesse Delelegne, Tassew Zewdie and Tekle Ayano;

- **International:** Ray Chesterfield, Per Dalin, Michael Huberman, Styrbjörn Gustavsson, Matthew Miles, Hallvard K. Kuløy and Adriaan Verspoor.

REFERENCES

Berman, P. and McLaughlin, M.W. (1977) *Federal Programs Supporting Educational Change*, Vol. IV: *The Findings in Review*. Santa Monica, CA: Rand Corporation.

Dalin, P. (1973) *Case Studies of Educational Innovation*. Volume 4: *Strategies for Educational Innovation*. Paris: CERI/OECD.

Dalin, P. and Rolff, H.-G. (1993) *Changing the School Culture*. London: Cassell.

Huberman, A.M. and Miles, M.B. (1984) *Innovation up Close: How School Improvements Work*. New York: Plenum Press.

Fullan, M.G. and Stiegelbauer, S. (1991) *The New Meaning of Educational Change*. New York: Teachers College Press (London: Cassell).

Lockheed, M.E. and Verspoor, A.M. *et al.* (1991) *Improving Primary Education in Developing Countries*. Washington D.C.: Oxford University Press.

Miles, M.B. and Huberman, A.M. (1984) *Qualitative Data Analysis: A Sourcebook of New Methods*. Beverly Hills, CA: SAGE Publications.

Verspoor, A.M. (1989) *Pathways to Change: Improving the Quality of Education in Developing Countries*, World Bank Discussion Paper 53. Washington D.C.

Chapter 2

Experiences from Field Work in Typically Successful Schools

The Emilio Rocha School Case, Colombia
Patricia Rodríguez

The department of Boyaca, situated in the eastern part of Colombia, was the scene of a definitive battle against the Spanish in the struggle for independence. In this department is the municipality of Tenza, known for its beautiful colonial county seat and where a large percentage of the population is involved in the production of handmade woven goods, as well as agriculture.

Searching for the school

We arrived in Tenza in search of the rural school of Emilio Rocha. We followed the instructions of local residents and found ourselves waiting at the side of the road at 6 am for the bus. The dilapidated bus picked us up and travelled through lush green countryside along a narrow, unsurfaced road. After some 30 minutes we got off the bus and followed a narrow, undulating path thick with mud from the previous evening's rains. We were guided along the trail by some children who were also making their way to the school. During the 15 minute walk, they explained that the school was located in a chicken farm, and that the farmer, named Rocha, had donated the land. The farmer had also given the money to build the school, and as a result it was named after him. We also learned that the hamlet in which the school was situated was inhabited by peasant farmers who, with the assistance of their children after school, grew subsistence crops to supplement the meagre income made on the chicken farm.

Before the change

When we arrived at the school, we were told that, as in all rural schools in Colombia, there had originally been one teacher who also served as school head, responsible for communicating with parents and carrying out a great number of administrative duties, and one other teacher. These two teachers used a standard curriculum to teach the first through fifth grades. The teachers were said to have stuck to a rigid schedule of activities, demanding that children stayed in their seats and committed lessons to memory. They had had little contact with the community or with the children outside the classroom and worried only about providing their superiors with the required paperwork. At that time fifty children had attended the school. Some were there most days but many, because of work obligations, attended infrequently, and some appeared only a few times before dropping out. For all the children, attending school was entering into the unknown and there was a general fear of failing. Some attended only because they were forced to do so by their parents. The teachers, with their lack of understanding of the students' situations, often concluded that rural children were not equal to their city counterparts. The combination of these factors resulted in serious wastage at Emilio Rocha. Many students turned their backs on education because of pressure to work or through lack of stimulation, and potential literate contributors to Colombian society were lost.

The situation was not helped by school supervisors who came only to check that teachers were present. Parents had little involvement in school operations with their only knowledge of the school being the grades that their children received. Many parents and students tried to take advantage of the limited opportunities the school presented. Students continued to try over and over again when sent back to the first grade. Parents stopped asking what was happening to their children after teachers answered initial questions with comments like 'He's stupid', 'She was absent a bit', or 'He stopped coming for a while'. Parents accepted these explanations because they knew little of the school and could expect nothing more.

During this period, in 1980, something changed at Emilio Rocha. An occasional teacher, named Álvaro, began to come to the school to teach the children music, dance and physical education. This started a change that continued when in 1982, despite rejection of a new programme called Escuela Nueva by most teachers and local officials, the headmistress of Emilio Rocha attended the courses offered by the programme. This training was the start of the profound change to the school that we encountered on our visit.

In 1983 another new teacher arrived at the school. In an effort to move closer to his family, Augustín, who held a degree in primary education, was able to arrange a transfer to Tenza and was assigned to Emilio Rocha. His traditional background had not introduced him to the Escuela Nueva programme that he encountered at the school. He knew nothing of the history of the programme, its methodology or the changes that it hoped to bring about. With no time to send him for training, his colleague, the headmistress, advised him of his responsibilities as they started the daily task of giving classes. Although reluctant initially, he soon developed an interest in the new programme. He liked the democratic approach of dealing with the children which created a participatory learning environment and found that he could communicate with the children on an individual basis and take a personal interest in each of them.

Despite his enthusiasm, Augustín found that implementing the programme wasn't easy. The school needed money for the 'learning corners' and the parents had none to offer. Help from the community was needed in other areas as well, but they were not in favour of the programme because they had heard the negative comments made by teachers in the region who were tied to the old teaching model and were afraid of anything new. The local authorities also refused to help either because they lacked knowledge about the new programme or they saw it as a threat. The teachers of Emilio Rocha were alone. They had to start with what was available which meant introducing the Escuela Nueva model gradually and transforming the school environment in stages. As one of the teachers reported, 'We organized the student government, the learning corners, and what materials we could and started to adapt the classrooms by reorganizing the furniture and decorating with local materials. We began the programme with second and third grades while using traditional methods with other classes because they had only sent us learning guides for those two years.

During the first year, the children resisted the changes. They were insecure working on their own and helping to create their own learning experiences. 'For us [the teachers] it was difficult to change from being instructors to being facilitators and give space to the children. It took time and dedication.' Both teachers were uncomfortable with a flexible schedule because 'it seemed to imply a certain disorganization, and the children seemed unable to develop their own schedule.' It was also difficult for parents to see their children engaged in activities other than the traditional ones of memorization and copying both in the classroom and for homework. The change also bothered the rest of the community because the children no longer sat quietly in classrooms but were in the community asking questions. This did not seem like learning to them, more a waste of time. It was also difficult for the children to elect one another and then follow the direction of a peer in activities that had formerly been reserved for the teacher. This was a building period, an adjustment and bringing together of teachers, parents, community and children that took two to three years.

The year 1986 was a year of several changes. The headmistress left the school and was replaced by a headmaster who had a personalized approach to education. Although he had not worked with the Escuela Nueva programme, he was familiar with it and had adopted some of the methodology to carry out work in the natural sciences for the local university. In addition, he knew the school. It was Álvaro. His arrival was fundamental to the survival of the programme, and he began a series of new strategies to create a complete Escuela Nueva. He invited the parents to the school and familiarized them with the guides their children were using, he involved them in the learning process and made them participants in the life of the school. They developed activities to raise money, made materials, built playing courts and became teachers showing the students how to sing and dance in the traditional ways of the region. He was also active with local authorities, pushing for complete training in the Escuela Nueva methodology which, with the help of a local supervisor, he was able to obtain. Regional and national leaders of the programme helped, as did local businesses and individuals, and he obtained desks, building materials, books for the school library and help in arranging a school restaurant that was run by local mothers.

Álvaro and Augustín formed a real team that helped the EN model solidify. They planned, organized and invented in the dynamic way outlined for teachers in the EN method. These two teachers still teach fifty children in five primary grades. With parents, community members and superiors they have one objective – to defend and improve the Escuela Nueva. Álvaro, though insisting that there is still much to do, said that it is easy to see the change in the children. 'They have woken up', they study and work hard in school because they can see the relationship between theory and practice. 'They have new values, they develop their skills, they are sure of themselves, they love the school and they motivate us. Now we have leaders here, later they will be leaders in the community. Now they question us and participate actively, they are creative. Now we have to be careful that they don't lose incentive because their classmates are moving faster.'

Arrival at Emilio Rocha School

A short distance from the path, on the left side of the road, we saw the school. It is a white house with red trim; it has a large patio which serves as an entrance way and contains a multipurpose sports court and two large classrooms which are light and airy. We saw a corridor with murals that appeared to have been drawn by parents, students and teachers; a kitchen busy with the movement of mothers rushing about with water, milk, sugar and rice; all were laughing. We also noticed a dining room containing a lot of clothes, instruments, posters and paints. In the map room we found women dressing nervously in costumes, while being hurried by the children. We then discovered that there was to be a celebration in honour of a national holiday.

We were witnesses to a communion — a communion of the school, parents and children, filled with emotion and friendliness and some shyness caused by the presence of two strangers, us. We were the onlookers for the performance and they offered us their songs, acts and dances. We learned why Álvaro had insisted on incorporating the community into school life through music and folklore. He played the music and the parents and children sang and danced. We, at the insistence of the student government, were included in the ceremonies and had to say a few words about our visit and what we had seen at the school.

We returned the next day for the start of lessons. When the small coordinator of discipline rang the bell and announced 'time to work', the children lined up by height and grade. The children in charge of personal hygiene checked the hands, fingernails, ears and hair of their classmates. They entered the classrooms and each gathered his or her materials, then they were greeted by the teacher. They exchanged information, asked questions, laughed, received pats on the head or shoulder, then they sat down to work, each one on a chosen assignment. They got up freely to consult with peers or with the teacher. Some went to the mathematics learning corner and counted sticks, others went to the science corner to identify different stones, another went to the library for a dictionary and others went outside to look for materials to complement their lesson. One girl interviewed us about the city and recorded our answers in her notebook. She then began to work on mathematics, trying to measure with a yardstick. Her concentration was broken when we asked to test children of third and fifth grade. On returning to work she seemed confused, she got up and went to the teacher, who explained the marks on the yardstick and gave her a new sheet of paper. He also showed her how to measure pieces of wood. He left the room and returned with a metal yardstick used for sewing. She recognized this and they discussed how the two were the same. When she finished her work, the teacher came over and they talked about how the yardstick could be read and what it could be used for and then read the *Teachers' Guide* together. He was a teacher-facilitator.

This day in a class of children from second to fifth grade showed us the dynamics that can be created between teacher and student. The teacher directed the children to the path they should follow in undertaking a task — if this was necessary — then he corrected, encouraged or challenged them to look for solutions, always with encouragement such as 'you're doing good' or 'yes, you can do it'. We also saw the academic orientation of the children when they worked in small groups; with discussion, defence of positions and finally a synthesis of ideas. We observed an absence of fear in asking questions and a spirit of voluntarily helping classmates with an 'I'll explain it to him, Teacher', with the teacher watching to ensure the correctness of the explanation.

We decided to visit the first grade classroom to find out how Augustín was teaching the children to read. When we went in, we were almost flattened by a group of 14 children running towards the courtyard, where they were to have a reading class. We were astonished. 'What, reading in the patio? without texts?' Yes, it was a class of dynamic reading that used small flashcards with syllables, short words, long words and new words. The children competed, laughed and identified real-life objects, matching them with the right words. Many didn't want to stop when recess came and they had to eat the snacks their mothers had prepared and go and play. The teachers played an active part in the children's games during recess.

After two days at the school, we left with great hopes for education in rural Colombia. The efforts of the two teachers together with the help received from regional and national authorities had allowed the school to flourish. But the most important elements were the commitment of the teachers to the programme, and their love of the children and their sense of mission as teachers. After buying some handicrafts in Tenza, we boarded the bus and returned to the city, with thoughts of the happy, active children, sure of themselves and eager to learn, who had been created by the Escuela Nueva that we had left behind in the lush green valley.

The Tegulet I School Case, Ethiopia

Tekle Ayono

Introduction and background

About half an hour's drive from the district capital of Debre Berhan is the agrarian area of Tegulet I, with its many grass-thatched tukuls (huts) on either side of the narrow road. Throughout the drive children, helped by their dogs, can be seen herding cattle in the fields and trying to chase away the monkeys and baboons that destroy the crops. Tegulet I is surrounded by mountains, hills and valleys. Its school is located in a small village in which modern human service programmes are rare or non-existent. The community does however have traditional services.

Within the school compound three are three blocks of buildings next to each other. The first one is built of breeze-blocks and has separate pit latrines for boys and girls. The second block, also built of breeze-blocks, contains classrooms for the senior grades, the headmaster's office and a staffroom. The third block is built of wood and mud and houses the school pedagogical centre, a small library and classrooms for the lower grades. The area in front of these buildings is grassed and behind is the school farm which grows beans and peas. The teachers' quarters provide free housing for the headmaster and teachers and are located within the school premises behind the farm. A few community members live in private tukuls adjacent to the three school blocks, and the entire school compound is enclosed by a sturdy stone and wooden fence.

Socio-economic conditions The only ethnic group in the area is Amhara and the language spoken is Amharic. The community follows Orthodox Christian religion combined with certain traditional local beliefs. The main occupation is subsistence farming, especially crop planting and raising poor-quality cattle. A few people combine their agricultural activities with small-scale trading.

The school and educational environment The school has played an important role in the area's literacy programme. At the start of the twenty-second year of the literacy campaign, 8,630 adults had been taught to read and write. Student achievement in this school is high. In 1989, all the students in the sixth grade passed the national examination. However, absenteeism and dropouts are a consistent problem.

Tegulet I school level changes as seen locally In 1984 lesson planning was not popular and teaching aids were not often used. The teaching-learning process was mostly oriented to rote learning and the mode of teaching was based on lecturing to the whole class with little attention paid to the individual. This has now changed and teachers make better use of lesson plans and aids to enhance their teaching. Recitation and memorization are less emphasized and there is more classroom demonstration. The teachers and headmaster emphasize group work in each subject.

In the past there was no political education in the curriculum. However, in 1990, political education was introduced for the fourth to sixth grades. A radio programme for schools became effective in 1984 though it was not directly based on the curriculum content until 1986. It has been improved since 1985, but problems with its content and vocabulary have been reported. For example, the students find the accent of the foreigner presenting fifth-grade English hard to understand; fifth-grade maths is difficult for students; and third-grade science requires that students answer some questions for which even their teachers do not have basic information.

The headmaster and teachers are positive about the changes. They think that political education has made the students more aware of the concepts of class struggle and revolution. However, there has been much recent change in Ethiopian politics. A new policy of mixed economy has been declared, and the Ministry of Education has issued a directive that Marxist political education must not be taught in schools.

Before 1984 students had poor academic abilities, little motivation for school work, and did not take part in any practical activities. Today's students have good academic abilities, they produce charts, dyes from plants, pottery and hand crafts, and their interests, motivation and eagerness for education have been praised by parents and confirmed by teachers:

> Students have a strong need and motivation for education. There is a strong push from children to go to school and those who finish literacy campaign programmes are motivated to go to formal school. There is strong competition among our own children and if we try to keep some at home to help us, they rebel and we are forced to send them to school. (Parents)

In the past there was no school pedagogical centre (SPC), and when it was first set up it was weak, with no emphasis on teaching aids. The school library did not open until 1986 and at first its services were poor. The school had only one radio and school books and textbooks were not looked after properly. The school has now bought basic tools and materials, it has an SPC, and teaching aids are prepared and used. The small library lends books to students, community members and teachers and is run by a committee. Textbooks rented to students are kept clean and covered, and the school has also bought a second radio from its own internal income. These changes mean improvement and development and teachers regard the reforms highly.

Co-curricular activities and labour education were also weak until 1985. There was no systematic record keeping, documentation or good discipline. That has now changed, and there are a variety of active clubs, such as agriculture, sports, mini-media, Red Cross and home economics. A good labour education programme was introduced in 1985. Teachers passed a resolution not to drink with students during working hours and the school now runs for the whole day. Some of the problems experienced with labour education were solved by taking the following steps:

> At the beginning, rather than teaching about labour education directly, it was approached indirectly. We worked on some socially useful things (cleaning and fencing streams and wells) with the community and convinced them of its benefits. We carefully taught them about labour education and today it is well accepted ... there has been good planning and implementation of labour education since 1984. (Teachers)

These changes are meant to give support to classroom learning as well as boosting income generation for the school. The improved documentation services mean that information can be located more easily, and teachers are also happy about the improved discipline.

In the past teachers did not cooperate with each other or share experiences, and there was no emphasis on jointly producing and using teaching aids. The teachers didn't have living quarters in the school compound so they lived with local residents. As a result, they had different outlooks on school organization and implementing changes: for example, some teachers drank with the students while others opposed it. In 1984, the teachers began to discuss school problems in meetings and find solutions together. They also started to give additional services to the school during their free time and to share experiences among themselves and with teachers from other schools. Unlike today, in 1984 the school did not make use of a question and answer competition to develop the inquisitiveness of the students and raise their achievement and knowledge. There are now lots of posters and teaching aids on the walls outside classrooms, indicators of teacher innovation. The headmaster and teachers make good use of mini-media by which means educative information and news are posted on the bulletin board weekly. These changes have raised the students' interest in learning and their understanding of new things.

The previous headmaster could not get much support from the community, as misunderstandings existed. In 1988 the school had cut down the big tree in the school compound under which the community previously worshipped, and fenced the compound. There was therefore no superstitious worshipping or paying sacrifice within the school compound. Most of the families who used to live in the compound were moved out and given land elsewhere. Their anger at these actions spilled over to their attitudes towards the school. The inspector talked to the head and the peasants and it was agreed that they should get new land. The headmaster coordinated teachers, students and the community to build houses in their new sites.

Now, inspectors visit the school twice a year to talk to the headmaster and to evaluate plans. They also talk to teachers in a meeting, sometimes observe classes, look at student exercise books and give feedback. Through discussion with the parents, the headmaster has been able to get financial contributions from the community.

The community's needs for education has grown constantly. People have seen the values of education in the lives of others and have been motivated. Today the community welcomes and respects teachers and provides them with free housing. Community relations with the school have improved greatly and the community has also solved the school's financial problems. The teachers and headmaster are encouraged by the increase in the school's internal income, and the parents have recognized that the introduction of reforms has improved the standard of schooling. Their positive feelings are also shown by the increase in attendance and by their strong desire for a junior secondary school. Dropout rate was high due to economic problems and a lack of awareness in the community about education, with most dropouts from poor and disadvantaged groups. Teachers have now created awareness amongst parents to send children to school. Absenteeism and repetition rates have decreased, and female participation is increasing.

The change process at the local level: what the process of implementation looked like

When the reforms were initiated the school had a shortage of teachers, and student enrolment was low. The low enrolment had prevented the expansion of the school beyond the sixth grade. There were also some misunderstandings between the school and community members on the management committee, and some new teachers had a poor understanding of the reforms. The District office held conferences to acquaint the headmaster with the changes, and he in turn educated the teachers. The teachers were then able to talk to some of the local farmers about the changes at the school and they were able to convince other parents to enrol their children. These actions not only improved the community's outlook on education and attracted more students to the school, but also encouraged people to build houses for the teachers.

Another problem at the outset of the reforms was a shortage of equipment and facilities in the school. The school asked the community members to contribute what they could to help solve the problem. The school pedagogical centre was built and the school obtained some tools from the district office and this helped to produce teaching aids. Some misconceptions about labour education during its early implementation were described by teachers:

> Some parents complained about their children getting cold while participating in the labour education programme and threatened to withdraw them from the school. Parents were also worried as they thought that their children were not getting enough academic learning and they were used for manual labour which they could do at home. (Teachers)

As described earlier, this problem was solved skilfully by the school. Some helpful activities such as digging wells and cleaning streams for drinking water were carried out for the community. As a result, their feelings about labour education changed for the better.

The aspects of the reform that the teachers felt were most significant were the development of teaching materials for social studies in the first to third grades, and the changes to the labour education programme. Before the reform there were central guidelines for developing social studies teaching materials and labour education. Locally produced materials have helped students and teachers to get to know and appreciate their locality and understand its problems. However, while socially useful activities through the labour education programme have helped to convince parents of its value, students now show less interest because they feel they have to do too much work.

The school used the political atmosphere positively to implement the changes. There was socialist emulation and competition among the teachers and the ministry rewarded meritorious headmasters and teachers every year. The school also used the organizational structures of different associations at the local level to mobilize community support.

How the programme and the school fit and adaptations made Labour education was intended to combine theory and practice while helping the community to finance the school. There was some discrepancy between the community's expectations and the intention of the programme:

> Due to the low educational level of the community, at the beginning there were some discrepancies between expectations and intentions of the changes. Labour education was not seen as teachers educating the children, as they thought education is limited to the classroom. The community thought that the school was using children to do physical labour just to get relief from classroom academic work. (Teachers)

These misconceptions were cleared up and it has been reported that labour education has solved some local practical problems. An important adaptation made to the labour education programme was changing its time in the schedule, allotting Friday afternoons rather than seventh period every day. Another important adaptation was working on activities that were based on community needs.

Political education has helped students and teachers to become more aware of the political and social conditions in the country. A local adaptation related to atheism in the Marxist political education curricula. The people in the locality are strict followers of religion, therefore teachers avoided unnecessary confrontation by deleting the atheist aspect.

Community needs for and its involvement in education have been increased. Community members now assist in the management of the school, the community provides land for the school, generates income by providing a labour force and each farmer contributes Birr 2.50-3.00 per year. The community promises to build more classrooms and teachers' quarters, and to send more children to school. The school management committee meets every month and decides on various important school-related issues. Local officials have convinced parents, through peasant associations, to send their children to school and have also convinced adults to attend literacy classes. Many children have gone on from the literacy programme to join the first grade. Thus, enrolment is increasing, and female participation especially in the literacy programme is very satisfactory.

The extent and quality of implementation

Material and financial support for the school from the community is now quite high. Extra classrooms, free living quarters for teachers and a small library have been built. Though there is shortage of paper, the SPC provides the teachers with adequate materials and equipment. Teachers make good use of teaching aids from locally available materials, and have become proficient in the preparation of lesson plans. They have benefited from the changes by deepening their knowledge, improving their teaching methods and sharing experiences and cooperating with other teachers. Their increased technical mastery has greatly increased their motivation and interest. They would be disappointed if the changes were to be cancelled or reversed, unless it were for a better goal.

The general standard of teaching materials is high. Social studies teaching materials for the first to third grades are highly relevant. There are some exceptions: textbooks for fourth-grade mathematics and third-grade science do not fit with student abilities and skills in these grades. The school radio programme, lesson planning, curriculum, SPC and labour education have an implementation rate of 100 per cent and a high success rate.

Impact and institutionalization

The changes and processes are desired to produce certain outcomes which can be broadly categorized as student, teacher and school outcomes. This section of the report concentrates on outcome and institutionalization at the school level.

Student outcomes One aspect of student outcome is a change in student knowledge. The students generally have good abilities and knowledge, and most of them pass Grade 6 national examinations. The changes have helped students to increase their knowledge of the environment and society, and they are also well informed about health and nutrition. The changes have also helped students to practise what they have learned by making charts, dyes and pottery. They can generate more income for themselves by applying the knowledge they have gained in agriculture, handicrafts and labour education. The various sports facilities have helped students to acquire good physical fitness.

Students no longer drink alcohol during working hours as they used to in 1984, and some of their superstitious traditional beliefs have been changed. The school radio programme has motivated students to learn because they enjoy the programme itself. They support weak and poor community members through labour education and are happy to lend this support. Students respect manual labour rather than despising it though they sometimes resent the amount of work they have to do. They have a strong need and motivation for education and they now insist on schooling.

Though one usually looks for improvements in students, these are not always observed. For example, one older boy who had joined school late hated labour education and manual work because he thought he had already mastered these skills at home and wanted to concentrate on academic learning. He challenged teachers about labour education and was not convinced by them of its value. His feelings towards schooling deteriorated and he was expelled.

Drop-out rate has always been high for economic reasons, with many families unable to afford to send their children the long distances to a secondary school. Now that the community has come to recognize the value of education the enrolment figures have started to increase, going from about 200 in 1987 to over 300 today. Some of the changes that political education demanded had a negative effect. Marxist political education introduced some elements of atheism. But the students in Tegulet I are ardent believers in orthodox Christianity and it was difficult to de-emphasize religion. Therefore the students had reservations about political education for religious reasons. However, the new policy declaration by the government meant that Marxist political education was dropped from the school curriculum during the regime of Mengistu (the former President).

Teacher outcomes The changes have deepened the teachers' knowledge, improved their ability to make teaching aids, strengthened their capacity for planning and enhanced their understanding of student needs and motivation. They have also begun to cooperate and exchange experiences, have developed the skills needed to link theory with practice and have gained good skills in information documentation. In general teacher skills and behaviour have been improved greatly as a result of their participation in the implementation of the changes. They have good and positive attitudes towards work. However, the new lesson plan format seems rigid and boring for teachers. The headmaster has reported that the routine demand of lesson planning seems to have turned teachers against formal presentation of plans although they may not dislike planning itself.

School outcomes The school has successfully and gradually changed the outlook and beliefs of the community. The discipline of the school also has improved greatly; teachers and students used to drink alcohol at school and leave early, but this has changed completely and working hours set by the Ministry of Education are fully observed. The labour education programme is well accepted, and the school has many active clubs such as Red Cross, nutrition, mini-media, agriculture, etc. There is good and systematic record keeping. The school has also helped to improve the environment by planting more trees, and has erected a fence to protect the property from animals. Land secured from the community will enable the school to generate more income. Internal income through selling grass, agricultural and hand-crafted products and financial contributions from parents enable the school to supply teaching materials. The newly improved sports field and SPC are also enabling the school to implement changes.

Though the school has achieved these and other positive outcomes, there have also been some negative aspects. The school management committee does a commendable job, but there are some problems. Sometimes the committee does not meet on time to decide on important school issues, and because of this the school had to suspend selling crops and collecting funds from the community. The cashier also occasionally fails to collect and deposit money in the bank.

Institutionalization There was no Marxist political education when the reforms started. By 1990, Marxist political education had been introduced in the fourth to sixth grades and it had become a regular part of the reform. Recent developments in the political life of the nation, in particular a new political and economic policy based on mixed economy, meant that the Marxist political education that had existed in the school during data collection was no longer a regular part of the programme by the time the results of the study were analysed. In fact, there is now a completely new government in Ethiopia.

Provided there are no radical political changes in the country all those involved are committed to continuing the reforms. The capacity of the SPC and the library will be developed; the increased community needs and participation will grow, thus helping the programme to continue; the assets owned by the school should ensure that internal income generation continues. A yearly programme has been posted in the headmaster's office and documents are filed well. The headmaster is pleased to be able to share his experiences with new teachers and gives them direction. They are informed about local environment, cultural values, how to adapt to the locality, etc. They are also shown how to prepare lesson plans, keep records and serve in various clubs.

Explanations for success at the school level

Enlightened leaders in the locality had the desire to improve their lives and their people, and thus the reforms were well accepted and implemented. Since most people in the locality were illiterate, the literacy campaign launched by the government was very popular and this helped to increase enrolment in the school. One other factor accounting for success at the school level was the political atmosphere and the resulting organizational structure in the country. Many popular organizations such as peasant, youth and women's associations were set up, and they helped to reach the people and convince the community to participate in school affairs. Children's awareness and motivation for schooling has been raised and they exerted pressure on their parents to send them to school.

Local authorities were close to the changes. The district administration encouraged the school to continue with the changes, and the region and district were empowered by the Ministry of Education to fully implement them. They held annual conferences in which various groups participated and this helped to create a sense of unity about the changes. Conferences were reinforced by the headmaster and SPC at the school level, and APC (district pedagogical centre) at the district level. Changes were initiated at the central level and implemented at the school level. The regional office evaluated the implementation of changes through the district and kept in close touch with the changes. Pressure and resources from the region received by the district office were passed on to the school. The regional office facilitated the sharing of successful experiences among districts.

The headmaster was a good source of continuous assistance for teachers, introducing guidelines, providing up-to-date information about the changes and coordinating experience exchange among teachers. The APC and the SPC trained teachers to make and use teaching aids. Inspectors visited the school twice a year and gave teachers necessary advice and on-the-spot assistance. The teachers helped each other whenever they faced technical problems while implementing the changes. This continuity of assistance from various sources improved the teachers' commitment, mastery and implementation skills. Teachers are now committed to school work and they honour teaching. Their feelings and confidence about education have improved. Mastering the reform concepts has raised teachers' capacity to implement the changes qualitatively.

The qualification and professional standard of those who provide assistance was considered to be high. The assistance was defined or requested by the school to meet its needs and was also endorsed by higher officials. On-the-spot assistance by inspectors was need-based; it dealt with day-to-day problems the school encountered when implementing the changes. This raised the motivation of both the teachers and the headmaster to implement the changes and improved teachers' skills in planning, record keeping and handling community issues. The assistance had a pedagogical and capacity-building emphasis. The headmaster claimed that the assistance was more classroom-oriented and pedagogical than administrative. However, it was observed and confirmed by teachers that inspection assistance was mostly management audit. Teachers got assistance and training on how to teach political education from an expert in this subject area. This encouraged teachers and helped them to gain more knowledge in the preparation and presentation of the subject, thus building their confidence to teach it. The training for the headmaster at the district level, the training for SPC coordinators by APC experts and the seminars and workshops on political education, radio programmes and other subjects all helped to strengthen the school's capacity to implement the changes. These capacity-building elements raised experience and interest in the programme and encouraged SPC coordinators to concentrate on their work in a planned and organized way. It also helped to intensify and popularize some components of the reform.

The role of the headmaster and local administrators emerged as one of the critical indicators of success in implementing the changes. There was stability among the headmasters who served in this school, which helped them to understand the community and its culture, to secure more land for the school, to fence the school and secure its property, to execute long-range plans with continuity and to gain more experience in implementing and following up changes. Inspectors were stable though the district administrators were not. Their relative stability has enabled the headmaster, inspectors and district administrators to follow up activities and to finish their plans with continuity. The dedicated and committed headmaster was close to, stayed with, and defended the changes. He led, guided and coordinated teachers during the implementation of the changes. His active presence and involvement had some positive implications for the implementation of the changes. It created competition among teachers, some of whom won merit rewards, and this in turn encouraged and motivated teachers for further success in implementing the changes. Local administrators were also close to the reforms, gave attention to building in the changes, stayed with and defended the changes. They were interested in the reforms and appreciated what was happening in the school, often commenting on changes during their visits. They also gave timely replies and positive responses to school requests and letters. The district officers and inspectors came to the school and encouraged teachers to implement the changes; they also offered practical, on-the-spot advice to solve problems. These actions helped to raise the commitment and confidence of the school in implementing the changes.

The headmaster was responsible for setting up the reading room and he prepared a good filing and documentation system in the school. He created a good division of labour and encouraged teachers to supplement the changes. He also brought in programmed use of the reading room for the third to sixth grades, and this helped to develop the students' reading habits and to increase their knowledge. There is a systematic recording of school properties and activities. The headmaster gave due attention to curriculum, budget and directives. He checked the work of teachers carefully and ensured timely delivery of materials to the school. The local administrators carefully checked up on what the school was doing, its record keeping and inventory system.

Assistance and administrative roles provided by the headmaster and district administration are two of the factors that are rated highly as reasons for success. The commitment of the teachers, headmaster and district administrators was another key factor. They all stated that they would be disappointed if the changes were reversed. They all believe in the importance of the changes and stayed with and defended the changes made. The headmaster and the teachers were empowered to decide on school affairs without being too far from central guidelines. The money generated through labour education and community contributions could be spent for school priorities without asking permission from the district office.

There are also some organizational factors that accounted for the successes of Tegulet I school. Personal networking is one such factor. The headmaster is the transmitter of the directives and guidelines given at the district level through seminars, conferences and workshops. He has close contact with the school management committee and the community at large. The headmaster and senior teachers got together, coordinated the community and convinced them to contribute more. They also mobilized new teachers to believe in the changes. The climate and political scene in the country was helpful, as the Workers' Party of Ethiopia had passed some directives to help the implementation of the reforms. It encouraged schools to boost their internal income. A healthy relationship between the community and school created favourable conditions for implementing changes. There was no major resistance to the reforms, although securing land for the school had caused some problems at the beginning.

Prospects for the future

The teachers have good faith in the programme and believe that the changes will continue to be implemented in the school in the future. Their positive outlook was expressed in the following way during a group interview:

> SPC will develop in capacity, more students will enrol and community needs for education will grow. District leadership will grow and develop through experiences, the community will help the school to be more self-reliant. (Teachers)

More farmland and water for irrigation for income generation, extension of the school to junior secondary, more trained teachers in all fields, resettling those families who are presently living in the school compound are some of their hopes. Their worries are based on their hopes. Shortage of farmland for the school, lack of water for gardening, the limitation of the school to sixth grade and high drop-out rate after seventh grade when children are sent to a distant school worry the teachers.

The headmaster also thinks that the changes will continue into the future; he will push the community and teachers to continue with the changes. He hopes that the school will be extended to the level of eighth grade and that the school will have trained teachers in all subject areas. He also hopes to get irrigation water to help the school boost its internal income, and is worried by the limitation of the school to sixth grade only. More resources, trained teachers and finance; more cooperation between the school and the community; and continuous and close follow-up from higher officials will all be needed to help the school fulfil these hopes and allay the worries.

The parents and school management committee members predict similar things for the future. They have stated that those farmers who live distant from school will continue to pay cash, and those near the school will provide labour services. In a group interview, the parents expressed the following views:

> The strong points of the school should continue and parents will do their best to continuously improve the implementation of the changes. We are also sure that the headmaster will continue pushing the committee members to implement the changes with more cooperation with the school. (Parents)

The parents hope that those families who live in the school compound will move out and settle in better places, that the school will expand to the level of junior secondary (grades 7 and 8), and that the headmaster will continue to coordinate school activities in cooperation with the community as he is doing at present. Their worries include limitation of the school to the sixth grade, and unemployment of young, educated students. They believe that increasing cooperation between different peasant associations, providing more land for the school, building more living quarters for teachers and upward expansion of the school step-by-step will help them reach these goals.

The Hasnahena Government Primary School Case, Bangladesh

Mumtaz Jahan

THE DISTRICT AND THE LOCAL CONTEXT

The Hasnahena government primary school is situated in the district of Tangail, near to the capital city Dhaka. Predominantly an agricultural district, Tangail produces rice, wheat, cotton, cane, groundnut, oilseed, tobacco, banana, coconut, jackfruit, etc. But the district is also well known for its cotton products, especially cotton sarees, and weaving is the major livelihood of most people in the district. The school is located in a weaving community consisting of predominantly low-caste Hindus. The community is very poor and most of the adults are illiterate. The few who claim to be literate studied up to classes IV and V. The literacy rate of the district is 20.2 per cent, compared to the national average of 23.8 per cent. The district has 1085 primary schools and the total enrolment in these schools is 277,000.

The most significant aspect of this community is that in spite of poverty and illiteracy, it is very eager to provide education for the children. The education officers of the area claimed unanimously that this was the best school in the *upazila* (region) and this was confirmed by the field-visit and classroom observations of the researcher. The school is in a better position in terms of physical facilities such as classrooms, benches, chalkboards, a toilet, a tubewell and a playground.

UNIVERSAL PRIMARY EDUCATION (UPE) AND THE REFORM

The formal primary education of Bangladesh comprises five years' schooling (classes I to V). The low literacy rate (23.8 per cent) is further aggravated by the high growth rate of the population, which means that the existing primary education facilities are inadequate to cope with the increasing number of primary school age children. In order to improve the overall situation at primary level, the government decided to introduce UPE, to provide facilities for universalization of primary education and raise the quality of education at that level. The UPE programme was initiated in 1981 (1980-85 five-year plan period) as a pilot project in 4053 schools of 44 upazilas with external assistance and it was carried over to the third Five-year Plan (1985-90) to cover all the primary schools of the country. The objectives of UPE (first and second projects) were as follows:

- enrolment of 70 per cent of primary school age children
- to ensure the successful completion of the five-year cycle of primary education by the majority of children enrolled
- to reinforce internal efficiency of the schools through better teaching-learning practices, school management and supervision aimed at qualitative improvement of primary education.

Certain specific measures were taken within the framework of UPE (first project) under the second five-year plan. These were:

- creation of separate directorate of primary education
- creation of the curriculum development centre
- creation of the posts of assistant upazila education officers (AUEO)
- appointment of more female teachers
- delegating some authority to upazila parishad for management and supervision of primary education
- training of teachers and supervisors through cluster training
- introduction of community learning centres (CLC)

- expansion of physical facilities of primary schools
- bringing private schools under government management
- distribution of free textbooks and uniforms.

The major thrusts of the UPE (second project) programme during the third five-year plan period were:

- wider coverage
- necessary repairs and renovation of existing schools
- construction of additional classrooms
- provision of other facilities
- supply of free textbooks and teachers' guides
- training of teachers and supervisors.

The most important work undertaken during the project period was qualitative improvement of the primary education through comprehensive curriculum renewal and modification and producing a competency-based curriculum accompanied by liberal promotion policy (LPP) and continuous pupil assessment (CPA).

The project schools under the first UPE project were selected in a phased manner and were given reform inputs such as physical facilities, expansion of school buildings, seating, blackboards, tubewells, toilets, etc., to allow more children to be enrolled in the schools. Children from disadvantaged families were offered government incentives in the form of free textbooks and clothing to enable them to take advantage of the educational facilities. Unfortunately, the provision of free clothing was withdrawn at a later stage. The recruitment of female teachers was a major component in the 'reform bundle' and was considered essential for encouraging the enrolment of girls. Another important reform input designed to improve the quality of teaching was cluster training, through a network of some 10 schools. The community awareness and its involvement in primary education were expected to grow through the formation of school managing committees and parent-teacher associations. The supervision and reporting systems were also strengthened by the reform through the appointment of AUEOs. These are included in the initial 'reform bundle'.

Over a period of ten years (1981-90), other reform components such as a modified curriculum and textbooks, teachers' guides, block teaching, liberal promotion policy and continuous student assessment were added to the UPE project (second), giving the 'reform bundle' the final shape shown in Figure 1.2.

SCHOOL LEVEL CHANGES AS SEEN LOCALLY

Hasnahena was one of the 4053 government primary schools that were identified as IDA (International Development Association) project schools in 1981. Before the project began the school had no toilet and the tubewell it had was out of order; children were not provided with free textbooks and there was no provision for in-service training of teachers. School supervision was irregular; there were no teachers' guides or reporting system; and there were no local

Physical facilities
Classroom space
Furniture
Playground
Tubewell and latrine

School management
Reporting forms
Maintenance
Evaluation (student assessment)
Liberation Promotion Policy

Curriculum
Relevance (life and need) oriented
Co-curricular activities (singing, dancing, sports, gardening, etc.)

Instructional materials
Textbooks
Teachers' guides
Teaching aids

Quality of teachers
PTI training
Cluster training
Supervision
Teaching–learning practice
Female teachers
Teacher attendance and punctuality

Community involvement
School managing committee
Parent–Teacher Association

Figure 1.2

committees such as the school managing committee (SMC) or the parent-teacher association (PTA).

As a result of the reform, the school received additional physical facilities such as more classrooms, benches, black-boards and a much-needed toilet and tubewell. The other measures which had a qualitative impact on the school included textbooks, cluster training in the form of refresher course, teachers' guides, and the academic supervision of the AUEO. Community involvement was ensured through the SMC and PTA.

The outcomes of the reform, seen by teachers and local administrators at the school level, include punctual teacher attendance, increased enrolment, more regular supervision, and higher retention rate and better performance of the learners. The people interviewed commented that free textbooks 'worked like a miracle', but stories from other schools do not support this. Although they received similar inputs provided through the 'reform bundle', the other schools included in the study did not show similar results. These initial findings led the researcher to question further how a rural school actually succeeds and what factors are responsible for success.

THE CHANGE PROCESS AT THE LOCAL LEVEL

The school received the reform inputs on a piecemeal basis. The teachers and the local administrators did not have an initial opportunity to see the 'reform bundle' and correlate this with the goals of the reform. The initial inputs were physical facilities and free textbooks. Over a long period of time, the 'reform bundle' has taken shape and it is easier now to connect it with the desired goals. The people involved are gradually aware of what UPE means and what the major objectives (raising enrolments, cutting down repetition and drop-out rates etc.) are.

The inputs provided for the qualitative improvement of primary education (cluster training, teachers' guides, block teaching, etc.) were recognized as strategies for the success of UPE by the teachers and administrators at a much later stage. One administrator expressed both positive and negative opinions about the quality of teaching by the teachers of this school. This implies that the quality of teaching-learning practice, which is the key implementation process of UPE, is still debatable. Many of the administrators related the quality of teaching to the use of teaching aids, but the classroom observations showed that even without teaching aids learners can be stimulated and made to learn. Good textbooks can be effective tools for learning.

At the initial stage, the headmaster and the local level administrators received orientation training, but when asked about it later, none of them could remember the title of the training material or the theme of the workshop; they could only remember the visit of a foreign consultant!

Hasnahena primary school is a big school with almost 900 students. It received enough physical facilities and the school's own funds were used to extend the school building. Even then the classrooms were overcrowded when 50 per cent of the children were present. The situation is not the same in other schools of the upazila. This raises a number of questions:

- Why has this school been termed the best school in the Upazila?
- Why don't similar inputs bring similar results?
- Who, in what way, caused the differences with respect to implementation and outcomes of the reform?

These inputs were designed as means for attaining the goals or objectives of UPE. The material inputs are unable to produce anything unless they get a group of persuasive users. The users of these inputs are the teachers who are responsible for making things work in the classroom situation of all schools. Hasnahena primary school has got a very persuasive headmaster who earnestly worked with the AUEO to improve the overall situation of the school. He implemented the reform well and made the school a very successful one in the locality. His active role and initiatives strongly suggest that even in the absence of the reform, this school under his leadership, would still be the best one in the area.

The ways in which the inputs were used was a factor in the school's success in implementing the reform. A good teacher learns from the teachers' guides, cluster training leaflets and advice/instructions from the headmaster and supervisors. The same materials remain unused by a disinterested teacher, thus similar inputs can have very different outcomes. It is obvious in the case of this school that the difference in implementation and outcome was created not by material inputs, but by human beings.

Consequently replication of innovations or reforms has become a challenge to the planners because human qualities differ from person to person. The roles played by the headteachers, teachers, supervisors and community of twelve schools each with different degrees of commitment, sincerity and accountability were the major factors behind the observed differences in the implementation and outcomes of the reform. It is not material input or even funding, but people who matter most, as the Hasnahena experience shows.

FACTORS THAT HELPED AND HINDERED THESE CHANGES AS SEEN BY TEACHERS IN THE SCHOOL

What factors were perceived by teachers in the school as contributing to its success? Everybody agreed that the headmaster held the key to its success, but it is interesting to look at those aspects of his behaviour that played the most vital roles. His presence in the school from morning to evening, and his command and influence over the teachers helped the reform to take root in the school smoothly and rapidly. His personal initiatives in the form of making a betel-nut garden for providing the school with extra income strengthened the teachers' and community's confidence in both him and the school. The regular weekly discussion-cum-training meeting of the teachers initiated by the headmaster, and the introduction of a reward for the class teacher who could enrol the largest number of students strengthened the teachers' motivation and improved their performance. Figure 1.3 illustrates how the headmaster acted like a catalyst in the improvement cycle.

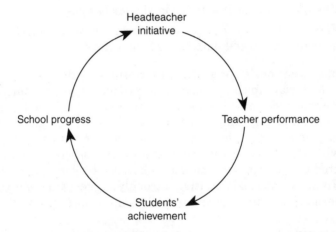

Figure 1.3

The headmaster of Hasnahena primary school has worked at the school since 1962. His role in the implementation and outcomes of the reform is reflected in the comments of assistant teachers, support givers and supervisors:

- the headteacher advised them from time to time to make them aware of reform activities... It led to teachers' preparation.
- He planted fruit trees and expanded school house from the profit... which increased teachers' confidence.
- The headteacher discussed with us.
- I got training from the headteacher once or twice a month.

- The headteacher's guidance and efforts are the key to the progress of the school.
- He observes classroom teaching.
- The headteacher organizes staff development class every Thursday.
- He planted betel nut trees in one corner of school yard, he has extended one classroom from the earnings of that.

The headmaster's worries reflect his character when he says: Teacher association has brought grouping and not recognized good teachers. His desire above all, is for good teachers for the school. His perceptions about the future of the school support his interest in it when he comments 'use of teaching aids will further improve teaching in the near future, and in 2 or 3 years, all the primary age children of the locality will be enrolled.' He sees the school's future need as gardening plots and sport goods, as well as more classrooms, furniture and building repairs, proving him to be an efficient teacher who also possesses the ability to make the school environment more attractive to the students. His desire for clothing for the poor students shows him to be a sensible teacher who cares for the disadvantaged learners.

When the support givers say 'teaching-learning is better (here) than in the other schools, it is a reflection on the types of assistance provided by the headmaster and the local support givers/supervisors. These are:

- supply of resources and facilities
- provision of training
- exerting control
- providing solution and support to the teachers initially and at a later stage of the reform.

All the aspects of headmaster's role have been rated as 'high' on the three-point scale used for identifying the degree of difference between the twelve headteachers.

The Thursday staff development meetings have created a forum for the teachers to discuss a wide range of subjects. Academic issues and problems emerge along with family and personal matters. The cluster training in this school has created a channel for carrying messages from the central level to the school level, providing the teachers with additional knowledge and skills. The teachers reported that being late for school was unheard of at this school and the researcher's observations support this. The headmaster's physical presence at the school from morning to evening indirectly influenced the teachers to be punctual and to stay until the end of the school day. The supervisors also visit this school frequently.

Thus the leader generates the growth cycle affecting all others around him. However, it should be mentioned that what a dedicated and able headteacher can achieve in a school, will not necessarily be possible for an equally committed and capable teacher. Although an institution is manned by a group of persons, they are very much influenced by the capabilities, skills, leadership qualities, behaviour patterns, attitudes and even temper of the person who heads the institution, and under whom they work. The same is true in schools. If the headteacher is not committed, others are not expected to be so. A very committed and sincere teacher cannot do much by his or her individual efforts, because colleagues are likely to follow the example of the headteacher. Thus individual efforts have limited results and little influence on others unless the individual holds the top position in the institution or school.

The role of the head of the institution of Hasnahena primary school corroborates the fact that if quick and sustainable change in a school is to be brought about, there is no alternative but to place a committed and sincere person at the top. Only then can multiple changes at every step affecting teachers, students and the school be expected. By virtue of his or her position, the head of the institution does not always have to speak aloud what is and what is not to be done. If the staff regard their leader as a dynamic personality, they tend to follow without specific instructions. Anyone who does not follow is regarded as a 'rebel' and finds himself or herself isolated and suffers from self-inflicted punishment. Taking this sort of risk is not very common among most professionals in this society: people like to go along with the group and conform to group behaviours.

So, the head of an institution can confidently act as a 'change-agent' or a 'reformer' because he or she attracts followers. The same is applicable to schools. The teachers follow the headteacher and implement his or her plans, and gradually the so-called 'rebels' join their hands with the group. The headteacher's role at Hasnahena primary school has brought it to the top in outcomes, implementation and institutionalization among the twelve schools in the study. The other factors that have played important roles in the success of this school are:

- The receptivity of the community. It is well known that when the consumers are eager to buy, the goods will be sold easily.
- The local administrators of this locality (UEO, AUEO) were equally committed as the headteacher. They visited the school often (confirmed by teachers) and thus kept the teachers dutiful.
- The cluster training has created a channel for carrying innovations in primary education from the central level offices to the school. It is functioning as a regular in-service training programme in this school. All teachers, willing or unwilling, have to attend and this training programme enriches them, and influences their classroom performances to some extent.
- The government child survey has made the teachers aware of the major concern of the UPE, i.e. enrolment of all children over five years old, and as a result they have started to encourage parents to send their children to the school.
- The free distribution of textbooks has made school accessible to the children of the poor weaver community.

- The free distribution of new teachers' guides has helped the teachers to improve the planning of their lessons.
- In a society where women enjoy very limited rights and no privileges, the presence of a large number of female students in the classroom is an indicator of the success of the reform.

These factors have helped this school to overcome its other limitations and problems.

The reform faced some difficulties at the initial stage because the DPEOs and UEOs did not have clear ideas about the reforms necessary for the improvement of the schools. This combined with a delay in the supply of materials and the poor quality of the building work contributed to the slow pace of the reform. Another problem is that the primary school teachers' association politicizes the teachers and different groupings develop among them. As a result, the professional development of teachers is no longer at the centre of the agenda.

The parent-teacher association (PTA) was set up with the main aim of creating awareness among parents and thus encouraging them to send their children to school. Although the PTA is not working in this area, the community is still very keen for its children to be educated, and is carrying out the role of the PTA without holding meetings. The community is producing the results that the authority expected to achieve through PTAs. However, the SMC and PTA are given the authority to look after the functioning of schools without making the teachers accountable to them. The committees have no power to take disciplinary actions or other measures against the teachers. For the most part, in poor, rural communities that must spend the day earning enough to live on, PTAs are still a planner's dream.

The reform has increased the teachers' workload. In addition to their normal work, they have to send different types of progress and status reports to the higher authorities and they have yet to master new concepts such as Liberal Promotion Policy and Continuous Pupils Assessment. This is affecting teaching-learning practice and its outcomes. One teacher mentioned that cluster training was taking up too much of his time, perhaps indicating that the training is not yet worthwhile.

The goals and objectives of the reform were not stated clearly to the local people at the outset. This is a common weakness found in all reform programmes. The policy guidelines covering this aspect are seldom used at the field level and even the trainers and supervisors do not always use and follow them properly. In this case, the central office did not take the trouble to convey the messages properly to all concerned. Furthermore, the relay system of communication and training, which is commonly used in populous countries, loses important issues and messages in the process, and the objectives, purposes and processes are not written in language understandable to the field level implementors.

THE RELATIVE SUCCESS OF IMPLEMENTATION AND OUTCOMES

The school, teacher and student level outcomes of this school indicate the relative success of implementation of the reform. The school level outcomes in Hasnahena primary school are: new classrooms, benches, tubewell, toilet, two female teachers, about 900 students including large number of girls, school reporting, SMC and PTA. The school has achieved a high degree of success in implementation of the reform in the areas of delivery of inputs, teacher performance and productivity, compatibility with other classroom routines and content. It has achieved a moderate degree of success in the areas of technical mastery, teacher engagement and interest, and a low degree in the wider use of reform among teachers. The positive changes at school level and the school's capacity for further change, show a high degree of success.

The student outcomes of this school are: regular attendance, fewer failures and more passes, more students receiving scholarships through competitive examination, active participation in both classroom and co-curricular activities. The school has achieved a high degree of success in various aspects of student outcomes, namely student knowledge, student behaviour and skills and attendance. The degree of success is moderate in other student outcomes, such as student attitudes, motivations and unexpected student changes.

The teacher outcomes are: punctual teacher attendance, improved subject and pedagogical knowledge, satisfactory teaching and team spirit. Although the PTA is non-existent, teachers have started urging parents to send their children to school. It is an indication of improved and responsible teacher behaviour. Cluster training has affected both the school and the teacher outcomes in the form of a congenial atmosphere in school and raising the standard of teacher performance. The school has been rated as high in three teacher outcomes — teacher knowledge, teacher skill and teacher attitudes, and has achieved a moderate degree of success in teachers' 'negative changes'.

The school has also achieved a high degree of success in all the components of institutionalization of the reform, indicated by improved teaching-learning practice and acceptance of the reform by all concerned. The betel-nut garden raised for extra income for the school for use in extending classrooms, rewarding teachers and weekly discussion meetings is a unique example of both teacher and school outcomes at the Hasnahena primary school. Comments from interviewees such as: 'Teachers are more punctual, interested', 'teachers are using ideas of cluster training', 'teaching-learning is better than in other schools', 'all items are supplied to the school', 'teachers are getting help from AUEO on all issues', 'enrolment has increased, teacher absenteeism has decreased,' 'the headmaster's guidance and efforts are key to progress', all imply that, whoever is playing the major role, the school has proved to be an excellent one in the Upazila as well as the best of the twelve schools of the study.

EXPLANATIONS FOR SUCCESS AT THE SCHOOL LEVEL

The success story of this school includes such components as increased enrolment with higher participation of girls, extension of school buildings, more regular and punctual teacher and student attendance, more scholarships, fewer failures and more passes. As discussed earlier the school received the same assistance as the others at different stages of implementation. In addition to this, free primary education, the role of the headteacher, UEO and AUEO; community involvement; and, above all, political support in introducing UPE in 1980 were factors that contributed to its success.

One question that may be asked is whether the headteacher would have been as effective without the reform and the assistance provided through it. In this particular case, the headmaster with his initiative, high degree of commitment and personal interest made good use of the reform bundle. The differences in school, teacher and student outcomes were mainly due to the roles played by the respective headteachers. For example, in one school, the administrators and people in the community tried hard for the improvement of the school but their efforts failed. This shows that if the school personnel, especially the head of the institution remain inactive, disinterested and unmotivated, the school situation cannot change even if it gets support from the authority, community and others concerned.

PROSPECTS FOR THE FUTURE

The reform components have become part of the school's regular routine. Provided the inputs are available and the committed headmaster stays, the school is expected to improve in teacher, student and school outcomes. However, what is less certain is what will happen when the headmaster retires. Will the school be able to sustain this development without his leadership? It is difficult to predict the future, but institutionalization of reform components will continue to produce good results for a long time. The teachers who have been working under the present headmaster are expected to carry on the work with the same spirit and dedication. The existing physical facilities and the reputation of the school will attract larger numbers of students in the future; and the routine discussion meeting and cluster training are expected to continue. The school personnel have developed an affinity for receiving and implementing change programmes, but everything will depend on the behaviour, attitude and motivation of the future headteacher.

The reform has also helped the policy planners to understand urgent and basic needs of a school, as well as the supplementary and future needs. This experience is expected to generate more interest and better planning in future. The implementation of the reform through the network from the Ministry of Education to the DPE to the DPEO to the AUEO and finally to the headteacher and School, helped bring central level officials closer to the field level personnel and to see for themselves what happens at the grass-roots level. This is bound to have impressive effects on primary education.

SUMMARY

In Hasnahena primary school, the reform helped the school personnel by providing appropriate and useful inputs while the committed headmaster and his colleagues used this opportunity to implement the reform successfully. The receptive community provided additional support to the school personnel and ultimately to the reform. Thus the reform, the headteacher's role and community pressure have worked together to bring the school to the level of 'excellent' in the Upazila.

Part 2

The Country Reports

This section, Chapters 3 to 5, presents a summary of each country report. The reader is adviced to consult with the individual school studies (a total of 31) and the analysis presented by the country teams. (The Country Studies are available from IMTEC.)

The purpose of this section is to provide reference materials for the international analysis (Chapters 6 to 9). In particular the sections describing the reforms are important background information for Chapters 6 to 9.

Chapter 3

The Escuela Nueva School Programme in Colombia

Carlos Rojas

This section presents a brief description of the origin of the Escuela Nueva programme, its main characteristics and form of operations. References for the description include *Manual de Orientación y Asesoría de Escuela Nueva* (Vásquez, 1984), the review by Colbert (1987) in the book *La Educación Rural en Colombia*, and the bulletin *Educar*, published by the National Ministry of Education in 1980.

THE LARGER SYSTEM PICTURE
The country context

The Colombian Educational System has its legal base in the national constitution and in the special decrees such as Law 088 of 1976, 1419 of 1978, 80 of 1980, and 1002 of 1984. Recently, a new law — 24 of 1988 — resulted in the restructuring of the national Ministry of Education.

The formal education system is made up of the following levels:

1. **Preschool education** This level refers to the education that is offered to children under six years of age. Its fundamental objective is to promote and stimulate the physical, affective and cognitive development of the child. In this way, it prepares children for the social context of the school and for their future school learning experiences. Table 3.1 shows the evolution of preschool opportunities in Colombia in the last few years. This education level has had the extensive participation of the private sector. Preschool education remains an urban phenomenon in Colombia with only 8.5 per cent of those enrolled from rural areas.

2. **Basic education** This cycle begins at the age of six years and includes all five primary grades and the first four secondary grades. The recent Political Constitution of Colombia of 4 July 1991 established that '... the State, the society, and the family are responsible for education and that education will be obligatory between the ages of five and fifteen and will include, at a minimum preschool and nine years of basic education.'

Between the end of the 1950s and the late 1970s, primary education was characterized by a significant growth in coverage that was superior to that obtained in other countries of Latin America. Unfortunately, this growth has not been maintained during the last 15 years. In accordance with a recent document from the national planning department, '... from the middle of the 1970s the rate of growth of education for Colombians has been notably reduced.

Table 3.1 Relative frequency of students enrolled in public and private preschools

Year	Public	Private
1982	38.6	61.4
1983	39.9	60.1
1984	42.2	57.8
1985	43.4	56.6
1986	44.4	55.4

Source: Estadísticas de la Educación 1982–86, Ministerio de Educación, División de Estadísticas y Sistemas, Colombia

In primary, the annual rate of enrolment has been less than 1 per cent. In secondary, where the greatest need exists, it was only 5 per cent between 1975 and 1984, and has been at 2 per cent for the last five years.' (Documento MEN-DNP-UDS_DEC, 2518, 19 March 1991)

It is in primary basic education where public education has its greatest participation. Approximately 4.2 million children are enrolled in primary education and 86 per cent of these are in public schools. The remaining 14 per cent have access to private schooling.

In terms of residence, the statistics of the Ministry of Education indicate that almost 36 per cent of those enrolled in primary school are from rural areas, while 64 per cent live in cities. Even with ongoing efforts to improve basic primary education, there remain a series of difficulties in relation to high rates of drop-outs, repetition, and absences. Only 18.3 per cent of the children in rural areas complete their primary education. In urban areas the figure is 62.4 per cent. In general the average grade reached by a rural child is less than second grade, while in the urban areas the average grade completed is fourth.

3. **Middle and intermediate education** This cycle prepares the student to continue his or her studies in higher education and/or for technical work. The vocational middle education programme offers different alternatives such as: science, arts, industry, commerce, agriculture, etc. Basic secondary education includes sixth through ninth grade. Intermediate education (tenth and eleventh grades) is considered to be a continuation of the middle school modalities. In general terms, sixth through eleventh grade are considered secondary education. Sixty per cent of the secondary students attend public schools and 40 per cent attend private schools.

It is important to point out that this level of education is almost non-existent in rural areas. Less than 1 per cent of secondary students have access to schools in rural areas. According to the national department of planning, 2.6 million students were enrolled in secondary studies in 1990. This number represents less than 50 per cent of the demand for schooling at this level.

4. **Superior or higher education** This is considered the last level of the Colombian education system. It prepares students in different fields of knowledge. The division of its services in recent years is shown in Table 3.2. Close to 60 per cent of the students studying at this level do so in private establishments. In Colombia, as in the majority of Latin American countries, there has been a rapid expansion at this level. At present there are nearly 240

Table 3.2 Percentage of students enrolled in public and private education facilities at the higher level

Year	Public	Private
1982	39.1	60.9
1983	39.6	60.4
1984	39.2	60.8
1985	40.9	59.1
1986	40.9	59.1

Table 3.3 Rate of illiteracy in the population of ten years and more

Census	Total in age group	Per cent illiterate
1951	7,792,000	38.5
1964	11,598,000	26.6
1973	14,513,000	17.7
1985	21,151,000	12.2

institutions of higher education in the country, of which 30 per cent are public and 70 per cent private.

According to the last census, conducted in 1985, Colombia has a population of 27,867,326. Of these 32 per cent live in rural areas. One of the chronic problems that have confronted the National Ministry of Education is the high rate of illiteracy among the population. As shown in Table 3.3, this remains at 12.2 per cent despite various literacy campaigns conducted by different governments.

The degree of repetition in the educational system is also somewhat alarming. As Table 3.4 shows, in 1978-1983, only 18.3 per cent of the children in rural areas who entered school completed their primary education. During the same time period, 62.4 per cent of the urban children completed the five years of elementary school. The average grade of completion suggests an even darker picture for the rural areas, with on average less than two years of school completed, compared to almost four years in the urban areas.

In terms of absolute numbers in primary education, there are 36,979 primary schools in operation in the country. Of these, the majority are public (90.5 per cent) with the remainder being privately run. Sixty-nine per cent of these schools are in rural areas, which reflects the dispersed nature of the population and the need for multi-grade classrooms.

There were 4,002,543 students enrolled in primary school in 1986. Of these, 86.4 per cent were in public schools and 13.6 per cent in private schools. Almost two-thirds of the students (2,564,896) were in urban schools with the remainder (1,437,647) enrolled in schools in the rural area. To serve this population there are a total of 135,924 teachers. The majority of these (84,867) are in the urban areas, while 51,237 work in rural schools. Thus, the teacher-student ratio is 1:30 and 1:28 in urban and rural areas, respectively.

The origin of the programme

Recommendation No. 52 of the International Conference of Ministers of Education, celebrated in Geneva in 1961 and supported by UNESCO, established

Table 3.4 Internal efficiency of the primary education system

Time period	Retention		Years of schooling	
	Urban	Rural	Urban	Rural
1961–1966	41.3%	3.2%	–	–
1969–1973	53.2%	11.0%	3.1	1.6
1978–1983	62.4%	18.3%	3.8	1.7

Source: Estadísticas de la Educación, Ministerio de Educación Nacional, Colombia, 1987

the need for opening 'Unitary Schools' that offered a complete primary education in the poorest rural areas of developing countries. As a result, this model started to be implemented in Colombia with technical assistance from UNESCO. The country created the first unitary school in the Instituto Superior de Educación Rural (ISER), Pamplona, in the department of Norte de Santander. By the middle of the 1960s, under the direction of Professor Oscar Mogollón, the programme had expanded to 150 schools.

In general terms the objectives of the unitary school were to:

- expand the coverage of the primary school system;
- lower the elevated indices of drop-outs, repetition and absences;
- offer an active learning not based on memorization;
- respect the learning speed of each child;
- provide the five grades of primary education in schools with one or two teachers.

Pedagogically, the programme required the development of cards or guides to deal with the specific areas of self-instruction, directed activities, expansion and recovery. This material was adapted and expanded by the students and teachers in the schools where the elementary school teachers were trained.

With the relative success of the programme, the national government decreed in 1967 its expansion to the rest of the country. At the end of the decade, the department of Antioquia, through its university, and the department of Risaralda began working with the programme, making adaptations as they saw necessary. However, during this process of growth some problems arose. The principal problem was the different focuses that the various people and groups working with the programme wanted to give it. This resulted in a lack of consensus about the definition and orientation of the 'Unitary School'.

The attempt to generalize the experience of the unitary school throughout the country identified several shortcomings in the programme. There were deficiencies in teacher training; in the involvement of local and regional administrators; in the relationship of the course content to the environment in which the children lived; and in the definition of the role of the teacher as a community promoter. As a response to these problems, and after evaluating the difficulties, the Escuela Nueva programme was begun in 1975. This programme had four principal components which were described in the first manual entitled *Towards a New School (Hacia la Escuela Nueva)*. A new educational model with different operative educational strategies and mechanisms for primary rural schools was proposed in the manual. One year later, in 1976, the 'New School' was recognized as a programme of the Ministry of Education.

Description of the Escuela Nueva Programme

Taking the principal education agents into consideration, Colbert (1987) described the objective of the Escuela Nueva programme as follows.

Objectives The fundamental objectives of the Escuela Nueva Programme are: to offer in the rural areas the five years of primary school education in rural areas with just one or two teachers, to decrease the rate of drop-outs, and to improve the quality of education. To accomplish these objectives the programme considers:

- an active teaching-learning process
- a flexible promotion system
- an emphasis on closer community-school relationship
- the fit of the educational contents to the rural needs.

At the student level, the programme specifically seeks:

- the development of active and reflexive learning
- the development of research, creative, analytical and applied skills
- the improvement of self-concept
- the development of attitudes of cooperation and solidarity
- knowledge and basic information of the curriculum areas.

At the teacher level, the programme expects to accomplish:

- the development of positive attitudes towards the new methodologies
- a role change from being just instructor to facilitator or guide
- a more active role as a community leader
- a positive attitude toward the rural area
- a better and more positive attitude toward the administrative officials and technical counsellors
- good management of the components of the programme
- mastery of the elements of the Escuela Nueva
  - organization of the student government
  - teaching with guides, learning corners and library
  - adaptation of schedules to the requirements of flexible promotion
  - adaptation of the guides to the environment and level of the students
  - capacity to manipulate several grade levels at once.

At the community level, the programme seeks to increase the community's involvement in the school's daily life and problems, as well as to increase the teacher's role within the community, so that the school becomes a centre of community integration.

Programme components The design of the new school programme started from the assumption that 'to introduce innovations to the children it is also necessary to introduce innovations in the stratagies for the teachers' training, in the administrative structure and in the teachers' community work. As a result, the programme has four basic components: training and follow-up, curriculum, administrative and community strategies.

(i) The training and follow-up component addresses teachers and administrative supervisors. The training is conducted through sequential workshops where the programme characteristics, methodology and strategies are presented. The teachers learn, among other things, how to manage the materials, students' guides and school library.

(ii) The second component relates to the curriculum. The programme designed written materials in the form of guides for the students and manuals for teachers and supervisors. To date, several versions have been released. The students' guides are one of the most important elements of the programme because they facilitate individual and group work.

(iii) The third component addresses administrative aspects. It aims to streamline the administration of the programme at the regional level and seeks to change the supervisor's prospective role to that of the teacher's facilitator and counsellor.

(iv) The fourth component relates to the community. This strategy tries to bring about the parents' involvement in school activities. The idea is to convert the school into a centre that promotes community development.

Characteristics of the programme methodology The following is a summary of the characteristics of the methodology of the Escuela Nueva programme:

- Active learning: the students have their own materials and work guides. They study in small groups.
- Teachers are guides and not instructors. They guide, supervise and evaluate the learning process.
- The promotion to the next objective or next course is flexible: the students move forward according to their individual differences and at their own pace.
- The students participate in the school organization through the school government.
- The classroom is organized in a dynamic way into areas of interest or 'corners' and subjects.

- The school might become an information centre for the community. The family records of each student provide basic data about the number of family members, their education and occupation.

Elements to implement the programme In order to implement the programme, each of the components includes a set of elements to be used by the teacher and the students as part of the methodology.

For the community component:

- School surroundings map (*croquis*): with the students and community help, a map of the school's surrounding area is sketched. This croquis allows children to locate the school in relation to the area dwellings. It also allows identification of the main access ways and determination of the distance that children have to walk to get to the school.
- Family records: the teacher must collect information about the characteristics of the households. This information about gender, age, education level, sports, associations etc., allows him/her to determine the potential number of school age children over the next years and the illiteracy level, as well as the needs and general characteristics of the area.
- County monograph: as a complement to the above information, the teacher must write a monograph of the area. In his or her work he or she has to describe the community organizations, cultural and sporting traits, nutritional habits, health conditions, employment situation, agricultural products, marketing, etc. This monograph then allows the teacher to plan school activities based on the characteristics of the region.
- Agricultural calendar: jointly with the community, the teacher must elaborate the agricultural calendar of the region and include the products and dates when the different agricultural tasks are performed. This is an essential element for the planning of scholar activities.

For the curricular and administrative components:

- Corners: these consist in the arrangement of areas of interest such as mathematics, natural sciences, social sciences, language, etc. Each of these 'corners' has didactic material for the student to develop his/her academic activities
- Constant observation material: in the main school classroom, the teacher must hang up posters with the alphabet letters, the numbers from 0 to 9, as well as the numbers 10, 100, 1000, 10000 etc.
- Library: within the programme philosophy, the library plays an important role as a consultation mechanism for both the teachers and the students to conduct investigations, to complement a theme or just as a place to read for fun.

- Students' guides: these consist of written material to direct the students in the activities that they must follow. Each academic area is divided into three parts and each part is divided into two or three units which are developed through the guides. The guide presents the objective(s) that must be accomplished, the basic information to accomplish the objective, practical and independent activities.
- School government: without any doubt, this is one of the most important and innovative elements of the new school programme in the process of students' formation. By this means, teachers, parents and students actively participate in the school direction and organization. The school government comprises a president, a vice-president and a number of committees in charge of specific aspects of the school life.
- Self-monitoring mechanisms: as part of the child's own self-monitoring there are four elements that the student handles permanently: a diary, an attendance control book, a suggestion box and a contest book.

The student's diary allows him/her to express his/her daily anxieties, concerns and problems. The attendance control consists of a table with that month's calendar and every child's name. Every day each student must put a mark to indicate his/her attendance. The suggestion box allows the student to communicate his/her wishes and problems to the teacher. The objective of the contest book is to identify each month those students who have done outstanding work in specific areas. These students are recognized on a special day called 'the achievement day' as the best mathematician, artist, journalist, etc.

Finally, the teacher controls the student's progress through the progress control book. When the student concludes a given activity he/she must show it to the teacher in order to get the authorization to go ahead with the next activity. This book allows the teacher to follow the student's advancement as well as the activities he must complete to get through the unit.

History of the educational change programme

In general terms, much of the planning of the Escuela Nueva and the definition of its components comes from the evaluation of the unitary schools.

In 1961, UNESCO sponsored an international conference for ministers of education in Geneva, Switzerland. The principal theme of the conference was the difficulty of providing primary education in rural areas with low population density. The outcome was a recommendation that Ministries of Education should be encouraged to create single teacher schools in which the teacher provided instruction to children of all primary grades. The recommendation also suggested that countries with little experience in this modality of schooling request technical assistance from UNESCO.

As a result of this conference, Colombia began to develop a unitary school programme, with assistance from UNESCO specialists. Specifically, Project I of UNESCO organized the first rural unitary demonstration school in the Instituto Superior de Educación Rural in Pamplona, Norte de Santander. The objective of the demonstration school was to train teachers and supervisors in new teaching procedures.

A primary school was annexed to the Instituto to serve as a laboratory school in 1962. Under the leadership of Professor Oscar Mogollón, who became director of the school in 1964, the programme developed in the experimental school was replicated in 150 schools in the state of Norte de Santander. Many of the elements of the unitary school were taken from the Argentine model of the unitary school Felipe Iglesias. The objective of this school was to facilitate active learning and respect for individual learning differences by organizing the school into work areas, using a system of individualized instructional cards, and developing a set of procedures for encouraging the children to participate in the organization of the school. The programme specialized in training teachers and supervisors to prepare materials and use them in multigraded classrooms.

In 1968, the school in Pamplona was visited by researchers from the University of Antioquia and the regional training centres and by representatives of the national Ministry of Education and the department secretariats of education. These visits had several outcomes. First, the government passed a decree that the unitary school approach would be used in all the schools in the country which had only one teacher and that low population areas would be emphasized. In order to implement this legislation, the secretariats of education were required to provide training for rural teachers in the procedures for teaching in unitary schools. During 1967 and 1968, the regional training centres gave more than 160 seminars to over 4500 teachers. These courses identified the need to develop a text for teachers. This text, published by CAPEC (Organización Administrativa y Pedagógica de la Capacitación), was distributed in various regions and was used in the initiation of several new projects at the departmental level. The University of Antioquia, for example, was contracted to design an experimental unitary school programme as part of Antioquia's response to the 1967 decree. This led to the eventual joint production of texts and modules which stressed linear programmed instruction by the university and the department.

In 1970 and 1974 specialists from UNESCO emphasized the community aspect of the unitary school model. These specialists stressed the idea of the school as a centre of the community and the importance of community-school integration. Others focused on the aspects of active learning and individual rates of learning in the classroom, which the Antioquia model attempted to achieve through programmed instruction. Thus, in Colombia several approaches to the problem of complete primary schooling among dispersed populations were being developed simultaneously on regional or local levels. As mentioned previously, however, there were a number of short-comings in each of these efforts which led to the development of the Escuela Nueva.

It is important to mention that in 1970, the departmental secretariat of education offered Professor Mogollón the opportunity to form an assistance team for carrying on the unitary school programme. The individuals who made up that team played a fundamental part in the development of the Escuela Nueva in Norte de Santander and later in its national expansion. The present national coordinator of EN, the regional coordinator of the programme, and the national training coordinator were all members of this assistance group for the unitary schools.

During the first year of initiation of Escuela Nueva, a number of activities that helped its consolidation were taken. The first draft of the aforementioned manual 'Hacia la Escuela Nueva' was written; the first training course was developed and given on the use of the library; and through a selection process, the regional coordinator of EN was chosen.

At the national ministry level, the programme coordination received financial assistance from the US Agency for International Development (AID) for printing the manual, the development of the first version of the student guides, and a series of training courses. AID assistance included a technical assistance team from a US university which consisted of two long-term advisors in the areas of educational systems and community unitary schools, and short-term specialists in evaluation and research design, curriculum, instructional materials and educational technology. Local specialists and institutions, however, were directly responsible for the implementation of the programme which built on their previous experiences with the unitary school efforts. It should also be pointed out that the first teachers who were involved in the programme had experience of the unitary schools. Thus, for these teachers, EN was not totally new.

The workshops, which prepared teachers and supervisors under the project, have been considered the most successful component of the project and a cornerstone of the Escuela Nueva programme. The training approaches that were developed in Pamplona were refined and teachers were brought into regional centres for training. A teachers' training guide was completed and 5000 copies were published to complement the workshops, during the first year of the project. Teachers who participated in the project were identified at the regional level and, over the course of the project, 354 rather than the projected 300 teachers, and 78 rather than 54 supervisors were trained.

The final evaluation of the AID project found that sufficient teachers and supervisors had been trained to administer the project. All of those interviewed agreed that the teacher in-service training component which takes place in three separate workshops has built the teacher commitment that has led to the successful implementation of the Escuela Nueva programme. Teachers are brought together in a comfortable setting and paid per diem which contributes to their sense of self-worth and enthusiasm. In the workshops, they were given tools for classroom management, for interactions with the community, and for use of the library. They were encouraged to work together and to develop their own ideas for instructional aids. The 78 supervisors who also received training were given orientation as to the functional aspects of the Escuela Nueva programme and the role of the supervisor as a facilitator in such a programme.

The development of the student materials was carried out through a contract with the University of Pamplona. The materials consisted of texts with programmed learning modules. The curriculum was completely new. It emphasized teachers, children and community members taking charge of their schools, and this approach was reflected in the name of the programme — Escuela Nueva or 'new school'.

In addition, a 100-book library was assembled for each school. This was achieved by negotiating with Colombian publishing houses for special rates and donations in consideration of the educational nature of the undertaking. The texts in this initial stage were mimeographed and there were two copies of each for each grade level. It was considered important that the distribution of the materials corresponded to the training as far as possible so that teachers could begin working with the new approach right away even if there were not enough materials available.

Between 1976 and 1978, the EN programme was developed in Norte de Santander. It was also initiated in the departments of Boyocá and Cundinamarca. Two factors strengthened the development of EN at this time, and later contributed to its consolidation. First, the commitment of the project coordinator and her friendship with the Minister of Education made it easier to obtain decisions on project issues. This increased even more when the project coordinator herself became Vice Minister of Education and had responsibility for the EN programme. Second, Professor Mogollón and two of his closest colleagues were transferred from their region to the Ministry of Education in Bogotá. As they were involved in the coordination of the EN programme, this created a nucleus of committed practitioners with ample hands-on experience with multi-graded schools at the central level. Professor Mogollón, because of his experience with EN, was given responsibility for coordinating training and participated directly in the Ministry team working to create regional EN support groups.

During these first years, the relationship between the central level, the regional coordinator and the teachers in the schools was on a largely personal basis. The regional coordinators were selected by the central level team on the basis of their performance in a training workshop. Those selected were given the responsibility for training the teachers and providing ongoing support. However, in the early days of Escuela Nueva, they were generally assisted in training by the founders of the programme who were members of the national team.

At the end of 1978, the EN programme had been established in about 150 schools in the department of Norte de Santander, and in 150 and 200 schools in Boyacá and Cundinamarca, respectively. Between 1979 and 1982, the programme expanded to nearly 2000 schools in a number of departments and regions of the country. With this expansion, the current national coordinator of EN felt that it was necessary to delegate responsibility for training teachers to 'multipliers' or individuals from the region who had been trained by the regional coordinator with the assistance of central level personnel. He recognized, however, that this implied that not all trainers were likely to have the fervour of the original trainers who had founded the programme. During this period, the

Escuela Nueva programme was financed by resources from each of the Departmental Secretariats of Education and through a loan from the Interamerican Development Bank.

The four years from 1982 to 1986 marked the acceptance of Escuela Nueva as a national programme as it was recognized officially by the Ministry of Education and institutionalized. Funds from the World Bank for a project called 'Plan de Fomento de la Educación Rural' (Rural Education Promotion Plan) strengthened the EN programme in the departments of Nariño, Sucre and Norte de Santander. This project adopted the Escuela Nueva as the educational alternative for the rural area, and other departments began to participate until the coverage reached 6000 rural schools. Between 1987 and 1989, the EN programme almost tripled its coverage. In December of 1989, the national coordination reported the existence of 17,948 schools in the programme. This represented 31,000 teachers who had been trained and 800,000 students.

The 'Plan de Fomento' project has recently expanded its coverage to the entire country through the 'Universalization of Primary Education' plan. This plan, as its name indicates, will increase coverage, lower drop-outs and repetition, and contribute to a general improvement in the quality of primary education. It is based on the adoption of the Escuela Nueva programme in all rural areas of the country. The resources needed to implement it will be provided by Colombia and by a loan to the country from the World Bank.

Country level factors related to success

The Escuela Nueva programme largely followed a process of initiation that was conditioned by external forces in the form of donor agencies working with national educators. As a result of UNESCO funding priorities, Colombia began its unitary school programme which has continued to be supported by different donor agencies as it expanded into the Escuela Nueva. The implementation strategy has been one of incremental expansion as the programme built on the experience gained by key personnel under the UNESCO effort to develop an ambitious integrated innovation. This reform package was then introduced on a small scale and has gradually expanded over time in a relatively stable economic and political environment.

In terms of outcomes, initial assessments conducted by AID at the end of its financing in 1978 and by the ministry central office in 1980 were on a small scale and focused on programme coverage and satisfaction of programme participants with inputs. In 1987, following expansion of the programme, a systematic evaluation of student achievement was conducted.

A number of factors have contributed to the institutionalization of the programme. Prior to 1982, the EN programme was dependent on several offices or divisions within the ministry. Originally, it was under the administration of the secretary general of the ministry; it was first transferred to the sectorial office of planning, then to the division of basic primary education, and finally to the division of centros experimentales piloto (pilot experimental centres). This movement was part of the strategy of the coordinating team for the EN programme. They attempted to move it to divisions where there was some support on the part of administrators and some money for programme development. Thus, they were able to keep the programme functioning and growing until there was enough support to institutionalize it within the ministry.

This support came with the plan de fomento which provided resources and focused attention on rural education. This led to its institutionalization within the ministry and within the administrative structure of the departments in which the programme was functioning. This recognition became public in an official document, *Educational Policy for Colombia 1982-1986* (Ministerio de Educación Nacional, 1983), which stated that: 'the programmes of proven quality within the framework of the national educational policy will be continued and strengthened' (p. 66). It was mentioned explicitly later in the document that the Escuela Nueva programme would be strengthened for the development of the rural areas.

As might be expected, interviewees at the central level pointed out that the expansion, or 'massification', of the EN programme implied modifications in the process of selection, training, delivery of materials and follow-up to the schools. The personal contact of the central level personnel in training of teachers and supervisors was gradually transferred to the regional coordinators. These individuals, in turn, trained supervisors and teachers to train others as 'multiplier' agents. According to the national coordinator, this process influenced the quality of training received by the teachers. The need to reach more teachers and the increased cost were factors that led to a reduction in the number of days dedicated to the training of teachers. The total training time for all of the workshops was reduced from 30 days to 12 to 15 days. This reduction was felt to have an adverse affect of on quality, and it is also likely that it affected motivation, because one of the objectives of the training is to show rural teachers that they are valued and that their input is respected.

National coordination The educators who initiated the programme in Pamplona subsequently formed part of a team at the central level that, throughout the formation of the EN programme, maintained the management of the innovation. They coordinated, planned, organized and implemented fundamental tasks such as training workshops at the regional and local level and developed the instructional materials.

As the programme was expanded to different states, regional coordinators were named to provide support. These individuals were part of the initial founding group in Pamplona. Thus, they had experience with rural schools and were totally committed to the programme. The national coordinator stated, 'We didn't start from zero as we had highly motivated people in the regions.'

Central support It is evident that another important factor in the success of the EN was the support given by the central level administrators to the regional coordinators. This then allowed the regional coordinators to provide the necessary support to local educators helping the teachers to implement the programme. The presence of the programme 'founders' in the workshops and in meetings with communities was constant throughout the initiation period. This, in addition to motivating the teachers, allowed those who knew the programme best to assist when pedagogical problems or incidents with communities arose.

Building of commitment The building of commitment was fundamental to the success of the programme. Commitment came about through the involvement of the programme originators at all levels to ensure success. Their enthusiasm and understanding was passed on to others as the programme grew.

Incremental expansion The educators who originated the programme and presently administer it at the central level, never envisioned a national programme. As one of them stated: 'The results have been far more than we expected ... we never saw the programme as growing to a national scale.' However, they still moved incrementally on the local level, involving schools little by little when the interest and resources were available.

The programme developed in a relatively stable environment, growing gradually with a rhythm that could be administered effectively at the central and regional level. However, its success attracted resources from the World Bank that allowed for a brisk expansion from 2000 schools in 1982 to almost 6000 schools in 1986, and 20,000 schools in 1991. This rapid expansion has, in the opinion of the central level administrators, led to deficiencies in training because of problems in organization and control.

Resources for the school The school's resources include guides, libraries and instructional materials. One of the pillars of the Escuela Nueva programme has been the provision of self-instructional student guides. As the guides are not expensive to produce, resources have been sought from a variety of sources including private organizations, departmental and national governments and international organizations. Costs have also been saved in that the same guide can be used by a number of children, either simultaneously in group work or in succession individually.

Outcomes at the system level

Interviewees felt that the EN programme has maintained its philosophy and basic principles over time. There is a total commitment to the programme at the national level and among regional coordinators. At both levels there are stable, permanent groups that include individuals who were among the early initiators of the programme. These individuals helped overcome opposition by individual teachers or communities who saw the changes under the EN programme as threatening. This nucleus of committed individuals also continued to pressure the ministry for additional resources to support the programme.

As the EN programme has shown its viability and 'quality', it has attracted economic assistance both within Colombia and from international donors. The money for the universalization programme will be spent almost entirely on assisting existing EN schools and expanding the EN programme to rural schools that do not belong to it. The programme has also received economic help from entities such as the Coffee Growers' Federation and the Foundation for Higher Education.

In terms of national organizations, the EN programme has led to radical changes in the conventional ways of training teachers. At the local level, the programme has trained and strengthened training teams which have slowly been incorporated into the regional education structure. The programme has also created groups in each region who are interested and involved in adapting the student guides to the needs of their locality.

Communication links have been developed between regional coordinators and the central level. These have changed from an almost exclusive reliance on personal contact to national meetings in which the national level personnel participate with implementing teams from each region. Generally workshops with the regional coordinators are held twice a year.

The administration of the Escuela Nueva Programme

In most departments, there is not a clear relationship in the organizational plan between programme and the other educational administrative units of the departments. The support received depends, to a large extent, on the secretary of education of the moment and the director of the experimental pilot centres, and in some cases, on the director of the regional education fund (fondo educativo rural — FER).

The administration of EN has had a distinct history in each region. In some departments its activities and administration depends on the secretariat of education, in others all of its activities are controlled by the CEPs, often with little contact with those who provide follow-up locally. Thus, in each department the EN programme has had a different strategy for dealing with the regional administration to gain supervision, resources or even for schools to join the programme.

THE LESSONS FROM 12 CASES
Overview of more and less successful schools

Although all of the schools in the sample were identified as 'good' schools, there was a consensus on the part of the research team that some of the schools had greater overall success than others. Three schools, Rocha, Cedros and El Camino, were considered excellent in their success with the programme. A group of seven schools — El Frutal, Patio Bonito, La Unión, Los Olivos, El Puerto, El Zipa and La Mina — were found to have had very good success with the Escuela Nueva, and two schools, El General and Santa María, have had good success. These ratings were all generally consistent with those made by the regional coordinators in identifying the sample, in that the first three schools had all been rated 'excellent' by the coordinators and the two schools rated lowest by the researchers were in the 'good' group identified by the coordinators.

The schools with excellent success had high levels of implementation which included support by local administrators to ensure that training and materials arrived during the initiation of the programme, and a great commitment on the part of the headmasters and the teachers. These schools' staffs also felt that students had made both cognitive gains, through the use of the guides and local materials and socio-emotional progress by participation in the student government committees and through experiences that included active self-directed learning. All of the teaching staff in the three schools felt that they had learned to be better teachers through their experience with the Escuela Nueva programme in that they recognized the importance of planning and of gearing learning opportunities to the individual experiences and reality of their students. These three schools had developed support for the programme in the community which, despite the general poverty, had resulted in improvements in their physical plants that distinguished them from the other schools in the sample. The Escuela Nueva programme was well institutionalized in each of the schools. All aspects of the programme had become routine in each of the schools, they had support of local administrators, and because of the universalization of the programme throughout the country, the schools were guaranteed resources in the foreseeable future.

The very good schools, especially the top three, are very similar to the excellent schools, differing principally in the level of cognitive gains seen by the teachers and in a more restricted physical plant. The other schools in this category also reported lesser cognitive gains and generally had at least one other area such as teacher commitment, physical plant or community relations where they were not as successful as the other schools listed as very good. All of the schools in this category had a high degree of programme institutionalization: Escuela Nueva was a regular part of school routine and they had the support of assistance givers and the assurance of continued resources through universalization.

The two schools that were considered good in their degree of success with the programme had relatively less assistance from local support givers than the other schools in the sample. This contributed to at least one member of the teaching staff lacking commitment for the programme at each school. In El General, socio-emotional gains in the children's independence and responsibility were seen. In Santa María children were seen to have become more irresponsible as a result of the programme, although some cognitive gains were identified. Both schools had experienced negative reactions to the programme by the community which hadn't been overcome at the time of the study and both had made only some aspects of the Escuela Nueva programme routine.

Key factors that explain good implementation

Assistance Generally, there is a high level of training across all schools. The various ways of receiving training or feedback (in-service training, supervisor assistance, assistance from directors of regional support centres, where they exist, and micro-centre workshops) have provided teachers in all schools with the opportunity to fine tune the programmes. Mitigating factors in the application of such training, as can be seen in El General and Santa María, are the lack of interest of the teaching staff in the former and the short duration of training (three days for all three training workshops) in the latter.

Administrative role There has been regional support for all schools and generally the position of regional coordinator for Escuela Nueva has been stable. With the massification of the programme, however, some teachers in the older programmes felt that the coordinators were spending less time on their schools. This was confirmed by local administrators who stated that as the number of schools in the programme in a region increased, the amount of attention each participant school received decreased.

The role of local officials has been largely neutral toward the EN programme. The exceptions are those who have received training in the philosophy of the programme and go on to become defenders of Escuela Nueva and pedagogical resources for teachers. In the more successful schools, there is generally at least one local administrator who has applied pressure on teaching staff to implement the programme as part of his/her role. Such pressure does not ensure implementation, however, as can be seen in the case of El General, where local officials including the regional coordinator and the núcleo director insisted that the school implement the programme, but because the headmaster wasn't committed to it implementation was less successful.

Thus, the combination of committed staff and local assistance givers is needed to ensure highly successful implementation. This is evidenced by the degree of implementation reached by Santa María and El General. In the first case, assistance was given only in the first year and thereafter teachers felt abandoned and their motivation decreased. In the second, despite the commitment of the staff, administrators did not visit the school and the headmaster didn't support the programme.

The key factor that distinguishes successful implementation is the role of the headteacher. In all of the more successful schools, the headteacher took an active role in implementing all aspects of the programme, both in and out of the school. This included training new teachers, selling the programme to the community and pursuing assistance from parents, adapting materials and making decisions about school operations. In those schools where the headmasters are indifferent or passive, implementation has been less successful. This is not to say that assistance is not important. However, where the headteacher is highly committed and active, this individual can increase the level of assistance, as was the case at Emilio Rocha and El Camino.

The conduct of the headteacher or teaching staff in their treatment of the children or the community can also be a factor in programme success. In each of the schools where the community didn't support EN or didn't support the programme strongly (El Zipa, El General, Santa María) there were complaints about the headteachers' treatment of the children.

Commitment Commitment of teaching staff to the programme is also an important factor. In all of the schools that were most successful in implementing the programme, all teachers were committed. This commitment is related to a number of factors: an initial feeling that the programme would provide them with additional tools for dealing with the methodological problems of providing instruction to multi-grade rural classrooms; the quality of training; the facility of working with the EN materials and other types of continuing support given by local administrators and the headmaster; and the results of the programme that teachers saw principally in the active participation of students in classroom activities.

Lack of commitment was related to a feeling that the programme was being imposed from above combined with a lack of materials or a lack of coordination between training and the receipt of materials. Similarly, these schools were not pushed by local administrators to implement the programme and the headteachers in these schools, perhaps because of these other factors, were indifferent towards it. The exception is La Mina where the programme was well implemented by the previous teaching staff but a total rotation of personnel put three teachers who were trying to move to urban schools in the La Mina at the same time.

Community support Community support is related to commitment and mastery of the programme by teaching staff. The programme, when well implemented, encourages interaction with the community. An understanding of the programme and a willingness to explain it to the parents has helped gain confidence and participation. This has generally been part of the headteacher's role in the most successful schools.

However, the most important factors are the commitment that the parents see in the teachers and, above all, the product of the school, i.e. the changes in behaviour that the parents see in their children. Where the components of the programme were not well explained to the parents or where parents perceived a lack of commitment on the part of the teachers, they have reacted negatively toward it. This was the case in Santa María where at the outset, the community supported the programme. At present, however, because of poor interpretation of the flexible promotion component, which has led to a lack of progress by the children, parents have rejected the EN programme.

Local adaptation Local adaptation has little relationship with success of implementation as it is an aspect of the programme which is explained in the teachers' guides. All of the teachers made such adjustments in the curriculum as they felt necessary, even where commitment to the programme wasn't high. Similarly, teachers feel able to take decisions about the structure of the programme. However, they are more active in carrying out these decisions where there is a high commitment among teaching staff.

Key factors that explain impact

The academic success of the children with EN is directly related to the mastery that the teaching staff have of the methodology and the philosophy of the programme. This section discusses the performance of teachers and their ability to function as facilitators for the children for each key element of the programme.

Guides In examining student impact, those elements of the reform related to student-level changes were contrasted for each school. As can be seen from cross-site display 3 (p. 274), all of the schools received student and teacher guides in the first year of the programme. Where all guides were not present, teachers used the strategy of combining traditional lecture style classes for the students without guides with the self-instructional activities of the Escuela Nueva. Thus, though an important contributor to student success, guides did not distinguish among the sample schools in which they were correctly used. However, the case of Santa María, where the teachers allowed the students to use the guides without any direction and stay at the same grade level for a number of years, shows the importance of understanding the instructional materials and being motivated to used them correctly if they are to have an impact on student learning.

Using the community as a resource for learning In those schools where information was available, using the community as a resource by conducting research with community members did not appear to be a discriminating factor in determining student impact. This is one of the activities identified in the guides and therefore was part of the programme in the 'excellent', 'very good' and 'good schools.'

Group work and active learning experiences are related very strongly to the commitment and mastery of the teachers. In those schools where the teaching staff had fully mastered the programme and were committed to it, group work with peer teaching occurred regularly as specified in the EN programme. The exception among the 'excellent' and 'very good' schools was the case of El Zipa, where though such activities took place, teachers felt that the students could not take part effectively because of malnutrition. Those schools that have had at least one staff member who was not committed to the programme (Patio Bonito, El General, Santa María) and thus taught in a teacher-centred way that did not encourage children to engage in collaborative group work or active enquiry, have been less successful in promoting positive student outcomes.

Learning corners The use and condition of the learning corners were also related to student outcomes. In those schools rated highest in student impact, the learning corners were used regularly. Again, this appears to be related to teacher commitment and mastery, as in these schools teachers worked with children to provide local materials for the corners and encouraged their regular use. In two schools, Los Olivos and La Unión, the corners were being redone at the time of the research and thus were not observed in use, despite high commitment and engagement on the part of the teaching staff. Where the teachers and director did not support the programme, the learning corners had fallen into disrepair and appeared to be areas for storing abandoned material from the school.

Flexible promotion. This is the aspect of the programme which varies most among the sample schools. In general, in the most successful schools the teachers understand the concept and have been able to implement a system whereby children advance in each subject as they are ready to do so. The exception is Cedros, where the concept is understood and various attempts were made to implement it. However, it has been rejected completely by the local community, and thus abandoned in order to preserve the EN programme. In some of the 'very good' schools, the concept is understood but seen as too difficult to implement. Teachers feel it is impossible to monitor and assist 30 or 40 children, each potentially at a different level within five or six subjects.

In the schools with the least impact on students, the concept of flexible promotion was badly understood and therefore poorly implemented. In the case of El General, the community's negative reaction to flexible promotion led teachers to let students move at their own rate during the year, but forced them all to finish together at the end of the normal school year. Thus, those children who had started moving ahead in a subject were held back until the bulk of the class caught up. In Santa María, teachers allowed children to stay in the same grade level for up to three years, with little direction, and as a result parents reacted negatively to both the teachers and the programme.

The concept of flexible promotion has been important in all schools in encouraging teachers to recognize and deal with individual differences in student learning. Where continuing assistance didn't occur, however, the application of the concept has not generally been appropriate. In several cases, such as Patio Bonito, El Zipa and La Mina, even with assistance, teachers made adaptations in the concept or discarded it based on their perception of children's abilities or needs.

Rural content As an integral part of the programme, with guidelines for teachers' adaptation of materials, this has been successful in all schools. Like community investigations, it does not therefore seem related to perceived differences in programme impact on students among the sample schools, with the possible exception of Santa María.

Student government This aspect of Escuela Nueva seems to be directly related to the socio-emotional impact of the programme. Teachers in all schools related participation in student government committees to a change in student behaviour. Where the student government was well implemented, students of all grade levels participated and carried out many school functions without assistance from the teacher. In two instances during the research, children were carrying out classroom activities despite the absence of their teacher. In those schools which were rated lower on their success with this aspect of the programme, the student government functioned in name only. Each committee was directed in its activities by the teacher and this individual made the operational decisions for each committee. In the other sample schools students were intimately involved in decision making.

Library The library appears to be related to student outcomes. In those schools with the highest student impact, the library is considered very important — it has a special place and its use is programmed into regular activities. In the 'very good' schools the library is used but not emphasized, while in the 'good' schools the library is not emphasized and appeared not to be used.

Self-evaluation This aspect of the Escuela Nueva programme was difficult to verify. Where it was observed or mentioned by teaching staff, however, it was always in a negative way. In some cases, teachers had developed their own tests and didn't attempt to implement self-evaluation. Given the low level of use and the negative attitudes even in some of the schools with relatively high impact, this aspect does not appear to be related to student impact.

Student-teacher relations In almost all of the schools there was an improved relationship between teachers and students. Teachers felt that they had become more accessible to students and in some cases recognized that they could learn from the children. Classroom observations supported these impressions. Students were observed to approach teachers with questions and to challenge them in both large and small group situations. The only exception was Santa María where teachers felt that relations were good, but students were not observed to approach the teachers and there were few opportunities created for questions.

Teacher-level elements of the reform were also examined for their relationship to outcomes. These included: training workshops; the teacher acting as a facilitator; active, engaged teaching; promotion of the programme in the community; and encouraging the community to participate in school events. There is very little to differentiate the schools in terms of training. All of the teachers received training and this allowed them to train new teachers when there was a change in personnel. The exception was Santa María, where though teachers received complete training, it was limited to three days compared to the 15 days seen during earlier initiation periods.

In almost all of the schools, the teachers act as facilitators for the children as suggested in the guides and the training workshops. However, there is a far greater tendency to use the traditional lecture method in those schools that have had less success with the programme. Similarly, these teachers have been less successful in encouraging active learning among the students.

Most of the schools have promoted the EN programme well in the community and have gained cooperation to the extent that the socio-economic status of the community permits. The exceptions have been those schools where teachers, because of insufficient training or follow-up by local administrators, have badly implemented certain elements of the programme which has led to the perception among community members that their children weren't learning. Where this has occurred, teaching staff have had little success in involving the community in school activities.

Key factors that explain institutionalization

Given the operational definition of institutionalization, there is a generally high level of institutionalization in all of the schools classified in cross-site display 1 (p. 268) as 'excellent' or 'very good'. The programmes are supported by regional and local administrators and by the teaching staffs. New teachers are trained through the formal in-service training, by supervisors or by their colleagues on the job, and are supported by the micro-centres.

As the Escuela Nueva programme is a total change for the school and a complete programme in itself, it is automatically 'built-in' in the sense that it doesn't stand out from other school routines. Because of the recent universalization of the EN programme, there is a general agreement that it will continue in all schools and that resources will be committed to this continuation. In certain schools, however, despite a high degree of institutionalization, there is some preoccupation that unofficial political opposition groups may influence the continuation of the programme in a region.

The general situation is different in the schools rated 'good' overall. These schools lack a strong role definition and commitment on the part of the headteacher, and have lacked the support by local administrators on a technical level that would enable them to consolidate all programme elements in the classroom. The headteachers in both schools have failed to support the programmes. However, the schools differ somewhat, in that the teacher in El General has tried to carry out all aspects of the programme and work with the community, but because of the director, there is ambiguity about the programme on the part of the parents. In Santa María, the headteacher and the teacher have misinterpreted the flexible promotion aspect of the EN programme and have allowed students to remain in the same grade for three years with very little direction from the teachers. This has caused a negative reaction throughout the community and they have asked that either the teachers be changed or the EN programme be abolished.

IMPLICATIONS

Several implications can be drawn from the results of this study. First, it appears that for a programme to be successful in the sense of becoming institutionalized at the central level, there must be an involvement of individuals committed to the project. In the case of the Escuela Nueva, the programme did not begin to be seen as an innovation of national scope until its founders moved to the Ministry and lobbied for support. These individuals also protected the programme, moving it within the Ministry to divisions where there was support until the results were sufficiently impressive that it gained a large constituency that supported its institutionalization. This implies that new programmes should be multi-faceted and flexible enough to fit into various areas of a Ministry's portfolio.

Second, it does not appear that a major innovation such as the Escuela Nueva can expect to be supported by a developing country even in a time span of almost fifteen years. Although Colombia helps finance the programme at both the department and national level, international donor support has also been necessary throughout the programme. Much of this support has been for programme expansion. However, the general complaints about the lack of new materials in the more successful schools that had been in the programme for a relatively long time suggest that the recurrent costs will remain high. This is especially true as the programme expands.

Another aspect related to expansion is the availability of experienced support personnel. In the sample schools, as the programme expanded, regional and local administrators were spread thin, and they tended to visit the older, better implemented schools less often. One solution is peer training, such as the micro-centres in the EN programme. There must also be a systematic plan for increasing assistance-giving personnel if the expansion is to be successful.

At the school level, the most difficult aspect of the programme to implement has been the flexible promotion component. There are a number of reasons for this including teachers' lack of understanding of the component, lack of acceptance by parents either because it is different from their own schooling or because they fail to see progress in the children, or lack of motivation on the part of students. This implies that special workshops on flexible promotion may be needed for both supervisors and teachers as the programme expands. Modules for discussions with the community on this component may also be a helpful addition to existing orientation materials. Self-evaluation has also been difficult to implement. It has generally been ignored by teachers or discarded for encouraging the students to do the minimum necessary to pass. As with flexible promotion, special workshops for the teachers on this aspect of the EN programme may be necessary if it is to be used effectively.

Lack of community support is a threat to institutionalization. In those schools where the programme was supported by the community, there was no threat to continuation. However, where the community had not accepted the programme completely, for whatever reason, there existed movements to do away with it. This suggests that ongoing assistance should monitor community attitudes as well as classroom activities, as the programme may appear to be successful within the school but lack community support.

Although the headteacher was found to be key to the success of the schools in the study, in small schools where the primary function of the headteacher is teaching, lack of commitment on his or her part may be overcome. In the Escuela Nueva schools which had staffs of two or three, and a headteacher with a limited administrative role, it was not always necessary that he/she be positive toward the programme. In some instances, a teacher was able to implement the programme even without support from the head.

A methodological implication of the study is that researchers who are concerned with measuring the achievement of children must take into account the number of years that a child has spent with the subject matter of a certain grade level. In the case of Santa María, the children scored well on the tests because they had spent up to three years working within a grade level with the material that the tests were designed to measure. This could not, however, be taken as an indicator of programme success.

REFERENCES

Colbert, C.V. (1984) Universalización de la Primaria en Colombia. El Programa de Escuela Nueva. In *La Educación Rural en Colombia. Situación, Experiencias y Perspectivas*. Bogotá.

Educar (1980) Bulletin from the Ministerio de Educación Nacional. Bogotá.

Ministerio de Educación Nacional (1983) *Plan de Desarrollo del Sector Educación 1982-1986*. Bogotá.

Vásquez, L.N. (1984) *Manual de Orientación y Asesoría de Escuela Nueva*. Ministerio de Educación Nacional. Bogotá.

Chapter 4

The Primary Education Reform Programme in Ethiopia

Anbesu Biazen

THE LARGER SYSTEM PICTURE
The country context

Social, political and economic factors Ethiopia is found on the horn of Africa lying approximately between 3° and 18° north latitudes and 33° and 48° east longitudes, with a total land area of about 1.2 million square kms. The country is divided into two major geographical regions: highlands and lowlands. The highlands occupy most of the northern, south-western and south-eastern parts of the country, covering 45 per cent of the total land surface of the country. The lowlands include the western fringes, eastern fringes, Awash valley, Afar and Red Sea regions, covering about 55 per cent of the total land surface.

The country has rich water resources, with numerous rivers that could be used all year round for irrigation in agriculture, production of hydro-electric power and fisheries if properly developed. There are also a number of crater lakes, highland lakes and rift valley lakes which have potential for such uses as tourist attractions.

The climate of Ethiopia is dependent on altitude and location. Traditionally the climate of the country is classified into five zones based on altitudinal differences. These are *bereha* or desert (below 1000 m); *kola* or tropical (1000 to 1500 m); *woina dega* or sub-tropical (1500 to 2500 m); *dega* or temperate (2500 to 3500 m); and *wirch* (above 3500 m), which is the coldest region.

The population of Ethiopia in 1990 was reported to be 48,000,000 of which the majority live in rural areas and a small fraction in towns (Central Statistics Office, 1986). According to Mehari (1989), the ratio of the urban-rural population has not changed much since 1975, because of the land reform of 1975 and the rural development undertakings of the government. Ethiopia has a relatively young population; 46.5 per cent are under 15 years of age and only 4.3 per cent are aged 65 years or over. The female population is a little over 50 per cent of the total population. It is also interesting to note that the annual population growth rate is 2.9 per cent and the average density of the population is 39 persons per square kilometre.

There are about 82 ethnic groups in the country. Each ethnic group has its own dialect and retains its cultural identity. About a dozen of the languages (Amharic, Oromigna, Tigrigna, Sidama, Afar, etc.) can be regarded as major tongues (Sjostrom, 1986, p. 5). Amharic is the national language and is used as a medium of instruction in all primary schools. English is also widely used among the educated group and is the language of instruction in secondary schools and in higher education.

Ethiopia's principal natural resource is agricultural land. The cultivable land comprises 66 per cent of the total area of the country, though so far only 11 per cent of it is farmed. Agriculture accounts for 75 per cent of the country's national income. The major products include food crops such as wheat, barley, 'teff' (the indigenous food), maize, sorghum, oil-seeds and pulses (Central Statistics Office, 1986). Livestock is also one of the major sources of income. The number of cattle, sheep and goats was estimated to be over 23 million, 10 million and 6 million respectively, in 1985 (Central Statistics Office, 1986). Poultry is raised on a large scale. Nearly all the rural population raise a small number of poultry, and modern poultry farming methods are also being used.

Ethiopia is one of the least developed countries in the world, and its industry is also poorly developed. The industrial sector comprises mainly manufacturing, mining and construction (Mehari, 1989). Though the country has a number of different mineral resources, the most widely extracted ones are gold and platinum, and the latter is extracted only on a small scale.

A radical political change has been underway in the country since 1974. After the overthrow of the feudal-bourgeois government, socialism was proclaimed to be the guiding political philosophy of the country, and via a process of gradual change a socialist system was developed. However, because of the current global experience of change and national pressures, a new policy of change has recently been introduced. The new policy proclaims mixed economic development giving an opportunity for the revival of private ownership.

In the period 1975 to 1987, prior to the new policy, over 90 major revolutionary activities were carried out. The two most radical were the land reform proclamation of March 1975, which made land public property, and the July 1975 proclamation that nationalized urban lands and extra houses. These have since been modified by a socio-economic policy change.

The National Democratic Revolution Programme (NDR) which clearly stated the development objectives of the country was introduced in April 1976. This was later re-enforced by Commission for Organising Workers' Party of Ethiopia documents and the programme of the Workers' Party of Ethiopia (WPE). The NDR and WPE programmes have given guidelines for expanding and improving the productive forces and the production relation within the framework of a socialist system. To this end, a number of proclamations were made nationalizing the commercial and industrial sectors of the economy and natural resources. This has been reversed by the new policy.

Within the various development fields outlined by the government of Ethiopia, education is given special attention. The tasks to be undertaken by the education sector have been defined in a number of policy statements. For example it has been stated in the National Democratic Revolution (NDR) programme:

> There will be an educational programme that will provide free education, step by step, to the broad masses. Such a programme will aim at intensifying the struggle against feudalism, imperialism and

bureaucratic capitalism. All necessary measures to eliminate illiteracy will be undertaken. All necessary encouragement will be given for the development of science, technology, the arts and literature. All the necessary effort will be made to free the diversified cultures of imperialist cultural domination and from their own reactionary characteristics. Opportunities will be provided to allow them to develop, advance and grow with the aid of modern means and resources. (Ministry of Education, 1979)

The education system intended in the socialist regime would have better served the interests of the broad masses by providing better knowledge, skills and attitudes to improve the quality of life and overcome backwardness. As has been stated in 'Education in Socialist Ethiopia' (Ministry of Education, 1984), there is every justification for saying that education has been provided with a radically different environment in which it can be effective in supporting the various ways in which the quality of life is being improved in Ethiopia today. In short, education is intended to promote socio-economic growth by developing intellectual, physical and spiritual capabilities of the youth and preparing them for the socialist system.

The education system The Ethiopian education system can be categorized as formal and non-formal. The formal education system covers the whole range of pre-school, primary, secondary, technical and vocational education (as well as higher education), while the non-formal education system covers literacy classes, distant education, evening classes and community skill training programmes (CSTC), etc.

The formal education structure is six years of primary education, two years of junior secondary and four years of senior secondary schools (6-2-4). Before the revolution there were a few pre-primary schools run by private organizations. After the 1974 revolution, however, pre-primary education was officially incorporated into the education system to cater for children aged from 4 to 6 years. A total of 87,355 children attended pre-schools in 1989. The same year there were 848 pre-schools with 1,888 teachers, and a pupil-teacher ratio was 46 to 1 (Educational Statistics, 1989).

Primary education is offered for children aged mainly between 7 and 12 years. The physical distances between home and school and other social problems can mean that children in rural areas start primary education late. The democratization of primary education is still far from being achieved. In 1989, the primary school participation rate was 34 per cent. What is encouraging is that there has been an impressive growth in student enrolment, number of teachers and number of schools. In 1974, the enrolment in primary education was 859,800. By 1989 this figure had risen to 2,855,846 with an annual growth rate of 8 per cent. During the same period, the annual growth rates of the number of teachers and schools were 9.5 per cent and 8.5 per cent respectively (Ministry of Education, 1989).

Education is free in terms of tuition fees in government schools, whereas students in non-government schools have to pay. In 1989, the share of student enrolment in non-government schools was 10.7 per cent, of teachers 9 per cent and of schools 7.1 per cent (Ministry of Education, 1989). The pupil-teacher ratio varies from region to region, within regions, and between urban and rural areas. In general the pupil-teacher ratio has been improving positively since 1974. In 1989, the national average was 43 to 1.

At the primary level the medium of instruction is Amharic, though English is taught from the third grade onwards. Students who successfully complete their primary education will have to sit for a primary school leaving examination at the end of the sixth grade in order to be promoted to the seventh grade.

The junior secondary education consists of general courses which are a continuation of the basic education received in primary schools. All students who pass the national grade six examination are entitled to be enrolled at this level. The enrolment rate has improved dramatically though the participation rate (20 per cent) is still very low. The growth rate of student enrolment was 11.2 per cent, number of teachers 8.8 per cent and number of schools 7.1 per cent in the past 15 years. The pupil-teacher ratio was 43 to 1 in 1989 (Ministry of Education, 1989). In principle, the age group of students attending school at this level should be 13 to 14 years, though for various reasons this is not respected. Of the 447,600 junior secondary schools, 10.3 per cent are non-government schools.

Schools catering for grades 9 to 12 are known as senior secondary schools. The official senior secondary school entry age is 15 years and the leaving age is 18. However, as with the primary and junior secondary schools, the senior secondary school age is not respected. The senior secondary school intake is totally dependent upon the students' achievement in the national examinations taken on completing the two levels of education, i.e. when students complete primary school (grades 1 to 6) and their junior secondary education (grades 7 and 8). The pupil enrolment at this level has shown a significant growth from 1974 to 1989; the student enrolment growth rate was 12 per cent, of teachers 9.7 per cent and of schools 6.7 per cent (Ministry of Education, 1989). In 1989, there was a total of 278 senior secondary schools. Of these, 10.1 per cent are non-government schools. The national pupil-teacher ratio at this level was 40 to 1 in 1989.

The senior secondary education is a tripartite system with academic, vocational and technical education. In grades 9 and 10 students take more general courses. All students take general vocational courses, and it is only in grades 11 and 12 that the tripartite system becomes obvious. The curriculum of the education offered in pre-revolution Ethiopia was condemned for being elitist. In response to public pressure and because of the need for trained manpower, the government opened new technical and vocational schools, offering three-year courses in 21 specialized areas after the tenth grade. In the 1988/89 academic year alone, 4100 students received technical and vocational training in 15 schools with 492 teachers. The pupil-teacher ratio that year was 8 to 1 (Ministry of Education, 1989).

Special education is given to physically, visually, and hearing impaired and mentally handicapped children. In 1989 there were 1537 students attending special education in 14 schools with 164 teachers. The pupil-teacher ratio was 9 to 1.

Post-revolution efforts and achievements

In the 15 years since the Ethiopian revolution, efforts have been made to improve the quality of primary school education and extend educational opportunities to all school age children. Further efforts have also been made to reorient the primary school education along a socialist line. To this end a number of changes have been introduced. New educational objectives have been set. A transitional curriculum has been developed and improved a number of times. In parallel to the transitional curriculum, a new socialist-oriented general polytechnic education curriculum has also been developed.

In order to bring about qualitative and quantitative changes in primary education, other changes have also been introduced. These include structural changes, staff development activities, curriculum changes and other elements such as labour education and co-curriculum activities, pedagogical centres (APCs and SPCs), mass media, school facility development, improving community involvement, etc.

The initiative taken to improve the quality of education in primary schools and implement the principle of equality of access to primary education to all school age children irrespective of sex, ethnic group or regional location, was based on the various policy statements of the WPE, the government and the Ministry of Education. In 1975 the Ministry of Education issued a working paper in which the new objectives were outlined as:

> The objectives of the new education must create needs of the broad masses by intensifying the class struggle linking education with work and translating science and technology into practice in order to improve and develop the living conditions of the people restoring handicrafts and arts for the use of the broad masses. (Report on tasks accomplished by the Ministry of Education since Meskerem 2, Education, June 1974)

Soon after this the general policy for the development of the educational system was spelled out in the programme of the National Democratic Revolution of April 1974. This was followed by the Ten-Year Perspective Plan for general education in which new educational objectives were stated and strategies for improving the education system were outlined. As well as qualitative development, it was thought possible to attain the universalization of general primary education by 1994. This was based on the principle that every Ethiopian has the right of access to primary education. This was further stated in the programme of the Workers' Party of Ethiopia (WPE) as:

> In accordance with the objective reality of the country, unsparing effort will be made to provide all school age children with eight years of education which will enable them to be employed after acquiring a certain level of education, on the one hand, and to successively pursue their education at higher levels on the other. In addition, special support will be given particularly to nomadic populations and those inhabiting border areas to ensure that educational opportunities reach all the citizens of the country equally. (Programme of the Workers' Party of Ethiopia)

With the efforts made to translate and make practical the above stated policy statements, encouraging quantitative achievements have been scored. Many schools have been built and the number of students and teachers has increased. The number of primary schools has increased from 2754 in 1974 to 8373 in 1988 (Educational Statistics 1989). The majority of the new schools were established in rural areas in an effort to maintain balanced urban-rural development.

In 1974 and 1988 the total number of primary school students was 859,800 and 2,855,846 respectively, showing an annual growth rate of 9 per cent. While this is a good achievement, there is still a lot to be done to attain the 1994 target of the universalization of primary education. The 1988 gross participation rate was 34 per cent. The other positive development observed in primary schools is the slight increase in participation rate of girls. Compared to boys, the percentage of girls attending school was ten in 1974, growing to 27 in 1988. Encouraging results are being seen in the balance between girls and boys in the lower grades (1 and 2). It is hoped that equal enrolments for boys and girls will be achieved in the near future.

In the period 1974 to 1984, the number of primary school teachers increased by 24.5 per cent, and was achieved through steady growth. During this time, the number of female teachers has also grown, though their number compared to that of males is still very small. In 1988, the ratio of female teachers to male teachers was 8 to 25.

As has been stated earlier, it could be said that Ethiopia has been launching a primary school education reform since 1974. The major objective of the reform is to bring qualitative and quantitative changes. To this end, a number of changes have been introduced. The major changes are described in the sections that follow.

The primary education reform programme

Major components of the primary education reform programme in Ethiopia Discussion with five key players at central level and a document study have shown that the major components of the primary school education reform in Ethiopia include the following.

Curriculum change The Institute for Curriculum Development and Research, and the Educational Materials Production and Distribution Agency have been very active in the development and distribution of syllabi, textbooks, teachers' guides, supplementary materials, teaching aids, etc. The creation of APC and SPC to give support for the teaching-learning process is another important aspect of the reform programme.

Teaching-learning methodology Efforts are being made to make teachers use different teaching methods as opposed to the traditional 'chalk and talk' method. The ministry is encouraging a participatory approach in which both pupils and teachers actively participate in the teaching-learning process.

Introduction of labour education Labour education has been introduced to integrate manual work with the elementary school programme in order to develop skills and promote an appreciation for physical labour by involving students in the school farm and garden, maintenance and other income generating activities.

Radio support The teaching-learning process in the classroom, especially that of primary schools, is being supported by radio programmes developed by the educational mass media services.

Community involvement in schools The community is being encouraged to support school administration and activities through school management and parents' committees.

Evaluation and monitoring The ministry has been able to institutionalize planning activities such as lesson plan, maintenance work, internal resource development, staff development, inter-school exchange of experience, staff meetings, etc. at school level. Various student assessment techniques, research and evaluation studies on the curriculum, teaching-learning methodology, etc. are also being intensified.

Planning and project management The ministry has made it a regulation that all units prepare annual plans and work accordingly. As a result, all departments and the various branches at central and local levels prepare annual plans and, with the approval of the responsible departments, implement them. Similarly projects are also prepared by the different branches of the ministry and sent to project management services for financial support.

School building Every year the Ministry of Education builds new schools and expands some of the old ones for increased student enrolment. In addition to the ministry's effort, the community also builds schools with the permission of the ministry. Attention is being given to the previously deprived rural areas.

Strengthening the administrative organization by creating new offices, restructuring and strengthening some of the existing offices, holding annual educational meetings and conferences, getting new rules and regulations, etc.

Staff development by giving pre-service and in-service training; running workshops and seminars for experts and teachers; and supporting staff at central, regional, awraja and school level.

Educational reform in Ethiopia The findings of the study based on the interview conducted at the central level are summarized in three displays: displays 1, 2A and 2B (pages 78, 87 and 93). In display 1, the major events in the reform process are chronologically presented followed by a discussion.

Criticisms of the education system prior to the reform period In the early 1970s the education offered at all levels was criticized for being elitist, academic and irrelevant to the Ethiopian socio-economic development need. The other main criticism of the education system was its failure to give service to the great majority of Ethiopian people, especially those living in rural areas. In 1974 the overall primary school participation rate was only 15 per cent. The figure for rural areas was no more than 7 per cent, whereas for urban areas it was more than 85 per cent. Most of the children attending school in rural areas were the children of families who had higher than average income and lived closer to urban areas. The children of peasants and nomads living in border regions and deep in the countryside had very little opportunity of attending school (NDR Programme, 1975).

Prior to the educational reform, equity issues were raised and discussed widely among the elite group and students of Addis Ababa University. More and more pressure was being placed on the government to provide an equitable education system irrespective of geographic position, social class, ethnic group and sex. It was argued that a new educational programme should be developed that would improve the living conditions of the Ethiopian people and that could be used to serve as an instrument for promoting socio-economic progress. It was also demanded that the content of the new programme should develop knowledge, skills and attitudes in children to make them happy and productive citizens after the completion of their education. The new education should also lay the foundation for further academic pursuits and different vocational and technical training.

As a result of public dissatisfaction with the previous education system, the government was forced to carry out a comprehensive review of the education system in 1971 to 1972. The study is known as the Education Sector Review. The review exposed that the then educational system did not satisfactorily transmit the cultural heritage and history of the country to the young generation. It was condemned as elitist, centralized, irrelevant and most of all, inequitable. The sector review recommended that 'education must aid in the transformation of the Ethiopian society by playing a vital role in the lives of all citizens. To do this, the present education system must be restructured and changed.' (A Draft Report: Education Sector Review. 18 June, 1972.) As a consequence of these recommendations the structure of the new education system to be developed was outlined by the then council of Ministers as follows:

1. The formal education system will provide:
   (i) 4 years of primary education
   (ii) 4 years of middle school education
   (iii) 4 years of senior secondary education.
2. A special two-year education will be provided to youth between the ages of 12 and 16 years.
3. A work-oriented non-formal education which is closely related to the formal education will be provided.
   (Education Challenge to the Nation: Report of the Sector Review, Ministry of Education, 1972)

The recommendation of the Education Sector Review was not acceptable because it was untimely and impractical in the prevailing socio-economic condition and political system. In fact, it aggravated the dissatisfaction and contributed to the rising tide of the general discontent which led to the overthrow of the old regime in 1974. The introduction of educational changes came with the socio-economic and political changes made in 1974. During that time different national slogans were coined to initiate, motivate and organize the Ethiopian people to combine their efforts and work hard to promote national economic development. In particular the slogan 'Ethiopia First' created a strong national enthusiasm for improving the living condition of the broad masses.

In the education field, questions such as 'What should be the new structure of the education system?'; 'What kind of curriculum should be developed?'; 'What should be the bases for decision making?'; and 'How should the administrative and management set-up be re-organized?' were widely discussed among students, teachers, elites and the community at large. The basis for introducing new changes in the education system was the fact that there was a new line of socio-economic development and also pressure from the community.

As a whole, the chronology of events prior to and over the reform period are summarized in display 1 (page 78), and the following discussion is made with reference to this display. According to the interviewees at central level, in 1975 the Ministry of Education ran a national seminar to brainstorm what 'Ethiopia First' meant and drafted a proposal for improving the education system. The participants in this seminar comprised teachers, headmasters and officials from the Ministry of Education, and they were organized into two task forces. The two task forces came up with two proposals. One of the task forces prepared recommendations for improving the administrative organization at central, regional, district and school level, while the other developed a proposal for curriculum reform.

A second seminar was organized in 1976 to discuss further the action needed to reform the education system. The following recommendations were made:

- Educational opportunity should be expanded to all school-age children irrespective of their sex, ethnic group and geographic position.
- Education should help to overcome some of the national problems. That is, it should help to strengthen national unity, economic development, etc.
- Education should serve as an agent of development by equipping children with basic knowledge and skills required in different sectors of life.

The participants of the seminar were organized into various committees and sub-committees. Some drafted educational decrees, some prepared guidelines for school administration and others prepared teaching-learning materials. It was after this seminar that a new educational slogan was created:

'Education for production'
'Education for scientific research'
'Education for political consciousness'

With this slogan, planning for an educational reform started. Step by step actions were taken to improve the education system in a more systematic way.

Planning phase The Ministry of Education's organizational structure has been modified since 1975. The previous structure was found to be inadequate to serve the fast expanding educational system and the ministry's new responsibility. Thus to make the education system more effective and efficient, new institutions have been established and some of the existing ones were re-strengthened (see display 1, page 78).

The Curriculum and Supervision Department was founded in 1974. After the Supervision Division was dissolved in 1982, the department became a national centre for curriculum development and educational research. The department became an institute in 1989, and has been able to develop teaching-learning materials for kindergarten, primary and secondary schools. It has managed to evaluate and renew the contents of most of the textbooks it has developed (Education in Socialist Ethiopia, 1984).

The other important institution created in 1974 was the Educational Materials Production and Distribution Agency. This is an organization set up to ensure the provision of textbooks, teaching materials, publications, furniture, equipment, etc. for all levels. In the preparation, production and dissemination of teaching-learning materials, the two institutions, i.e. the Institute for Curriculum Development and Educational Research and the Educational Materials Production and Distribution Agency play a vital role (ibid.). However, it has been unable to fulfil the growing demands of schools in terms of the provision of teachers and quality curricular materials.

The Institute for Curriculum Development and Educational Research has so far prepared 39 syllabi, 129 textbooks, 77 teacher guides and 39 supplementary materials for the transitional education programme and 50 syllabi, 41 student texts, 50 teacher guides and 2 support materials for the experimental education programme. Most of these materials have been printed and disseminated by the EMPDA. In fact the Educational Materials Production and Distribution Agency has produced 58,299,934 curricular materials for the formal education system (transitional curricular materials) and 9,176,822 curricular materials for the experimental education programme including other educational publications from 1971 to 1986 (EMPDA, 1989).

The Education Mass Media Service (EMMS) was reorganized and strengthened in 1975. It broadcasts centrally-developed educational radio programmes. Although the EMMS was created a few years before the revolution, it was only broadcasting to a few regions with three 1 kW power radio stations. After clear directives from the Ministry of Education to the Educational Mass Media Services, eleven new radio stations each with 10 kW power were installed and started broadcasting. This has enabled services to be provided for 90 per cent of the country's primary schools. EMMA is also responsible for educational television services (Department of Educational Mass Media, 1987).

The Schools' Construction and Maintenance Services (SCMS) is also one of the strong arms of the Ministry of Education which was re-organized in 1976. Ever since its creation, it has been very active in constructing primary schools at different sites all over the country. As a result the number of primary schools has from 2754 in 1974 increased to 8584 in 1989. During this period the average annual growth rate of primary schools was 8 per cent.

In order to develop the education system in a more systematic and controlled way, the Ministry of Education created the Office of the National Committee for Central Planning (ONCCP). The ONCCP has given guidelines for leading activities in a planned way and has instructed ministries to develop five-year and ten-year plans of work. Accordingly it is the duty of every department in the ministry to prepare annual and five-year work plans. Similarly, schools prepare yearly plans and teachers yearly, weekly and daily lesson plans. Every unit in the Ministry and schools at the grassroots level send progress reports of accomplishments of their yearly plans. At school level such a practice has helped to follow up teachers' progress and ensure the coverage of the curriculum as prescribed by the Institute for Curriculum Development and Research.

During the first few years of the revolution, there was a serious demand for schooling. In areas where the government was unable to open new schools or expand the existing ones, communities took the initiative to build their own and asked the government to provide teachers, textbooks and other facilities. This created a strain on the Ministry's limited resources, and the government introduced stricter measures on school expansion. Now, if communities want to build schools they have to get permission from the Ministry. Otherwise the government builds schools according to its budget in areas that need to be given priority.

The national enthusiasm was the reason for introducing most of the changes mentioned. Obviously, the policy committee of the Ministry of Education has played the leading role in organizing various working committees to develop objectives and guidelines for the different innovative activities implemented. Some of the innovative programmes have been partly funded by assistance from SIDA, UNICEF, EEC and IDRC, and with money borrowed from the World Bank, etc. However, the innovative programmes were not all implemented at once.

Innovative actions were introduced gradually from 1978 onwards. Experts from the German Democratic Republic started coming to advise on how the new curriculum should be developed and assist in the preparation of curricular materials. By 1989 new educational directives and objectives were set. These came out in four volumes. As a result syllabi, textbooks and teacher guides were developed and sent to schools. Since the curricular materials disseminated earlier were developed within a short period of time, they suffered from lack of clarity. (The textbooks in particular suffered from lack of quality because of shortage of expertise, experience, training and orientation in the field.) Gradually, using feedback obtained from evaluative studies and teachers' comments, improvements were made. Now, there is a quality control committee. This committee is responsible for ascertaining whether or not the minimum acceptable quality of materials has been met before it is printed and disseminated.

In the effort to make the education system more socialist-oriented, the general polytechnic education system was initiated. Since 1981, a new curriculum has been developed. A complete package has been developed and tried in 70 schools for grades 1 to 8. This curriculum is awaiting decision for nationwide implementation.

Early implementation With the aim of devolving authority and responsibility to the grass-roots level and involving the community and parents in school life, proclamations 54/1975 and 103/1976 were issued. These proclamations gave the chairmanship of the school administration committee to an individual chosen from the community, and the secretariat to the school director. Though this has made it possible to involve both parents and the surrounding community in school administration, it has created a problem in handling the daily management routines. Thus proclamations 54/1975 and 103/1976 were revised and amended by proclamation 260/1983. The new proclamation makes the headteacher the chairperson of the school administrative committee. The school administrative committee represents the government and the community whereas the parents' committee looks after its own interest in terms of pupils' learning. The chairperson of each parents' committee, organized by grade level, is also a member of the school administrative committee.

In the effort to devolve authority to lower levels of administration and to decentralize management, awraja (district) pedagogical centres (APCs) were created in 1977. APCs were started in Gondar with the intention of supporting classroom teaching with locally-produced teaching aids. When APCs were formally established at Awraja level, it was envisaged that they would be used as a method for mobilizing local initiatives and ideas to enhance the education of primary schools. Their main functions were to coordinate the inputs of all concerned individuals, groups, communities, local associations, popular organizations and educational officers in order to facilitate quality education in primary schools. At present APCs prepare and disseminate teaching aids, and run training for school directors, teachers and community leaders. School pedagogical centres which were created with similar objectives to APCs are serving teachers as centres for producing teaching aids. This is discussed in detail in later chapters.

Teacher education programmes The number of teacher training institutes increased from ten to 13 between 1974 and 1983 showing an average annual growth rate of 1.9 per cent, though currently only 11 are operational. As a result, the yearly enrolment of trainees for primary teacher education increased from 3100 in 1974 to 4142 in 1989 (Ministry of Education, 1989). However, there is still a need for more teacher training institutes if the government's commitment to provide basic education for all is to become a reality.

Community skill training centres (CSTCs) were also created in 1975, to offer skills of handling and using basic tools needed to improve the life of the rural population and to reinforce their knowledge of reading, writing and arithmetic. Between 1975 and 1989 a total of 408 CSTCs were constructed, and these had 151,671 participants, 31,034 of whom were female (ibid.).

In 1975, a circular was passed to all district administrators to provide ten hectares of land to all rural schools. This was intended to serve a dual purpose: to enable schools to generate their own internal income in an effort to facilitate the teaching-learning process; and to create a means for integrating theoretical classroom, especially agricultural, knowledge with practical field experience.

Later implementation District schools' offices and schools have been given more and more authority since 1978. For example they are now responsible for the transfer of elementary school teachers which used to be carried out at central and regional level. Decisions about school sites and their number are taken by district offices. Districts are encouraged to adapt and enrich the curriculum locally. As a whole, district schools' offices and schools are now responsible for preparing and executing their own plans. This is the result of the effort to decentralize authority to the grass roots level and the beginning of local school administration.

It has already been pointed out that the Ethiopian government is making every effort to universalize primary education to all school-age children. As a mechanism to get feedback for improving educational programmes, the curriculum evaluation and educational research division was founded in 1981. This division has carried out more than 16 evaluative studies. The evaluative research of the general education system in Ethiopia (ERGESE) is one of its outstanding achievements. It showed that while educational opportunity has widened, there has not been a corresponding improvement in the quality of the education system. The recommendations for improvement have been widely discussed and measures for professionalization of educational personnel, increasing supply of resources and efficiency of their utilization, re-examination of the curriculum with respect to national needs and the nature of the learner, rationalization of the organization and management of the education system, etc., are being taken. The division has also produced ideas and recommendations useful for policy-making and has collected feedback for improving the activities of the different departments of the Ministry of Education.

The changes introduced in Ethiopia are still in practice. Introducing new teaching methods in the classroom, use of teaching aids, the labour education programme, developing a new management system, etc. are all an on-going process.

Display 1 Key events/consequences

	Period	*Key event*	*Consequences*
Before	1974	Political change: seminar. New policies towards equality of opportunities, more practical emphasis, relevance to ordinary citizens. (10C)	1975: National seminar for developing ideas for education reform
	1974	Curriculum change	1975: National conference develop strategy for national reform and policies. 'Education for production, education for scientific work and education for political consciousness

The Primary Education Reform Programme in Ethiopia

Display 1 *(cont)*

	Period	Key event	Consequences
Planning phase	1975	Reorganization of Ministry of Education. New departments were added and old ones were reorganized and strengthened. In 1975 curriculum department and EMPDA, adult education department, etc. were established	A better organizational structure eventually envolved. Better textbooks for most subjects were prepared and distributed to all schools
	1975	Educational broadcasting expanded. Centrally developed radio programmes started to broadcast (6C)	The number of radio broadcasting stations expanded from two to eleven. Coverage now includes 90% of schools
	1975	School building programme initiated. School building intensified. Communities also started building their own schools (6C)	Number of primary schools in 1974 was 2754, increasing to 8584 by 1989, with an annual of growth rate of 8.5%
	1975	Planning at central level. The Ministry of Education started developing the education system in a systematic and controlled way	Government introduced a more strict measure on school expansion
	1978	Experts came from GDR	Adapted the general polytechnic education system
	1980	New educational directives and objectives were set (6C)	A new curriculum started being developed
Early implementation	1975	Proclamation 54/1975 and 103/1976. Improved proclamation 260/1983 made headteacher vice chairperson of administrative committee and role of parents expanded (6C)	The basis for a totally new school management structure and for parents' involvement in school affairs
	1975	A circular was passed to all rural schools so that they could obtain ten hectares of land from local authorities for production (6C)	It became the first base for school income generation
	1977	Creation of district pedagogical centres (APCs) and school pedagogical centres (6C)	103 APCs and 6000 SPCs providing schools with teaching aids and in-service training opportunities
		The number of teacher training institutes increased from ten to 13 between 1974 and 1983 with a growth rate of 1.99	Recruits were trained to be teachers in primary schools

Display 1 *(cont)*

	Period	Key event	Consequences
Early Implementation	1977	Community skill training centres were established	From 1975 to 1989 a total of 408 CSTCs have been constructed. Of the 151,671 participants in CSTC programmes 31,034 were female
	1978	Delegation of authority to regional and district education officers. Recruitment of teachers, transfer of teachers, planning at local level, etc (7C)	The beginning of local school administration
	1981	Establishment of central curriculum evaluation and educational research division (6C)	The division has carried out 16 education evaluative studies. Policy issues and recommendations were given to concerned departments
	1981–1990	Most of the changes introduced were gradually developed and improved	All changes initiated are nationwide and still put in practice

Factors accounting for success of educational reform in Ethiopia A summary of the findings of the country level factors accounting for the success of the reform are given in display 2A (page 87). The following discussion is made with reference to this display.

Strength of national organization The new administrative structure has created an effective mechanism for directing and implementing changes at school level. At central level, the Ministry of Education has established a body called the policy committee responsible for preparing directives, guidelines and policies for implementing and monitoring educational reform. The committee members are heads of departments and services such as the Institute for Curriculum Development and Educational Research, Educational Mass Media Agency, planning and external relation services, school construction and maintenance services, project management services, inspection department, formal education department, teacher education department, etc. and is chaired by the minister.

Policy issues and desired changes identified at different levels are first forwarded to the policy committee by the department concerned. The department responsible for initiating a change is normally expected to explain it and to clarify issues. After the committee has examined and thoroughly discussed the proposed plans and programmes, decisions are made. Such decisions are channelled to the appropriate body for necessary action. The inspection and the formal education departments are particularly responsible for ensuring the implementation of changes, rules and regulations passed by the policy committee, and the information exchange system as well as the way decisions are made and executed is a strength of the national education system.

Table 4.1 Courses conducted by management and training services 1981–1989

Year	Type of course	Duration	Number of participants
1981	Personnel management	15 days	108
1981	Financial management	15 days	108
1981	Auditing and financial control	15 days	93
1981	Purchase and store management	15 days	113
1981	Record keeping	15 days	100
1981	Educational administration for deputy regional and district education officers	15 days	200
1982–83	Inspection	12 weeks	120
1982–83	Secondary school management	6 weeks	280
1983	Financial management	3 weeks	103
1984	Planning and statistics	3 weeks	134
1985–86	Inspection	12 weeks	113
1987	Educational management and administration	2 weeks	54
1989	Materials management	0.5 week	80
1989	Financial management	0.5 week	100
1989	School administration	1 week	185
1989	Inspection	6 weeks	147
1989	National examination administration	1 week	26
	Total		2064

Source: Negussie Habteyes, 1990.

Capacity building of national organizations At the beginning, when new education goals were developed and the preparation and development of new teaching-learning materials was in progress, there was a lot of confusion. The main reason for this was that educators who were doing the ground work lacked experience and expertise in the field. In time, on the job training was given to most people who were developing innovative materials, and this has greatly improved efficiency and the outcome of the ministry. The experience accumulated in initiating, designing and implementing changes became a driving force for further work.

Building of commitment The Ministry of Education has been running orientation programmes, workshops, seminars and in-service courses to acquaint teachers, headmasters, district and regional education officers with the new programmes in an effort to build their skills and commitment for effective implementation. Examples of courses offered by the management and training services are given in Table 4.1. Annual education conferences held at various levels have also served as discussion forums for exchanging experiences and finding ways and means of minimizing problems encountered while implementing the changes. The participation of community members in seminars held at district level has made it possible for schools to get the support and commitment of the community in finance, materials and labour.

Strategic matching Generally the Ministry of Education develops change programmes based on need assessment. Once a change is identified and a programme is developed for it, the idea is to implement it nationwide. For example the Institute for Curriculum Development and Research developed and tested a totally new curriculum in 70 'experimental' schools. These materials were developed and tried out one after the other. The model of development was progressive. At present the curriculum package for grades 1-8 is ready for nationwide implementation and is intended to be implemented grade by grade.

Legal regulations Nearly all educational policies are made by the Ministry of Education. The legal bases for identifying, developing and implementing innovative programmes are the authority and responsibilities vested in the Ministry of Education. This is stated and explained in different government documents and proclamations (the NDR programme and the Ethiopian) referring to education.

Decision making Major decisions concerning the new educational objectives and directives, the curriculum, and other policy issues are decided by the Ministry of Education on the basis of the Ethiopian constitution and the party programme. Regional offices and district offices are responsible for planning and executing their own specific activities such as allocating budgets to different schools, assigning and transferring teachers to schools, determining school sites, running local training workshops, visiting schools, etc. Likewise schools devise their own annual plan of activities, and are also responsible for implementing the curriculum, labour education programme, teaching aids, teaching methods, etc. by adapting to local conditions.

Pressure for good implementation The need for educational change was proclaimed by different interested pressure groups and the community during the 1974 revolution. The aim was to make education more relevant to national development needs. To ensure quality implementation of the changes yearly education conferences are held at central, regional, district and school level. Participants of the conferences are expected to report what has and/or has not been achieved. Unless there is a very good reason, guidelines passed from the centre to the periphery are normally respected, and this is usually verified by quarterly reports from all concerned units.

Curriculum developments Curriculum development is a centralized business. Curriculum materials for elementary to secondary schools including syllabi, textbooks and teacher guides for all subjects and grades, supplementary materials, some prototype demonstration materials, science kits, the curriculum for teacher training institutes, and sixth and eighth grade national examinations are developed centrally by the Institute for Curriculum Development and Research. The curriculum has been developed along a socialist education system, based on the NDR programme and the new educational directives. Subjects such as political education are offered from grade four onwards.

At present there are two types of curriculum: the transitional curriculum and the new general polytechnic education programme which will eventually replace the old curriculum. In both the syllabus is seen as a state document to be strictly followed by all teachers of a particular grade. Similarly, it is expected that all students of a particular grade will use the specified students' texts within the constraints of shortages.

The steps of curriculum development include the setting of instructional objectives in each subject area; determining topics and sub-topics of each subject area; preparation of instructional materials in sample schools; improving materials with the feedback obtained; and introducing teachers to the newly developed instructional materials through in-service courses, workshops, seminars, etc. Representative teachers and SPC coordinators from most schools, and APC coordinators and inspectors are normally given orientation on the new programmes.

Division of labour There seems to be a strong division of labour in the system. Different units of the Ministry of Education have different responsibilities. For example, the Institute for Curriculum Development is responsible for preparing curricular materials and carrying out educational research and the Educational Materials Production and Distribution Agency is responsible for printing and disseminating curricular materials, etc. However, it is the duty of district education offices to adopt and implement centrally initiated changes. District offices can mobilize the local communities to support plans to build more schools, classrooms and also satisfy schools' of their own needs as well.

Infrastructure development The organizational structure of the Ministry of Education has a chain of hierarchy stretching from the centre to the periphery including departments, institutions, agencies, etc. at central level, regional and district schools' offices and schools. Some of the centrally organized departments and services have extensions at regional and district level, for example, inspection, planning, mass media, etc. The district pedagogical centres and school pedagogical centres also contribute to training and orienting teachers to innovative changes such as the preparation and use of teaching aids.

Availability and quality of materials At the beginning of the reform period, simple draft curricular materials were sent to schools. At the time, it was very difficult to supply adequate numbers of textbooks and teacher guides. Gradually, improved materials were distributed and the plan was to distribute at least one textbook for every two students.

The Evaluative Research of the General Education System in Ethiopia (ERGESE) has shown that the quality of some of the curriculum materials needs to be improved and steps have been taken accordingly. However, the quality of curriculum materials is something that has to be continually improved, especially the relevance of curriculum materials in order to keep them in tune with the prevailing socio-economic development of the country. There is currently a shortage of stationery; sports facilities; raw materials for producing teaching aids and home-economics products, etc. Since most schools try to use locally available raw materials for all of these, very little attention is given to quality.

Table 4.2a General education budget by level of education in US dollars

Level of education	1988	1989
Primary education	103,333,420	112,156,056
Junior secondary education	24,417,283	26,569,367
Senior secondary education	25,498,785	27,513,960
Technical/Vocational education	2,223,374	2,268,041
Teacher training education	4,045,707	6,661,904
Other	25,677,797	24,381,346
Total	185,196,366	199,550,674

Source: Basic Education Statistics, 1989, p. 24.

Table 4.2b Unit cost in US dollars by year and level

Level	Year			
	1985	1986	1987	1988
Primary	37.20	39.61	39.13	35.75
Junior secondary	64.25	61.84	58.45	52.66
Senior secondary	81.64	81.64	77.29	67.17

Source: Educational Statistics, 1988.

Resource allocation budgeting The nationwide allocation of money, human resources and curricular materials is determined by the Ministry of Education on the basis of pupil enrolment in the different regions. The general education recurrent budget by level of education for 1988 and 1989 is shown in Table 4.2.

Resource delivery The overall education budget has shown a slight increase as a percentage of the gross domestic product. However, it is difficult to say that the education budget has increased as a percentage of the total government expenditure. On the other hand, the rate of growth of student and teacher enrolment has created a strain on the limited education budget. The unit cost per student is declining and this is causing a number of problems. A large portion (more than 80 per cent) of the recurrent budget goes on paying salaries, leaving very little for purchasing stationery, paying for workshop and seminar participants, inspectors and other educational officers who are supposed to evaluate school activities and provide constructive feedback to teachers and headmasters. In general, there is a scarcity of government budget for running the day-to-day activities of schools and district schools' offices. It has been pointed out by district education officers and support givers that schools don't receive any financial assistance to cover office running costs. It is only APCs who receive Birr 1200 every year for training teachers and preparing prototype teaching aids.

When schools first began to implement the changes, there was a serious shortage of teachers. The 1989 educational statistics show that the situation has improved. The national average teacher-pupil ratio is 1 to 46, however it is much higher in urban areas than in rural areas. For example the ratio for Addis Ababa is 1 to 56. There are many reports indicating that there is a problem with the quality of teacher training for primary schools and the quality of programmes of training institutes.

The delivery of educational materials and resources is the responsibility of the Ministry of Education through the Educational Materials Production and Distribution Agency and the regional and district education offices. EMPDA delivers syllabi, teacher guides, textbooks, chalk, blackboards, science kits, etc., to regional offices. The regions deliver to districts, and districts distribute the appropriate share to each school according to its student enrolment. In some cases, schools don't get these materials in time for their opening in September; they get them around late October.

Effective communication It can be said that there is a two-way communication system. Information is disseminated from the centre to the grass roots by means of workshops, seminars, annual education conferences, circulars and the mass media. Schools in turn send quarterly progress reports and letters to district educational offices. District offices compile statistical information gathered from schools and either pass it to Regional Education Offices who pass it to the Ministry of Education or send it directly to the Ministry of Education. Every year the data is processed and reported as educational statistics by the planning and external relation services. The information is used for further planning and developing the education system.

Responsive adaption Drafts of new curriculum materials developed by the Institute for Curriculum Development and Research are usually sent to schools for comments. Teachers organized by departments discuss the materials and send their comments to the institute, where they are further discussed in workshops in which teachers and subject experts participate. Such practices have helped to reflect local interest needs, to correct mistakes detected and to improve weaknesses.

Although curriculum development is centralized, schools prepare social science syllabi and the content of learning for grades 1 to 3 based on the guidelines given by the Institute for Curriculum Development and Research. The idea is to make students familiar with their own localities, culture and historical developments. Schools prepare and use teaching aids. However, APCs collect teaching aids that can be displayed as good examples and models during annual education conferences, seminars and workshops. This has aroused the teachers' interest and improved their commitment to support classroom teaching with visual aids and practical experience.

User involvement Teachers are sometimes invited to draft syllabi and the contents of textbooks under the guidance of the Institute for Curriculum Development and Research. They are also involved in trying out draft materials, giving comments to experts of ICDR and in implementing new curricular materials and other innovative changes such as the labour education programme and the use of teaching aids. However, it is difficult to say that users feel they share ownership of curricular materials development.

Regional and district education officers, headmasters and teachers have participated in workshops and seminars to familiarize them with the educational changes and facilitate their smooth implementation. In addition to being introduced to changes and gaining some experience, users can suggest ideas that promote local adaptations. However, the teachers' involvement in curriculum development is unsatisfactory. To create the user ownership which is currently lacking, many teachers feel that they should be involved at the various stages of curriculum development. There is also a similar feeling among the experts working on curriculum design in Ethiopia.

Protection from turbulence In an effort to promote socio-economic development, teachers have been called to give service in mass organizations and development activities. This is sometimes done in school hours, which affects classroom instruction and the implementation of some of the changes. Under such circumstances, the Ministry of Education has negotiated with other organizations and local officials to relieve teachers of assignments that take up classroom hours and affect the implementation of the changes.

Decisions supporting institutionalization Important decisions essential for strengthening and continuation of the programme are made at the national level by the policy committee body. Specific matters such as training personnel, developing rules and regulations for monitoring, evaluating and getting feedback, determining the mechanisms to raise funds, etc. are left to the respective units of the Ministry of Education. For example, training of teachers is the responsibility of the teacher education department and promulgating new rules for controlling and inspection purposes is the duty of the department of inspection. Decisions made by the Ministry of Education are based on the different proclamations and working documents of the ministry itself. These include proclamation 54/1975 and 100/1976, the improved proclamation 206/1983, new educational objectives and directives, the ten-year perspective plan, the NDR programme, etc.

Assistance Professional assistance at central, local and school level is provided in different forms. At the beginning of the reform, assistance was obtained from resource people who used to prepare discussion papers. Gradually Ministry of Education experts were sent on educational tours to learn from the experience of other countries. Some were also given overseas training for specialized programmes such as curriculum development, educational planning, research and evaluation, pedagogy, etc. In parallel with this teachers and headmasters are trained at home in in-service and pre-service programmes. This is further strengthened with workshops and seminars intended to develop the knowledge, skills and attitudes of teachers and headmasters on some of the changes already introduced, and the APCs have played a significant role in this. These training programmes are carried out regularly, but they are not available for all teachers, headmasters and experts at the central level for the simple reason that there is a shortage of financial resources.

Monitoring and control Every educational change is associated with one of the departments at the centre which monitors and controls the implementation of the changes. The Institute of Curriculum Development and Research is responsible for following up the implementation of curricular materials, the EMPDA for printing and distributing textbooks, the formal education department for the labour education programme, etc. In addition to these, the inspection department through its regional and district representatives, follows up the implementation of the change programmes and provides feed-back to the respective unit at the centre. The inspection department also synthesizes the quarterly reports of regional education offices.

Display 2A Country level factors accounting for the success of the reform

Factor	Illustrative indicators (+, −)	Rating (H,M,L)
Strength of national organization	Policy committee initials changes. Different units of MOE follow up implementation of changes. Guidelines are passed from the centre to the REO and DEO. Inspection department reviews all progress reports and sends feedback (10C)	H
Capacity building of national organization	New offices and departments opened and others re-strengthened. Some staff members were given training or sent on study tours. The experience gained in initiating and implementing changes is a capacity (4C)	H
Strategic matching	Changes introduced are based on national needs. Labour education for relating theory with practice and internal income generation, SPC to facilitate the teaching-learning process, etc (6C)	H
Legal regulations	The authority and the responsibility explained in different documents are the legal bases of the MOE (8C)	H
Decision making and division of labour	Major decisions are made by the policy committee of MOE. Regional and district offices are responsible for executing and following up MOE policies (5C)	H
Pressure for good implementation	Annual conferences are used for exchanging information and pressurizing all units to implement the changes. Quarterly reports of activities are a must (2C)	H
Curriculum development	Syllabi, teacher guides, textbooks, supplementary materials, prototype demonstration materials, science kits, teacher-training materials, sixth and eighth grade national examinations are prepared centrally (8C)	H
Infrastructure development	APCs, inspection, statistics, mass media are represented at regional and district levels (6C)	H
Availability and quality of materials	Curricular materials are available at school level. The textbook-pupil ratio is 1 to 2. There is an acute shortage of stationery (4C)	H
Resource allocation and delivery	EMPDA is responsible for the distribution of curricular materials. 92.6% of the recurrent budget is used for paying salaries and allowances leaving only 7.4% for running costs. UNICEF, SIDA, WB, etc. are also helping financially in the development of the education system (2C)	H

Display 2A *(cont)*

Factor	Illustrative indicators (+, −)	Rating (H,M,L)
Closeness to implementation	Through annual conferences, quarterly reports, school visits, inspection evaluation and research findings, higher officials follow up the implementation of the changes (6C)	M
Effective communication	There is a two-way communication system. Directives, rules and regulations and new changes are disseminated from the centre. Quarterly reports from the grassroots level are sent to the centre (6C)	H
Responsive adaptations	Draft curricular materials are sent to schools for comments. Local interests are normally reflected using the feedback obtained. Model teaching aids are displayed at APC (2PC)	H/M
User involvement	Teacher are called to assist in drafting the contents of textbooks and asked to try them (2C)	M
Protection for environmental turbulence	When teachers are assigned to work in mass organizations, MOE officials negotiate with other organizations so that teaching hours are not affected (3C)	M
Decision supporting institutions	The various proclamations, guidelines, and the new administrative set-up EMPDA, ICDR, EMM, etc. are the main ones (7C)	H
Assistance	Discussion papers, educational tours, seminars and workshops, study leave, in-service and pre-service training, are considered as different forms of assistance (6C)	M
Monitoring and control	Concerned departments are responsible for guiding, monitoring and controlling changes they have initiated (4C)	H

The degree of implementation success seen from the national viewpoint

The major components of the primary school education reform in Ethiopia have already been outlined. These are:

- expanding educational opportunity to all school-age children
- improving the structure, organization and management of the Ministry of Education
- staff development by providing different training schemes
- building schools and providing better facilities
- developing socialist education
- developing a better production and distribution system for educational materials

- integrating theory and practice through labour education programmes
- encouraging schools to generate their own internal income
- providing radio support
- promoting active community participation in school affairs
- expanding research and evaluation activities to create an effective and efficient education system.

According to the interviewees, most of these changes have been implemented nationwide. However, the degree of implementation varies from region to region and from school to school.

System level outcomes Display 2C (page 94) summarizes the findings regarding outcome at system level.

Demand for schooling In the past 15 years there has been a big increase in the demand for schooling and communities everywhere are asking the government to build schools or they themselves build them. The demand is not limited to primary schools, but also includes junior secondary and senior secondary schools. Since the onset of the revolution, there has been a considerable growth in the number of primary schools, students, teachers and teacher-training institutes. In 1974 the total number of primary schools was only 2754 with 18,600 teachers and 859,000 students. In 1989 the total number of primary schools was 8584 with 65,993 teachers and 2,855,846 students. The average yearly growth rate of schools, teachers and students was 8.5 per cent, 9.5 per cent and 9.0 per cent, respectively (Educational Statistics, 1989).

The increased number of pupils has meant that most of the urban primary schools and some of the rural ones operate in two shifts. The shift system in turn has contributed to the enrolment of even more students. The literacy programme has also had an impact on student enrolment. The literacy programme is intended to provide basic literacy skill to the illiterate adult population. However, in some areas children also attend the programme. After completing and acquiring a certificate, some children join the formal education programme. On the other hand, educational wastage is very high in primary schools. The number of repeaters and drop-outs is high at all grade levels, but is particularly high in grades 1 to 3 (see Table 4.3).

Despite the efforts made, the national participation rate of primary schools is still only 34 per cent (Educational Statistics 1989, p. 1) According to the interviewees, the quality of education has also not improved as desired. There are a number of reasons for this, including large class size, low teacher morale, inadequate teacher-training, low unit cost per student, low educational budget, etc. (see ERGESE, 1986).

Capacity of central institutions and support system At central, regional and district level the Ministry of Education has developed a capacity for initiating, planning, developing, implementing and monitoring innovative

Table 4.3 Flow rates in primary schools 1987

Flow Rates	Grade 1	Grade 2	Grade 3	Grade 4	Grade 5	Grade 6
Repetition rate	0.1873	0.0949	0.0691	0.0643	0.0512	0.1027
Drop-out rate	0.2912	0.0323	0.0588	0.0657	0.0474	0.0755

Source: Education Statistics, 1987.

programmes. Experts have been given professional training, formally by attending local and overseas universities, and informally through workshops, seminars and short educational tours abroad. The experience gained so far is also a capacity for further educational development.

New roles and relations between central, regional and local institutions
Despite the fact that the Ministry of Education has been running annual education conferences, the focus of discussion used to be mainly administrative issues. Very little attention was given to what was going on in the classroom. This has been improved lately. Annual conferences are now used for sharing experiences, for passing new ideas and for paying attention to what goes on in the classroom.

It has become clear that the Ministry of Education is unable to run workshops and seminars or give training to all primary schools teachers. The strategy used to overcome this problem is to encourage schools and district educational offices to run their own workshops. In such workshops resource people, teachers and headmasters who have participated in seminars organized at central level and who have had training, present discussion papers and demonstrate new teaching aids, teaching methods, etc. Similarly, different departments of the Ministry of Education organize meetings, seminars and conferences in which experts, educational officers and policy makers participate to discuss the findings of different studies and practical problems.

Changes in innovation strategy There has not been a uniform strategy in the implementation of most of the changes introduced. The transitional curriculum was implemented progressively, with syllabi, textbooks and teacher guides developed and tried out, then implemented grade by grade in all schools. The innovative changes such as the implementation of the labour education programme, radio support, establishing SPC, etc., were intended to be implemented nationwide within a short period of time. This has been attained in most primary schools. However, the construction of APCs and radio broadcasting centres can take too much time.

Changes in funding The unit cost per student has declined in recent years and according to 1989 educational statistics, is now very low compared to that in other developing countries. The reason for this is mainly the inability of the government to allocate adequate educational funds. At the same time, the high growth in yearly enrolment is straining the limited budget. To minimize the problem, schools are encouraged to generate their own income by encouraging the community to contribute money and provide a labour force and raw materials; and by collecting school fees, book rent and by producing vegetables, crops, handicrafts, etc., for sale.

Assistance from external donors The Ministry of Education gets financial, material and technical assistance from different friendly governments and non-government organizations for the develoment of education in Ethiopia. The assistance of external donors varies from year to year. For example: the Swedish International Development Agency (SIDA) donated $5,236,091 in 1988 and $5,617,889 in 1989. Mostly the external donors give assistance to short-term programmes. The main donors are UNFPA, UNESCO, UNICEF, UNDP, ADFI, World Bank, OPEC and SIDA. The German Democratic Republic, USSR, UK, Italy, FRG, Japan and Finland also have given assistance and details of this are published in a report on SIDA assisted education projects (Ministry of Education, 1990).

Impact on students The new curriculum is considered to be more relevant to local and national needs than the pre-revolution curriculum, and was developed with the feeling that students' attitude toward learning and physical labour would improve. Although the impression has been gained that students can relate theoretical knowledge with practical experience, there hasn't been an investigation on the impact of the curriculum on student attitude, skills and achievements. However, the effort to relate theoretical knowledge with practical experience is continuing through labour education activities at all levels of the education system. The general feeling of most of the interviewees is that there has been a positive development in terms of student knowledge, skills and attitudes. According to the Ministry of Education, the repetition rates on the sixth and eighth grade national examinations in 1987 were 9.8 per cent and 13.8 per cent respectively (Educational Statistics, 1989, p. 30). In the same document it is shown that the 1989 figure of repeaters (15 per cent) is quite a bit higher than the figure for 1987. If this national exam result is taken as an indicator of acquired knowledge and skills, it contradicts what the interviewees have said in this regard.

Impact on teachers It has already been pointed out that in the past 15 years, efforts have been made to acquaint teachers with new educational changes and innovative programmes through workshops and seminars and with pre-service and in-service teacher education. According to a Ministry of Education report, in June 1989 alone a total of 4142 elementary school teachers graduated from ten TTIs and all of them have since been employed. In the summer of the same year a total of 3361 teachers received refresher courses in different TTIs and 1190 head teachers received one short course in the Debre Berhan and Awassa TTIs. When this is compared with a total of 8584 primary school head teachers and 65,993 teachers all in need of refresher courses and training, the effort seems like a drop in the ocean.

In general the attitude of most teachers towards the innovative programmes was positive from the beginning, with the exception of the labour education programme. However, in rural elementary schools in particular, where the outcomes of the labour educational programme are now being seen, teachers and students have come to like it and be involved in it. This has created a good working relationship and cooperation between teachers and students. Nevertheless, many teachers don't want to stay in the teaching profession, and the reason often given for this is low teacher morale because of the low salary. Most teachers point out that the cost of living is rising and the rate of salary increase doesn't match this rise.

Impact on schools A better working atmosphere has been created in schools. Proclamations 54/1975 and 103/1976, circulars such as the new school rules and directives passed from time to time have enabled schools to have better organization and division of labour and to involve local communities in school administration. In addition to government budget, schools are encouraged to generate and use their own income. For this, most rural schools have received additional land in accordance with the circular passed allowing schools to have ten hectares of land. School administration and parents' committees play a satisfactory role in the generation as well as the utilization of resources in many schools. As a result many schools have expanded their classrooms and activities giving more opportunities for student enrolment and quality teaching.

In spite of the fact that demand for enrolment has grown considerably in most schools, drop-out and repetition rates are high, particularly in grades 1,2 and 6 (see Ministry of Education, 1989, p. 30), and for girls.

Institutionalization/sustainability of the programme The fact that by 1989 the primary school participation rate had risen to 34 per cent shows the need for more schools. Every year a few more are built and the government is committed to build more and more schools until basic education for all becomes a reality. In schools, teachers are organized by departments and the division of labour is defined. Every year trained teachers are sent to schools and untrained teachers are allowed to attend summer courses. However, it appears that more effort is needed in this area.

Textbooks, science kits, hand tools, etc. are sent to schools; and efforts are continuing to make the curriculum more relevant to socio-economic development. Schools have been boosting their internal income through labour education programmes and co-curricular activities. In this, school administration and parents' committees play significant roles. The Ministry has intensified research and evaluation activities. In short, all the changes introduced are built into the education system.

Linkage between central, regional, district and school levels

The following discussion is based on display 2B. Linkage between central, regional, district and school has been investigated from different angles.

Assistance The Ministry of Education organizes annual educational conferences, seminars, workshops and training programmes. Mostly the participants are teachers, APC and SPC coordinators, inspectors, statistics

Display 2B Linkage between country, district and school levels

	How linkage is done			Researcher comments/explanations
	To districts	To schools	Consequences	
Assistance	A series of courses were given to different groups. From 1981 to 1989, 2110 participants attended courses for a duration ranging from 1.5 weeks to 6 weeks (C)	In addition to in-service programmes, APCs have given training to 5,027 headmasters, 23,830 teachers, 25,622 previously untrained teachers, 17,137 SPC coordinators and 4754 members of school administration committees (2C)	The different training programmes have helped to build capacity for better (quality) work (2C)	APC has served to give immediate training at least to community employed, untrained teachers
Administrative role	Guidelines, rules and regulations, textbooks and other materials are sent to REO and DEO Every APC gets Birr 1500 as its annual budget (3C) Schools are entitled to have ten hectares of land (6C)	Every school has two volumes of 'school rules and regulations'. They also receive their quota of textbooks (3) Most schools have now ten hectares of land (6C)	Schools make use of the centrally distributed materials and work according to the rules and regulations (3C) Schools have larger compounds which they use for different purposes (6C)	There seems to be a good chain of actions This has helped schools to use some of the land for generating internal income, sports, etc.
Commitment	Departments of MOE are committed to the implementation of the changes. They initiate follow up of the progress of changes and give additional guidelines for effective implementation (3C)	Schools are visited by experts from the department that initiated the changes. Practical problems are discussed with teachers	Schools themselves feel that changes such as the labour education programme, planning activities and involving the community in school affairs are their responsibilities	Most of the change programmes are effective and schools now have the support of parents and communities

Display 2C. Outcome at the system level

Illustrative indicator	Outcome	Rating H,M,L
Demand for schooling	From 1987 to 1989 annual growth rates of primary school enrolment, number of schools and teachers were 9, 8.5 and 9.5 per cent, respectively. Primary school participation rate in 1989 was 34 per cent. Community school demand is growing (10C)	H
Capacity of central institutions and support system	The re-organization of the MOE, experts' experience, training, and ability to plan and execute changes has increased the capacity for futher educational development. MOE produces domestic curricular materials, teaching aids, science kits, etc. (6C) The more MOE is unable to meet training, material and financial needs of schools (4C)	H
New roles and relations between central, regional and local institutions	Annual educational conferences are being used more and more as a forum for sharing experiences, passing new ideas, with greater attention to classroom situations (4C)	H
	Departments and units organize meetings, seminars and conferences to discuss research findings and practical problems (3C)	H
	Decentralization of authorities to regional and district offices, better understanding of community and school needs (3C)	H
Changes in innovation	There are two types of curriculum: transitional and polytechnical. The latter has been developed since 1980 and tried out in 70 schools. It was evaluated and improved; and is now waiting for a decision on nationwide implementation (6C)	H

Source: Agreed minutes from the Joint Annual Education Sector Review, Addis Ababa, Ethiopia, 1988.

officers and radio programmers. Similar activities are run by regional and district offices particularly for teachers and headmasters. Seminars and workshops are used for briefing participants on new educational developments, policies, rules and regulations. During such seminars at district level, papers are presented on subjects including the production and use of teaching aids, preparing annual plans, teaching methods, radio use, record keeping and pupil assessment. Seminars are also given at school level in order to replicate experiences and impart information to other teachers. As a result, there has been an information flow and transmission of knowledge, skills of planning and executing changes. In this way teachers at the grass-roots level become familiar with innovative changes and their implementations. School headmasters and teachers have made use of the guidelines, their training and the knowledge they have gained in seminars and workshops for implementing most of the centrally initiated changes.

Administrative role The Ministry of Education distributes textbooks and other centrally prepared or purchased materials to each region based on enrolment and the number of schools in each area. Regional offices in turn divide the resources between districts and schools using the same rationale. Sometime mis-allocations are observed. For example too many geography textbooks may be available in some schools while there is shortage in other schools. The same thing is true with new policies, guidelines, rules and regulations developed. All schools have received the centrally developed materials and are making use of them.

Commitment Experts from the central office often visit regional and district offices to encourage responsible individuals and groups to continue implementing the centrally initiated changes. Though it is mandatory to implement these changes in schools, the interviewees believe that they are only effective if implementors at all levels have a positive attitude and are committed to the work. With this in mind, the district administrators and support givers said that in addition to giving on-the-spot assistance during school visits, they also help teachers by clarifying queries and solving practical problems. By explaining the importance of the changes and the advantages the school will have on implementing them, it has been possible to keep the changes going on in most schools.

Received pressure The Ministry of Education requires all units at central level, regional offices, district offices and schools to submit quarterly reports of the progress of their annual plans. This serves as a mechanism for pushing all sectors to implement the changes according to given terms of reference. In addition experts and inspectors evaluate school progress by visiting schools at least once in a year.

Received resources It has already been pointed out that the Ministry of Education provides curricular materials, tools, teachers and builds schools. However, it hasn't been able to satisfy the growing needs of schools.

Success experience The Ministry of Education has been able to implement most of the centrally initiated changes in schools, and in most cases the curriculum, labour education programme, radio programme and support of the community have become a part of school life. However, respondents at the central level still feel that what has been achieved in terms of student outcome is not yet satisfactory.

Empowerment engagement Though implementors of the change were not directly involved in designing most of the innovative ideas, they do feel that the changes are important and necessary. District education officers, teachers, headmasters and community leaders are all working for the effective implementation of the changes. Communities are helping schools to build more classrooms and to generate internal school income, etc. In general it can be said that schools and communities have taken the changes as their own and are committed to their implementation.

Local adaptation of the programme All curricular materials are developed with the idea that teachers will use them uniformly across schools. Teachers are expected to enrich the materials with examples taken from their surroundings. It is also the teachers' duty to prepare notes based on the teacher guides, textbooks and other resource materials, and to prepare their own teaching aids and use appropriate teaching methods. Teachers must also prepare their own social studies materials for grades 1 to 3. Except in the case of the curriculum, teachers are entitled to adapt the other innovative change to local conditions and circumstances.

Community support The revised proclamation 260/1983 has enabled schools to involve the community in school administration in a more efficient way, and has become the basis for a totally new management structure and for parents' involvement in school affairs. Thus it has become possible to involve both parents and members of the surrounding community in solving some of schools' material and financial problems. They also assist in solving disciplinary problems, obtaining houses for teachers, and in some areas they even hire teachers to overcome shortages.

IMPLEMENTATION AT THE SCHOOL LEVEL
Cross-school analysis

From the nine case studies, it is quite clear that all the centrally initiated changes have been implemented in all the sample schools. What will be investigated in this section is the degree of implementation, impact and institutionalization, and all nine sample schools (Gedeo I, Tegulet I, Tegulet II, Gedeo II, Chilalo I, Tegulet III, Chilalo II, Gedeo III and Chilalo III) were taken for the cross-school comparisons. In fact, an initial sorting of the schools in terms of the success of implementation was made by inspectors during the sample selection in each district. For example, the inspectors in Gedeo district rank-ordered the three schools, by placing Gedeo I as an 'excellent', Gedeo III as a 'very good' and Gedeo II as a 'good' school in terms of implementing the changes. A similar grouping was made by each district. However, the results of the study showed some difference in ordering.

Purpose The purpose of the cross-school analysis is to identify factors that accounted for greater and/or less success in terms of implementation, impact and institutionalization of the educational reform components launched in Ethiopian primary schools over the past ten years.

Procedure The cross-school analysis was carried out after the nine case studies had been written and distributed among the study team for further enrichment. Prior to that, the schools were grouped into three preliminary piles with the help of the coach for the Ethiopian group. Before the actual sorting was made, all the completed displays were read and commented on by the coach. This helped a lot in clarifying vague ideas, straightening out misconceptions, and reducing and polishing the displays. After making a thorough study of each case study, a second attempt was made to sort the schools into three piles based on their relative success. This was further investigated according to the ratings each school received on a set of criteria outlined in the various displays used for the case studies.

As a preparation for developing cross-site display 1 (page 280), each group first worked out the details for each school on two or three big flip charts based on displays 5B and 6 (pages 356 and 357). These were summarized and

Table 4.4 Distribution of the schools rated according to implementation success, impact and institutionalization

Criterion	Rating				
	L	L/M	M	M/H	H
Implementation success			Chilalo II Gedeo III Chilalo III	Chilalo I Tegulet III Tegulet II Gedeo II	Gedeo I Tegulet I
Student impact			Chilalo I Gedeo II Chilalo II Gedeo III Chilalo III	Tegulet III Tegulet II	Gedeo I Tegulet I
Teacher impact			Chilalo II Gedeo III Chilalo III	Tegulet II Chilalo I Tegulet III Gedeo II	Gedeo I Tegulet I
School impact			Chilalo II Gedeo III Chilalo III	Tegulet II	Gedeo I Tegulet I Chilalo I Tegulet III Gedeo II
Institutionalization			Chilalo II Gedeo III Chilalo III	Tegulet II Gedeo II	Gedeo I Tegulet I Chilalo I Tegulet III

rated under each sub-category, i.e. (a) delivery of inputs, technical mastery, teacher engagement; (b) impact: student outcomes, teacher outcomes, school outcomes; and (c) institutionalization such as classroom consolidation, support of key people, etc. After thorough discussion, ratings and clarification were made by each group. Cross-site display 1 was generated by the study team. In this display the most pertinent data were summarized under input, impact and institutionalization and rated as high, high/medium, medium, medium/low and low.

Analysis of cross-site display 1 As has been pointed out above, cross-site display 1 summarizes the data explaining implementation, impact and institutionalization (see Ethiopian country report, cross-site display 1, page 280). For comparison purposes, the high, medium or low ratings were converted into a five-point scale, namely: high (3), high/medium (2.5), medium (2), medium/low (1.5) and low (1). To carry out the cross-site analysis, the distribution of the nine schools under each rating was examined (see Table 4.4).

The table shows that the schools are spread along M, M/H and H ratings for implementation success, with most of the schools (n = 6) falling under medium-high and/or high, and three schools under medium rating. Six out of the nine schools (Gedeo I, Tegulet I, Chilalo I, Tegulet II, Gedeo II and Tegulet III), are

Table 4.5 Summary of ratings for each school

Criteria	Gedeo I	Tegulet I	Chilalo I	Tegulet III	Tegulet II	Gedeo II	Chilalo II	Gedeo III	Chilalo III
Implementation success	3	3	2.5	2.5	2.5	2.5	2.0	2.0	2.0
Impact	3	3	2.5	2.7	2.5	2.5	2.0	2.0	2.0
Institutionalization	3	3	3	3	2.5	2.5	2.0	2.0	2.0
Aggregate score	9	9	8	7.5	7.5	7.5	6.0	6.0	5.0
Average	3	3	2.67	2.73	2.5	2.5	2.0	2.0	2.0

rated high/medium or high whereas the rest (Gedeo III, Chilalo II and Chilalo III) are medium. The frequency distribution of the schools of impact shows a somewhat different picture. Eight out of the nine schools (Gedeo I, Tegulet I, Tegulet II, Gedeo II, Chilalo I, Tegulet III, Chilalo II and Gedeo III) are rated medium or higher whereas only Chilalo III school is rated medium/low. In general, the changes have had a satisfactory impact on students, teachers and the schools.

The frequency distribution of the nine schools for institutionalization shows some difference from those of implementation success and impact. All the schools fall within three ratings: medium (n = 3), high/medium (n = 2) and high (n = 4). On the whole, most of the reform elements are well institutionalized in all the sample schools. In cross-site display 1, the nine schools were distributed over the 'excellent', 'very good' and 'good' categories. This was done by aggregating the ratings for implementation success, impact and institutionalization as shown in table 4.5. As can be seen, the schools differed along the three parameters implementation success, impact and institutionalization. Further analysis of the table showed that the rating could be grouped into three categories: schools with scores falling within the ranges of $3 \geq x > 2.5$, $2.5 \geq x > 2$ and $2 \geq x > 1.5$. This enabled the research team to put the schools in three groups namely 'excellent' schools (x = 3), 'very good' schools ($3 > x \geq 2.5$) and 'good' schools ($2.5 > x > 1.5$).

This resulted in a grouping of Gedeo I and Tegulet I schools as 'excellent', Tegulet III, Gedeo II, Tegulet II and Chilalo I schools as 'very good' schools and Gedeo III, Chilalo II, Chilalo III schools as 'good' schools. This was done by rating the 'excellent' schools as high, the 'very good' schools as high/medium and the 'good' schools as medium. There were no schools in the low category. All the schools have implemented the reform components as well as they could (see Table 4.4).

Excellent schools

In the following discussion the phrase 'excellent schools' refers to Gedeo I and Tegulet I schools. The factors that have contributed to the implementation success, impact and institutionalization of the changes have been investigated and are discussed in the following sections.

Table 4.6 Overall grouping of the nine schools based on the average ratings of the three major factors

Interval	School
x = 3 (Excellent)	Gedeo I, Tegulet I
2.5 ≤ x < 3 (Very good)	Tegulet III, Gedeo II, Tegulet II, Chilalo I
1.5 < x < 2.5 (Good)	Gedeo III, Chilalo II, Chilalo III

Table 4.7 Community financial support ($)

Gedeo I	Tegulet I	Tegulet III	Gedeo II	Tegulet II	Chilalo I	Gedeo III	Chilalo II	Chilalo III
580	1142	1256	5411	18840	6763		4830	9662

Implementation success The implementation success of the two excellent schools could be explained by the quality and quantity of the inputs of the community, the district education offices and the teachers of the schools. The community's need and participation has contributed greatly to the implementation success of the changes. The community has provided additional land to be used for income generation, contributed finance, materials and labour services for building additional classrooms, school halls, libraries, stores, etc. The School Management and Parent Committee have also been highly involved in the day-to-day management of the schools including the mobilization of the community to give more support to school development and to increase enrolment, and solving the problems of drop-outs, repeaters, etc.

This can be verified by looking at some of the specific community inputs in the two schools (Table 4.7). For example, in Tegulet I the community has provided free accommodation for teachers by building houses within the school premises and creating a conducive atmosphere for teachers so that they can concentrate more on the school activities. Although Tegulet I school is in an area where the annual per capita income is very low compared to other areas, as its financial contribution the community has voluntarily given up its traditional religious worshipping and given the land that was used for this to the school, and enabled six families from the school compound to move elsewhere by building houses for them. Similarly, the local community of Gedeo I school has contributed significantly to the school's development for the successful

Table 4.8 Conditions for classroom interaction in the excellent schools

	Gedeo I	Tegulet I
Textbooks-pupil ratio	1:1	1:1 to 1:2
Average teaching load	21	30
Teacher-pupil ratio	1:24	1:39
Average class size	37	39

implementation of the reforms. In the past five years the local community has raised over Birr 60,000 and built eight additional classrooms, a store, a SPC, a barn, a cultural hall and a school hall.

The district education office provides textbooks, manpower, chalk, hand tools and some other materials. It also facilitates the implementation of the changes and plays a monitoring role. Table 4.8 further examines the DEO input for the excellent schools. Though there is some disparity in terms of textbooks-pupil ratio, average teaching load, teacher-pupil ratio and average class size between the two schools, the study clearly showed that they are both in a much better position than the very good and good schools (see Tables 4.9 and 4.10).

The two excellent schools have a high division of labour, a good organizational set-up and a healthy working relationship. In both cases, teachers participate and lead different co-curricular activities and are organized in departments. They also help one another and share experiences in the production and use of teaching aids. The other aspect of schools input is the establishment of a school pedagogical centre (SPC) to provide professional support for the teachers. School pedagogical services are rendered by giving in-school training and orientation in the production and use of teaching aids, enrichment of the national curriculum and its adaptation to local conditions. Both schools have large quantities of a variety of quality teaching aids organized under different subjects. Some are displayed systematically on shelves, while others are put on tables, walls and on the floors.

Another important factor in implementation success is the school's ability to generate internal income and become self-supportive in terms of covering the schools' running costs. Both schools grow cereals and vegetables for sale. The money generated is used for purchasing stationery, raw materials for producing teaching aids, tools, reference books, supplementary materials, batteries for the radio and for paying for attendance at conferences and workshops organized at district level.

The implementation success of the two schools was also investigated in terms of technical mastery, engagement, interest, experience exchange and cooperation of teachers. The subject mastery of the teachers is at a highly satisfactory level and they have a clear conception of most of the components of the reform. Similarly, the pedagogical mastery of the teachers has improved. Teachers prepare and use lesson plans effectively. Their teaching methods, preparation and use of teaching aids have improved, and they also continuously assess their students' progress. In all their efforts to improve the teaching-learning process they consider student needs and motivation. In this respect academic competition has helped to motivate and encourage students to study harder.

The engagement and interest of teachers is reflected in their dedication to the school's work and the implementation of the changes. The majority of teachers in both schools spend most of their after-school hours working on co-curricular activities and other school work. They work collaboratively, exchange experiences and solve problems encountered in the process of implementing the changes. Most of them feel that the changes should continue to be implemented unless something better is found.

While most of the points discussed above are shared by both the excellent schools, Tegulet I has had a better experience in giving orientation to new teachers. Unless teachers are made aware of the local culture and social practices in the community, the implementation of the reform components can face difficulties. As the reform had aspects conflicting with the local culture, it was felt necessary to make teachers aware of the difficulties they could face and give advice on how to tackle them.

Impact

Student impact The cognitive development of the students in these schools has been reported to be good. Students' grasp of subject matter is shown by their achievement in national examinations and classroom tests. For example in the past five years only 5 per cent of the Gedeo I school students who took the national sixth grade examination failed, and in 1989, all those Tegulet I students who sat the sixth grade national exam passed.

In the psychomotor domain, the students' practical skills in producing teaching aids and their participation in labour education activities have improved. In the latter case children are assigned to activities that are appropriate to their age level and physical strength. For example, while the older children mow crops, the younger ones carry it to where it is piled up.

The students in these two schools have a positive attitude towards attendance, the number of drop-outs is decreasing and students also have a positive attitude towards physical labour. The students of Tegulet I have also dropped some of their superstitious beliefs, for example worshipping trees.

Teacher impact The teachers of both schools claim that their theoretical and practical knowledge has increased as a result of the implementation of the changes. This has been witnessed by the achievements of their students in national and classroom examinations and tests.

Teachers plan and organize lessons systematically and handle the teaching-learning process to a satisfactory level. It has already been pointed out that teachers use teaching aids regularly and assess their students' progress by giving tests. They use radio programmes and academic competitions effectively to supplement classroom teaching. The interest and effort they are showing to improve the teaching-learning process is considerable. The teachers invest a lot of their spare time in helping and working on school activities. They also keep good records of student progress and attendance. In addition they mobilize the community and work with them closely in labour education activities.

School impact Both the schools have an effective organization. School administration committees, parent committees, departments, school pedagogic centres (SPC) and libraries are well established in the schools. They have constructed additional classrooms and introduced a productive labour education programme, in terms of mobilizing skills, generating internal income and developing self-supporting ability.

Institutionalization So far the analysis has dealt with the degree of success of implementation of the reform and its impact. On the following few pages the factors that have contributed to the excellent schools' performance are discussed. As has been pointed out by Verspoor, the ultimate goal of the change process is the sustained application and integration of the innovation into regular classroom and administrative practices. In this regard, all the centrally initiated changes have been institutionalized at school level. However, the degree of institutionalization, as in the case of implementation process and impact, differs from school to school. Institutionalization of the reform components has been investigated in terms of classroom consolidation, likely continuation, support of key people, resources committed, 'built-in-ness' to procedures, roles and assistance for new teachers.

The classroom consolidation of Gedeo I and Tegulet I schools has been found to be very high with respect to lesson plans, preparation of teaching aids in SPCs, involvement of teachers and students in co-curricular activities and labour education. The teachers use radio programmes effectively and to some degree teaching aids. They also regularly assess students' achievement and try to use different teaching methods. However, the use of different teaching methods and teaching aids seems to have been affected by lack of adequate pre-service and in-service training.

The teachers, the headmasters, the community members, district education officers and other key people feel strongly that the changes will continue to be implemented. In fact, it has been reported that the changes will not be discontinued and if they are, there will be disappointments. It has been emphasized that the changes will be implemented better and more intensively in the two or three years to come. The district education officers including inspectors, district pedagogic centre (APC) coordinators, community leaders and other authorities like the reform programme and want to maintain it. However, though the support of the headmaster, the SPC coordinator and department heads is satisfactory and is available as needs arise, the pedagogical support of inspectors and other professionals outside the school is not regular or as desired by members of the two schools.

The sources of resources in both schools are the Ministry of Education, the community and the school itself. Teachers, textbooks, some tools, chalk and other materials are supplied every year by the Ministry. The financial support and labour services of the community have been obtained every year and are guaranteed for the immediate and long-term future. The school has made it its duty to generate its own internal income through labour education activities and other extra-curricular activities. All the reform components such as planning activities, increasing enrolment, using curricular materials, radio programmes, teaching aids, application of a labour education programme and participation of the community in education are part of the regular routine in both schools.

Generally, new teachers coming to the two schools are given orientation in the school's practices and expectations by the teachers. Tegulet I, in particular, briefs new teachers on the local culture and social practices, thus enabling them to behave in a way which does not conflict with the social expectations in the area and to win the support of the community by their efforts to socialize and adapt to the locality.

Very good schools

The characteristics of the very good schools — Chilalo I, Tegulet III, Tegulet II and Gedeo II — were studied along the same three parameters as the two excellent schools, i.e. implementation success, impact and institutionalization.

Implementation success The implementation success of the reform components in these schools was investigated in terms of the community input, district education office or ministry input, the schools, organizational set up, facilitation, teachers' technical mastery and student input.

The community input in these schools is quite high. All of them get financial, material and labour services support from the community. In Gedeo II, the community built six additional classrooms and a school hall. In Chilalo I the community contributed $284,155 to build additional classrooms, and there is similar input in the other schools. In all the schools the community is represented in school life through the school administrative committee and parent committee. These have helped to mobilize the community to provide additional land for the schools, give labour services for farming, harvesting crops and planting trees, to intensify labour education activities and to secure lodging for teachers, etc. For example, the community in Tegulet II constructed houses and provided free accommodation for teachers. In the other cases, the community ensures that teachers at least get rented houses. In general, there is a lot of similarity between these schools and the excellent schools in terms of community support.

The district education office provides teachers, textbooks, tools, chalk and other materials for these schools. At central level in-service teacher education programmes are provided for untrained teachers or teachers who are interested in becoming school headmasters. At district level, workshops and annual educational conferences in which the headmaster, teachers' representatives and some school administrative committee members participate are organized.

In general the district education office input in terms of textbook supply is remarkable though the directives are to issue one textbook for every two pupils. This has been realized for most subjects in these schools, though there is a shortage of agriculture, home economics and political education textbooks. Table 4.9 shows the district education office's input in terms of the textbook-pupil ratio, teacher-pupil ratio, average class size and the average teaching load for the very good schools.

As in the case of the excellent schools, Tegulet II, Gedeo II, Chilalo I and Tegulet III schools' organizational set-up, ability to generate their own internal income, facilitation, establishment of SPCs and production of teaching aids are strong indicators for the success of the implementation of the changes. The difference is that the degree to which these have been realized in the very good schools is less than in the excellent schools. The other important factors for success are the technical mastery, the engagement and interest of teachers, and the experience exchange and cooperation among them. As in the excellent

Table 4.9 Conditions for classroom interaction in the very good schools

	Tegulet III	Gedeo II	Tegulet II	Chilalo I
Textbook-pupil ratio	1:1–1:2	1:1	1:1–1:2	1:26
Teacher-pupil ratio	1:47	1:30	1:49	1:60
Average class size	47	51	65	70
Average teaching load	30	19	25	25

schools, the teachers in the very good schools have an adequate knowledge of the subjects they teach and are fully aware of the reform programme and its components. The quality of their pedagogical practice is somewhat moderate in terms of using teaching aids, student assessment, use of different teaching methods, understanding students' needs and motivations. On the other hand, all teachers prepare and use daily, weekly and annual lesson plans and keep good records of students' progress.

At the time the reform was introduced, the primary school participation rate was quite low, there was a high drop-out rate, low motivation, poor achievement in the national examinations and a lack of interest in labour education activities and manual labour.

Impact The following discussion considers the impact of the reform components in the very good schools.

Student impact The cognitive knowledge of the students in the very good schools and their psychomotor skills were rated high/medium while their attitude to implementing the changes was highly positive. There are differences between the achievements of the very good schools in their national examination results. For example for Gedeo II school, though the overall number of passes in the sixth grade national exam is comparable to that of the other schools in this category, an overview of the past three years' results shows a downward trend.

In all these schools, students participate in labour education and co-curricular activities. This has given them practical skills to make them productive. The skills they have gained in sports and gardening are not limited to school, but have also been transferred to their home areas.

The overall attitude of the students in these schools towards education is positive. The students keep themselves and their schools clean, are disciplined, have high respect for their teachers, actively participate during the teaching-learning process and show eagerness to learn. In Chilalo I each student has responsibility for planting and taking care of a tree until it is fully grown.

In Tegulet II, Chilalo I and Tegulet III schools, enrolment is increasing and the drop-out rate is falling every year. However, in Gedeo II school the drop-out rate and the repetition rate is high compared to those of the three other very good schools and the two excellent schools.

Teacher impact The teachers have improved knowledge of the subjects they teach. They are well aware of the objectives of the curriculum and are working hard to achieve them. Lesson plans and teaching aids are used in the classrooms. Teachers use radio programmes and academic competitions effectively to supplement classroom teaching.

The teachers have become increasingly able to prepare and use teaching aids. Their skill in mobilizing the community to work with them is improving all the time. Their ability to lead and participate in labour education and co-curricular activities, share experiences among themselves and work for the school has improved. In general, their attitude toward the educational changes made is positive. They make good efforts to motivate and encourage their students to study and work hard. They quite often use their free time to work for the school purposes.

School impact The outcome at the schools level is satisfactory. The organizational set-up in the schools has been improving, though there is a lot still to be done. All have been able to construct additional classrooms and enrol more students. For example Gedeo II school has managed to build a library, a store and a handicraft room. Tegulet II has built an SPC, three classrooms and teachers' quarters. Chilalo I has also constructed additional classrooms, library, laboratory, department and co-curricular offices (rooms).

The schools have become more self-reliant. They use the money they have generated for purchasing stationery, batteries for the radio programmes, etc. There is adequate experience for implementing and sustaining changes in these schools.

Institutionalization The study shows that there are a lot of similarities between the experiences of the excellent and very good schools in terms of the implementation success and impact of the reform components. The difference is a matter of degree. This is not surprising since in Ethiopia most of the changes are centrally initiated. In addition there are different mechanisms for ensuring uniformity. The annual educational conferences held at central, regional, district and school level are all used for such purposes.

The classroom consolidation of the changes has been relatively high. As in the excellent schools, teachers make use of the school pedagogical centres for producing teaching aids, though the application of teaching aids in classrooms is not at all satisfactory. For most teachers the basic reference materials are student textbooks and teaching-learning processes. However, teachers appreciate the services of the SPC and believe that it contributes to achieving the objectives of the educational programme.

Teachers assess their students' progress from time to time and keep good records. In contrast to those in the excellent schools, the teachers in the very good schools use relatively few teaching aids. In general, there is no doubt about the continuation of the changes. All teachers and education officers agree that the changes are important and will continue to be implemented unless something better replaces them. In fact most of them would feel disappointed if the changes were reversed.

The support of key people outside the school in terms of observing classroom instruction and providing feedback has been minimal. However, in all the schools, school administrative committee members and the headmaster are stalwarts in backing the changes. They find ways and means of solving the schools' financial and material problems. The headmasters advise teachers on technical and pedagogical matters. The teacher-to-teacher assistance and cooperation in the production of teaching aids and participation in co-curricular activities is reported to have shown an improvement in all cases.

The major sources of resources in these schools are the Ministry of Education, the respective communities, and the schools themselves. The resources will continue giving the required support. Presently almost all the components of the reform are well-established in the school's system. And as a rule, whenever new teachers come to the schools they are given orientation as to the rules, regulations and practices. This has enabled them to start their work smoothly and be integrated into the school community.

Good schools

The characteristics of the good schools — Chilalo II, Gedeo III and Chilalo III — were also studied along the parameters of implementation success, impact and institutionalization.

Implementation success To some extent the good schools also share the experiences of the 'excellent' and the 'very good' schools in securing financial, material and physical labour services from the community. The school communities have all expressed the need for educational development and given material and moral support. Chilalo II, Chilalo III and Gedeo III communities have not provided the schools with ten hectares of land, according to the guidelines given by the Ministry of Education: the Gedeo III community has managed to give about three hectares of land; and Chilalo III has been given five hectares of land.

In Chilalo II and Chilalo III, the communities have given Birr 10,000 and Birr 20,000 respectively. The community in Gedeo III has also provided some financial aid to the school though it is less than that provided for Chilalo II and Chilalo III schools. In all three cases, the community's material support was substantial and the labour services rendered were excellent. As in the excellent and very good schools, the district education office provides teachers, curricular materials, some tools, chalk, etc. Some of the pertinent input of the district education office is outlined in Table 4.10.

In these schools, the average class size is quite a lot higher than it is for the excellent and the very good schools, with the exception of Chilalo I and Tegulet II schools. The textbook-pupil ratio is also relatively low, except in Gedeo III, and this has been reported to be a problem. However, the average teaching load is low, because these schools have a large number of staff members. For various reasons, including health problems, urban schools are assigned a high number of teachers.

The in-service training experience of these schools is similar to that of the excellent and the very good schools. To enable them to implement the reform components, the good schools have made efforts to generate their own income and meet their financial needs so that they can cover their running costs. They have been able to purchase their own stationery, raw materials for making

Table 4.10 Major inputs of awraja education office to the 'good' schools

	Gedeo III	Chilalo II	Chilalo III
Textbook-pupil ratio	1:1	1:1–7	1:4–7
Teacher-pupil ratio	1:38	1:55	1:49
Average class size	77	65	75
Average teaching load	16	21	24

teaching aids, batteries, etc. The organizational structure of these schools is similar to that of the excellent and very good schools. However, Chilalo III and Chilalo II schools have ministry-employed typists, store keepers, guards and health assistants, a privilege gained as a result of their high enrolment, long years of service and, in the case of Chilalo II, to its being a junior secondary school.

The teachers in these schools are familiar with all the reform components. Teachers prepare lesson plans, teaching aids, make use of radio programmes and participate in labour education activities. They have reported that their ability to implement the different aspects of the reform has improved and they have developed a positive attitude in the process. However, teachers are not keen to make use of teaching aids. In general, the teachers' involvement in different co-curricular activities, their dedication and commitment is satisfactory, though low compared to that of teachers in the excellent and the very good schools.

Impact The student outcome of the good schools was also examined in terms of cognitive knowledge, skills and attitudes. It was found that the students' academic knowledge is lower than in the excellent and the very good schools. In general, it has been reported that the students in these schools have less motivation and interest for education. Their participation in labour education is also quite low. On the other hand, the enrolment rate in these schools is very high, the students regularly attend classes and the repetition rate is low. This shows that there is some leniency in the promotion policy, especially of Chilalo III and Chilalo II schools.

The teachers of Gedeo III, Chilalo II and Chilalo III schools have a good knowledge of the subjects they teach. Most are familiar with the curriculum and are making use of the syllabi, teachers' guides and students' textbooks. As in the excellent and very good schools, the teachers prepare lesson plans skilfully and try to use different teaching methods and student assessment techniques. They participate in different co-curricular activities. However, the teachers' involvement is less in these schools and their willingness and dedication to invest more of their spare time in school activities is low.

The outcome in Gedeo III, Chilalo II and Chilalo III schools is lower than in the excellent and very good schools. Though all three schools have managed to get some land from the community, they are still far from having ten hectares of land. Experience exchange among teachers and their collaboration in settling academic and disciplinary problems is also lower than in the other schools, but all three schools generate adequate internal income which has made them self-supportive. Their programme of campus beautification and classroom maintenance is effective. The three schools are well organized. There are school administrative and parent committees. Although the schools have constructed additional classrooms, they have been unable to reduce the large class-size; for example, Gedeo III school had to reject over 250 applications for enrolment.

Institutionalization Some of the components of the reform, such as preparing and using lesson plans, teaching aids, radio programmes, different teaching methods, improved student assessment techniques, etc., are moderately used. The use of the labour education programme to relate classroom knowledge to practical experience has not been as effective as desired in these schools.

Many respondents do not doubt that the implementation of the changes will continue. The changes are relevant to the schools' needs, thus they are supported by the school community and the staff members of the district education office. Unless something better comes up, the continuation of the existing components of the reform is taken for granted. In fact the users would feel bad if the changes were reversed without any good reason.

These schools get financial, material and labour services from their respective communities, who have been found to be a continuous source of income. Similarly, the district education office has sent textbooks, tools, chalk and other materials on a regular basis. This has helped both the student and schools a great deal and it is felt that such provision will continue in the future. In general, the changes are well established and have become a daily routine. Whenever new teachers join these schools, they get assistance that can at least help them get started. However, the assistance new teachers get in these schools is much lower than in the case of the excellent and the very good schools.

Based on cross-site display 1 (see page 280), the cross-school analysis showed that there is a difference in the degree of implementation success, impact and institutionalization of the changes between the nine schools: Gedeo I and Tegulet I as excellent schools; Chilalo I, Tegulet III, Tegulet II and Gedeo II as very good schools; and Chilalo II, Gedeo III and Chilalo III as good schools. The findings of the study show that the factors accounting for the implementation success, the impact and the institutionalization of the changes are somewhat different.

The other effort made during the analysis was to see if there was a correlation between implementation success and impact. As can be seen in Table 4.5 (page 98), there is a very high correlation between the two. A similar effort was made to see if the mean score of implementation and impact correlates with the scores for institutionalization. In this case also, there was a high correlation. In general this can be accounted for by the relatively long period over which the implementation process was carried out. Thus, it was found to be unnecessary to try explaining implementation and impact. Instead it was considered important to explain institutionalization.

Table 4.11 Summary of school outcome: implementation, impact and institutionalization

	Excellent schools	Very good schools	Good schools
Implementation success	High teacher engagement and interest. Spend lots of their extra time for school purposes	Good teacher engagement and interest	Low teacher engagement and interest
	Excellent collaboration among teachers	Strong headmaster-teacher and teacher-teacher collaboration	Modest teacher-teacher collaboration
	Very good teacher performance and productivity. More innovative adaptation of the curriculum except teaching English starting in grade one	Satisfactory teacher performance and productivity	Moderate teacher performance
	Headmaster systematic and efficient in organizing, facilitating and leading activities		
	High DEO and regional administration involvement		
Impact	High student knowledge as seen in national exams and classroom tests	Good academic performance, but moderate in Gedeo II	Low academic knowledge as seen in national exam results
	Good student feeling and attitudes (overcoming superstition beliefs)	Good student interest and motivation for education except in Gedeo II	Low student behaviour and motivation
	Small class size and student population.	Low class size and student population except in Chilalo I	Large class size and student population
	Tegulet I school works full day whereas F.G. works in two shifts. Tegulet I has overcome most of the serious problems it had.	Work in two shifts except Tegulet II and Tegulet III	Two shift system. Acute shortage of textbooks
	Rural agrarian	Semi-rural agrarian	Semi-urban with mixed economy

Table 4.11 *(cont)*

	Excellent schools	Very good schools	Good schools
Institutionalization	Strong DEO and regional administration office support provided more land for G.B. school by moving out six families from the school	Sufficient land except in Gedeo II	Poorer fit in terms of enrolment, securing land, practising labour education, community participation.
	Highly self-reliant in facilitating and financing school activities	Good internal income	
	Good assistance for new teachers' pedagogical matters and in orienting to the social life	Satisfactory assistance to new teachers	Low assistance to new teachers

Factors accounting for implementation, impact and institutionalization of the reforms

The three major points of discussion, i.e. implementation, impact and institutionalization, were explained in the preceding section of the report. This section concentrates on the factors that have accounted for the success of the reforms, based on cross-site display 2 (page 282).

Assistance The Ministry of Education and district education offices have given the schools and the school communities different forms of assistance and the amount of assistance given to each school varies. The teachers and headmasters in the nine sample schools have received in-service training from the centre through the DEOs. The DEOs have also conducted seminars, workshops and annual educational conferences for headmasters, SPC coordinators, teachers' representatives and representatives of the school management committee on administration, planning, programming, preparation of teaching aids, etc. Inspectors visit the schools and give advice on the handling of school work, record keeping and documentation, and give feedback on the overall school activities. There is headmaster-teacher and teacher-teacher assistance in the schools. The headmasters supervise classes and school activities and give advice and feedback to teachers. APC coordinators and the headmaster in turn train teachers at the school level on the preparation of teaching aids.

Although the above assistance is common to all the schools, there are points of assistance which differentiate the schools from each other. For example, Gedeo I, Tegulet II and Chilalo I get more assistance than the others in the following aspects:

- Teachers have received in-service training in some special subjects such as political education and physical education.
- There is a monthly 'teach each other'-programme and exchange of views among teachers in their departments.

Administrative role The DEO officials send guidelines, circulars and rules and regulations to the schools. They inspect and check school activities, give advice, respond to demands, revise the administrative set up of the schools, ensure proper delivery of resources and facilitate experience exchanges within and out of schools. They assess headmasters' and inspectors' reports, conduct meetings and discussions with school staff and communicate with community officials. However, in the case of Tegulet I, there is one more point which makes the administrative role stronger than in the other schools. Because of a particular local problem that existed in the school, the DEO has maintained constant contact with the regional administrative officials to provide a long-lasting solution for the school by creating a conducive school environment for an effective teaching-learning process.

Commitment The DEOs have a positive feeling, ownership and dedication towards the reforms. They defended and protected the changes at a time of difficulty and uncertainty. They would like the programme to continue and the changes to be more effective. Headmasters and teachers use their spare time for school activities such as preparation of teaching aids and participation in labour education. The school management and parent committees are dedicated and concerned. They work closely with the school with positive feelings and interest. Gedeo I, Chilalo I, Tegulet III and Gedeo II have indicated strong commitment with respect to headmasters, teachers and the community's interest and feelings.

The headmasters regularly plan programmes and supervise, follow up and facilitate school activities. They check lesson plans, evaluate teachers, observe classes and conduct regular meetings, organize, coordinate and lead community activities through school management committees. They also chair staff meetings, curriculum committees and school management committees.

Pressure DEOs send guidelines, circulars and directives to all schools and push the schools and the community to implement the changes. They remind the schools of their responsibilities, demand continuous progress reports, evaluate the schools' activities and give feedback. Similarly, the headmasters encourage the staff and students to carry out school activities and community services. They also evaluate teachers' record keeping, labour education and co-curricular activities.

Resources DEOs, communities and the schools themselves are the main source of resources. This means getting manpower, textbooks and other curricular materials such as tools, equipment and model teaching aids from the DEOs; and farmland, finance, materials and free labour from the community. Schools also generate their own income. Two of the good schools (Chilalo II and Gedeo III) have received fewer resources than the others. With the exception of Chilalo III, the remaining schools have received better resources in the form of high community inputs in terms of expansion and construction of school buildings, the purchasing of stationery and facilities, and hiring support-giving staffs such as guards. In the case of Chilalo III primary school, the DEO has provided additional support-giving staffs and facilities such as a dresser who runs the school clinic, a typist, a store-keeper and a guard. These aspects make Chilalo III primary school somewhat different from the other schools in terms of resources received.

Success experience In general, the teaching/learning process in all schools has been facilitated with the establishment of departments, the SPCs, libraries, the construction of additional classrooms, stores, school halls, etc. The schools also generate their own income, prepare teaching/learning materials, prepare teaching aids from locally available materials and plan their activities. The staff of these schools have gained more experience through implementing the changes, i.e. skills in planning and teaching, programming, coordinating, cooperating and preparing teaching aids. There is exchange of experiences, teacher-teacher training and beautification of the school compounds by planting trees. In the case of Gedeo I, teachers' and students' theoretical and practical knowledge has shown an improvement as a result of their high involvement in labour education, teaching aid production and other co-curricular activities.

Empowerment As far as empowerment and engagement is concerned, all schools are rated as high except Chilalo II, Gedeo III and Chilalo III which are rated as moderate. DEOs are responsible for conducting educational conferences, workshops and seminars and the dissemination of circulars and directives to the schools. They also explain and clarify issues pertaining to the changes. They send written encouragement and empower schools to make decisions on some issues such as income generation, building and maintaining rooms, preparing local teaching materials based on central guidelines, allocating funds and administrative issues. The school management committees are empowered to give decisions on schools' financial and managerial issues. Headmasters and teachers are engaged in planning and deciding school activities. The school management and parent committees deal with students' disciplinary problems and the teaching/learning process, as well as coordinating parents. Headmasters and department heads are engaged in evaluating teachers. The staff and the students act as models for the community by being engaged in socially useful community services.

Local adaptation Headmasters and teachers have revised and adjusted certain aspects of the reform programmes. Labour education has been adapted to suit local needs. The central guideline says that labour education is supposed to be conducted out of school hours, but parents greatly need the labour of their children after school hours. To comply with central guidelines and needs of the community schools such as in Gedeo I, Tegulet I, Tegulet II, Gedeo II, Gedeo III and Tegulet III have adjusted the programme to be carried out once or twice a week for about two hours during school hours.

Teachers prepare local teaching materials based on guidelines, for example social studies grades 1-3 and home economics grades 1-6. With the exception of Tegulet I, Tegulet II and Tegulet III, all schools have adopted a two-shift system to manage shortage of resources and to give educational opportunities to more children. Central guidelines on financial contributions, for example payment for sport, have been revised, and the community now provides payments in the form of labour services at school level. In the case of Tegulet I and Tegulet III there is a relatively high local adaptation of the content of the curriculum. For example, atheistic ideas had to be taken out of political education so that it would suit the local beliefs and practices. Furthermore, practical teaching of handicrafts on religious days had to be changed in order to avoid religious offences.

Community support In all the schools studied, the community support was found to be very high. The communities have positive feelings and attitudes. They support the schools financially, materially, and by giving free labour services and managing the schools through school management and parent committees. They encourage greater enrolment and the expansion of school buildings and facilities. They feel responsible for the well-being of the schools, the staff and the students. For example, in the cases of Tegulet I, Tegulet II and Chilalo I, the communities have constructed living quarters for the teaching staff. In the other schools the communities give priority to teachers for renting houses.

Organizational context The working relationships between DEOs and schools, school management committees and headmasters, teachers and headmasters, teachers and teachers, teachers and parents, and teachers and students are good. DEOs have facilitated experience exchange within and out of the schools. The school management committee also provides the schools with finance and material, and gives free labour services.

There is a good division of labour (there are clubs, departments, various committees, etc.) and responsibilities within the schools are shared. The headmasters are transmitters of directives, guidelines, rules and regulations from DEOs to schools. They coordinate activities between communities and schools, orient teachers on the school's activities and also facilitate means of exchanging experiences in the schools. There is conformity to rules and regulations passed by DEOs. In general, the Ministry of Education policy, educational proclamations and the establishment of mass organizations have created a conducive atmosphere and good organizational working relationship in the schools.

Though there is farmland for income generation there is further demand for vertical and horizontal expansion of schools, DEOs' and SMCs' support, expansion of school compounds, materials and educational facilities, training for teachers and improving their living standards, a balancing of the teacher-pupil ratio, and an improvement in the promotion policy. Most schools have also expressed their worries about water supply, administrative and support-giving staffs, accommodation for teachers, the distance students have to walk from home to school and vice versa, and the aspiration for higher grades (junior and senior secondary schools).

On the whole, organizational context, support and administrative roles are found to be the key factors accounting for the success of the changes in all the schools. Commitment, success experience, received resources, received pressure and assistance are found to be second-order factors, while local

Table 4.12 Summary of rating of factors accounting for the implementation, impact and institutionalization of the changes

Criterion	Gedeo I	Tegulet I	Tegulet III	Gedeo II	Tegulet II	Chilalo I	Gedeo III	Chilalo II	Chilalo III	Total
Assistance	2.5	2.5	2.5	2.5	2.5	2.5	2.0	2.0	2.0	21.0
Administrative role	2.5	3.0	2.5	2.5	2.5	2.5	2.5	2.5	2.5	23.0
Commitment	2.5	3.0	2.5	3.0	2.0	2.5	2.0	2.0	2.0	21.5
Received pressure	2.5	2.5	2.5	2.5	2.5	2.5	2.5	2.0	2.0	21.5
Received resources	3.0	2.5	2.5	3.0	2.5	2.5	2.0	2.0	2.0	22.0
Success Experience	3.0	2.5	2.5	2.5	2.5	2.5	2.0	2.0	2.0	21.5
Empowerment engagement	3.0	3.0	3.0	3.0	2.5	2.5	2.0	2.0	2.0	23.0
Local adaption of the programme	3.0	3.0	3.0	3.0	3.0	3.0	2.5	2.5	2.5	25.5
Community support	3.0	3.0	3.0	3.0	3.0	3.0	2.5	2.5	2.5	25.5
Organizational context	3.0	3.0	3.0	3.0	3.0	3.0	3.0	3.0	3.0	27
Average	2.80	2.80	2.70	2.80	2.60	2.65	2.30	2.25	2.25	

adaptation of the programme and empowerment engagement are third-order factors. A closer look at cross-site display 2A (page 282) also shows that commitment, received pressure, received resources and success experience are strong factors in most of the very good schools for the institutionalization of the changes.

Summary

The study shows that the nine schools have much in common in terms of implementation success, impact and institutionalization of the reform components. It has been found that all the changes have been implemented in all schools. However, there are some differences in the degree of success of implementation, impact and institutionalization. Gedeo I and Tegulet I were found to be excellent, Chilalo I, Tegulet III, Tegulet II and Gedeo II schools were found to be very good, and Chilalo II, Gedeo III and Chilalo III were good schools. The most important findings of the study are summarized as follows.

Engagement and interest in working and promoting the changes and other educational activities is one of the strongest characteristics of the very good schools. These factors were also found to be important in the good schools. However, teachers spend a lot more of their free time preparing lesson plans, working on labour education and on co-curricular activities in the very good schools than in the good schools. This is done without any additional payment or other fringe benefits.

The teacher-teacher and the teacher-headmaster collaboration in pedagogical activities, such as the preparation of teaching aids, solving academic problems and experience exchange, and participation in social and economic life was also found to be much better in the excellent and very good schools than in the good schools. Teachers perform their daily routines well and are very productive. It appears that teachers and headmasters know their responsibilities and work accordingly in the interest of their schools.

The link between the centre, the regions, the districts and the schools has already been discussed in detail. Education conferences are run at central, regional, district and school levels every year. This is done to acquaint the participants with new educational developments, policies, rules, regulations and managerial skills. Other provisions such as textbooks and teachers are also sent to schools every year depending on local needs within the financial constraints of the Ministry of Education. The Ministry of Education requires all units at central, regional, district and school levels to submit quarterly progress of their annual plan. This has served as a mechanism for pushing all sectors to implement the change. However, the supervision and monitoring of schools' work by the district education office was minimal, though this does not appear to have affected the success of the changes introduced in schools.

The Ministry of Education, through the regional and district education offices, distributes textbooks and other centrally prepared materials. Regional and district offices regularly contact schools on administrative matters and respond to their immediate needs. They also remind the schools of their responsibilities and weaknesses during annual conferences, workshops and school visits. However, they don't directly interfere in classroom activities.

All units at central, regional, district and school levels prepare annual plans and work accordingly. This culture has helped schools to be more organized and to follow up teachers' day-to-day progress. As a result of schools' self-evaluation of the accomplishments of their plan, they have become more careful in planning realistic programmes and activities.

The other important finding of this study is that of the community participation and its input in school life. The revised proclamation 260/1983 has enabled schools to involve the local community in school administration in a more efficient way. Local communities not only share school management responsibilities, but also assist the schools materially and financially. They assist in solving disciplinary problems, help teachers to obtain houses, and hire school guards and teachers to overcome shortages. In almost all the schools, the local community also provides free labour service for income-generating activities.

The Ministry of Education provides on-the-job training for untrained teachers. Training is given during the long vacation for three consecutive summers. Those who have completed the programme are normally awarded certificates leading to salary increment. Teachers also get on-the-job assistance from the school pedagogic centre coordinator. The SPC coordinator in turn gets his or her training from awraja (district) pedagogic centres. The APCs run workshops for SPC coordinators to develop teachers' skills in teaching aid production and use. Normally, the financial assistance for such purposes comes from the Ministry of Education, donor agencies and the schools themselves. At school level, the headmasters and the school management committees provide financial and material support for practical activities. This has made it possible to involve teachers and students in the preparation and use of teaching aids at the grassroots level. In general, teachers feel that they need more training and that they should be given refresher courses periodically. However, educational officers point out that financial constraint is a major obstacle in meeting these needs.

Teachers in these schools have been able to adapt the curriculum successfully by preparing the contents of grades 1-3 social studies and grades 1-6 home economics courses. Contrary to the central guidelines, the English teachers in Gedeo I school have decided to start English lessons in the first grade in order to enable children to learn language skills as early as possible. In addition these teachers put extra effort into teaching the Ahmaric language because for over 90 per cent of the children, Amharic is their second language.

Success in the very good schools is partly attributable to the planning ability of the headmasters. This was expressed in organizing school activities, coordinating community and teacher inputs, evaluating and giving feedback, orienting new teachers to the various school activities, leading and giving directives for effective and efficient implementation of the changes. The good schools have also had a similar experience.

Most of the very good schools have managed to get ten hectares of land from the community for practising labour education and sports activities. This has enabled them to generate adequate internal income which they use for different purposes. It has not been possible in the good schools to get adequate land since all of them are in semi-urban areas.

The academic knowledge, interest and motivation of students differ in the two categories of schools. In the very good schools, the majority of the students who have taken grade six national examinations have got good results. Compared to the other schools, the number of passes in classroom tests has also been high and this is a result of good teacher inputs. Academic knowledge of students is high in the very good schools and low in good schools.

Compared to those of the good schools, students of the very good schools have good interest in, and motivation for education. These schools have smaller student populations and class sizes and are either typical rural or rural village schools in which the majority of the local community is totally dependent on farming. The good schools are urban schools with a high student population (1000-2500), a large class size (62 to 80) and a shortage of textbooks. The occupation of the communities is based on mixed economy. They are either farmers, shopkeepers, traders of agricultural products and service givers, or a mixture of any of these or other occupations.

It has already been pointed out that all the changes are institutionalized in all the schools. The factors that have enhanced the success of the changes in these schools have also been discussed. However, there are some special points that have contributed to the difference in the degree of success in the two groups. In Tegulet I school the regional administration and the district education offices have mobilized the local community to give the school additional land and build houses for six families who used to live in the school compound. They have also made additional effort in changing the superstitious beliefs of the local community. In this regard, the community has shown a considerable change of attitude.

The other important factor observed in these schools is the fact that they are becoming self-reliant. The very good schools generate adequate internal income to facilitate their activities. The assistance given to new teachers is another important point given attention. In most of the very good schools teachers are systematically introduced to the school practices by the headmaster and department heads. In Tegulet I school they are given special orientation about the social life in the community. The locality is one of the areas where staunch traditional beliefs are exercised and which newcomers are expected to accept and comply with. Without a clear understanding of the social and cultural context, it would be very difficult for teachers to be effective in implementing the changes. The headmaster and teachers have reported that orientation of new teachers has helped them to adapt to the new culture and to be successful in school work.

Recommendations

The findings of this study show that there has been adequate experience in initiating, implementing and institutionalizing changes. So far, most of the changes have been centrally initiated. Though this had advantages, it also caused implementation problems in the initial stage. In future, changes should be initiated both at school and central level, or teachers at the grassroots level should at least be consulted at the planning stage. It is also important to lay the proper foundation before executing changes. In addition to financial and material preparation, teachers should be oriented and convinced about the significance and use of the reform components.

The institutionalization of changes is the ultimate goal. Organizational context, community support, local adaptation, empowerment and success experience have played a great role in this in the very good schools. These characteristics should also be reinforced in good and low achieving schools.

The inspection role played by the district education offices in all the sample schools has been minimal (once a year for a couple of hours) and has had little impact on classroom teaching. It is strongly recommended that instructional inspectors make frequent classroom visits so that they can give the teachers the feedback necessary to improve their teaching skill and efficiency. The inputs of APC and SPC have been considerable. However, a lack of adequately trained coordinators, means the centres have been unable to provide the desired level of technical assistance. Thus, the coordinators should be given adequate training and materials to carry out practical activities.

Nearly all teachers in the sample schools have demanded that refresher courses should occasionally be given to all teachers. Furthermore, the present one-year teacher training has been reported to be inadequate for creating efficient and skilled teachers. Thus, it is strongly recommended that the training is upgraded to a two-year programme.

The annual conferences held every year at central, regional, district and school levels have been reported to be a useful way of strengthening awareness of new roles and expectations, and encouraging experience exchange, etc. These should continue in a more coordinated way by paying more attention to what goes on in the classroom rather than concentrating on management, audit and administrative matters. In addition, APCs and SPCs should be more active in organizing workshops aimed at improving teachers' pedagogical skills. The necessary fund for this should come from the government, donor agencies and the local communities.

The rural schools Gedeo I, Tegulet III, Tegulet I and Gedeo II, have smaller student populations, class sizes, higher learning interest, effective teacher engagement, strong community support and accommodation for teachers. These factors have contributed greatly to the success of these schools in implementing the changes and it is recommended that local communities should play a greater role. It has also been found out that the textbook-pupil ratio in some of the very good schools (Gedeo I, Gedeo II) is one to one, but this is not the case in the good schools. Thus the research team recommends a better supply of textbooks.

The school's income generation has become a reliable financial source for the sample schools. The money generated is used for purchasing stationery and for facilitating other school activities. These experiences should be further developed and shared with other schools. Though the shift system is not a remedy for problems like teacher and material shortage, it does offer the rural communities opportunity to send more children to school. Those who are engaged in household duties while their brothers and sisters are attending schools in the morning, can go to school in the afternoon, and it has been suggested that rural schools adopt a shift system as a temporary solution for rural families.

The good practices these schools exercise in running annual conferences, monthly departmental meetings, weekly academic competitions and school beautification activities should continue in a more organized way. The theme of these exercises should be to serve and promote pedagogic excellence. New teachers assigned to schools need good orientation about the rules, regulations and activities run in the school. They should also be given adequate information on the social life of the local community.

Involvement in school administration and management has helped to mobilize the community to contribute finance, materials and provide physical labour services. These good tendencies should be intensified. Teachers' collaboration in running school activities, engaging interest in the teaching/learning process and using a lot of their free time for school purposes has also contributed to the successful implementation of the reform components in the excellent and very good schools and should be encouraged and transferred to other schools. However, teachers' application of teaching aids and student assessment techniques have not been satisfactory, and APC and SPC coordinators, headmasters and department heads should encourage the adequate preparation and use of teaching aids.

The efforts made to relate theory to practice should be continued in a concerted way by teachers, headmasters and others. Students should also be encouraged to transfer the knowledge and skills they acquire in schools to the home. For example, labour education activities should be used as a source of income for rural students which they could use for financing their education.

REFERENCES

Central Statistics Office (1986) *Ethiopia-Statistical Abstract*. Addis Ababa.

Central Statistics Office (1990) *Facts and Figures*. Addis Ababa.

Curriculum Department (1976) *Grade 5 Geography Textbooks*. Addis Ababa.

Curriculum Department (1986) *The Evaluative Research of the General Education System in Ethiopia*. Addis Ababa.

Department of Educational Mass Media (1987) *Evaluation of Primary School Radio Programmes*. Addis Ababa.

EMPDA (1989) *Textbook Publishing and Printing in Ethiopia*. Addis Ababa.

Last, G.C. (1960) *A Geography of Ethiopia for Senior Secondary Schools*. Addis Ababa: Ministry of Education.

Ko-Chih and Chinapah (1985) *Universalization of Primary Education and Literacy*. Addis Ababa.

Mehari, T.Y. (1989) *Rapid Population Growth and Its Impact on Socio-Economic Development in Ethiopia*. Addis Ababa, pp. 11-15.

Ministry of Education (1979) *The New Ethiopian Educational Directives*. Addis Ababa.

Ministry of Education (1979) *WPE Programme of Education*. Addis Ababa.

Ministry of Education (1979-1989) *The Ethiopian National Literacy Campaign Retrospect and Prospects*. Addis Ababa.

Ministry of Education (1984) *Basic Information on Education in Ethiopia*. Addis Ababa.

Ministry of Education (1984) *Education in Socialist Ethiopia*. Addis Ababa.

Ministry of Education (1985) *Basic Education Statistics*. Addis Ababa.

Ministry of Education (1989) *Basic Education Statistics*. Addis Ababa.

Nigussie Habteyes (1990) *Assessment of In-Service Training Provision for Educational Managers by the Management and Training Service of the Ministry of Education 1981-1989*. Addis Ababa.

Rosser (1989) *Awraja Pedagogical Centres*. Addis Ababa.

Sjøstrøm, R. (1986) *A Pilot Study of Effects of Primary Schooling in a Rural Community of Ethiopia*. SIDA.

Chapter 5

Universal Primary Education in Bangladesh

THE LARGER SYSTEM PICTURE

The country context

Social, political and economic factors Bangladesh, with an area of about 144,000 km^2 is the most densely populated country in the world. It is located in the north-eastern part of the South Asian subcontinent. It is bounded by the Bay of Bengal on the south and India on the west, north and east, except for a short border with Burma to the south-east. The population, growing at the rate of 2.6 per cent per year, is currently estimated at 115.5 million and by the year 2000 it is likely to be 136.4 million (projection made by Planning Commission). Nearly 85 per cent of the population is dependent on agriculture or agro-based occupation. The present size of population is grossly incommensurate with the level of production. Family planning together with population education will remain major elements of the development strategy of Bangladesh for a long time to come.

According to World Bank estimates, life expectancy per thousand at birth is 52 and the infant mortality rate for 1990 is 122. Widespread poverty together with malnutrition, scarcity of resources and lack of education are elements of the vicious circle causing under-development. According to the 1991 census, the literacy rate for all ages is 24.6 per cent (male 30.2 per cent, female 19.2 per cent), for ages five and above is 27.8 per cent (male 34.6 per cent, female 28.03 per cent), for ages 15 and above is 33.8 per cent (male 36 per cent and female 22.9 per cent).

Bangla is the mother tongue of the people, and the official language and medium of instruction at all levels of education. English is taught as a second language and widely understood, particularly in urban localities. About 87 per cent of the population of Bangladesh is Muslim, 12 per cent Hindu, 0.6 per cent Buddhist and 0.3 per cent Christian. Islam is the dominant religion and its values and ideals pervade all spheres of state and social life.

Bangladesh was a part of British India from 1757 to 1947. In 1947 it became a part of Pakistan known as East Pakistan. It emerged as an independent and sovereign state on 16 December 1971, when the nine months long War of Liberation ended. During its 20 years of independence, Bangladesh has experienced periods of constitutional government broken by periods of martial law. It currently has a parliamentary form of government with a prime minister as the head of the government. There is a national parliament consisting of 330 members (300 members are elected by direct adult franchise and another 30 female members are indirectly elected by the parliament). This parliament is known as the National Assembly of Bangladesh.

Bangladesh is divided into four administrative divisions. Each has a senior civil servant called the divisional commissioner. These divisions are sub-divided into 64 districts, each with a middle level civil servant called the deputy commissioner at the chief administrative office. The districts are progressively sub-divided into 460 sub-districts (*upazila*).

With a per capita annual income of US$ 170, the country is bracketed with the lesser developing countries (LDC) of the world. About 55 per cent of the GDP is derived from agriculture and only 9 per cent from manufacturing; cottage industries contribute about 4 per cent. An estimated 85 per cent of the civilian labour force is employed in agriculture, and there are only 0.3 acres of arable land available per capita. Economic dependency ratio is calculated at 229 per cent. Income, wealth and consumption are not evenly distributed in the country in terms of urban-rural location and socio-economic strata.

Overall urban in-migration stands at 30.52 per cent and that for rural at 8.70 per cent. Flight of the labour force from agriculture and the number of educated unemployed are increasing and are calculated to constitute nearly 20 per cent of the civilian labour force, aged 10 years and above.

The structure and functioning of the educational system during the programme period The focus of the development of primary education has, by and large, been on the expansion of the traditional system which consists of five years of schooling. However, emphasis has also been placed on science and work-oriented education during the second and third Five-Year Plan periods covering the decade from 1980 to 1990. The thrust has been on expansion of educational facilities, such as increasing the amount of seating, desks and benches, provision of furniture and increasing the number of teachers, particularly female teachers. Simultaneous efforts have made in areas such as improvement of curriculum and textbook development, pre-service and in-service teacher training, and improved administration and supervision of schools.

The formal education system comprises five years of primary education (classes I-V), seven years of secondary and higher secondary education (classes VI-XII), two to five years of higher education in different areas of specialization, and some postgraduate degree programmes. There are two public examinations leading to the award of the secondary school certificate (SSC) on completion of class X and the higher secondary certificate (HSC) on completion of class XII. Before nationalization of primary schools by the Government of Bangladesh in 1973, they were traditionally being run by the community. Of the present total of 45,077 primary schools, 37,634 are run by government management. At the secondary level, schools are run primarily by the community; only 295 high schools and eight intermediate colleges (offering grades VI to X, and XI to XII respectively) are managed by the government.

The existence of 13,828 ebtedayee, offering primary level education, and 5873 senior madrasahs offering a parallel system of secondary and higher education with a religious bias, funded by the people, shows the level of community support for education in the country. Vigorous attempts are underway to bring the madrasah education system (Islamic system of religious education) nearer to the general system of education by making the adoption of a national curriculum and textbooks a condition for obtaining government recognition and financial support.

The Ministry of Education is responsible for primary, secondary, vocational, technical and higher education including madrasah education. During the last decade new directorates, departments and professional institutions have been established to improve educational administration and management. New legislation has also been enacted to decentralize the administration of primary education through the creation of upazila (sub-district) primary education committees headed by elected upazila chairmen; upazila education officers act as member-secretaries. Upazila administration is currently undergoing change and is yet to take a definite shape.

Public sector expenditure for education has increased considerably in absolute terms, i.e. it increased from US$ 188 million in 1980-81 to US$ 435 million in 1989-90. In terms of GNP, the expenditure on education was 1.1 per cent in 1980-81, increasing to 2.2 per cent in 1989-90 at current price. Expenditure on primary education alone in 1980-81 was US$ 70 million and had increased to US$ 212 million by 1989-90. The share of primary education in the second five-year plan (1980-85) was 48.81 per cent, while it was less than 20 per cent in the previous plans, i.e. 18.58 per cent in the first five-year plan (1973-78) and 13.22 per cent in the two-year plan (1978-80). Following implementation of universal primary education, the Government of Bangladesh has given top priority to primary education with increased allocation.

For the first UPE project (1981-86), IDA assistance amounted to US$ 40 million, in addition to some assistance from other supporting external agencies. The second primary education project, which started in July 1985 and is expected to be completed in June 1991, involved the agencies IDA (US$ 78 million), UNICEF (US$ 13.17 million), SIDA (US$ 6.70 million) and UNDP (US$ 1.83 million). The objectives of the project were the expansion and improvement of primary education for the achievement of universal primary education (UPE). The main components of the project were civil works and furniture, instructional materials (books), training and orientation.

Description of the change itself

Universal primary education (UPE) is one of the major goals of the government of Bangladesh. To this end it implemented two UPE projects under its second and third five-year national development plans in the ten years from 1980 to 1990. The country is now in the middle of the implementation of the third UPE project under the fourth five-year development plan, 1990 to 1995. The goals of the first and the second UPE projects were:

- to increase primary school enrolment, particularly that of girls, from 60 per cent to about 70 per cent of the 6- to 10-year-old age group;
- to ensure that the majority of children who are enrolled in schools complete the five-year cycle of primary education;
- to improve the quality of primary education through better

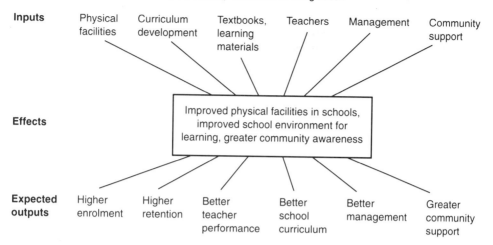

Figure 5.1 *Input-output model.*

management, effective supervision and improved classroom instruction.

In order to achieve the above goals, the government provided necessary inputs to 4300 schools during the first project and to all others during the second project plan. The inputs consist of both physical and human components. The physical inputs include civil works instructional materials and curriculum development, while the human inputs include improving management, quality of teachers and community involvement in the affairs of schools. An extensive reform has also been brought about in the management and administrative system to oversee and supervise primary education of the country from central to upazila level. The inputs and the network of administrative and management systems provided by the UPE project are expected to result in higher enrolment and retention of the children in school, better teacher performance, improved school management, improved school environment and greater community support. These input-output relations are shown in Figure 5.1.

The six categories of inputs in Figure 5.1 were termed the 'reform bundle' and are shown in more detail in Figure 5.2. Successful implementation of the UPE programme over the last ten years has brought about changes in each component of the bundle at the school, local, district and central levels. However, the bundle contains some items provided to the system (and schools) by other supporting agencies such as UNICEF during the period.

School level change

Physical facilities It was estimated that to enhance the enrolment from 60 per cent to 70 per cent, 2.5 million additional children would be enrolled in the primary schools throughout Bangladesh. This means an average enrolment of an additional 70 children per school, requiring extension of existing school

Physical facilities
Classroom space
Furniture
Playground
Tubewell and latrine

Quality of teachers
PTI training
Cluster training
Supervision
Teaching–learning practices
Female teachers
Teacher attendance and punctuality

Instructional materials
Textbooks
Teachers' guides
Teaching aids

Curriculum
Relevance (life and need oriented)
Co-curricular activities (singing, dancing, sports, gardening)

School management
Reporting forms
Maintenance
Evaluation (study assessment)
Liberal promotion policy

Community involvement
School management committee (SMC)
Parent–teacher association (PTA)

Figure 5.2 *The reform bundle: changes at the school level.*

buildings or construction of new buildings or construction of new buildings and provision of necessary furniture. As well as school buildings and additional furniture (benches and desks, blackboards, tables, cupboards and chairs), tubewells and latrines were also provided. All these facilities were essential for creating a learning environment in the schools.

Instructional materials The majority of the people of Bangladesh belong to the rural areas and nearly 70 per cent of the rural people are poor people who cannot afford to buy textbooks for their school-going children. In order to encourage enrolment the primary school children were given textbooks free of cost under the UPE programme. Previously the parents were required to buy textbooks for their children. Distribution of free textbooks encouraged enrolment in schools, particularly that of poor children and girls. The project also supplied exercise books to primary school students free of cost at the initial stage.

Similarly, the project provided the primary school teachers with free teachers' guides and teaching aids, both of which helped improve the teaching-learning process in the classroom.

Teachers' quality Before the introduction of the UPE programme a large number of primary school teachers were untrained, but all of them were given training during the programme period. To facilitate their one-year training, five new primary training institutes (PTI), including one for training female teachers only, were set up, increasing the number of PTIs from 47 to 52. The original 47 were co-educational and they continue to be so. The Academy of Fundamental Education (now NAPE) was strengthened and entrusted with the tasks of improving instruction at the PTIs and of conducting research into the improvement of the primary education curriculum.

Cluster training Cluster training is a new concept. A cluster consists of about 20 nearby primary schools. In order to supervise the activity of the schools in a cluster an assistant upazila education officer (AUEO) was appointed to be responsible for all of them. The AUEO organizes the cluster training for the teachers of each school once a month in the school premises. Teaching methods, lesson planning, designing and preparing teaching aids, and management of school activities are the themes of the training. The teachers' guide is used as one of the resource materials for this training. The concept of cluster training is an innovative component of the UPE programme.

Female teachers The government adopted a policy of including female teachers in primary schools. Before the introduction of the UPE programme the country had few female teachers in the primary schools of the country. It was hoped that an increase in the number of female teachers in primary schools would attract more girls to the schools. During the project period the target was to raise the number of female teachers to 50 per cent of the total number. The current target is 60 per cent.

Teaching-learning practices In order to improve the teacher competency, a series of in-service training was organized at each of the PTIs. All the primary teachers were brought under this training programme. Teaching methods, lesson planning, preparing teaching aids, evaluation techniques, etc. made up the content of this training programme.

Curriculum After the launching of the second UPE programme, the curriculum was revised thoroughly to make it responsive to the life and needs of the children. Accordingly, textbooks are being produced and published following the revised curriculum.

Liberal promotion policy Many children left school if they failed to get promotion from grade one to grade two on the basis of an annual examination. To check drop-out, a liberal promotion policy was introduced for students in grade one. With this system all children enrolled in grade one get promotion to grade two, reducing the drop-out rate to a great extent.

Community involvement Previously the management of primary schools in Bangladesh was largely entrusted to the respective communities. After independence, primary education was nationalized in 1974 and it became the responsibility of the government. After nationalization, the community had nothing to do with the management of primary schools of the country. In order to regain the community support, school management committees (SMC) and parent-teacher associations (PTA) were formed as aspects of the reforms.

Local level change In the current upazila level, one upazila education officer and one assistant upazila education officer supervised the activities of the schools and performed other administrative functions. After the initiation of the UPE programme, several more AUEO were created, and at present there is one AUEO for every cluster of about 20 schools. As a consequence, it has become possible to strengthen the supervision of schools and to organize regular cluster training.

District level change Before the introduction of UPE there was one district inspector of schools (DI) for the administration and coordination of primary education of each district. Now posts of district primary education officer (DPEO), assistant district primary education officer (ADPEO) and other supporting staff have been created to coordinate and supervise primary education of the district. The DPEO keeps direct links with central level administration and subdistrict level offices.

Central level change Ministry of Education and Directorate of Primary Education (DPE) are the two central level organizations concerned with education. The Ministry of Education is the policy formulation agency and the DPE is the implementing organization. Before the introduction of the UPE programme there was a single directorate of education. Its responsibility was to oversee and look after the entire education of the country. Only a section of the directorate was entrusted to look after the primary education of the country. The DPE is headed by a director general (DG), and below the DG, there are two directors. One director is in charge of administration and the other is in charge of planning. A number of deputy directors, assistant directors and research officers with professional backgrounds have been taken on to strengthen the DPE. A strong administrative and supervision network has been developed throughout the country by connecting the districts with the DPEs.

The story of the educational change programme

Primary education is understood today as the graded school system that followed from the recommendations known as Wood's Education Despatch of 1854. The Education Commission of 1882 recommended that the control of primary education be entrusted to local bodies, such as the district and the municipal boards. Between 1917 and 1927, the government passed the Compulsory Primary Education Act to be implemented in selected rural and urban areas for children of both sexes. In 1944 a comprehensive plan of education (known as the Sargent Report) was prepared for providing pre-primary education for children between the ages of 3 and 6 years and universal compulsory and free primary education for the 6 to 14 year age group, divided into junior basic for 6 to 11-year-olds and senior basic for 11 to 14-year-olds. This was to be achieved over the next 40 years.

With the emergence of Bangladesh as an independent country in 1971, a new national policy on education was recommended by the Bangladesh Education Commission. The Bangladesh constitution provided for free and compulsory primary education to be achieved early. To this end, the government nationalized 36,000 privately managed primary schools and their teachers in 1973. Two development plans, namely the first five-year plan (1973-78) and the two-year plan (1978-80) were aimed at rehabilitation of facilities destroyed or damaged during the Liberation War of 1971 and expansion of physical facilities to accommodate increased enrolment.

The Government decided to introduce universal primary education (UPE) during the second five-year development plan period (1980 to 1985) and allocated

46 per cent of resources from the development budget in the education sector. The World Bank joined hands with the government to develop and finance a UPE project in 44 upazilas (UZ). The scope and size of the project was expanded into a single national project with the IDA and other donors providing about 80 per cent of the project cost during the third five-year plan (1985 to 1990). The school mapping based on a set of criteria and other factors was drawn up to guide upazila parishads in preparing a list of schools requiring reconstruction/repair in a particular year. The criteria were not strictly followed and many deserving cases did not get priority in the selection. Later on, districts were also involved in the selection of schools.

Through in-service and later cluster training (introduced in 1982) and by the issuing of government circulars, teachers and field supervisors were informed about the objectives and salient features of the reform project and their respective roles in it. A series of orientation meetings were held throughout the country with UZ chairmen, UZ executive officers, SMC and PTA chairmen and members informing teachers about their roles and responsibilities in implementing the project. In addition to this, information booklets were developed and distributed. The project director continued personal correspondence, with UZ chairmen informing them about policy measures and implementation procedures at UZ level. Provision was made for project related training (PRT) which included recurrent (once a month) school-based training given by assistant upazila education officers (AUEOs). PRT, which is conducted at the central, divisional and district levels and also at PTIs and NAPE covers all categories of personnel working for UPE.

A Directorate of Primary Education was created in 1981. A curriculum development centre was also created in 1981 and this subsequently merged with the Textbook Board in 1983. The number of curriculum development staff was increased, and a nucleus of AUEOs was created to carry out intensive supervision of a cluster of about 20 to 25 primary schools. Textbooks were made free for all primary school students in 1985 and an apex institution called National Academy of Primary Education (NAPE) was established to provide leadership to PTIs, maintain uniformity and ensure quality of teachers' training as well as to assist the newly created teachers' training division of DPE in organizing in-service training activities of all categories of supervisory personnel.

As a part of the first reform programme the school management committee was reconstituted and strengthened and a new organization called the parent-teacher association was introduced to bring back community cooperation in primary schooling. The implementation strategy was altered slightly one year after the introduction of UPE and project IMPACT (instructional management by parents, community and teachers) was also dropped midway through implementation as the innovation failed to catch the imagination of the community who were sceptical about its long-term benefits.

UPE has been treated as a 'core'-project and allocations were made in the Annual Development Programme. Thus the project was always protected. In order to facilitate a flow of funds to meet the requirements of civil works, an impressive fund (amounting to US$ 7 million) was allocated to the Special Account in Foreign Exchange (SAFE) in Bangladesh Bank.

A summary of the degree of implementation success seen from the national viewpoint

The study includes interviews with central level informants, people who have followed the UPE reform over a long period of time. Their descriptions and interpretations are recorded here and form a useful background to our findings at the school level. In no way do these comments intend to be a general evaluation of the relative degree of success of the UPE reform. They are, rather, the perspectives of central decision-makers.

The extent and quality of implementation of the programme In 1981, a directorate of primary education was created to facilitate the implementation of the UPE programme. In 1983, a government order was issued, as a first step, for decentralization of management of primary education. The responsibility of managing the primary schools was given to the upazilas. In the same year, a National Curriculum Development Centre was created under the Ministry of Education. The purpose of the NCDC was to design and plan relevant and appropriate curricula for the primary, secondary and higher stages of formal education. This organization was subsequently merged with the National Textbook Board which included a separate curriculum wing. The government further issued directives for the implementation of liberal promotion policy in 1986, and in 1989 took another important decision related to primary teachers' recruitment rules, making a provision for 60 per cent of the total recruitment of teachers to be women.

The UPE has been given due importance as 'core' project in the annual development programme of the Ministry of Education. It has been a constitutional obligation which started with the nationalization of 36,000 privately run primary schools in 1973 followed by the introduction of UPE in 1980. These efforts led to the introduction of the Compulsory Primary Education Act by the Parliament of 1990. Much emphasis has been given to ensure the recruitment of qualified, trained teachers, especially females. The salary of primary teachers was raised substantially to attract quality people as primary teachers. To strengthen the reporting mechanism, a management information service unit has recently been created in the DPE for monitoring the UPE programme and establishing effective control on its overall progress.

The government has given UPE topmost priority in the education sector. As a result, the newly created organizations like DPE and NCTB are actively engaged in various activities related to UPE. The political commitment of the government was reflected by involving zila parishad, district administration and upazila (sub-district) parishads in the implementation of UPE. The donor agencies have shown great interest and have continued to provide financial support to the primary education sub-sector.

Although the history of primary education dates back over 100 years, the current UPE programme emphasizes the need for universalization of primary education. Some specific measures were taken for the success of UPE. These include expansion of physical facilities, supply of free textbooks, curriculum renewal and corresponding teacher training and infra-structural support, and community involvement through the formation of SMC and PTA. The main thrust of the UPE programme was to extend the physical facilities available for primary education. In carrying out construction and repair works, schools were selected in consultation with upazila parishad and district authorities. A new regular reporting system for collecting data from the school and its catchment area was introduced. Some other decision making responsibilities, for example posting and transfer of teachers, were delegated to upazila administration. All these policy decisions were taken at the ministry level. However, the implementation of these decisions rests with the DPE. The directorate and DPEOs conduct the implementation activities of these programmes and thus try to establish a linkage between central and local level administration.

The different components of the UPE programme have been entrusted to various organizations: for example, overall administration by DPE, curriculum development by NCTB, primary teachers' training by NAPE, educational statistics by BANBEIS and physical facilities by the facilities department of DPE. In the implementation process of UPE a close linkage has been established among all these organizations and institutions. The programme also emphasizes regular supervision as an important means for improving teaching-learning and motivation of the teachers. To accomplish this, the post of AUEO was created. The AUEOs are primarily responsible for providing academic supervision, in-service training to the teachers and guidance for reporting to higher authorities. The instructional materials which include textbooks for the student and teachers' guides for the teachers were made available free of cost. However, the funds for day-to-day expenses and co-curricular activities are inadequate, and the quality of school buildings is unsatisfactory because the contractors were appointed by the central office of DPE and were not accountable to SMC or local administration.

In a poor country like Bangladesh which has a very high population growth rate and limited resources, a massive programme like UPE could not be launched without foreign assistance. During the second primary education project (1985 to 1990), 80 per cent of the total expenditure of the programme was met from IDA credit and the remaining 20 per cent from government funds. The internal resources, or the government fund, were spent on teachers' salaries and other expenses for upazila, divisional and district primary education offices. The external financial assistance was used primarily for physical facilities and for free distribution of instructional materials.

The AUEOs are supposed to establish a close relationship between the upazila education office and the schools and provide cluster training (in-service) each month for teachers to improve the classroom teaching-learning activities. A system of regular reporting on schools' progress (another new measure) was introduced in 1986. The National Academy for Primary Education (NAPE) has been established to provide in-service training and action research on primary education. In the programme implementation much importance has been given to the involvement of the parents and the community, and provision has been made in each school for the formation of a SMC and a PTA, with guidelines for their effective functioning. Moreover, teachers have been involved in the development and modification of the trial editions of new textbooks and guides.

System level outcomes According to the national informants, the UPE programme provided schools with the necessary physical facilities for raising enrolment rate. The rise in the gross enrolment ratio from 62 per cent in 1980 to 70 per cent in 1989, implies that social demand for schooling has also been increased. The ratio of girl students has also shown an increase (and now stands at about 46 per cent of the total enrolment). The drop-out rate has also shown a downward trend.

The programme has spelled out the duties and responsibilities of the DPEO which cover all aspects of administration, inspection, teachers' training and reporting. The services of the UEO and AUEO have been placed under the upazila parishad, so the DPEO faces difficulty in establishing his authority for supervision and control over the UEO and AUEO. The replacement of the traditional annual examination resulting in pass or failure in grades one and two by liberal promotion policy through continuous student assessment has not yet been accepted by the parents, who are still in favour of merit-based evaluation.

During the second and third plan periods external agencies have shown increasing interest in primary education. This was reflected in the increased IDA fund for the second primary education project. The whole country is now aware of the importance of primary education. Parents are more keen to send their children to school, and this interest has been largely created by the free distribution of textbooks. Local and central administrators and school personnel have also become aware of the basic requirements of primary schools, teachers and students. Different organizations like NCTB and DPE are developing their capabilities and undertaking a number of activities to ensure the success of the UPE programme. The programme could establish a close linkage between central and local administration through the present administrative structure. It has earned the confidence of external donors as well as the political support of the government.

Impact

On students The student impact as seen by national level interviewees may be summarized as a slight increase in the enrolment and attendance rates and a decrease in the drop-out and repetition rates. The central level interviewees mentioned the increase in enrolment and higher participation rate of girls and students from poor families as the outcomes of the project. They identified the decrease in drop-out and repetition as a positive impact of the reforms. Some of the interviewees thought that the drop-out rate had not been decreased as much as was expected. They observed that free textbooks improved the participation rates of the students in all schools.

Some research studies have focused on student outcomes. The following quotes indicate the nature of the findings:

> In five IDA villages, ... 71 per cent primary age group attended school in mid-1984, whereas in non-IDA villages ... 30 per cent attended school.
>
> Non-enrolment, drop-out and attendance rates in IDA villages showed better figures than non-IDA villages.

Enrolment increased since 1980 in the IDA area by 161 per cent and in the non-IDA area by 144 per cent, the rate accelerated in recent years.

The drop-out rate in the IDA schools reduced from 20 per cent in 1981 to 5 per cent in 1984, whereas in the non-IDA schools it increased from 18 per cent in 1981 to 22 per cent in 1984. (Qadir, 1984)

There had been an increase of enrolment in 1989 compared to 1988 in the sample schools ... 8.73 per cent in the rural areas.

... the participation rate of primary age children stands at about 72 per cent ... (Haque and Jinnah, 1990)

On teachers The major teacher impact as seen by national level interviewees was the increased number of female teachers, which had contributed particularly to the increased enrolment of girls. The interviewees also mentioned that the teachers were more regular and punctual in their attendance and that they improved their knowledge and skills for better teaching. They think that cluster training and teachers' guides have contributed a lot to the overall improvement of teacher behaviour and performance. Some of them mentioned that teacher motivation was still poor. They also thought that close and regular supervision by the AUEO improved teacher attendance and performance.

Research on teachers has among other topics looked at the impact of *female* teachers:

There was a positive correlation between the number of female teachers and the corresponding number of female students in a school. (Miah *et al.*, 1984)

None of the heads of the 100 schools studied was female. The headteachers reported their satisfaction with regard to assistant female teachers' quality. (Ministry of Education, 1984)

Female teachers appeared to be more regular in attendance compared to male teachers of the same school.

Teachers with better/higher general education seemed to teach better. (Haque *et al.*, 1987)

On schools The national level interviewees identified school impact as the construction and repair or expansion of school buildings and latrines, and the supply of benches and other furniture. These measures improved physical facilities for the students and the teachers and encouraged higher participation rates. The free textbooks and teachers' guides together with cluster training had improved enrolment as well as teaching, which in turn brought about changes in the overall conditions of the schools. They thought that the school management committee (SMC) and parent-teacher association (PTA) were formed with a view to improving community involvement in children's education, though these bodies were not functioning too well. Supervision of schools for academic improvement was strengthened because of the allocation of a smaller number of schools to each AUEO. As a result the teachers' attendance and their classroom performance has greatly improved.

Research on school impact of the reform and the role of parents in Bangladesh indicates the following trends:

> Joint plan of action by Brac staff, UEO, AUEO, headmasters, teachers on home visits, co-curricular activities, scheduling SMC and PTA meetings, cluster training, etc. have largely contributed to the successful implementation of supervision and management system of primary schools, improved student, teacher attendance, community parent participation. (Latif 1991)

> Parents perceived literacy as a means of getting better job and raising social status. Poverty (31 per cent), lack of motivation of the parents (25 per cent) were cited as the most important reasons for illiteracy or lower attendance of schools by the children. (UPE *et al.*, 1988)

> Parent-teacher association hardly functions in practice.

> 100 per cent of guardians expressed the view that children should go to school. Attitude towards education of girls was very favourable. (Haque and Jinnah, 1990)

> ... majority of the parents were willing to send their children to any educational programme if necessary facilities like free supply of all educational materials and dress were made available ... about 56 per cent wanted school near their homes ... (Haque and Jinnah, 1990)

> The general feelings that schools were to be looked after by the government and that the teachers did not depend upon the managing committee for the administration of the schools, fostered a weak link between the villagers and the school. (Ahmadullah *et al.*, 1984)

Institutionalization of the programme The central level interviewees thought that primary schools would make progress in all respects in the next ten years, though the physical facilities would not change. The training programmes and curriculum development would also continue. As the reforms had and still have full and stable political support, these should continue, particularly as the reform has now established proper linkage between the central and local levels through the reformed administration, supervision, cluster training, reporting and monitoring systems. Some of the central level interviewees gave the opinion that general awareness of the middle class about the importance of primary education had been improved during the last few decades.

Moreover, the requirements of the reforms led to the creation of some national organizations like the NAPE and the Directorate of Primary Education. These permanent organizations are providing strong support to the UPE programme. The staff development programme, through cluster training, has become regular and routine work of the directorate. Some of the interviewees mentioned that the sustainability of the reforms was dependent on the supply of free textbooks. If this continues, so should the reform.

Unanticipated outcomes – positive and negative The reforms suffered from teacher shortage in many schools, which hampered classroom activities. The specified quality of physical facilities could not be ensured in many schools, because neither the SMC nor the headmaster had any authority or means to exert influence on the construction engineers, suppliers of materials and contractors, who were appointed and controlled solely by the central authorities. Some interviewees mentioned that nationalization of primary schools relieved the community of the responsibilities they once carried for primary education of the locality. Some of them resented the appointment of female teachers. One mentioned that the parents were mostly unaware of the reforms and the programme had little opportunity for local adaptation. Another said that the sudden increase in enrolment of children in all schools as a result of the reforms had caused an acute space problem in the schools.

Major criticism is currently being expressed in the public debate, as well as in the research and donor communities, about the quality of primary education. Concerns are expressed about imbalances, corruption, politicization and conflicts. Also the policy study called the Qudrat-e-Khuda commission stresses the need to see primary education as a right and to drastically improve the system. Others point to the need to bring primary education responsibilities back to local village control. These discussions show that there are some basic dilemmas facing Bangladesh education, and they include imbalances:

- between private options for education and regular government education;
- between rich and poor children;
- between girl and boy participation;
- between allocations for lower and higher education;
- between teacher and student responsibilities;
- between hardware and software project inputs;
- between local, central and external initiatives, commitments and responsibilities;
- between non-formal education and government primary education.

It is not our task in this study to evaluate the UPE reform in general. Our task is more limited: to understand how successful UPE schools work. We hope to explain why these schools are successful, and thereby learn some important lessons about how the primary system in general can be improved.

Country-level factors that seem to have accounted for success, as seen at the national level

Interviewees at the national level perceive the strengths of the reform to be the political commitment, division of labour and creation of different organizations and an infra-structure, resource allocation and delivery, and curriculum renewal.

The government's political commitment to UPE led to the creation of specialized organizations such as the DPE for administration and supervision, the NCTB for curriculum, and NAPE for primary teacher training. An administrative network has been set up connecting the central, divisional, district and upazila levels in order to ensure successful implementation of UPE. Thus between the Ministry, the DPE and the school, there are divisional, district and upazila education officers to play intermediate roles. In 1981, a curriculum development centre was created with a view to making the curriculum relevant, life-oriented and more suitable for the nationals of a newly independent country.

National level interviewees all mentioned the creation of the posts of assistant upazila education officers as a constructive strategy by the central level people. The AUEO has been given the responsibility of providing academic training to the teachers of about 20 schools in the upazila per month. This has strengthened the academic training of the teachers and means that administrative supervision and management is now the sole duty of the upazila education officer. This mechanism appears to have helped both local education officers to discharge their duties more comfortably and efficiently than ever before. The cluster training provided by the AUEO gives the primary teachers an opportunity to enhance their teaching skills and works as a medium to disseminate all new ideas and developments in different areas of primary education. The National Academy for Primary Education is being utilized as the core institution for further training of teachers.

Cluster training has been the focus of several research studies in Bangladesh. The following quotes indicate the nature of the conclusions:

> Contents of teacher leaflets and cluster training helped increase teachers' knowledge and skills. (Akhter, 1987)

> The concept of cluster training has generally taken root, though in an uneven manner. (Akhter, 1987)

> Their training helped them in reducing school drop-outs and increasing student participation rate ... in improving management of the schools. (Huq et al., 1984)

The supervision role of the AUEO has also been the focus of studies:

> The supervisory services given by AUEOs ... (a) observing teachers in teaching situations, (b) observing teacher's use/misuse of appropriate or inappropriate teaching aids (c) holding discussions with teachers after class observation ... (d) asking students questions, (e) organizing teachers training programme

> Responses of headteachers are that some schools were visited by the AUEOs twice a month, some others once a month and still others not even once a month. (Akhter, 1984)

> A regularly monthly and half yearly system of reporting from the schools and the field officers on all important aspects of primary education was found to work. (Haque, 1990)

The other factor emphasized in the interview is the creation and development of organizations on the basis of specialization. By building an infrastructure the quality of cluster training and activities of specialized organizations can be controlled and enhanced by implementing newly designed plans and appointing better quality people. The two major infrastructures created and strengthened by the reform were the parent-teacher association and the school management committee. Following the nationalization of primary schools in 1973, all the traditional responsibility of the community in respect to primary education was removed. This created a new problem: the community was unaware of the primary schooling which was being designed to serve it. To regain community participation, the old body, the school management committee has been strengthened, and a new body called the parent-teacher association has been formed with a view to establishing a close relationship between parents of the children and the primary school teachers. It is obvious that without the motivation of parents, the higher participation rate of both girls and boys will remain a dream. The interviewees admitted that although these bodies were not working well, they should gradually improve in the future.

These two strategies are regarded as the indicators of the high commitment of the government. Moreover, the legal regulations followed which include 1983 ordinance for decentralization of management of primary education, introduction of liberal promotion policy and primary teacher recruitment rules for increasing the quota of female teachers are evidence of government support. These were some of the strategies for increasing enrolment, participation of girls and local participation in primary education.

Another factor emphasized by the interviewees is resource allocation and delivery. According to the interviewees, there is no alternative to physical facilities such as buildings, latrines, tubewells, classrooms, benches, desks and textbooks free of cost. They appreciate the inputs or resources of the UPE project as the 'core' requirements of the schools. The major activity of the UPE was the extension of physical facilities undertaken in all primary schools. The interviewees mentioned that all the inputs corresponded to the objectives of UPE. For the delivery of the resources, a map was drawn up stating the requirements of each school, though priority lists have not always been maintained.

All the interviewees regarded the supply of free textbooks as one of the most important resources. They think free textbooks acted as the main motivating factor for the poor parents and their children in rural areas and it seems that this is the key to the UPE programme. The delivery system of resources was moderately successful and schools have received nearly all the resources according to the school mapping, though the quality of building and furniture was not always satisfactory.

The supply of free textbooks and facilities have been the focus of some studies:

> Supply of free books and uniforms encouraged poorer sections of parents to send and keep their children in school. (Ahmedullah *et al.*, 1984)

The supply of textbooks in UPE (IDA) project schools was fairly satisfactory.

Textbooks did not reach students in time. (Balaghatullah, 1984)

Most of the learning materials (input) supplied to the sample schools were found to exist.

100 per cent of the teachers expressed that the learning materials supplied were useful and relevant. (Alauddin, 1985)

Furnitures supplied to schools did not in all cases meet the specifications of material, quality and measurement. (FREPD, 1984)

A large number of serving teachers are eager to get teacher's guide on each school subject. (Rahman, 1986)

Some of the interviewees also mentioned the development of relevant and life oriented curricula and textbooks, and considered this an important factor of UPE.

The national level interviewees focused on the factors with more of an administrative and less of an academic nature, which were the focal points of the project. They were either involved in designing these strategies or acted as the administrators of those related organizations engaged in the implementation of UPE. They gave much importance to the creation of the post of AUEO but were unable to discuss the strengths and weaknesses of cluster training, an important input of the UPE project. Similarly they did not highlight the roles of NAPE and NCTB because they did not have any experience of their activities.

Although an MIS is constituted in the DPE, the national level interviewees did not attach much importance to it. The administrators are keen to frame a programme and create relevant facilities but less concerned about the progress of the programme. Hence monitoring and evaluation have not been developed and did not attract the attention of the policy planners at the initial stage.

The only classroom activities that impressed the interviewees were teacher attendance and enrolment. This is because at the national level people are able to identify major and measurable outcomes but not the process and immeasurable outcomes. Consequently factors such as teacher-pupil involvement, teacher motivation and commitment did not receive much attention from the central level interviewees. Finally, the interviewees thought that because the UPE programme has been created as a 'core' programme for the country, it will never face any difficulties, financial or otherwise. It will stay and continue.

The development of the infrastructure like the creation of NAPE, NCTB and DPE, helped the implementers to carry out different types of activities. UPE is a target which needs a multidimensional approach to tackle all the existing problems of primary education and complement the system with planned strategies. For example, physical facilities and resources like free textbooks were provided with a view to increasing enrolment in primary schools and attracting poor children. These have worked well in all schools.

To raise the achievement level of the primary school children a relevant curriculum is needed, and this is still being developed. The improvement of

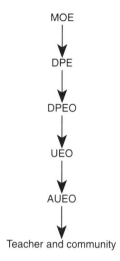

Figure 5.3 *The administrative network.*

in-service training of teachers is a complementary strategy adopted in the reform, which will in turn affect the achievement level of the children. The role of NAPE and the AUEOs and the mechanism of cluster training were major strategies designed to enhance the classroom performance of both teachers and children. These factors have worked in all primary schools with a variety of success rates.

Linkage between national and regional/local strategies as seen from the national level

Finally, in our central interviews, we asked for elements of the reform that were instrumental in linking central initiatives to local implementation. An administrative network has been set up linking the Ministry of Education, DPEO, UEO, AUEO and school teachers. The policy planners expected this to facilitate the implementation of the activities for achieving the three objectives of primary education and at the same time establish a closer relationship between the policy planners and the implementers. The network is expected to work as shown in figure 5.3. This administrative infrastructure has taken permanent shape in the primary education system of the country through which all the programmes, instructions and directives generated at the central level reach the schools. The national level interviewees identified the following as the linkage factors which worked more significantly than others.

Assistance Assistance is one of the major ways through which linkage between centre and school has been established. Assistance in the form of training and supervision provided by the DPE and DPEO is not as high as it is at upazila and school level. This is because the new AUEO posts are placed in the upazila, closer to the schools. As a result, their effects are felt much more by the schools and upazila education officers than by the district and central level offices. The rating varies from high to low, differentiating one school from another, but the reality is that the mechanism for improving the school climate has been established with the help of this officer and the cluster training system. Through supervision and academic training schools and upazilas have moved closer to each other, creating a better opportunity for the administrators to have a real glimpse of school problems.

In many schools the assistance, i.e. the cluster training and supervision, is not that strong. It relies on good headteachers who have implemented the reform successfully. In addition this training requires academically sound and interested people who are few and far between in the communities. So, although the practice has been introduced, it is only working in schools which have an academically sound AUEO and a good headteacher.

Administrative role All the administrators from central to local level are tied by the administrative role which includes attitude, commitment, controlling and monitoring implementation, providing instructions to the teachers, visiting schools and education offices, school reporting, solving problems and providing materials and local funds. This linkage factor is again weak at the district level but strong at upazila and school level because of the presence of UEOs and AUEOs close to the schools. The administrators visit nearby schools and successful schools especially. With the creation of the post of AUEO, the relationship between the administrator and the school has become stronger than ever.

Commitment Commitment of the personnel at school, upazila, district and central level is an important factor that links all concerned with UPE. This factor is weak at both district and upazila level and strong in specific schools where there are very committed headteacher and teachers.

According to the interviewees, government commitment reflected in directives and orders, facilitated the implementation of the reform. But not all central level officials were that committed, compared with the contributions of a generally committed school head. In spite of this weakness, an awareness of the need for UPE has been created among people at all levels. As a result commitment in the form of accepting the reform as a priority by teachers, AUEOs, UEOs and higher officials is no longer rare. Moreover, this reform has helped officials to develop a much stronger team spirit than before.

Commitment is strong in schools and less strong at district and central level, because the transfer of personnel is more frequent in the latter than in schools. The individuals who have planned and designed the reform must have higher commitment than a new person who has to carry on the implementation process, but was not involved in the process of initiation.

Received pressure and resources The normal practice for establishing a link between the policy planners and people at different implementation levels is the issuing of circulars, orders and instructions and through solving implementation problems and providing political support. These are indicators of pressure normally imposed by planners/administrators on the implementers. This has been found to be weak in both the district and upazila levels and strong in schools, the actual implementers of the reform. This implies that pressure is put on the teachers by administrators at all levels, because if the teachers fail, the reform also fails.

The resources supplied by the central level as inputs of the reform have generated a channel for linking schools with the higher administrative bodies. Resources, mainly new building, new furniture, latrines, tubewells, teaching-learning materials, contingency grants and other financial help, reached the schools in most cases much later than desired, and some of them were of poor quality. The resources were the major input of the reform without which the opportunity for all poor children to receive primary education would remain a dream. These were considered by all as the basic necessities of the school, and were provided to all schools during the reform period.

Success experience The national interviewees were able to identify some of the major and measurable, visible outcomes of the reform at school level as increased overall enrolment, increased enrolment of girls and poor children, appointment of more female teachers, teachers' punctual attendance, higher achievement rate, extra classrooms and other physical facilities. These outcomes are the joint products of reform inputs, the newly created infrastructure, assistance, commitment and the administrative role. This success experience is weak at district level but strong in at upazila and school level, where actual implementation is taking place.

The interviewees confirmed that everything comes from above and the project people listened to the concerns and requirements of local people/schools. Lately upazila parishad has been delegated with the authority of the management of primary schools with a view to increasing local participation in primary schooling. The interviewees mentioned that although the SMGs and PTAs are not functioning in most of the school catchment areas, they have still been formed in the hope that parents will be interested in their children's education and schools in the future.

IMPLEMENTATION AT THE SCHOOL LEVEL

Overview of more and less successful schools (cross-site display 1, see Bangladesh national report, page 288)

Introduction In arranging the ten schools in order of success in implementation, impact and institutionalization considered together as a combination of criteria for classification, the schools have been placed in three groups:

- 'excellent' schools
- 'very good' schools
- 'good' schools, which still have some weaknesses.

Excellent schools Four schools (Hasnahena, Champa, Aparajita and Palash) have been placed in this group, and they continue to be excellent when implementation and impact are considered as the criteria of classification. The four schools have received all the 'inputs', with the exception of the first school, where the headteacher extended the building out of the income from the betelnut garden on his own initiative. Two schools are using the block teaching regularly, while the other two have moderate ratings on this issue. Three of the schools have high ratings on curriculum-related training, while one has a moderate rating. It is interesting to note that in spite of the strong presence of curriculum-oriented training, the teachers' technical mastery has not improved that much in the excellent schools. There is little difference between the ratings of excellent and very good schools on this factor.

Community involvement is higher in excellent schools as compared to very good schools, and supervision is higher in excellent schools than in schools in the other two groups.

Very good schools Three schools (Chameli, Ulatchandal and Rangan) form the group of very good schools when implementation success, indicating student, teacher and school impact, and institutionalization are considered together. These schools are regarded as moderate in the extension of physical facilities, and are equal to the excellent schools in the supply of free textbooks.

These schools are rated as high/moderate in active teaching, nearly the same as the excellent schools, which reflects the presence of motivated headteachers and teachers in both groups.

On school impact, the rating of this group is somewhat higher than that of the good schools in terms of enrolment, girls enrolment, role of active head, teacher-community relation and physical facilities, but in school discipline this group is equal to good schools and on the role of female teachers this group has been rated a little lower than the good schools. The rating of AUEO supervision is lower than that of the excellent schools and at the same level as in the good schools.

In terms of student impact, the rating of this group is lower than in the excellent schools and higher than in good schools (on student achievement, attendance, retention, repetition rate, student motivation). This group is equal to the excellent group in the increase of enrolment, with a high rating.

Good schools The three schools that form the group of good schools are Padma, Shapla and Jaba. This group of schools have lower ratings on physical facilities, AUEO supervision, community involvement, headteacher motivation, curriculum-oriented training and teachers' technical mastery than the very good schools.

In all student impact criteria these schools have lower ratings than the other two groups of schools. The same is true for teacher impact and school impact. However in teachers' association activity the very good and good schools are equal, rating higher than the excellent schools.

Conclusion One interesting finding is that teacher association activity is nearly non-existent in excellent schools, while it is moderate in all the very good and good schools. Cluster training organized by the AUEO is a discriminating factor under institutionalization between excellent, very good and good schools. It is closely related to supervision, which is also high in excellent schools, and gradually lower in very good and good schools. It corresponds to the ratings of teacher punctuality.

Though there are a large number of inputs in the reform bundle, some of them have a more direct and stronger impact on implementation than others. Free textbooks, new classrooms and physical facilities, motivation of headteacher, curriculum-oriented training and recruitment of female teachers have a strong impact; while community involvement, recruitment of new teachers, teachers' technical mastery and child survey are weakly implemented. In short, the data show that where there is a low quality of implementation, impact is low and institutionalization is low.

Key factors that explain good implementation, impact and institutionalization

Introduction Four schools (Hasnahena, Champa, Aparajita and Palash) form the excellent group when the schools are arranged in order from the best to the least good in terms of implementation success and (student, teacher and school) impact. This group of schools has been rated high on implementation; high, high/medium, medium on student impact; high, high/medium, medium on teacher impact with one exception, i.e. low on teachers' association activity; high, high/medium, medium on school impact with a few exceptionally low scores on female teacher and PTA and SMC.

Three schools (Chameli, Ulatchandal and Rangan) form the group of very good schools when arranged in order of success in implementation and impact. This group of schools has been rated high, high/medium, medium, medium/low and low on implementation; high, high/medium, medium and medium/low on student impact; one high, high/medium, mostly medium and (one) low on teacher impact; (two) high, high/medium, medium, medium/low and (two) low on school impact.

The remaining three schools (Padma, Shapla and Jaba) form the group of good schools, but have some weaknesses. The group has been rated (three) high, high/medium, medium, medium/low and low on implementation. On student impact, teacher impact and school impact, the ratings are high/medium, medium, moderate/low and low.

Implementation Taking implementation success as the criterion for classification, the excellent schools have a score of 23 high, while the very good schools have seven high, and the good schools have three high (see worktable 11, Appendix 4, page 327). This discrimination shows that though on some specific indicators, the excellent schools have been rated low, on most of the criteria/factors of implementation and impact these schools have larger number of high scores to explain their excellent rating. The difference between excellent schools and very good schools is 16, which means that the difference is large and significant with respect to implementation success. On the other hand, the difference between the scores of the very good and good schools on the same issue is not significant (4) enough, which implies that the excellent schools are too high on the success scale compared to the very good and good schools.

141

Impact The excellent schools score 24 high on student impact, 11 high on teacher impact and 33 high on school impact. The very good schools score seven high and 13 high/medium on student impact, only one high and 12 high/medium on teacher impact and only two high and 16 high/medium on school impact. The good schools score no high and four high/medium on student impact, five high/medium on teacher impact and one high and 10 high/medium on school impact.

These data show that the reform has been implemented almost as envisaged but the impact on students, teachers and schools has been less satisfactory than was expected and that the better schools are more homogeneous than the weaker schools with respect to both implementation of the reform and the impact on the targets. Moreover, the data indicate that the classification of the three groups of schools is quite reasonable in terms of impact of the reform.

Institutionalization The picture here is even clearer. The excellent schools score 26 high, the very good schools score three high and seven high/medium, and the good schools score no high and three high/medium. This shows that only in the excellent schools is there a satisfactory degree of institutionalization. This finding raises serious concerns about the institutionalization of the UPE reform, knowing that our sample of schools is considered to be the successful schools.

Factors explaining success of implementation, impact and institutionalization The data show that the excellent schools have been rated high on the criteria or indicators of implementation such as extension of physical facilities and free textbooks/guides, mostly high on female teachers, AUEO supervision, headteacher motivation and curriculum-oriented training, and mostly moderate on teachers' technical mastery (see worktables 38 to 47, page 340ff).

The excellent schools This group of schools has a total score of 14 high on assistance; 11 high on supervision; 13 high on commitment, 11 high on received pressure; 19 high on received resources; 20 high on success experience; and 10 high on empowerment; with very high scores on role of headteacher and role of administrator. Assistance in the form of monthly cluster training, supervision by UEO and AUEO, and headteachers' role, training and staff development activity have been identified as the strongest factors for successful implementation of the reform in excellent schools.

The data reflects that this group of schools has received all the resources or inputs of the reform which were then utilized and sometimes extended by the motivated headteachers. Furthermore, the commitment of the headteachers attracted the attention of the local supervisors, and as a result, the schools received much closer supervision and academic help than the other two groups. These schools faced fewer problems in getting resources because of close contact with the supervisors.

Headteachers' class supervision is the other factor which is very high in this group of schools. The classroom is the actual place of reform implementation, so it is evident that when the headteacher is inspecting classroom teaching, the result will be reflected in higher teacher motivation, punctual attendance and better performance in the classroom, which in turn will affect students' achievement and participation. Finally, this is likely to increase enrolment of students, reduce the drop-out and repetition rate; which is what has actually happened in these schools.

The very good schools The three schools in this group together have scores such as four high and three medium on assistance; five high on supervision; four high and 6 high/medium on commitment; two high and six high/medium on received pressure; six high and five high/medium on received resources; two high and eight high/medium on success experience; with fairly high scores on role of headteacher and administrator.

The data imply that these schools have moderately active headteachers and received almost all the reform inputs, but less than excellent schools. These schools received moderate attention from the administrators and the moderate degree of success experiences of these schools justifies this. It is further reflected in a moderate degree of success in enrolment, recruitment of female teachers and girls enrolment, achievements, drop-outs and repetition, punctuality, scholarships and extra classrooms. Acceptance of the reform by these schools is not so strong as that of excellent schools, but all the ratings indicate that these schools have implemented the reform with a moderate degree of success.

The good schools The group of good schools have scores such as six medium on assistance; three medium on supervision; three high/medium and 17 medium on commitment; 13 medium on received pressure; two high/medium and ten medium on received resources; two high/medium and nine medium on success experience; four medium on community/participation; with moderate scores on the headmasters' and administrators' role.

The data imply that these schools have received much less attention from the supervisors than the other two groups. Commitment is quite high in these schools but the lower ratings on other factors are responsible for the difference in the successful implementation of the reform between this group and the other two.

Conclusions The first group, the excellent schools, have higher ratings on the factors which play an important role in the implementation process than the other two groups. Some of these factors are assistance, supervision, commitment, role of headteacher and administrator, received resources, received pressure and community support. Although community support was only rated high in two schools (Hasnahena and Palash), the poor Hindu weaver communities have shown eagerness in sending children to the schools. This has helped the schools to increase enrolment, and has contributed to both the implementation success and impact, at least marginally, in both these schools. It indicates that local participation may have a significant impact on the reform.

In addition, the headteachers of both of the two schools mentioned above were awarded best headteacher prize. This indirectly created a pressure for doing a better job on the two headteachers. There is less worry about the flow of assistance, resources and supervision in the excellent schools, because the administrators and supervisors feel confident about the better utilization of everything in these schools. It is a two-way relationship — the school personnel attract the supervisors, so the supervisors visit them frequently which helps the school obtain resources and solve problems, leading to the progress of the school. In other words, it means better performance, more attention and more pressure.

Lack of parental awareness about the education of their children, non-functioning of the SMC and PTA, and influence of primary teachers' association have higher scores in very good and good schools. These have rendered negative effects on the implementation and impact of the reform in these schools.

Analysis of the above data leads to the following conclusions:

(i) Assistance in the form of in-service help for teachers and headmasters (which includes regular monthly training in school premises, occasional special training, supervision of classroom and other activities, pedagogical help, advice etc.) contributes to implementation success and impact. The excellent schools appear to have received better assistance than the very good schools and the latter received slightly better assistance than the good schools.

(ii) The administrative role defined as typical behaviour of the headmasters and the local administrators (AUEOs) (which includes stability, presence, facilitation, monitoring/regulating, supervision and support) has a moderate effect on implementation success and impact. The quality of administrative role in the excellent schools, compared with that in either very good or good schools, tends to be of a higher order. But the very good and good schools do not differ substantially in this factor. This role in all schools is of moderately high quality.

(iii) Supervision/support (when considered as key factor separately from assistance as defined earlier) has only a slight effect on implementation success and impact. The excellent schools appear to have received a higher degree of supervision/support than the other two categories of schools. However, this factor is present in all schools, gradually decreasing from very good to good schools. It has contributed to the difference between the groups in terms of implementation and impact.

(iv) Commitment (defined as positive feelings toward the reform programme, ownership and priority given to it) appears to be high in excellent schools and almost equally high in the other two groups.

(v) Empowerment/engagement (defined as concerned people's feelings that they were actively involved in decisions about carrying out the programme — trying it out, revising it, improving it), as a factor capable of contributing to implementation success and impact, is found to have been present moderately in the very good and good schools and quite high in the excellent schools.

(vi) Local adaptation of the programme (defined as revisions or changes in the programme that make it more effective) as a key factor is found to have been slightly higher in excellent schools than in the other two categories of schools. This factor by itself cannot explain the outcomes since the reform came from above and was accepted by all schools.

(vii) Parent support (defined as positive, encouraging attitudes of parents and community leaders toward the programme) is found to have been high/moderate to low, and a factor that discriminates the excellent schools from the very good schools. (No data was available for the good schools.)

(viii) Received pressure (defined as feelings on the part of the headteacher and teachers that they are expected by important others to 'do it right') is found to be present as a high impact factor in the excellent schools and a moderately high impact factor in the very good schools and good schools. So this factor clearly accounts for differences in implementation success and impact.

(ix) Received resources (defined as funds, equipment, materials and people that actually arrived at the school to help implement the programme) are found to have been highly present in the excellent schools, and moderately present in the very good and good schools. This factor also contributes to the differences in implementation and impact.

(x) Success experience (defined as short-term results of the programme that 'worked' and gave people a positive feeling. These can occur through mastery of practice or through seeing good results with students) are highly present in the excellent schools, quite high in the very good schools and moderately present in good schools. This factor accounts for the differences in implementation success and impact to some extent.

(xi) Other cultural factors (e.g. presence of Hindus in the community) appear to have contributed highly to the outcomes in the case of two schools in the excellent group.

(xii) Other negative factors such as poverty of community, conservatism of parents, lack of awareness of parents, lack of interest in the SMC and PTA, undue interference of the local leadership of the primary teachers' association, appointment of too many female teachers often seeking leave or transfer to urban areas although their presence raises enrolment of children including girls, overcrowded classrooms, lack of local involvement in physical facilities development, floods etc., tend to adversely affect implementation and impact.

Implications for national-level strategies and practices needed to support successful local implementation/impact and institutionalization

Introduction The key factors listed in cross-site displays 1 and 2 (pages 288 and 290) actually represent the components of the bundle of reforms. The conclusions drawn in this part of the report show that all the key factors (or their various combinations) are needed at a certain minimum level for successful implementation, good impact (on students, teachers and school), and institutionalization of the reforms. Hence some of these key factors are found to have been present in all three categories of schools equally, while other factors tend to contribute differentially to the degree of success in implementation/impact and institutionalization. In drawing implications the key factors, which clearly tend to explain good implementation/impact, and good institutionalization, have been considered first.

Implementation/impact and institutionalization The major factors working for the success of the reform are:

- cluster training
- role of headteacher and supervisors
- supervision
- commitment
- community support and resources
- pressure
- success experience.

Assistance tends to contribute to implementation success and (student, teacher, and school) impact. The excellent schools compared to the very good schools and the latter compared to the good schools have received better (or possibly more) assistance. However, in spite of this difference between the three types of schools, all the schools in the excellent group and one of the three very good schools have received assistance of high quality, while the remaining two schools in the very good schools group and all three schools in the good group have received assistance which has been rated between moderate and moderate/low. The variation in the assistance received shows that there is a positive relationship between the level of assistance received and the degree of successful implementation and impact of the reforms.

Looking at the bundle, improvement in the quality of teachers is one of the most important aspects of the reform programme. Several strategies have been taken to achieve this. Provision of in-service training system known as cluster training for headmasters and teachers at their respective school premises once a month conducted by the local AUEO; use of leaflets prepared by experts as a resource material for the cluster training workshops; solution of day-to-day problems faced by the headmaster and the teachers in managing curricular, co-curricular and other activities; strengthening and improving the PTIs and other connected research and training organizations; other in-service training and orientation programmes for local administrators and supervisors (including the AUEO and the headmaster of each school); intensive supervision of classrooms and school; in-service training courses at the PTIs and NAPE to improve the teaching competencies of all primary teachers; and, above all, creation of a large number of AUEO posts in order to strengthen academic training and supervision, and free distribution of Teachers' guides have positively contributed to the qualitative improvement of the teachers. Provision has also been made to recruit the outstanding and experienced headmasters as AUEOs. This aspect of the programme has boosted the morale of primary school teachers who looked at it as a provision for their promotion. The services of resourceful headmasters have been utilized to train their colleagues in the same school as well as in the neighbouring schools.

The major implications that can be drawn are as follows:

(i) The most common factors found in all the schools are cluster training and supervision. These have been rated high in excellent and very good schools, and the quality of this training is instrumental for success. This should not only be continued but should be strengthened by putting more emphasis on pedagogical knowledge and skills of classroom teachers, making this assistance more need-responsive and locally adaptive.

(ii) Emphasis should be placed on the capacity building of head teachers and supervisors because the data show that the role of headmaster and supervisor is important for the successful implementation and impact of the reform in excellent schools.

(iii) The data from the excellent schools indicate that commitment of teachers and administrators leads to better implementation and impact of the reform. Provision of rewards for better teachers and supervisors should be considered and need-based research and studies should be undertaken on a small scale with the help of the interested and committed teachers, PTI and NAPE personnel and the findings used as feedback for the improvement of school activities.

(iv) A linkage between the local PTI and the cluster of schools should be set up and occasional seminars/workshops held on primary curriculum, problems and issues of primary education, role of headteacher and supervisors, mechanism of better supervision etc., with a view to improving the quality of the primary education system.

(v) Regular reporting on the school's progress is a common factor in all the schools, and has become a routine activity. For better monitoring and feedback a linkage mechanism should be developed between the related offices such as the Ministry of Education, planning cell, DPE, NCTB, BANBEIS, NAPE etc. A joint local and central staff development committee should also be considered.

(vi) The school displays as well as the cross-site displays show that cluster training is a strong common factor in all the schools. One headteacher of an excellent school arranges a weekly staff development class and all the headteachers of the excellent and very good schools supervise classroom teaching implying that there is a close relationship between academic training, guidance and better teacher and student performances. In this context, opportunity for the improvement of professional qualifications of teachers, headteachers, AUEO, UEO may be expanded. Exchange programmes between excellent and good schools, and rural and urban schools, should be designed with a view to improving the teaching-learning process, use and development of teaching aids, knowledge about children's behaviour etc. Books, journals and documents should be provided to the teachers to enhance their academic knowledge.

(vii) The data clearly show that there is close relationship between the physical facilities and the success of the reform. The school mapping should state accurately the requirements of the schools, and resources should be allocated on the basis of the identified needs.

(viii) Free textbooks have been regarded as a very effective factor for the enhanced participation rate of the poor, disadvantaged children in all three categories of schools. Some mechanism should be evolved to continue this help to the poor when the foreign donors withdraw grants for this component.

(ix) The excellent schools have received much more pressure for doing a better job than the other two groups. This has direct implications on the implementation and impact. Special characteristics and needs of weak schools should be focused on and discussed in the training programme of AUEOs and UEOs.

(x) In the interviews, some of the teachers expressed their hopes/needs for the schools in the form of an assistant headteacher to reduce the workloads that arise out of the school reporting, cluster training, continuous students' assessment and liberal promotion policy and to ensure security of school resources. The observation confirms that as the schools operate in two shifts, the teachers do not get any time off to do tasks other than teach. Provision of one assistant headteacher could be useful for improving primary schooling. Security of school resources could become the responsibility of the PTA and SMC.

(xi) The cross-site displays 1 and 2 (pages 288 and 290) show that extension of physical facilities is a common factor in all the schools with variation in degree of presence. It is one of the items under implementation success in cross-site display 1 and under resources in cross-site display 2. It has also been mentioned by all the teachers in school displays as essential to the schools. Regular repair and maintenance could be the duty of the community, answered through the SMC and PTA. One headteacher of an excellent school has created a school fund and extended a classroom out of that fund. This implies that the SMC might take initiative to create income generating programmes in schools so that the schools can take care of regular repair and extension of physical facilities on their own.

(xii) The data from excellent schools confirm that when the community is eager to receive school education, it becomes easier to implement the reform. Motivational programmes for the parents should be undertaken by the SMC, PTI, NAPE, DPE, NCTB, mass media, political parties, Social Welfare Ministry and Ministry of Education and Women's Affairs. The SMC should be given more authority than it enjoys at present.

(xiii) Success experience has a positive impact on successful implementation and impact to a large extent. It sharply differentiates the excellent schools from the other two categories. Provision should be made to distribute scholarships to high achievers at the end of the third grade and some scholarships should be fixed for girls only, to encourage girls' participation.

(xiv) The negative factors that emerged out of the findings of the study presented in the school displays and the interviewees' concerns expressed in the interviews both at the national and local level, include poverty of the community, lack of parental awareness, non-functioning of the SMC and PTA, undue interference of local primary teachers' association activists, appointment of too many female teachers who seek leave or transfer to urban areas, overcrowded classrooms, lack of community participation in the physical facilities of the schools, children leaving at midday meal time, natural calamities such as flooding. Schools can develop joint programmes for the parents on health, family planning, seeds and fertilizers etc., with the help of agencies working on these issues. Motivational programmes for the parents, SMC and PTA should be properly designed and introduced without further delay. The SMC should be delegated with more authority so that with the help of AUEO and UEO, it can take measures to reduce the undue interference by primary teacher activists.

In practice both male and female teachers seek transfer to urban areas which is true of all professions. Females seek transfers because they are keen to join their husbands who normally work in a city or urban area. This problem can be reduced by employing local women as teachers for the primary schools. Maternity leave is the right of all women, but in an overpopulated country, the female teachers should act as role models in their locality. Therefore population education and family planning might form a course in the in-service and pre-service training curricula of the primary teachers.

There is no doubt about the need for classroom space and benches if all children are to be allowed to attend school for a quality education. This should be taken up by the DPE as well as by the SMC of the locality. The children who leave at meal time will stay in the schools if some provision for school meals is arranged either by seeking community help or, for example, by shifting school times.

As floods have become a regular calamity causing considerable educational wastage, school sessions should be reorganized omitting July and August from the school calendar.

(xv) All the above factors are implicated in the process of institutionalization of the reform. The programmes suggested above should be adopted to further strengthen those factors which are working and to supplement the factors which are weak, and new mechanisms or strategies should be adopted to remove the factors which are adversely or negatively affecting implementation, impact and institutionalization of the reform.

REFERENCES

A tracer study of 100 assistant female teachers appointed under the UPE project, Draft report. (1984) BANBEIS in cooperation with UNESCO, Ministry of Education, Dhaka.

Ahmadullah, A.K., *et al.* (1984) Institute of Social Welfare and Research, Dhaka University. Newly constructed physical facilities and enrolment of children in primary schools (case study of three schools).

Akhter, S. (1987) Institute of Education and Research, University of Dhaka. A study report on evaluation of the academic aspects of the cluster training programme. Vol. 1: Summary of findings, conclusions and recommendations. UNDP-UNESCO illustrative study.

Akhter, S., *et al.* (1984) Institute of Education and Research, University of Dhaka. A study on the role of the assistant upazila education officers in academic supervision of the primary schools under UPE (IDA) project.

Alauddin, K. (1985) National Academy for Primary Education, Mymensingh. An illustrative study on the utilization of the learning materials under UPE (IDA) project (1980-1985), Bangladesh.

Balaghatullah, M. (1984) Human Resources Division, BIDS, Dhaka. Study report on supply and utilization of textbooks under the UPE (IDA) project.

Case study on supply, distribution and utilization of school furniture for UPE (IDA) project primary schools (1984). The Foundation for Research on Educational Planning and Development (FREPD), Bangladesh in cooperation with UPE, Dhaka.

Haque, S. (1990) For and on behalf of the National Task Force, Dhaka. Wastage in education.

Haque, S. and Jinnah, M.A. (eds) (1990) Synopses of three research studies on primary education, non-formal education, technical/vocational education. The Foundation for Research on Educational Planning and Development (FREPD) in cooperation with the Ford Foundation.

Haque, S., *et al.* (1987) UNDP/UNESCO Project BGD/85/018, Dhaka. Reform of primary teacher training in Bangladesh, Final Report and Recommendations, Part 1, Study on Teacher Effectiveness.

Huq M.N., Chowdhury, S.A. and Karim, M.R. (1984) National Institute of Educational Administration, Extension and Research (NIEAER), Dhanmondi, Dhaka. Illustrative study: UPE (IDA) project, training of ATEOs as primary school supervisors.

Latif, A.H. (1991) Institute of Education and Research, Dhaka University, IIEP, UNESCO. A case study on Bangladesh Rural Advancement Committees' Facilitation Assistance Programme on Education.

Miah, A., *et al.* (1984) Institute of Social Welfare and Research, Dhaka University. Situation of female enrolment and dropout in primary schools (a case study of three schools).

Qadir, S.A. (1984) Division of Human Resources. BIDS, UPE in Bangladesh. An enquiry into the issues of enrolment, dropout and repetition.

Rahman, S. (1986) Institute of Education and Research, Dhaka University. Reform of primary teacher training programme in Bangladesh. Supportive illustrative study 1 of 4, profile of primary school teachers.

Rahman, S. (1990) Institute of Education and Research in cooperation with UNICEF, Dhaka. A study on recurrent cluster training programme.

Study on non-formal education. Final report (1988) Universal Primary Education Project, Prokaushali Sangsad Limited, Dhaka, Bangladesh & UNESCO.

Part 3

International Analysis and Recommendations

Chapters 6 to 10 contain the international comparative part of this study. They describe and analyse how the central informants see the process and the outcomes of the reform. The reader has a chance to compare these perspectives with those of the local informants, by first reading Chapter 6, and then comparing this with the views presented in Chapter 7. The information from local informants — students, parents, teachers, heads and local administrators — is the basis for our country and cross-country analysis of outcomes in Chapter 7.

In Chapter 8 the data from all levels is used to explain the outcomes. The attempt is to link key factors in the process to defined outcomes, and to provide a picture of the dynamics of the change process. Chapter 9 revisits the 'Verspoor study' and compares findings; then looks closer at the nature of each key variable that may explain outcomes, looks at the role-implications of the findings and compares the change strategies that lead to success. Chapter 10 contains a discussion of the implications at the country-specific as well as at the international level.

Chapter 6

The Success Seen Centrally

So far we have seen how the reforms have been implemented in one typically successful school in each country (Chapter 2), and we have described the reform and the reform process for each of the three countries, as presented by the country HSI teams (Chapters 3 to 5). This chapter builds on the documentation of Chapters 3 to 5 and the interviews conducted at the central level. Its purpose is to look at how the central informants in the study describe and assess the implementation of the reform. It looks at the results of each study once again, goes back to the research questions (see Chapter 1), looks across the country data, and attempts to find some further clarity about the basic questions in this study. Are there interesting common trends or contrasts that might provide further insight into the question: 'Why have the schools succeeded in implementing and institutionalizing the reform?'

How do the central decision makers in each country (Country level study) see the reform, and how do they explain the success? The factors studied are specifically those that Verspoor found to be critical to the 'national level'.

COLOMBIA

The basis for the Colombian reform was much the same as that in Ethiopia and Bangladesh. The existing system did not take rural needs into account, the illiteracy rate was high (26.6 per cent in 1964), and only some 18.3 per cent of students who started primary schools in the rural areas ever finished five years of schooling.

The Escuela Nueva programme (EN programme) was built on an earlier concept, the 'Unitary school', first developed by UNESCO in 1962 and tested on a fairly limited scale in Colombia during the next two to three years. Through these experiments an important training programme took place that qualified a core group of Colombians as educators. Through personal contacts the experiment became known to the Ministry of Education, a visit by central decision-makers took place and a comprehensive training programme that qualified the future leaders of the programme was implemented. From then on (1968) the EN programme got some national attention and assistance from the USAID. A series of workshops on the EN concept was implemented to include practical tools, extensive teacher cooperation and skill training. Teachers received per diem compensation which boosted teacher morale, and teacher commitment was developed. Gradually during the 1970s the EN programme expanded and got more support, still functioning as a local/regional project.

However, it was still a regional, and relatively speaking, small-scale experiment (although by 1982 some 2000 schools were involved!). From 1982 onwards, with evaluation reports and key people supporting it, the EN programme got 'official National status' and it expanded very rapidly. During the 1980s as many as 15,000 new schools joined, and the programme enjoyed financial and professional assistance (e.g. from the World Bank).

How do central decision-makers assess implementation success?

Central informants in the Colombian study see the following outcomes of the EN programme:

1. Stability and commitment. A long and difficult path towards national legitimation of the EN programme has succeeded, and thereby provided a chance to renew rural education in the country. At present there are stable, committed individuals and groups centrally and regionally who support the EN programme and help to maintain it. It is on its way towards institutionalization. These groups 'help to overcome opposition', in a country that unlike Ethiopia, is not easily governed by proclamations.

2. Economic security. The EN programme is today enjoying financial support from the government, many private organizations in Colombia and international organizations. It can base its planning on a healthy economy, again an important aspect of institutionalization.

3. Innovations in teacher training. The successful EN training programme has resulted in new forms of teacher training. These forms are gradually being used in ordinary pre-service training programmes throughout the country, and have a major long term impact on the quality of primary education in general.

4. Local curriculum adaptations. The EN programme has helped teachers to understand the needs for locally adapted curriculum and materials. It has created new norms, gradually changing the role of the teacher from an 'implementer' to a 'developer'. This is seen as part of teacher professionalization, an important factor to improve the quality of schooling.

In their responses, the central informants took the success of the EN programme itself for granted. What was mentioned was its stability, institutionalization and spin-offs within the Colombian system of education. It may be a natural response since the question (in their minds) has not been the quality and impact of the EN programme, but the issue of acceptance and legitimation at the national level.

What country level factors have accounted for the success?[1]

The data are somewhat unclear on this point; however, the existing data has been interpreted in the following way:

1. Assistance. Mainly local training, extensive and skill-oriented, with systematic guides and learning materials associated with the training programme, is the most important form of assistance. This is a core aspect of the programme and is seen as critical for success. It has been reduced from 30 days to 12 to 15 days in total, which gives cause for concern.

2. Responsive adaptation and user involvement. These aspects are critical for the professionalization of the teacher, a core concept in the EN programme. Teachers are encouraged to create, adapt and develop their own additional materials and to share their work and experiences. These factors contribute to user commitment, which is seen as a factor developed through user involvement.

3. Resource delivery. The programme would not have survived without independent financing, from national and local groups and from international donor agencies (including the USAID and the World Bank). It is a key factor in the 'success story'.

4. Closeness to implementation. In most cases the EN experts stayed close to the teachers and the schools, and followed up and assisted teachers. How the follow-up was done, how extensive it was and what quality it had depended mainly on the regional organization of the EN programme.

5. Protection from environmental turbulence. The move to the Ministry and the acceptance of the EN programme as a national programme is seen as a way of protecting the programme and securing stable financing for it. The move helped the programme to gain economic support (e.g. through a World Bank-sponsored programme), and to get the needed professional support. It found a 'home' in the division of Experimental Pilot Centres of the Ministry of Education. For a programme to become national and to be institutionalized, it needs not only recognition, but legal, economic and professional support. Moreover, it needs to be 'positioned' in the hierarchy in such a way that it can reach its objectives.

6. Curriculum development and availability of materials. The EN programme is based on a structured curriculum and materials for individualization and group work. The teacher needs training to master the 'new system'; it is a radical departure from traditional teaching. The materials component is, therefore, seen as critical.

7. Decisions supporting institutionalization. The recent move to the

---

[1] 'Factors' refer to the factors reported in display 2A, see Appendix 6, page 348.

division of Experimental Pilot Centres in the Ministry of Education is seen as critical for the quality of the programme. This will enable the programme to gain a regular status and the necessary foundation for institutionalization. At the same time the control is moved from the central core group to regional groups. There is fear that this may reduce the impact (e.g. training with less competent and committed trainers). Also the system probably cannot pay for the full-scale training programme. Already it is cut down from a total of 30 training days to a total of 12 to 15 days.

8. Other factors. As shown in Table A (page 171), several factors in the interpretive model are not applicable for the Colombia case. As far as 'strategic matching' is concerned, it probably belonged to the group called 'permanent pilot' for a long time, and when accepted by the national authorities moved to what may be called 'incremental expansion' (at a very rapid speed!). In fact without the adoption of the EN programme by the central authorities it may have stayed as a 'permanent pilot'.

The EN programme faces many challenges in the years ahead. Recent research reports indicate that the central organization is inadequate, and that the regional organizations differ widely. This is the opposite of the Ethiopian system, with its strength and weaknesses. While Ethiopia has a centrally planned systematic administrative and professional support structure, the Colombian case is grown from local groups and has local variation in local organizational structure.

Linkage between country, district and school levels

The concept of 'linkage' is basically taken from a context where the central level initiates a reform, has to go through several layers of administration, and finally is able to communicate with schools. The assumption is that the better these linkages, the more chances there are for successful implementation.

This concept does not work well in the Colombian project. It was not initiated from a central place, and did not have to go through various levels to reach the school. It actually started in the school, or rather it started with an engaged group of educators close to schools. The 'linkage' issue, or the question of how the 'message' could travel through the system and finally result in institutionalization, is a very interesting story, but one difficult to verify fully from the data in the study. (Data from display 2B (p. 351), mainly school level data.) The following 'linkage-factors' are seen:

1. Assistance. Training played a key role, it gave the opportunity for a free flow of information, through two-way communication between the initiators and the teachers. The extensive training periods and the networks developed played a critical 'linkage function' in the programme. It was basically a relatively small group of well trained professionals who trusted each other and who influenced the

development of the programme through training and coaching.

2. Administrative role. Administrators played a minor role in the first few years. Some regional networks were developed among administrators, EN experts and teachers. These were important in terms of linkage. Later, linkages to the ministry became important.
3. Commitment. This is a key notion in the EN programme. The initiators and the core group 'transmit' commitment through role-modelling, enthusiasm and motivation (in particular through the training programmes). Success in the classroom 'transmitted' enthusiasm to students and parents.
4. Received pressure. This played a minimal role. During the first years, the programme was mainly seen as a 'volunteer' project, the regional organization was often ad hoc and varied considerably from place to place.
5. Received resources. The key resource is teaching/learning materials which usually reached the classroom. This material went a long way towards helping the teacher to follow the instructional goals and values of the EN programme. Now the resources are distributed from the central level (partly financed through external donors) to the schools.
6. Success experiences. Training results led to enthusiasm. Results were often seen by both teachers and parents. This created further motivation and interest for the programme.
7. Empowerment and engagement. See comments on 'commitment' above. Teachers have the key role in success and are acknowledged for it. Teachers feel real responsibility. The 'linkage' occurs through the transmission of new concepts and a new teacher role.
8. Local adaptation. This is an important concept in the EN programme, although the teaching-learning system is fairly rigidly defined. The teacher can still adapt and develop his or her own materials and find local solutions.
9. Community support. Parent participation is critical. The linkage here is from classroom success experienced by the students and the teacher, transmitted to the parents who develop further motivation and interest for the programme and the school.

If 'linkage' is interpreted as being the processes by which an 'innovation message' is carried through the system, with the aim of national dissemination, then this would probably best describe the Colombian process.

Reform strategies in Colombia — a summary

The very term 'reform strategy' seems rather inappropriate in the EN programme context. There was no 'grand plan' as in Ethiopia; it was mainly a pedagogical concept and the initiators had no idea or ambition that the programme would become a national programme. It was a strange mixture of local initiative and international developments (UNESCO). It was also based on some real needs, as in Ethiopia. However, it worked its way quite differently through the system, from bottom up.

1. Local experiments with demonstrated classroom impact. The EN programme was based on some fundamental problems in rural education that the national system had not resolved. With ideas from local groups and based on an international initiative, a local core group started experimentation, tried some fundamental new approaches to rural education, and could demonstrate success. It was basically a 'grassroot movement', with strong professional support (e.g. from a university) and support from international organizations. Since the project had no established national role, the leaders could not speak with formal authority. The alternative was professional influence that could best be established through demonstrated 'success experiences'.

2. Strong project leadership. The project developed as a cooperative effort among a small group of highly qualified and committed individuals, who had the motivation, the skills and the strength to stay on and work themselves (literally) into the system into strategically placed roles. They played the key 'administrative role' over a long period, and they stayed close to the schools.

3. Professionalization as the main route to success. Through the development of a core team and a series of local and national workshops for teachers (a total of 30 days of skill workshops), an in-service training programme emerged and teachers were given a full and responsible role that led to the professionalization of the rural teacher. This in turn led to commitment.

4. International and professional alliances. This (probably) was done for several reasons; however, it is assumed that the 'free market system' in the early stages of the EN programme placed EN as one of several competing innovations for rural education. Strong international and professional alliances gave extra legitimation and power to the programme.

5. Influence through personal networks. The way from a local experiment to a national programme was long and cumbersome. This was partly achieved through the increasing number of schools and individuals joining. More critical were probably the personal links between the project director and the Minister of Education, and the gradual 'penetration' of EN people into central and regional organizations. It was a cumbersome process, step by step, over more than 20 years!

In summary, the EN programme in Colombia is an example of a 'bottom up' strategy for educational reform that succeeded. (A model of the reform process is presented in Chapter 8, page 199.)

ETHIOPIA

Colombia, Ethiopia and Bangladesh have all tried to reach the classroom and influence the learning outcomes; however, they have done it in very different ways. The Ethiopian primary education reform is a system-reform, and, therefore, has a number of components (see Chapter 4, pp. 66 to 119). Some of these have been underway for more than 15 years, and others for a shorter period (see display 1, Chapter 4, page 78). It was a major initiative by the new Marxist/Leninist-inspired government that came into power in 1974. Although the former government had made a critical review of primary education in 1971/72, describing the system as elitist, too academic, irrelevant and not meeting the needs of the rural population, it was with the new regime in 1974 that power and energy was first put behind the reform movement. With the slogan 'Ethiopia first', and a large national seminar that outlined three principles:

- education for production
- education for scientific research
- education for political consciousness

the reform really started (for details about the reform, see Chapter 4, pp. 71 to 78).

How do central decision-makers assess implementation success?

Overall the central level informants feel that most of the components have been put into place. There is a feeling of success, that the country has accomplished something significant and that the plan really works. At central, regional and district level the Ministry of Education has developed a capacity for initiating, planning, developing, implementing and monitoring innovative programmes. The system has developed an 'innovation capability'. This is seen as a major accomplishment.

At the same time it is documented that only 34 per cent of the primary school age population attend primary schools (Educational Statistics, 1989). The drop-out rate and the repeating rate is serious (particularly for girls). National evaluation studies also show that the achievement results are less satisfying, and that the investments do not increase at the same speed as the enrolment does.

What country level factors have accounted for the success?

It is unclear from the data how the central informants interpret the various decisions, events and factors in terms of their implications for the reform. It is also a very comprehensive reform effort over a long period of time, and it is hard to separate the issues many years later. We have found the following explanations, as expressed by the central informants ('Factors' from display 2A are given in parentheses, see also Chapter 4, page 87):

1. Political stability throughout the reform period is a dominant contextual variable. The reform studied is in a country that for more than 15 years has been governed by the same party (and mostly the same people). Although the country has been going through civil wars and hunger catastrophes, the same government has remained (until 1991). This has allowed, not only for decisions to be followed up, but also for long range planning. It has also allowed for a gradual process of developing commitment ('building of commitment'). In such a situation, all main decisions, from the outset, have been aimed at *institutionalization* ('decisions supporting institutionalization').

2. Strength of national organizations. This is seen as a factor that has contributed significantly to the reform. A well developed 'infrastructure', a rational 'division of labour' and qualified staff (gradually developed on the job) are seen as main characteristics. Because of the political stability, and the 'drive' that supports the reform, the layers of administration have developed a competence that is unusual. The Ethiopian system of educational administration has an unusually qualified core staff ('capacity building of national organizations'). These national organizations have an impressive record of curriculum development, resources for building programme, the development and distribution of materials (resource delivery), and the development of policy guidelines and laws (legal regulation).

3. Availability and quality of materials. In addition to these qualitative improvements at the central level producing improved curricula and learning materials, the Ethiopian system also provides a local capability. The district office has its own 'pedagogical centre' (APC) that develops local materials, uses teacher ideas and products, gathers teachers for practical materials development workshops, and trains the SPC director for his/her role (school-based materials development). The schools have regular sessions with teachers and students developing their own classroom materials. This system is seen as both unique and important and it works, according to central informants. However, the demand is much higher than the supply.

4. Pressure for good implementation is another factor that has contributed. It has been clear, from the outset, what the expectations are; schools have been reminded, expected to adopt and deliver and have been asked to report regularly. This system of monitoring is seen as critical by central decision-makers ('monitoring and control').

5. System management has been critical. Very close communication among all levels of management of the system, regular management meetings, seminars and conferences, and clear decision-rules have been part of 'system-management' (to include 'effective communication'). Decisions have been systematically analysed, discussed and executed. 'Institutionalization' has been the objective from the start.

6. Staff development ('Assistance') in different forms, in particular through the district-level APC and the school-level SPC have contributed significantly to the success. The role played by the headmaster and the teachers is also significant. They participate in in-service training; however, they learn together on the job, working together to implement the reform. Although demand is larger than supply, the system of staff development is seen as unique and important.

7. Responsive adaptation is seen as an important part of the system. Gradually the schools have received more power, as have the district offices. The central interviews show that this aspect of the reform in the later years is seen as a value in its own right (e.g. in relationship to ethnic minorities). It is less a strategic issue (getting support for the reform) than a valuable aspect of the reform itself.

The Ethiopian primary education reform is a comprehensive and systematic national development programme with a large number of factors contributing to implementation and institutionalization. However, there are also some 'weak factors' and the following were mentioned by central informants:

1. Resources have not been adequate, in fact the per student level of financing has been declining, and many classes are overcrowded, leaving little hope that the qualitative objectives can be met. If resources are not allocated *expansion* of the system would cause severe problems.

2. Closeness to implementation. This has happened through the administrative rules and regulations; however, supervision is mainly administrative. Closeness to the classroom is partly missing, but maintained by the APC in many districts.

3. User involvement. Here again, some teachers are involved, but the large majority are seen as 'implementers' of the reform.

4. Protection from turbulence. Ethiopia has been through many 'national campaigns'. These are political campaigns involving masses of people for a given cause. Teachers were often seen as important participants in these activities. Teachers have only partly been 'protected'; therefore, classroom work has been disturbed.

5. Strategic matching is a concept introduced by Verspoor (World Bank, 1988). The Ethiopian situation (in the context of the primary education project) was stable (politically and economically), and the innovation must be considered ambitious and innovative. In Verspoor's definition the effective change strategy would be 'incremental expansion' (using a 'small scale experiment' approach and gradually increasing the number of schools). The Ethiopians did not use the 'incremental expansion' strategy (except for a fairly minor project in the last four to five years), but decided to go nation-wide as soon as possible, with the entire bundle. Since this,

for practical reasons, is not really possible, the reform faced some tough times, and had to 'learn from each other's own trials and errors and adapted over time'.

Linkage between country, district and school level

One part of the study concerns the possible linkages between the various levels of the system, e.g. how do intentions from the central level 'communicate' within the system? The data here are collected from all these levels within our sample of school districts and schools, as well as from the central level. For Ethiopia the following is reported:

1. Assistance is a key factor in the process of linking the various levels of the system. Central authorities arrange a yearly education conference, the districts subsequently organize district seminars, the APC implements workshops of various kinds and the school-based SPCs have on-going collegial training sessions on various aspects of the reform. It is seen as a very strong linkage factor.

2. The administrative role is also a key variable in linkage. It is a strict regime, administrators are both well trained and informed and are expected to follow-up. Schools are visited regularly and send annual plans and quarterly reports on progress. Although several schools report that the visits by the district officer are mainly concerned with administrative matters (and seen as pedagogically ineffective), people from the APC, especially, try to assist teachers professionally. The main impression, though, is that the administrators of the system are there to communicate the 'message', see to it that schools perform and report back.

3. Commitment in the sample schools is reported to be high, but it is unclear what the central informants feel about this factor. It could be a result of local and organizational factors only, or a matter of 'linkage', i.e. that commitment to the reform somehow is communicated through the system, for example by role-models, through training, etc.

4. Received pressure is no doubt a major factor, felt at the district level and at the school level and communicated through the administrative ladder (as described above). Expectations are high, and performance expected. Pressure is placed on schools from both national and district administrators as well as from parents in the school management committee.

5. Empowerment is to some degree achieved and is basically a result of the decentralization process. Decentralization is clearly a relative matter, and even a fairly limited degree of local power may be seen as very positive and create a feeling of ownership and empowerment. This is certainly true for most of the sample schools, and is also expressed by the central informants. The system has clearly defined what parents can do, what teachers can do and what the *headmaster*

can do and influence. In total it is a shared responsibility at the school level, which gives the key actors a role to play.

6. Local adaptation is encouraged through the system, although it is limited and controlled (e.g. local social science curriculum for grades 1 to 3). In particular parent participation may be an increasingly important factor in the decentralization process that would allow for more local control of schools. It is unclear how the 'linkage'-effect is achieved, but it does encourage exchanges among schools.

Reform strategies in Ethiopia — a summary

The new government was, as the former, a very centralized Government. It was also very systematic in its efforts, and it laid down a 'grand plan' that was as comprehensive as could be imagined. Reading the data from the 'central interviews', the reform strategy is seen basically as the following:

1. All aspects of the reform served national objectives. These objectives were ideologically defined, but were generally acceptable for the large majority of the people (with some exceptions, e.g. 'labour education'). The objectives were clear, centrally defined and communicated effectively throughout the system. The project enjoyed political stability over more than 15 years, a factor that enabled political objectives to be realized.

2. Central authorities gave legitimation and support. The reform was a giant undertaking, took both quantitative (e.g. expansion) and qualitative aspects into account, and therefore was dependent on large-scale physical resources (e.g. for a comprehensive building programme, and the development of textbooks, new teaching-learning materials, etc.), new attitudes, knowledge and skills throughout the system that would support the new primary school. To a large extent this was, as expressed by the central informants, actually accomplished, with some exceptions (see below).

3. Central authorities built a system of reform. Such a mammoth undertaking would probably not succeed without a large scale investment in the 'educational infrastructure'. A series of new central institutions were established to 'produce and deliver' the reform components. All regional and local educational authorities were strengthened, and new structures were also established at the regional and local level (e.g. the 'pedagogical centres' at the district level (APC) and at the school level (SPC)). To 'reach out', the authorities needed a system where the information could flow both ways. The development of the 'educational infrastructure' is seen by the central informants as a key component of the strategy (and actually as a major outcome as well).

4. Central authorities maintained control. The Ethiopian government built a 'strict regime', with a highly qualified administration. Not only were most important decisions taken through government

declarations, but all schools, headmasters and teachers were expected to do exactly what was proclaimed. The syllabus was given, rules and regulations were centrally decided, and all critical elements developed and distributed by central authorities. Schools were given freedom to implement the reform, with some room for local adaptations (e.g. the social science curriculum for grades 1 to 3, see below). Control was accomplished through a system of educational administration, with regular inspection (not very effective) and through quarterly school reports that each school had to submit and which the inspectorate analysed.

5. An effective system of communication. The system is partly built on a strict set of administrative rules and procedures. As important is the regular contacts that administrators have with each other and with headmasters and (sometimes) teachers. The local APC seminars play an important communication function at the local level, and the yearly national education conference plays an important 'hearing-function' at the country level. The leaders of the educational system met to exchange views, to provide feedback to the government and to be given new directives.

6. An effective system of national and local training and support. The system has provided an on-going and stable support structure where training plays a key role. The yearly education conference is an important forum for educational discussions. Ideas from this conference are 'carried down the system'. The APC and SPC seminars are 'two-way' seminars where teachers' ideas are used, further developed, shared and 'disseminated'.

7. Local adaptation as a strategic alliance. There could be many reasons for potential failures. Aspects of the reform might be opposed by local groups (e.g. due to ideological differences), the sheer complexities of the reform could cause serious problems (e.g. late arrival of critical materials), the system could break down because of a lack of necessary resources, the system could be so popular that the expansion could kill the pedagogical intentions. There were (and are) many potential problems. The government tried to develop ownership of the reform ideas through active community participation (e.g. in the management committee), and thereby compensate for potential implementation problems (e.g. local income generation when central resources were inadequate).

8. Decentralization as a productivity measure. Gradually central authorities have given regional, local and institutional leadership more authority (e.g. transfer of teachers, yearly school plans, etc.). Also the yearly education conference is no longer a one-way information exercise, but a two-way exchange of views. It is done, mostly because at this stage of institutionalization, broad local competence in decision-making is vital for the further stabilization and development of the reform.

In summary, this is a centrally initiated, developed and managed reform, systematically implemented with considerable administrative pressure, as well as with economic and professional support. It was based upon real needs, ideologically motivated and professionally founded.

BANGLADESH

The primary education project in Bangladesh is a reform effort that is different from both the Colombian and the Ethiopian projects. There are, however, similarities to both these projects. The needs of rural children, the need to provide basic education for all children, the need to improve the quality of rural education, reduce drop-out and raise standards were also important factors in Bangladesh in the early 1970s, and became an important agenda for the new nation.

Universal primary education (UPE) was part of the second and third five-year development plans. In fact in the second plan as much as 46 per cent of the development budget was allocated to UPE (1980 to 1985), and IDA contributed as much as 80 per cent of the project costs. The Bangladesh project has been called 'mildly innovative' by the Bangladesh HSI team. In contrast to the Colombian project that is very radical in its approach to instruction, and to the Ethiopian project that systematically tries to alter most components of the delivery system as well as the teaching-learning process, the Bangladesh project is basically an effort to improve what already exists, and complement it to enhance its productivity.

What country level factors have accounted for the success?

The central informants in Bangladesh provide the following picture:

1. Universal primary education (UPE) as a top priority throughout the entire project period. In spite of government changes, UPE has enjoyed top priority, resources for UPE have been 'protected', and this has contributed to higher motivation and enthusiasm for the reform ('protection from environmental turbulence', and 'resource allocation'). In a country like Bangladesh with very limited resources, and a number of crises and problems, this is not a small achievement!

2. Strength of national organizations. The establishment of more effective central machinery to plan, develop and implement the reform is the most important aspect. A comprehensive 'project related training' (PRT) component helped to qualify staff for the project ('capacity building'). This has, as far as the central informants see it, resulted in a more regular delivery of materials, as well as higher quality products (partly to include 'availability and quality of materials').

3. Strategic matching. In spite of political turbulence at the national level, the local political situation has been fairly stable. The changes introduced have been modest — a mildly innovative reform, as stated

by the HSI team. It is a gradual development process over a long period of time or 'progressive innovation' in Verspoor's terminology. In practice this means that a number of successive changes have been introduced, each rather modest in itself, whose cumulative effect over time can result in considerable change.

4. Pressure for good implementation. The Bangladesh case is one of fairly strict administrative rule. The central administrators put pressure on the district administrators, who in turn put pressure on the local people (e.g. AUEO). This is done during inspection visits; however, the main mechanism is the regular reports from schools ('monitoring and control'), and the meetings and training sessions among the AUEO and the headmaster and teachers.

5. Curriculum development. The Ministry of Education established a new organization, named NCTB, to carry out the development of the new curriculum. Well trained people and external funds added to the quality of the process. Textbooks were developed centrally.

6. Closeness to implementation. The newly established AUEO that combines supervision with training, and communicates with the administrative levels above, is a key to the reform and a 'factor' that has contributed to the success. The introduction of the AUEO is a major improvement of the administrative system. He or she is supposed to supervise his cluster of schools and have regular visits and training sessions with each school (to include 'effective communication', and partly 'infrastructure development').

7. Decisions supporting institutionalization. It was clear from the outset that the UPE project would be institutionalized. All major decisions, therefore, had this assumption 'built in' (at least from 1985).

8. Assistance. Training is also seen by central informants as a key factor. This was first organized as project related training (PRT) for key decision-makers, and then in the form of 'cluster training', with heads and teachers of about 20 to 25 schools, led by the AUEO. He or she had regular supervisory responsibilities and conducted local training sessions for teachers in each school once a month.

Linkages in the Bangladesh project

As stated above, the Bangladesh project is a centralized project. Linkages are therefore primarily top-down. The central level decides and 'informs' or 'instructs' lower levels to implement the decisions. The following elements characterize the system of linkage:

1. Policies and guidelines are decided by the Ministry of Education, and Directorate of Primary Education. The Ministry also provides the funds.
2. The Directorate implements the decisions through the hierarchy of divisional/district, upazila offices. The curriculum unit of NCTB

develops curriculum and materials, and disseminates these through seminars, workshops, PTIs, NAPE. Educational supervisors and teachers are involved in these workshops.

3. The district puts considerable pressure to maximize implementation results.
4. The upazila education officer works with the AUEO to implement the decisions, the AUEO conducts training sessions and both of them supervise the schools.
5. The AUEO plays a key role in providing academic training to the teachers and communicating from the field through the hierarchy described above. Schools also submit regular monthly reports to the AUEO and UEO.

Several central informants feel that the system is ineffective, that the 'supervision' is 'more fault-finding than fact-finding', and that it does not serve any useful purpose.

Other aspects of the Bangladesh 'linkage-system' as seen by central informants include:

1. Assistance. In particular the cluster training conducted monthly by the AUEO helps to bridge the gap between central decisions and local implementations.
2. Administrative role. The AUEO, with responsibility for the supervision of 20 to 25 schools, plays an important communication function in the system.
3. Commitment. Through the many regular meetings and workshops a positive cooperative climate develops that gradually builds commitment.
4. Received pressure. Through the administrative system of information and control, the schools know that their activities are known. Pressure sometimes develops some strange behaviour, as for example, when the attendance register is inflated to produce 'positive results'! Pressure is received and felt.

The report also suggests several negative 'linkage factors':

The 'resources received' are seen as inadequate; decentralization is done without giving the means to do it (and therefore there is little 'empowerment'); there is no 'Local adaptation', therefore local culture and needs are seldom taken into account; and 'community support' is decided centrally, though it is very limited in the field. The system is highly centralized and has a limited ability to free up local motivation and resources.

Reform strategies in Bangladesh — a summary

In Bangladesh the UPE project became a national commitment, and had top priority throughout the entire period (1980 to 1991) as seen by central informants. Based on the central data available, the following reform strategy is observed:

1. All aspects of the reform are controlled centrally. The Ministry of Education and the Directorate of Education had all power, took all policy decisions, worked out the necessary guidelines, regulations, curriculum and materials, and instructed the next level on how to interpret and manage the reform. As in Ethiopia, the central authorities gave the project legitimation and support (assisted by external donors).

2. Central authorities strengthen the administrative system. The project needed additional resources, a stronger administration (at all levels), additional competence and modified rules of behaviour. An important aspect of the reform strategy was to build a more modern management system to implement the reform. Although it has some similarities to the Ethiopian model, it is less innovative, introduces fewer role changes and does not really build a new concept of management, with the possible exception of the AUEO.

3. Implementation happens through regular monitoring and control. This is quite similar to the Ethiopian model. The various levels of management have a monitoring and reporting role. The Bangladesh system introduces a new role, the assistant-upazila education officer (AUEO) that is close to the schools (has about 20 to 25 schools for supervision), and plays an important role as a 'communicator' in the project.

4. Implementation is enabled through information and training. Again the AUEO plays an important role through the so-called 'cluster training' system, in which teachers and heads in their small local school receive training and information regularly. One important effect of these regular meetings, seminars and training sessions is that it builds a 'community of professionals', and an informal system of support is developed.

The Bangladesh reform is also different from the Ethiopian reform in several ways. It does not have the same systematic capacity building; it has a weaker resource base; and most importantly, it has not built a system that encourages local participation and adaptation. It does not lead to empowerment; it is a top-down system that does not build local strength.

THE COUNTRY LEVEL FACTORS — A SUMMARY AND COMPARATIVE NOTE

Table A provides a summary picture of the country level factors selected for the study, and that may have accounted for the success of the reform (as assessed by country level informants). The information is taken from Display 2A (page 348), where all 'factors' are assessed, describing the nature of the variable in each concrete setting ('illustrative indicators') and a rating is given.

Table A What country level factors have contributed to the success of the reform?

Colombia

Factor	Impact	
Strength of national organizations	NA	Local and regional focus
Capacity building of national organizations	MLI	Small scale due to budgetary constraints
Building of commitment	HI	High commitment by initiators and core group. High teacher commitment, due to active role and success experiences
Strategic matching	NA	First 'permanent pilot', then 'incremental expansion'
Legal regulation	NA	
Decision-making	HMI	Decision-making clear — close relation between designers and local level
Pressure for good implementation	MI	Fairly relaxed. Dependent on regional organization
Curriculum development	HI	Strong part of design. Guide. Individual material. Completely new
Division of labour	MI	Central and local organization strong. Some regions weak
Infrastructural development	MI	Created experimental centres and demonstration schools
Availability and quality of materials	HMI	Mostly available. Regional differences
Resource allocation	HI	Independent funding. National and international
Resource delivery	HI	
Closeness to implementation	HMI	EN experts follow-up. Dependent on regional implementation organization
Effective communication	MI	Good personal networks. Unclear what the relationships are to regional and central administration
Responsive adaptation	HI	Teachers encouraged to produce own materials
User involvement	HI	Active role. Teacher in charge. Professional
Protection from environmental turbulence	MI	Early financial problems. Now national budget
Decisions supporting institutionalization	MI	Decision to 'nationalize' programme and central funding
Assistance	HI	Local, intensive skill-oriented work
Monitoring and control	MI	Fairly relaxed. Dependent on local organization
Other (political stability)	HI	Stable political and economic environment
Other (external donor)	HI	Active involvement of several donors, including the World Bank

Key: HI — high impact; HMI — high/medium impact; MI — medium impact; MLI — medium/low impact; LI — low impact; NA — not answered.

Ethiopia

Factor	Impact	
Strength of national organizations	HI	Ministry of Education, curriculum development, materials production and distribution, department planning
Capacity building of national organizations	HI	Staff development, fellowships, donor assistance, experts
Building of commitment	HMI	Gradual development over project period
Strategic matching	NA	Nation-wide from start
Legal regulation	HI	Series laws/proclamations/regulations
Decision-making	HI	Clear, central rules, consistency throughout
Pressure for good implementation	HI	Clear, specific expectations, inspections, reports
Curriculum development	HI	National curriculum development, local adaptation, APC
Division of labour	HI	Very effective good relations at national/district/school level
Infrastructural development	HI	National organization, strengthen district, APC, SPC
Availability and quality of materials	HI	Materials production and distribution agency, APC, SPC
Resource allocation	MI	Inadequate. Expansion too rapid
Resource delivery	HMI	Adequate, good distribution
Closeness to implementation	MI	Mostly administrative. APC pedagogical relations
Effective communication	HMI	Regular supervision and training. Quarterly reports
Responsive adaptation	HMI	Local curriculum development. Time-scheduled adaptation. Labour education
User involvement	MI	Fairly active community involvement in SMC and contributions
Protection from environmental turbulence	MLI	Often disturbed by 'national campaigns'
Decisions supporting institutionalization	HMI	Most decisions have 'institutionalization' in mind. Reform period 15 years
Assistance	HI	National conference, local district APC, school-based SPC
Monitoring and control	HI	System of quarterly reporting and regular supervision
Other (political stability)	HI	Political support, high priority over 15 years
Other (external donor)	HMI	Major contribution, relatively modest compared to national investment

Key: HI — high impact; HMI — high/medium impact; MI — medium impact; MLI — medium/low impact; LI — low impact; NA — not answered.

Bangladesh

Factor	Impact	
Strength of national organizations	HI	Major improvement of Ministry of Education, Directorate, curriculum development and materials development and distribution
Capacity building of national organizations	HMI	Comprehensive project-related training, international studies, management training
Building of commitment	MI	Variation — high headmaster and AUEO commitment
Strategic matching	MI	Progressive innovation, from pilot to nationwide
Legal regulation	HI	Regulation, Act
Decision-making	MI	Decentralization to upazila level and AUEO
Pressure for good implementation	HI	Administration plays key role in planning, implementation and monitoring. High expectations. Pressure on lower levels
Curriculum development	HI	Strong. New curriculum, effectively developed
Division of labour	MI	Responsibilities at central and regional level
Infrastructural development	HMI	Strengthened/new national organization. New local role (AUEO)
Availability and quality of materials	HMI	Improved quality of textbooks and learning materials. Reliable delivery
Resource allocation	MI	Inadequate — does not match enrolment increases
Resource delivery	HMI	Regular, reliable distribution of materials
Closeness to implementation	HI	AUEO supervision and seminars play key role
Effective communication	HI	AUEO plays important role, with regular visits to about 21 schools. Seminars with heads/teachers each month
Responsive adaptation	LI	No room for adaptation
User involvement	MLI	Very limited teacher, parent and community involvement in shaping reform
Protection from environmental turbulence	HI	Resources have been 'protected' throughout the reform. Important for motivation
Decisions supporting institutionalization	HI	Assumption built in from start (1985)
Assistance	HI	PRT for key decision-makers. Cluster training regularly for heads and teachers
Monitoring and control	HI	Regular school reports. Inspection. Regular supervision by AUEO
Other (political stability)	HMI	High political support to UPE through entire period
Other (external donor)	HI	Dominant role by IDA (80 per cent). Critical for size of programme

Key: HI — high impact; HMI — high/medium impact; MI — medium impact; MLI — medium/low impact; LI — low impact; NA — not answered.

Colombia

The summary picture for the Colombian project is given in Table A (page 171). It is not seen as strong at the national level, in fact much of the information about this level (in terms of what factors may have accounted for success) is missing. What has played a key role is resources from donors (partly true also for Ethiopia).

The strength of the EN programme is in the classroom and close to the classroom. The role of the teacher — his or her involvement, commitment and professionalization — is a key to success. Also, as for Ethiopia new and better teaching-learning materials play an important role. The locally available training programme is skill-oriented and quite essential for implementation success.

The administrative role is unclear in the EN programme. It is highly dependent on the regional organization and therefore varies greatly. Usually EN experts follow up, when needed. However, it depends on the region. The EN programme does not have its origin in the government (as for the Ethiopian reform). It started locally and has subsequently grown throughout the entire system. In contrast to the Ethiopian system it has not 'built a system of reform', it is relatively weak on 'infrastructure', division of labour and other 'system-factors'.

Ethiopia

This is a very comprehensive reform effort. According to the central informants a number of factors may have contributed. The Ethiopian reform is strong in all aspects related directly to the central level (e.g. 'capacity building of national organizations'). It maintains strength throughout the administrative system, and stays close to the reform intentions through a systematic management effort. The only perceived weakness at this level has to do with the amount of resources available (as the enrolment grows). The Ethiopian support system (e.g. the local APC and the SPC) is also seen as strong, in fact in combination with a strong management and reporting system, it seems to be a very strong combined factor.

The relative weaknesses (apart from the resource needs) in the Ethiopian system, seen from the central level, seem to be related to local school factors, e.g. user involvement, protection from environmental turbulence, closeness to implementation and commitment.

Bangladesh

The Bangladesh project is built around a national initiative and administered in a highly centralistic way. Its strengths seem to be political consensus for a high UPE priority, protection of resources, a strong national organization, a strengthened administrative structure and competence, and a new administrative and professional role, the so-called AUEO at the local level. Although the AUEO is locally placed and has the responsibility for about 20 to 25 schools, he or she is there to communicate the central message and to report back. His or her main work is regular supervision and rendering 'cluster training' to the teachers. The central informants find the AUEO one of the very strong factors of the system.

The Bangladesh project has few strong factors accounting for success at the classroom level, and the local level. Commitment, user involvement and local adaptation are fairly 'weak factors', as far as contributing to success (as interpreted by the central informants). The Bangladesh project is very large, it is somewhat modest in its innovations and it builds on the assumption of gradual improvements. Its strengths as seen by central informants are an improved administrative structure, management competence and a new innovative role — the AUEO, with a particular emphasis on the local training component, the cluster training.

The three countries — a factor comparison

This chapter only deals with the information from central informants. 'Strengths and weaknesses' of these countries are compared based on this information; however, conclusions can only be drawn using information from all levels (see Chapters 7 to 9). Because one factor is seen by central informants as 'strong', it does not mean that it helps to explain success. The factor may have been strong, but irrelevant.

The first impression from Table A is that two of the countries have much in common — Ethiopia and Bangladesh, while the third is very different — Colombia. This is now considered factor by factor.

1. Factors directly associated with the activities of central decision-makers (e.g. 'strengthening national organizations'), called 'macro'-factors (Table B)
2. Factors that link the central decisions to the local level, and thereby 'transmit' the message from the policy level to the implementation level (Table C, 'linkage'). Table C includes 'linkage-factors' from school display 2B, i.e. it has information not only from central decision-makers, but also from local level and school informants. In cases where a direct comparison can be made between two factors, one from the central level and one from the local level, this has been done (see Table D).

These tables are very condensed and provide the reader with a summary perspective of the variables. The purpose is to see what is common among these three reform efforts (as seen by the central informants) and what seems to distinguish them.

The macro-factors indicate that there are a few common factors for all three systems. The strong factors for all three systems (there are no commonly weak macro-factors) are:

- curriculum development
- political stability
- external donor support.

Table B 'Macro-factors'

Factors	Colombia	Ethiopia	Bangladesh
Strength of national organizations	NA	HI	HI
Capacity-building of national organization	MLI	HI	HMI
Legal regulation	NA	HI	HI
Curriculum development	HI	HI	HI
Infrastructure development	MI	HI	HMI
Resource allocation	HI	MI	MI
Decisions supporting institutionalization	MI	HMI	HI
Decision-making	HMI	HI	MI
Pressure for good implementation	MI	HI	HI
Division of labour	MI	HI	HI
Protection from environmental turbulence	MI	MLI	HI
Monitoring and control	MI	HI	HI
Political stability	HI	HI	HMI
External donor support	HI	HMI	HI

Key: HI — high impact; HMI — high/medium impact; MI — medium impact; MLI — medium/low impact; LI — low impact; NA — not answered.

As has already been seen, 'curriculum development' in the Colombian context is defined somewhat differently than in the two other countries. In Colombia, originally, the curriculum was to a large extent defined by a professional group outside the Ministry. It is only in the last few years that the Ministry has adopted the programme. In the other two countries it was the Ministry that initiated the curriculum reform.

The difference between on the one hand Colombia, and on the other hand Ethiopia and Bangladesh, is best seen in an analysis of which macro-factors discriminate between the two groups. Strength of national organizations, legal regulation, pressure for good implementation, capacity building of national organizations, monitoring and control and decision-making are all strong factors in Ethiopia and Bangladesh, and factors that are relatively weak (or not answered) in Colombia. One factor, 'resource allocation', is strongly represented in Colombia, and moderately represented in the two other countries. Thus the picture of two countries with fairly strong centralistic reform strategies versus one country with a 'bottom-up'-strategy is confirmed.

Table C 'linkage'-factors, where the information is coming from both central and local informants, underlines this finding. These are factors that informants at the central level (marked 'C') believe to be important factors 'helping the system together', and factors (marked 'L') that the local informants experience as 'bridging' the intentions of the reform with the realities of the local site. Information comes from display 2A (central informants) and 2B ('linkage', local informants). The information about 'linkage' from the local informants is qualitative

Table C Linkage-factors

Factors		Colombia	Ethiopia	Bangladesh
L	Administrative role	MI	HI	HMI
C	Resource delivery	HI	HMI	HMI
C+L	Assistance	HI	HI	HI
L	Received pressure	MLI	HI	HI
C	Closeness to implementation	HMI	MI	HI
C	Effective communication	MI	HMI	HI
C	Availability and quality of materials	HMI	HI	HMI
L	Local adaptation	HMI	MI	LI
C	User involvement	HI	MI	MLI
L	Committment	HI	HMI	MI
C	Building of commitment	HI	HMI	MI
L	Success experience	HI	HMI	NA
L	Empowerment, engagement	HI	HMI	LI
L	Received resources	HI	MI	HMI
L	Community support	HI	HI	LI

Key: C — central informants; L — local informants; HI — high impact; HMI — high/medium impact; MI — medium impact; MLI — medium/low impact; LI — low impact; NA — not answered.

in nature, e.g. how linkage is effected in districts, also illustrating the consequences. The quantification of this data is based on the frequency of linkage and the consequences seen by the local informants (quantification has been checked by each team leader).

There are three commonly strong linkage factors for all three systems, as seen by the central informants:

- assistance
- resource delivery
- availability and quality of materials.

In all systems 'assistance' is mainly understood as in-service training, often locally based, and often followed-up by a local supervisor and/or the headmaster. Resource delivery and learning materials are seen as highly important elements by the central informants, and seen as 'strong' factors in the reform.

The differences between the two groups become even clearer if the information from Table C is considered. The strong factors of the Colombian reform (as seen by the central informants), compared to the other two countries are:

- user involvement
- empowerment and engagement
- success experience
- local adaptation
- building of commitment.

These are factors strongly associated with activities at the school level, factors that are critical for implementation. The Colombian reform strategy, in other words, as seen by the central informants, is stronger in terms of its ability to involve the user, to create a feeling of success and empowerment, to develop commitment and to use this energy for local adaptation. The two other systems, in particular Ethiopia, has elements of these factors (e.g. 'building of commitment' and 'local adaptation'); however, it is clearly stronger in Colombia. The only 'linkage' factor that is clearly stronger in Ethiopia and Bangladesh, is 'received pressure', the effect a fairly strict regime (Ethiopia) and on-the-job supervision (AUEO in Bangladesh) has on the system.

What factors play a decisive 'linkage' function?

To be able to distinguish the views of central informants, on the one hand, from the local level and school level informant, on the other, those factors that are basically the same have been pulled out and asked at all levels. To what extent, in other words, are the views of central informants confirmed by the local and school level informants? Only the 'linkage' factors are considered, to determine to what extent a given strategy has 'worked its way through the system', or 'communicated' the essential message.

Five factors that are supposed to play a linkage function were selected:

- **Factor A: Resource delivery (seen centrally) versus received resources (seen locally).** From Table D it can be seen that central informants feel that this has been a very important part of the reform and has contributed to the success. However, in Ethiopia and Bangladesh local informants do not see the resources as playing a 'linkage' function. This is not the case in the Colombian case, where the materials play such an important role in the whole reform.

- **Factor B: Assistance, as seen centrally and locally.** This factor is seen as contributing to the reform and playing a strong role in 'linkage' (centrally). In Bangladesh this role is played by the AUEO, in Colombia by a variety of EN resource persons and in Ethiopia through the DEO and the headmaster. There is a common view on 'assistance' as an important linkage factor from both central and local informants in all three countries.

- **Factor C: Pressure for good implementation (seen centrally) versus received pressure (seen locally).** This is seen as a strong factor both centrally and locally in Ethiopia and Bangladesh. In Colombia it is seen as moderately important centrally, but does not seem to play a strong linkage role, as seen by the school people in the Colombian schools.

- **Factor D: User involvement (seen centrally) versus local adaptation (seen locally).** These are in principle two different factors. However, it is assumed that the intention of user involvement (as designed) would by definition mean 'local adaptation'. Table D shows a consistent pattern. In Bangladesh, by design, user involvement is not

Table D Cross-check factors

Factors		Colombia	Ethiopia	Bangladesh
(a)	Resource delivery (C)	HI	HMI	HMI
	Received resources (L)	HMI	MI	HMI
(b)	Assistance (C)	HI	HI	HI
	Assistance (L)	HI	HI	HI
(c)	Pressure for good implementation (C)	MI	HI	HI
	Received pressure (L)	MLI	HI	HI
(d)	User involvement (C)	HI	MI	MLI
	Local adaptation (L)	HMI	MI	LI
	Empowerment, engagement (L)	HI	MI	LI
(e)	Building of commitment (C)	HI	HMI	MI
	Commitment (L)	HI	HMI	MI

Key: C — central informants; L — local informants; HI — high impact; HMI — high/medium impact; MI — medium impact; MLI — medium/low impact; LI — low impact; NA — not answered.

strongly represented in the reform, and does not play a role as a linkage function. In Ethiopia 'user involvement' is moderately present, as seen by the central informants. The result is moderate local adaptation, as seen by the school people. In Colombia user involvement is seen as a very strong factor contributing to success. Local adaptation is also seen as strong by the school people.

- **Factor E: Building of commitment (seen centrally) versus empowerment and engagement (seen locally).** These two factors are not identical either; however, close correlation is assumed. In other words, high emphasis on 'Building commitment' should result in high 'Empowerment and engagement'. Table D confirms this. Bangladesh is seen as moderate on 'building commitment', and school people feel little empowerment and engagement. Ethiopia is seen as fairly strong in 'building commitment' and school people feel moderately committed and engaged. Finally the Colombian system is seen as strong in terms of building commitment, and school people feel empowered and engaged.

There is clearly a question of what is meant by 'linkage'. The definition here is 'methods, procedures, mechanisms through which national, regional (or district) and local schools are tied together, coordinated (as contrasted with operating independently or alone)'. Four of the five factors that can be directly compared between the central informants and local informants, show that there is a high correlation between the intentions (as seen centrally) and the reality (as experienced locally). In other words, at the policy level, at the management level (e.g. 'pressure'), at the professional support level (e.g. 'assistance'), and at the personal level (e.g. 'commitment'), there are strong and important linkages.

These findings confirm that there are at least two quite different reform efforts, with two quite different sets of dynamics, as assessed by central informants. These are a 'top-down' strategy on the one hand (Ethiopia and Bangladesh) versus a 'bottom-up' strategy on the other. There are also clear differences between Ethiopia and Bangladesh:

- Ethiopia has built a strict regime, uses a highly qualified and professional management staff and systematically works on all levels of the system to include participation of all actors, including those at local level.
- Bangladesh has developed a nationwide and complex UPE project, basically through a traditional administrative system (partly strengthened), but with an innovative and new supervision element at the local level (the AUEO). Its user participation is weaker than Ethiopia's.

Chapter 7

The Outcomes of Educational Reform — Seen Locally

So far we have learned what central informants believe to be the outcomes and how they explain these outcomes. These informants have often played a central role in the reform effort. In some cases, they 'own' the reform, having been centrally involved in its initiation, development or implementation. We have seen briefly that the central 'messages' have 'travelled down the system' (i.e. Ethiopia and Bangladesh) through one form of 'linkage' or another. In order to get a comprehensive picture of what actually has been achieved, we need to get down to the school level.

How do parents, students, teachers, local leaders and support personnel assess the outcomes of the reform efforts? We have already seen that 'outcomes' are widely defined, ranging from better achievement in core subjects to improved behaviour of students, better communication with the community, improved financing of schools, punctuality of teachers, a more active student role in the teaching-learning process and better school management, to mention but a few!

The intention has not been to assess the value of these outcomes, but to *describe* to what extent these outcomes are found in real school situations — and not only in the heads of planners and decision-makers. We want to move into the classrooms to actually see what goes on, to walk around among students and parents in the schoolyard and in the community to talk and observe. Some of these objectives can be assessed through 'hard data', such as achievement scores, drop-out rate, retention, etc. In all cases where these kinds of data are available, they have been used as a basis for documentation. In Colombia, students were also tested in core subjects with standardized tests, to compare the sample schools with country averages.

Most of the data are, however, based on the opinions of parents, teachers, headmasters and district personnel, and reactions of students. The data are based on rather lengthy interviews, often twice with each respondent over a period of a few days (see Chapters 3 to 5). There are, clearly, methodological problems associated with this method, including subjectivity and memory errors, unavailability of baseline data, and fear of openness to an external investigator. However, since the data are based on the opinions of a fairly large sample of individuals, all with different roles and interests in the reform, we have confidence in them.

Outcomes have been defined as follows:

1. Degree of success in implementation. Are the 'inputs' to the reform really delivered? Do teachers have the needed technical mastery?

Are teachers motivated and are they productive using new methods and materials? How well do the new practices 'fit' with the way instruction so far has been done? Are all teachers involved or only a few?

2. Student impact. To what extent do students learn more, something different, or more or less relevant to their life-situation? How do they behave? To what extent are students motivated? Are they attending school regularly, what has happened with the repeat rates, and are there negative student changes?

3. Teacher impact. How knowledgeable are teachers about the new content and methods implied in the reform? Can they actually do what is expected of them in their (new) role? What are their attitudes and what do they feel about the reform? Are there negative changes related to teachers?

4. School impact. To what extent are there positive changes in the school's organization, e.g. the climate, the way decisions are taken, the way parents are involved and the way teachers cooperate? Has the school strengthened its ability to carry out other changes? Are there negative aspects related to the school level and associated with the reform?

5. Institutionalization. To what extent are the changes 'built in', and a natural part of the school life? Are new behaviours consolidated in the classroom? Is it likely that the changes will continue? Does the reform have support from key people? Are resources committed? Are procedures modified to fit the new practices? Do new teachers get the necessary support to cope with new practices?

Methods of analysis

The informants at the local level and school level are students (observation), teachers, parents, headmasters, support personnel and district personnel. A summary of the outcomes is recorded in display 6 (see Chapters 3 to 5). To qualify the changes, the researchers have summarized the elements of the changes and their meanings in display 3 (page 353). The degree of success of implementation is recorded in display 5B (page 356).

It is hard to clarify and assess outcomes. The very first task, therefore, in the interviews, was to ask the informant to talk about how it was 'then' (before the reform), and how it is 'now'. The interviewee had the chance to discuss these changes quite freely. Towards the end of the interview, the interviewee was given a 'probe' to check if there were other changes as well that he or she may have forgotten. This produces a fairly large amount of data, which were then summarized in the displays 3 and 5B. The interview data was recorded together with the classroom observation data on the relevant issues. Towards the end of data collection a summary of 'outcomes and institutionalization at the local level' was filled out, which is the main source of information in this chapter. Each research team needed several sessions to agree on these ratings.

The Outcomes Seen Locally

Figure 7.1 *Worktable 8 Ethiopia, teacher impact*

	Schools								
	Excellent			Very good				Good	
Factor	1	2	3	4	5	6	7	8	9
Use of local teaching/learning aids	HI	HI	MI	MI	MI	MI	LI	MLI	MLI
Teaching/learning process/class management	HI	HI	HMI	HMI	HMI	HMI	HMI	MI	MI
Teacher-teacher cooperation	HI	HI	HI	HMI	HMI	HI	MI	HI	MI
Teacher-headmaster cooperation	HI	HI	HMI	HI	HMI	HMI	MI	MI	MI
Participation in academic competitions	HI	HI	HI	HMI	HI	HI	HI	NA	NA
Ability to motivate students	HI	HI	HMI	MI	HI	MLI	MI	LI	LI
Interest in labour education	HI	HI	HMI	HI	HI	MI	LI	LMI	LMI
Personal cleanliness	HI	HI	HI	HI	HI	HI	HI	HI	HI
Mastery of subject matter	HI	HI	HMI	MI	HMI	HMI	HMI	MI	MI
Commitment	HI	HI	HMI	HI	MI	HMI	MI	MI	MI
Involvement	HI	HI	HMI	HI	HI	HMI	MI	HI	HMI

Key: HI — high impact; HMI — high/medium impact; MI — medium impact; MLI — medium/low impact; LI — low impact; NA — not answered.

These data are then summarized again in cross-site display 1 (see Chapters 3 to 5). Based on the mentioned school displays and the cross-site display 1, each element of 'outcomes' was systematically recorded in a series of 15 'worktables' that were used for analysis of outcomes in this chapter (see Appendix 4, page 322). Figure 7.1 shows one of these displays, in this case worktable 8, 'Ethiopia, teacher impact'.

The various factors associated with teacher behaviour related to the Ethiopian reform are recorded at the left side of the table. Each column (a total of nine) represents one of the sample schools in Ethiopia. They are ranged from left to right in terms of their overall implementation outcomes score. Each research team went through a systematic process ranging the sample schools in relation to the outcomes. For an example of this project, see 'Ethiopia', Chapter 4, pp. 96 to 119. The first two columns on the left represent the two excellent schools in the Ethiopia sample, the next four represent the very good schools, and the last three columns the good schools, measured in terms of outcomes.

The first question we ask, is the following: Is there a factor that appears strong or weak across all schools? There is one clear candidate: 'personal cleanliness'. This is a behaviour expected by the teachers and that expectation seems to be fully met. Another strong candidate is 'involvement', which is somewhat weaker at the lower end, but fairly strong overall.

The second question we ask is: Is there a factor that discriminates among the three categories of schools? Glancing at worktable 8, it is clear that there are marked differences among the three categories of schools. The two excellent schools have a much higher teacher impact than the very good schools and the good schools. The difference between the very good schools and the good schools is not so obvious; however, the sum is clearly higher in very good schools than in the good schools.

There are several discriminating factors

- use of local teaching-learning materials
- interest in labour education
- mastery of teaching and classroom management
- cooperation, in particular teacher-headmaster cooperation
- ability to motivate students
- commitment.

Most factors discriminate the excellent schools from the rest, many discriminate among all three groups (e.g. 'use of local teaching-learning materials'), and in this case, none discriminate between the excellent and the very good schools on the one hand and the good schools on the other. A candidate may have shown 'participation in academic competition'; however, we don't know how that factor works in two of the good schools (not answered). Appendix 4 presents all 15 worktables for the analysis presented in this chapter.

The starting conditions

We are dealing with schools that, relatively speaking, have had considerable success in implementing and institutionalizing the reforms. The schools are not alike and they differ considerably in their reform success. Some 'excellent' schools have implemented and institutionalized almost all reform components, some 'very good' schools have also come far, and some 'good' schools have done well, though some elements are less successfully done. Could it be that the schools were very good schools to begin with and worked from advantaged positions? Could it be that we would also find the distinctions 'excellent', 'very good' and 'good' in the initial conditions?

Let us first remind you of the sampling criteria explained in Chapter 1. We were looking for rural schools in poor countries, with resources well below average. We asked for good schools in terms of their ability to cope with the reform, not in terms of their relative strength of resources.

The initial situation

We also checked the situation in all 31 schools when they started to approach the reform (display 4). Looking at the first criterion 'situation' reveals the following:

1. Eight out of 31 schools had severe and/or inadequate start conditions (resources, staff deficiencies, buildings, etc). They comprised 22 per cent of the excellent schools, 43 per cent of the very good schools and none of the good schools.
2. Good starting conditions, with positive attitudes (also from the community) were found in nine out of 31 schools: 22 per cent of the excellent schools, 28.5 per cent of the very good schools and 37.5 per cent of the good schools.

Table 7.1 Entry strategies

Intervention	Excellent	Very good	Good	Total
Information/training	7 schools (78%)	10 schools (71%)	6 schools (75%)	23 schools
Briefing community	5 schools (55%)	9 schools (64%)	4 schools (50%)	18 schools
Improve resources	2 schools (22%)	4 schools (28.5%)	1 schools (12.5%)	7 schools
Adaptation of reform	2 schools (22%)	4 schools (28.5%)	None (0%)	6 schools

3. Slow start with scepticism and hesitation from teachers (and often the community) was found in seven out of 31 schools: 44 per cent of the excellent schools, 14 per cent of the very good schools and 12.5 per cent of the good schools.
4. A few schools started with large ideological conflicts (three good schools in Ethiopia), a situation that could probably have influenced the implementation success.
5. In two of the 31 schools there was insufficient data to assess the initial conditions (Ulatchandal, Padma, both in Bangladesh).

From these data we can say that the initial conditions, in terms of the problems mentioned, were not in favour of the excellent or very good schools. Relatively speaking, the good schools (with the exception of Ethiopia) had the best start conditions. If they differ in success, it was not due to their initial conditions (as far as this can be assessed).

Working with display 4, we have also analysed what the local decision-makers did initially to cope with the types of problems encountered. The percentage of schools in the category using this, among other intervention methods, is shown in parentheses in Table 7.1. The most common initial strategy is information and an 'information-like' in-service training, used in 23 of the 31 schools. To brief the community is important in all countries and in all types of schools. Eighteen of 31 schools briefed the community very early, and was done almost equally in all three types of schools. Very few schools used other intervention strategies initially. A few schools (seven) improved the physical conditions (buildings, classrooms, etc.), and only six schools attempted to modify the reform. None of the good schools tried to adapt the reform to local needs. The initial strategies also showed that the schools were fairly similar in their approach to coping with the initial challenges. Differences in outcomes, therefore, are most likely to depend on what happens during the many years of reform.

IMPLEMENTATION SUCCESS AS SEEN LOCALLY

The purpose of this section is to analyse the data for each country, and each main variable (e.g. 'student impact') within each country. We will look at the outcomes that are commonly strong or weak within the total sample of schools, and at those factors that seem to discriminate within the sample of schools. The reader is encouraged to use the worktables in Appendix 4 to help read this section. The worktables also provide a basis for more detailed analysis, e.g. the characteristics of the excellent schools.

The outcomes are presented in the following order:

1. degree of success in implementation
2. student impact
3. teacher impact
4. school impact
5. institutionalization.

Colombia

The EN reform is an attempt to improve the quality of educational delivery and thereby improve student outcomes; it works as directly as possible with teachers and students. In terms of 'implementation' we find the following (worktable 1):

1. Teachers' mastery shows impact in all schools, and discriminates among all three categories of schools.
2. Teachers' commitment is a strong factor and also discriminates among all three categories of schools.
3. Training delivery is a strong factor, and shows high to medium impact in all three categories of schools (one of the two good schools shows low impact).
4. Delivery of materials is an uneven factor, strong in the excellent schools, strong to low impact in the very good schools, and low impact in one of the two good schools ('not answered' in the other school). The factor discriminates among all three categories of schools.

In terms of 'student impact' (worktable 2) we find the following:

1. The EN reform has had significant impact on student learning in almost all sample schools. The explicit outcomes may vary from school to school, but in total the reform has had a high impact in three to five different student outcome measures in all schools except one.
2. Two student impact factors, namely student leadership and socio-emotional gains, are strong in all schools except one. These are clearly central to the reform, and also indicate a strong element of student behaviour change (e.g. student leadership).
3. Cognitive outcomes are generally observed as high to high/medium impact in ten of 12 schools, and this factor seems to discriminate the excellent schools from the very good and good schools.

As far as teacher impact is concerned (worktable 3), we find the following:

1. Teacher motivation shows high impact in both excellent and very good schools, and medium to low impact in the good schools.
2. Teacher behaviour (indicated by the other five variables in the table) shows high impact in the excellent schools, high to medium impact in

six of seven very good schools and medium impact in the good schools.

The schools we are studying in Colombia are very small rural schools, often with only one headmaster and one teacher. 'School impact' (worktable 4) is seen in the following areas:

1. Student governance is a factor that shows impact in all 12 schools. It is clearly stronger in the excellent and very good schools than in the good schools, and is therefore a discriminating factor.
2. Improvement of the physical structure shows high impact in all categories of schools, and in a total of seven schools.
3. School community relations discriminate the excellent schools from the other schools; however, this factor also shows high impact in three of the very good schools.

Looking at institutionalization (worktable 5) we are concerned with those structures and procedures that have stabilized and routinized the innovation. We find the following:

1. The factor that we have called routinization discriminates the excellent and very good schools from the good schools. However, it shows a high to medium impact in all schools.
2. Community support shows impact in all schools and discriminates the excellent and very good schools from the good schools.
3. Support (local administrative support and assistance given) shows high impact in all but one very good school.
4. Resources (committed or promised) show high impact and discriminate the excellent and the very good schools.
5. Teachers orienting new teachers shows high impact in two of three excellent schools.

In summary, we find several factors with high impact in the Colombian case. Common high impact factors are teachers' technical mastery, training delivery, student socio-emotional gains, student leadership and student governance, the routinization of the programme and community support. These high impact factors are all closely related to the classroom and the school.

The Escuela Nueva programme for rural schools in Colombia has a clear and significant impact at the school level, both in terms of student and teacher impact, implementation and institutionalization. The factors that discriminate among the three categories of schools are:

- implementation (delivery of teaching-learning materials)
- student impact (cognitive gains)
- teacher impact (motivation and commitment, teacher mastery and behaviour)

- school impact (community support and school-community relations)
- institutionalization (routinization of the programme and resources committed or promised).

Ethiopia

The reform effort in Ethiopia is very different. It is centrally initiated and developed, aiming at a much broader set of goals than the Colombian reform. Also in this reform student outcomes are essential, and the development of a new management structure, new management behaviour, a new support structure and the role of the community in school management were among other components envisaged by the central planners. How do local informants perceive the outcomes in the sample schools?

When we look at the worktable on 'implementation' of the Ethiopian reform (worktable 6), the overall impression is that all major components have been implemented with high to medium impact in all schools. It is a very comprehensive reform, and it has worked in the sample schools. A more detailed analysis of the worktable provides the following information:

1. Use of the new curriculum and the use of radio programmes show a high impact in all schools. District office support of training shows a high/medium impact in all schools, and new assessment techniques have had medium impact in all schools.
2. Implementation of labour education, classroom management, community support and division of labour discriminate among the three categories of schools, the excellent schools showing the highest impact.
3. The factors that discriminate the excellent schools from the others are: teachers' technical mastery, school management, use of teaching aids and the SPC.
4. DEO support of materials discriminates the excellent and the very good schools from the good schools.

Looking at student impact (worktable 7), the picture is less comprehensive, and in general, the factors show less impact than for implementation. We find:

1. There is no common high impact student factor for all nine schools, with the exception of 'enrolment' which has increased and shows high or medium impact. The reform has had a medium impact on the promotion rate, a low to low/medium impact on the drop-out rate and a medium (to high) impact on attendance. The impact on repetition has been highest in the good schools.
2. Examination results discriminate among all three categories of schools.
3. Attitude to labour education and attitude toward schooling discriminate the excellent and the very good schools from the good schools.

Teacher impact in the Ethiopian reform (worktable 8) shows the following results:

1. Teacher impact is an overall strong factor, and shows high to medium impact in all schools. More specifically personal cleanliness and teacher involvement show high impact in all schools.
2. The following factors discriminate among all three categories of schools:
   - ability to motivate students
   - the use of local teaching/learning materials
   - interest in labour education
   - commitment
   - mastery of the teaching-learning process and classroom management
   - staff cooperation
   - mastery of the subject matter.
3. Participation in academic cooperation shows high impact in the excellent and very good schools (two of three good schools did not answer).

Turning to school impact (worktable 9), we observe an overall high to medium impact factor. All nine schools show no less than medium impact on any one of the 12 sub-factors in the worktable. More specifically we find:

1. Improvements of the physical structure, generation of school income and organizational changes including new departments show high impact in all three categories of schools.
2. Co-curricular activities and community relations (very good schools show highest impact) discriminate among all three categories of schools.
3. The following factors discriminate the excellent and very good schools from the good schools:
   - the use of labour education
   - school beautification
   - school climate
   - the school management committee.
4. The library and enrolment (where the excellent schools show the lowest impact) discriminate the excellent schools from the rest.

Worktable 10 indicates that the reform has been institutionalized to a large extent. Impact on a total of 17 sub-factors varies from high to high/medium and medium, in all but two factors (in two schools). It gives a picture of a reform that has become daily practice. More specifically we find:

1. The strongest institutionalized components that show a high to high/medium impact in all schools are:

- the curriculum
- radio programmes
- materials support from the community
- labour support from the community
- DEO support in general
- textbook delivery from the DEO
- instructional materials from the DEO
- SMC support
- headmaster support
- training
- orientation of new teachers (two of three good schools did not answer).

2. The following factors discriminate among schools:
   - Community financial support (excellent and very good schools versus the good schools)
   - SPC coordination (among all categories)
   - labour education (excellent and very good schools versus good schools).

In summary the common high impact factors in the Ethiopia case are:
- the use of the new curricula
- the use of radio programmes
- teachers' personal cleanliness
- organizational changes (to include new departments)
- the school generating income
- improved physical structure
- enrolment
- the support of the headmaster
- community support
- DEO support in terms of textbook delivery and instructional materials.

In other words, an extensive and comprehensive list of high impact factors, indicating that the Ethiopian reform is well implemented in all categories of schools in our sample.

The common medium impact factors are the DEO support of training (high/medium) and the use of assessment techniques. The common low impact factors are the reduction of the drop-out rate and the reduction of the repetition rate.

The Ethiopian reform is quite comprehensive, it shows high impact in the sample schools, and institutionalization has come far. The following factors discriminate among the three categories of schools in Ethiopia:

- Implementation (community support and cooperation, commitment and cooperation, DEO materials, classroom management, teacher mastery and use of teaching aids, school management, labour education, SPC and division of labour).
- Student impact (examination results, attitudes towards labour education and attitudes towards schooling).
- Teacher impact (staff cooperation, mastery of the teaching-learning process and classroom management, teacher commitment, staff cooperation, use of local materials, mastery of the subject matter and interest in labour education).
- School impact (labour education, co-curricular activities, school climate, school beautification, the work of the SMC, the library and enrolment).
- Institutionalization (community financial support, SPC coordination, labour education).

Bangladesh

The expectations for the Bangladesh primary education project were also quite comprehensive in nature, and to some extent there were the same type of expectations as in the Ethiopian reform (e.g. increased enrolment, improvement of the quality of instruction, improved supervision and management, community involvement, etc.). What do we learn from our local informants in *successful* schools?

Worktable 11 gives the impression of a reform with a large number of components and with a varied degree of implementation. The pattern among the three categories of schools is also less clear than in the Ethiopian case. A more detailed analysis reveals the following:

1. Free textbooks and guides is a factor showing high impact in all schools, a compulsory part of the reform which clearly has reached the sample schools.
2. New classrooms and facilities is also a strong factor in all schools, however this factor discriminates the excellent schools from the other schools.
3. Headteacher motivation is generally strong (high to high/medium) in all schools.
4. Curriculum-oriented training is a fairly strong component, and this factor discriminates the excellent schools from the other schools.
5. The recruitment of female teachers is a moderately strong factor that discriminates the excellent schools from the others.
6. AUEO supervision is a fairly strong component that again discriminates the excellent schools.
7. There are some factors that are generally weakly implemented, according to our local informants:

- community involvement (discriminate the excellent schools)
- recruitment of new teachers
- teachers' technical mastery
- support from local institutions
- child survey.

8. Co-curricular activities discriminate the excellent and the very good schools from the good schools.

Worktable 12 (student impact) also indicates a fairly large distribution of outcomes. Our analysis indicates the following trends in the material:

1. There is no high impact factor common to all ten schools. There are, however, factors that indicate medium impact across schools in all categories:
   - active student participation
   - student motivation and student attitudes
   - interest in co-curricular activities
   - student cleanliness
   - student creativity
   - participation in talent competition.
2. The factors that discriminate the excellent schools from the other schools are reading and attendance.
3. The following factors discriminate among all three groups of schools:
   - student achievement and scholarship awards
   - arithmetic
   - student behaviour
   - repetition rate
   - enrolment (excellent and very good schools versus good schools)
   - retention.

The strongest discriminating factors are student achievement (including achievements in reading and arithmetic) and enrolment.

Teacher impact (worktable 13) appears as a factor with limited discrimination among schools. The immediate impression is that most factors show medium impact in most schools, with some exceptions:

1. Teacher motivation and teacher punctuality show high impact in the excellent schools, and this factor discriminates these schools from the very good and good schools.
2. Teacher behaviour in the classroom, i.e. the use of the described methodology, and active teaching are the next strongest factors (high to high/medium) and common to all schools.
3. Pedagogical knowledge and subject matter knowledge discriminate among all three categories of schools.

School impact (worktable 14) indicates a higher degree of impact, and our analysis shows:

1. Instructional materials are commonly a strong factor (high to high/medium),
2. Several factors discriminate excellent schools from other schools
   - regular reporting
   - improved teaching
   - teachers' attendance
   - teachers' acceptance of supervision
   - school discipline
   - school environment
3. The following factors discriminate among all three categories of schools:
   - active headmaster
   - increased enrolment and increased enrolment of girls
   - school-community relationship
   - physical facilities.
4. Commonly low impact factors are:
   - teachers' collaboration (medium impact)
   - female teachers' recruitment of girls
   - parents' participation in PTA and SMC.

The last worktable summarizing outcome variables is worktable 15, institutionalization. Compared to the other worktables for Bangladesh the excellent schools show higher impact, and few common factors appear:

1. Cluster training and regular reporting are fairly strong across the board, however they discriminate the excellent and the very good schools from the good schools, as does the promotion system.
2. Materials support and continuous assistance appear to have medium impact in all schools, while the use of SMC/PTA and the recruitment of new teachers both show fairly low impact.
3. The following factors discriminate the excellent schools from other schools:
   - the teaching/learning process
   - community resources
   - the support of key people
   - built-in the main factors of the reform
   - teachers' punctuality
   - regular supervision
   - co-curricular activities
   - child survey.

In summary, common high impact factors are relatively few in the Bangladesh reform. The strongest factors are inputs such as free textbooks, new buildings, classrooms and facilities. Another common strong factor is headmaster motivation. However, there are a number of common medium impact factors, including student impact factors such as changes in student motivation, attitudes, participation and behaviour, and their interest in co-curricular activities and participation in talent competition. There are also many teacher impact factors scoring medium impact, including teachers' relationship with the community, teacher-teacher relationships and collaboration, their relationship to students and their planning skills. In terms of school impact, there is one common medium impact factor, namely the relationship to the community. In terms of institutionalization two factors turns out to be commonly seen as having medium impact, these are materials support and continuous assistance.

Several factors are commonly seen as having low impact. These include community involvement and the support of local institutions, the recruitment of new teachers, the use of child surveys and the use of the school management committee and the parent-teacher association.

Several key aspects of the reform in Bangladesh have been implemented in our sample of successful schools, on average at a medium impact level within the defined outcome measures. What seems to discriminate the excellent (and to some degree the very good schools) from the other schools are:

1. Implementation success, defined as AUEO supervision, curriculum oriented cluster training, the recruitment of female teachers and co-curricular activities.
2. Student impact, in terms of student achievement (including arithmetic and reading), student behaviour (including attendance), reduced repetition and increased retention, attendance and enrolment.
3. Teacher impact, both in terms of teacher attitudes (motivation, punctuality and attitudes toward supervision), teacher behaviour (teacher attendance, use of described methods and use of active teaching), and teacher knowledge (pedagogy and subject matter knowledge).
4. School impact, in terms of teachers' and headmasters' attitudes and behaviour, improved teaching, regular reporting, school discipline and the school environment, increased enrolment, physical facilities.
5. Institutionalization in terms of Cluster training, regular reporting, improved teaching/learning process, the support of key people, 'built-in-ness', teacher behaviour, supervision and co-curricular activities.

A CROSS-COUNTRY ANALYSIS OF OUTCOMES

The purpose of this section is to look at outcomes across the countries. It will look at each outcome measure separately, and at both the factors that appear commonly strong and the factors that discriminate the three categories of schools.

Implementation

We are studying three quite different reform efforts and three different reform strategies. Therefore, there are also clear differences in terms of implementation. We see both commonalities and contrasts:

1. Teacher mastery shows high impact in almost all Colombian schools, it is a discriminating factor in Ethiopia (from high to medium impact), and it shows medium impact in Bangladesh. This is consistent with our earlier analysis. The Colombian reform strategy is a fast way to reach the teacher, where the training and the materials component are tightly coupled. The same is true for Ethiopia, though the coupling is not so clear, the curriculum-coverage is wider and the number of teachers in the schools is much higher, with the probability of a wider distribution of outcomes. The same explanation applies to Bangladesh as well.

2. Teacher motivation shows high to medium impact in all three countries, discriminating the three categories of schools in Colombia and Bangladesh. We are studying a sample of high performing schools, and see a positive motivation among teachers as a pre-condition, or at least an enabling condition, for other outcomes.

3. The classroom is changed in all three systems: in Colombia due to a combination of new teacher behaviour and new materials (the guide); in Ethiopia because the curriculum, use of radio education, etc. appears in all schools; and access to free textbooks and classroom construction has improved the materials condition in Bangladesh. These changes are all important as indicators of outcomes in these three systems; however, there are substantial differences in terms of what classroom changes have been achieved.

4. Training is another factor that cuts across all three systems. It appears to be strong (mostly high or high/medium) in all three countries, in all categories of schools. It does discriminate the excellent schools in Bangladesh. Training is seen as a key to success in all three systems. In Colombia there is now fear that the training programme will be cut back (with negative consequences for the reform). In Bangladesh it is seen as a key element of the AUEO role, instrumental to the reform, and in Ethiopia it is part of the local support given by the DEO and partly a function of the school pedagogical centre.

5. Materials support shows high impact in all categories of schools in Bangladesh (free textbooks), and is also a high to medium impact factor in the other two countries. However, in Colombia and Ethiopia it is a discriminating factor. There are differences in terms of *what kinds of materials* are available and *how these materials are developed*. In Bangladesh the materials are all centrally developed, while in Ethiopia and Colombia some of the materials are locally developed and the curriculum adapted. These differences have

consequences for other variables (e.g. technical mastery and classroom instruction, see Chapter 8).

6. Several country specific outcome measures discriminate between the categories of schools, e.g. use of labour education in Ethiopia, recruitment of female teachers in Bangladesh and the competence of the headmaster in Colombia.

Student impact

These outcome measures distinguish the reform efforts even more clearly:

1. While student cognitive and socio-emotional gains are found to be strong (high to high/medium) in all three categories of schools in Colombia, there is no common strong achievement factor in the other two countries. Both in Bangladesh and in Ethiopia examination results discriminate between the three categories of schools.

2. There is high to medium impact in several student attitudes and student behaviour indicators in all three countries. In Colombia student leadership behaviour is seen as high to medium; in Ethiopia both student attendance and attitudes toward schooling (discriminating factor) show high to medium impact; and in Bangladesh active student participation, student motivation, participation in co-curricular activities and student cleanliness show medium impact.

3. In Ethiopia and Bangladesh the enrolment rate has been strongly influenced (data from Colombia are missing).

4. The repetition rate has been only modestly influenced in Ethiopia and shows medium impact in Bangladesh (data from Colombia incomplete).

5. The drop-out rate has been only modestly influenced in Ethiopia, and this factor shows medium impact in the excellent schools in Colombia. Cross-site display 2 for Bangladesh indicates increased retention and lesser drop-out in some school cases.

Teacher impact

The following outcomes are seen:

1. Teacher motivation appears in all three countries as a discriminating factor. It appears as a high impact factor in Colombia and as a medium impact factor in the other two countries. (Teacher commitment in Ethiopia is treated as teacher motivation).

2. Teachers' classroom behaviour shows an impact in all three countries. It is a strong factor (high to medium) in Colombia (the specific behaviour assessed varies), a high to medium impact factor in Bangladesh, and a high to medium factor in Ethiopia, and it

discriminates among the three groups of schools, in the latter two countries.

3. Teachers' personal behaviour (e.g. punctuality, cleanliness) shows high impact in both Bangladesh and Ethiopia (no data from Colombia).
4. A number of key teacher behaviours within each system do discriminate among the categories of schools, e.g. work with the community in Colombia, ability to motivate students and interest in labour education in Ethiopia and planning skills in Bangladesh.

School outcomes

The reform efforts are different and also have different consequences for the school as a whole:

1. A common high impact factor in Colombia and Ethiopia is the improvement of the physical facilities. This is a high to medium/low impact factor and also a discriminating factor in Bangladesh.
2. School community relations show impact in all three systems: high to medium impact in Ethiopia, high to low in Colombia and medium in Bangladesh. It is a discriminating factor in Colombia and Bangladesh.
3. Several high to medium impact country specific outcome measures discriminate between the three types of schools, e.g. student governance in Colombia, use of labour education in Ethiopia and regular reporting in Bangladesh.

Institutionalization

All the reform studies have been practised for many years. There are, therefore, common results in this category as well:

1. All three systems have to a large extent routinized key elements of the reform. This factor shows high impact in Colombia and Ethiopia. Excellent schools in Bangladesh have institutionalized the reform at a high impact level, the other schools at a medium to low impact level.
2. The system that has commonly achieved most in terms of institutionalization is the Ethiopian system where we find high to medium impact as a common trend within all central aspects of the reform in all categories of schools, with the exception of labour education. This also appears to be accepted; however, it discriminates between schools. Although community support is also a commonly strong factor in Ethiopia, its ability to provide cash (finance) is a discriminating aspect.
3. More specifically the following factors show high to medium impact in all three countries:
   - community support (discriminates in Colombia and Bangladesh)
   - training and assistance (discriminates in Colombia and Bangladesh)

- district support (textbooks, materials) commonly strong in Ethiopia, showing high/medium impact in Bangladesh, and generally high (but uneven) impact in Colombia.

What factors discriminate?

Finally we shall look at those factors that discriminate within each of the outcome measures, and we will combine several sub-factors to arrive at a summary picture of the outcome measures that discriminate among the excellent, the very good and the good schools in all three countries:

- student achievement
- teachers' motivation and attitudes
- teacher knowledge (implied factor in Colombia)
- teacher mastery
- school-community relations.

Differences in terms of outcomes among the three categories of schools for all three countries can be seen in the classroom, i.e. what students learn and how teachers teach, as well as at the school level in terms of the relationship between the school and the community. This is not surprising; however, it is clarifying. The best schools have teachers with high motivation, personal attitudes that are helpful to the school as an institution, they are knowledgable and they master their teaching well. These teachers produce results! Also they contribute to higher cognitive learning among students. This study underlines that there is a clear correlation between a competent teacher on the one hand and student achievement on the other. Teachers make a difference.

We also find that school-community relations are better in the excellent and very good schools. This may relate to other factors (see Chapter 8); however, as we have seen from Colombia, when parents see results of a reform, they become interested in it. We will assume that competent teachers also make a difference to parents, and thereby to the relationship between the school and the community. As we have seen, positive relationship with the community may mean active parent participation (e.g. in school management as in Ethiopia), in school finance and in other kinds of support.

We should recall that the best schools also show high impact in a number of other areas, and that the factors that explain the variation in outcomes may be many. To say for example that it all depends on the teacher, is too simple. The question is how some of the rural primary schools in very poor areas have achieved so much in terms of teacher, student and school outcomes. How do schools improve?

Chapter 8

Explaining Implementation, Impact and Institutionalization

INTRODUCTION

At this stage of analysis we are ready to describe and analyse the characteristics of the change process in the sample schools. As explained earlier, we have discussed a number of factors that may have helped or hindered the reform process in the schools. These range from type and degree of external assistance, administrative roles, inputs in terms of resources, to community involvement and the organizational context of each school (see cross-site display 2, Chapters 3 to 5).

As in Chapter 7, we shall use the same ordering of schools used by the country research teams, grouping them into excellent, very good and good schools according to their degree of outcomes (see Chapter 6). We shall continue to use this ordering of schools as we look into the factors that may have influenced the outcomes as seen by the local informants. Our descriptive task is to get a comprehensive understanding of how each factor 'worked' in the three groups of schools (e.g. was assistance different in the excellent schools than in the other two groups of schools?), and also of what the total profile of the three types of schools was in terms of the change process, when we see all these factors together.

The unit of analysis is still first the country and second the factor. In other words, we will try to get a grasp of the change strategy used in each of the countries studied, and hope to understand how the change process worked in practice, what each main factor meant in the process and how it all hangs together. This last task, to look at the interdependencies of factors, will be presented as a conceptual map at the end of each country section.

The data come mainly from the local level, i.e. the teachers, headmasters and local support personnel. It is their description of how the various factors helped or hindered the change process that this analysis is based on. The factors have been discussed earlier, and a list of these factors is given in appendix 6 (operational definitions). They are discussed in the different contexts in chapters 3 to 5 (see for example 'Ethiopia', Chapter 4, pp. 75 to 78). The ratings used range from high impact to low impact, meaning that the factor is highly present and has helped, been positive or contributed to the change process and specific outcomes, or on the other hand, has been less useful, possibly irrelevant and even negative.

The main tools of analysis are the worktables (see Appendix 4), which summarize the ratings of each main factor, and describe the content of each factor for each of the three countries. These data are drawn from cross-site display 2 (Chapters 3 to 5), which builds on display 7D and also partly 7A, 7B, 7C and 8 (see Chapters 3 to 5, and separate school reports).

The analytical task is to consider to what extent differences in strategies and processes made a difference, or at least were related, to the differences in outcomes (as documented in Chapter 7). We will try to identify causes and effects. In doing so, the analysis is based on the case histories of the different schools (what happened first and second), what seems to the informant to have been helpful or hindering. Was the factor alluded to or observed repeatedly, did the informants say it was a cause, and was there some conceptual reason that could plausibly be said to be at work? Secondly, we have discussed these relationships with the research coordinator in each of the three countries and have thoroughly discussed alternative hypotheses. The 'maps' or figures presented in this chapter linking the factors together and presenting an integrated picture of the reform process are the result of these studies and discussions.

COLOMBIA

Assistance is clearly a high impact factor in the EN reform (see worktable 16). Initial training is a common factor for all categories of schools, and has a high impact. On-going support comes from different sources, though mainly from the micro-centres. This on-going in-service Assistance is less common, and discriminates the excellent and very good schools from the good schools. In other words, the good schools have mainly initial assistance, and limited on-going assistance.

The role of the headmaster has been studied as an independent factor in the change process. Worktable 17 provides a rating where the headmaster function is broken down into five sub-categories. These categories come from the reading of the narrative text for each of the 31 schools in our total sample, and are:

1. Stability and commitment. The extent to which the headmaster has been in the school over a long period of time (minimum five years), and has a generally positive attitude to the reform.
2. Policy implementation and control. The extent to which the headmaster is pushing for implementation and supervises/evaluates the efforts.
3. Coordination and facilitation. The extent to which the headmaster is actively helping to get the reform efforts together, helping to resolve problems and also representing the school and the reform to the outside community.
4. Attention to resources. The extent to which the headmaster is active in finding resources for the implementation of the reform.
5. Pedagogical support. The extent to which the headmaster assists teachers, provides follow-up and feedback and seeks help from the regional support centres when needed.

Looking at the Colombian reform, the following picture emerges:

1. The common factor for all three categories of schools is stability and commitment (not answered in two schools). These ten headteachers have been in their present school for a minimum of five years, and most of them have helped to introduce the EN reform.
2. The headmaster factor appears stronger in the excellent and the very good schools than in the good schools.
3. The role most commonly played by the head is the pedagogical support role.
4. The more administrative aspects of leadership are less apparent in the schools studied.

The picture is of a headmaster who is a colleague, committed to the reform and actively trying to assist teachers pedagogically and to resolve problems as they occur.

The role of the local school administrator in the reform efforts was also studied using the narrative text of the 31 cases and the same five sub-categories as for the headmaster analysis (worktable 18). Looking at Colombia the following picture emerges for the district administrator role:

1. Stability and commitment is a common high impact factor for the district administrator role.
2. The most common function played is the pedagogical support role, particularly through supervision visits and in-service training sessions.
3. There is some attention to the administrative functions (in four schools); however, this function does not seem to have played an important role.

The overall impression of the administrative role in Colombia, looking at both the headmaster and the local administrator role together, is the following:

1. The pedagogical support function is clearly given priority over any other function, and it is undertaken by administrators with a high degree of stability and commitment to the reform.
2. The excellent schools have administrators with a higher impact on the reform than in the other two categories of schools.
3. The roles do not have complementary dimensions, e.g. with an inactive or indifferent headmaster one could expect a more active, supervisory and task-oriented district administrator. We find no such relationships; on the contrary, a school with a high impact headmaster playing a given role (e.g. pedagogical support) often has a high impact local administrator playing the same role, and a weak head is often accompanied by a low impact district administrator.

Supervision (worktable 19) or regular ongoing visits with pedagogical inputs by the local administrator or by a resource person at the micro-centre is commonly a high impact factor. This seems to support our findings about the functions played by the district administrator, i.e. the pedagogical support role. Commitment (worktable 20) is also commonly a high impact factor in terms of both headmaster commitment and teacher commitment. Headmaster commitment discriminates the excellent and the very good schools from the good schools.

Received pressure (worktable 21) from various external agents, e.g. the regional coordinator or the director of the Regional Support Centre, is present and seen as having high impact in both the excellent and very good schools. It is almost absent in the good schools, in fact in one of these schools the teachers pushed the head! This finding is somewhat surprising, compared with our analysis of the district administrator role. It can, however, be understood as pedagogical pressure, i.e. push for implementation, insisting on EN, etc., or a conscious effort to ensure implementation of the reform, by doing it right.

Received resources (worktable 22) seems basically to mean two types of resources: the student guides which were given in the first year are important in all three categories of schools, and seem commonly to have high/medium impact; and donations from the community, often facilitated by the headmaster, are also a fairly common and high/medium factor. Success experiences (worktable 23) in terms of student cognitive and socio-emotional development are present in all categories of schools. This factor does discriminate the excellent and the very good schools from the good schools. Also, a number of site-specific experiences are seen as success, including community acceptance, the appointment as a Demonstration school, visits, supervisory feedback, etc.

Empowerment (worktable 24) appears to have one strong component, namely that the teachers and the headmaster decide all important things. This factor shows high impact in both excellent and very good schools, and discriminates them from the good schools.

Local adaptation (worktable 25) has one common high impact factor, namely local adaptation of the students' guide. This guide is central to the implementation of the EN reform, and at the same time, it provides the possibility for local adaptation and underlines in a real sense that the teachers and the headmaster decide all important things. Community support (worktable 26) shows high impact in both the excellent and the very good schools, and negative reactions in at least one of the two good schools. Parent and community acceptance has, however, not been easy or automatic. In five schools the community changed from a negative to a positive attitude.

The dynamics of the EN reform process

We are now at a stage where we know the outcomes of the EN reform, and we know the factors that may have contributed to these outcomes. We also know what factors discriminate the best schools, in other words, the factors that may be central to understanding the success. Figure 8.1 illustrates how the single factors identified are connected to each other.

The progression in Figure 8.1 is roughly chronological. Factors that were antecedent or part of the context prior to the reform are placed on the left. Moving to the right, we see factors that represented early initiatives. The centre of the figure includes factors we believe the study clarifies as the most significant factors in understanding the reform (see display 7D) as implementation

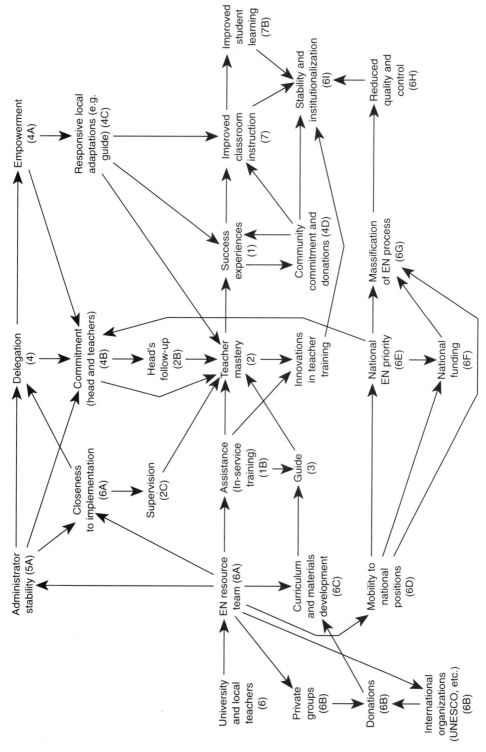

Figure 8.1 *Colombia: the EN reform process. Numbers given to some factors correspond to the numbers in the text.*

proceeded. At the far right we see the outcome factors — what the reform accomplished after it had been implemented for a number of years. The arrows represent the researchers' best judgment of what led to what over the course of the reform. We can now interpret the network of factors:

1. Central to the change process is the success experiences (1) felt by teachers as they begin to use the EN programme, using the guide and what they have learned from the initial training (1B). In spite of hesitation, even negative attitudes in the community, the early success experiences in the classroom convinced both teachers and parents that the change was really possible, and indeed positive. Teachers saw significant changes in children and these impressions were shared by the parents.

2. Central to these success experiences is teachers' mastery (2). The initial in-service training (1B) is a critical resource, as is the on-going support of the headmaster (2B) and the external supervisors (2C). We see clear differences between the excellent and the very good schools on the one hand, and the good schools on the other, in terms of both the headmaster role and the external follow-up.

3. The student guide (3) plays a key role in the EN reform, and a particularly important role in teachers' mastery. The guide provides concrete materials and help for the teacher to perform a new role. However it is also flexible enough for the teacher to adapt the guide to the local conditions. This does not lead to down-sizing, but to improved teacher skills.

4. A central condition for improving teacher skills is the clear decentralized nature of the school system in Colombia. Heads and teachers are trusted to take all important decisions, delegation (4) that leads to empowerment (4A), commitment (4B) and responsive local adaptation (4C). This is true for both teachers and heads. Their commitment is also increased by the fact that the community (after having experienced early successes) feel committed and provide donations for the school (4D).

5. This successful delegation happens in a system (the sample schools) where most heads have been in the job for longer than five years (5A) and feel committed to the EN reform, and where the District personnel are equally stable and committed (5A). We assume that the supervisors and the heads must know each other very well after years of cooperation.

6. So far we have explained the internal dynamics in a typical school. Drawing from the information in Chapter 6, the national view, we can now see how the overall EN programme is linked to our local sites:

    (i) A group of local teachers and university people (6) started the programme and became a knowledgeable EN resource team (6A) who started the innovations and got support from both local, national private groups and international donors (6B).

(ii) The team provided comprehensive training and materials support (6C) to the local administrators (5A) (who were quite stable in their positions), and to a large extent the implementation of the programme was delegated to local school personnel (4) (supervisors and headmasters), which meant closeness to implementation (6A).

(iii) As the popularity for the EN programme developed, members of the EN team moved into national positions (6D), made their influence through these positions and the EN programme became a national priority (6E), got national funding (6F) and thereby legitimacy.

(iv) The consequence was massification of the EN programme (6G), a reduction in inputs (e.g. training reduced to 50 per cent of original programme), changes that may negatively influence the quality (6H) and the stability and institutionalization of the programme (6I).

7. As this dynamic evolves over time in our sample of schools, teachers become more professional in their job and instruction improves (7), student cognitive and social-emotional gains improve (7B), and the EN programme itself is routinized and institutionalized (6I).

The EN reform is an example of a bottom-up driven reform, with changes in the classroom and integration among teacher and students as the key and central elements. Although it does demand new resources, i.e. a student guide and teacher in-service training, the additional costs to the system are moderate. Since it is a classroom and school-based programme, the interaction in the school and between the school and the community are essential for its success. To understand the conditions under which the EN reform is most successful, we will look for the factors that discriminate the excellent and the very good schools. The factors that characterize a successful EN programme are as follows:

- it has a better in-service training component
- it generally has a stronger and more pedagogical-supportive and committed headmaster
- it receives more on-going pedagogical pressure through external supervision
- it experiences more success in terms of changes in children
- it feels more empowered
- it receives more community support.

In other words, the EN programme is most successful when it is 'done right'. The problem of down-sizing the innovation is therefore very real, when the in-service training component is drastically reduced, and at the same time, the regional and local administration delegate responsibilities for implementation to the individual school. There does not seem to be any contradiction between empowerment and external pressure. The successful cases show that the form of regional pressure is one that teachers understand and accept, namely pressure for good implementation. The reaction is more 'someone out there cares', than 'someone out there takes over'. Successful rural EN schools experience empowerment, and at the same time accept and value external supervision.

Our assumption is that this can be understood because these are successful schools. They have well-trained teachers with a professional attitude, who are used to the active support of the headmaster. They also experience support from the community, they are valued. We believe that the critical factors were that the EN programme fulfils a real need, that teachers had positive success experiences relatively quickly, and that the enthusiasm for the programme spread to parents and the community. The teachers, however, would not have had success without support through extensive training, the guide and on-going support.

ETHIOPIA

Assistance (worktable 27) is also a key factor in the Ethiopian reform process. Teachers' in-service training is a common factor. It shows high impact in the excellent and very good schools and medium/low impact in the good schools. Part of this training is the annual educational conference. The components of assistance that discriminate the excellent and the very good schools, even further, are:

- teachers helping and teaching other teachers
- teachers work in the school pedagogical centre (SPC)
- feedback from the headmaster and the local inspector.

While the good schools do benefit from the DEO workshops and the annual conference, the on-going support mechanisms do not have the same impact as in the best schools.

The role of the headmaster (worktable 28) shows some common high impact components, such as the stability of the heads (all except one have been five years or longer in the school) and their fairly active (or even strict) insistence on following-up and controlling teachers' work. They also pay careful attention to the availability of textbooks and other teaching-learning materials, and they give suggestions, help and advice. These are all common high impact factors for all three categories of schools.

As worktable 28 indicates, the Ethiopian headmasters studied showed an impressive and active presence in the school. They are active in all five functions analysed. We see a headmaster who is not only pedagogically active, but also a leader who insists on policy implementation, who is actively coordinating and pushing, and who cares about the delivery and availability of resources. No single sub-factor discriminates among the three types of schools. Overall, the heads in the excellent schools are seen more as having a high impact, and they are more active.

The role of the district administrator (worktable 29) also indicates a more active external role than the one observed in Colombia, though lack of data from several schools prevents us from drawing any conclusions. Common to all categories of schools are:

- Systematic follow-up and control to ensure policy implementation. This happens through many mechanisms, e.g. yearly school visits, quarterly school reports and giving of directions (or guidelines, see below).
- Pedagogical support through various mechanisms, e.g. local training conferences, advice and help to schools, a yearly conference, supervision visits, etc. All categories of schools receive pedagogical support; however, the support is more comprehensive in the excellent and very good schools.

Attention to resources, in particular the delivery of textbooks and other learning materials discriminates the excellent schools from the very good schools and these from the good schools. Again we are seeing an administrator role in Ethiopia that is comprehensive in nature, that belongs to a systematic management tradition and that connects the individual school with the larger system (linkage).

Supervision (worktable 30) is a very common phenomenon in all categories of schools, and it is done by both the headmaster and the local district personnel. Common to all categories of schools are:

- The headmaster facilitates and coordinates activities and assesses teachers' work. The supervision function is clearly delegated to the headmaster, and the local inspector plays a relatively moderate role in this respect.
- The DEO provides guidelines for the work in the school. This is a high impact factor in all schools.
- The district educational officer supervises the progress of the school, on at least a yearly basis. The impact varies considerably. He or she also advises the administration and helps to problem-solve; however, the impact is generally seen as low.

This information helps us to distinguish between the supervision roles of the district administrator and the headmaster. The district administrator has a more formal role, works through guidelines (which are seen as having a high impact) and visits the school infrequently. The direct problem-solving efforts and advice-giving are seen as having relatively low impact. The headmaster is working actively and daily with the teachers, is much more present, and is therefore playing a much more active supervisory role.

The activities that discriminate the excellent and the very good schools from the good schools are:

- the head works closely with the teachers
- the head works closely with the school management committee
- the head encourages teachers

- the head shares responsibilities with teachers
- the head checks teachers' lesson plans.

In the best schools we find a headmaster who communicates better, who is willing to share responsibilities, who supervises and who is also supportive. This is a clear role-change for headmasters. He or she is no longer a distant administrator but an instructional leader who is able to play two different and complementary roles at the same time: to set standards and ensure that they are fulfilled, on the one hand, and to work closely with teachers and parents, encourage them, support them and share responsibilities with them, on the other.

Commitment (worktable 31) is another factor that shows high impact in many schools. In all categories of schools our data indicates that both teachers and the headmasters in general welcome the changes. Another common factor, though one with a more moderate rating, is the attitude of the school management committee and the readiness of the DEO to respond to requests.

The Excellent and the very good schools indicate higher impact than the good schools on the following factors:

- students' attitude towards the reform
- readiness of students, teachers and the headmaster to spend their free time with school activities
- readiness among the teachers, the head and the SMC to cooperate.

Commitment is hard to assess under a fairly strict regime. Even the fact that in the excellent and very good schools students, teachers and the head are willing to use their private time for school affairs is not necessarily a very reliable (or even good) indicator of commitment. Our observations of students and classroom situations, however, support the general positive attitudes that are reported in the interview data.

Received pressure (worktable 32) also indicates some common high impact areas:

- DEO exerting direct pressure
- submission of quarterly reports
- follow-up and pushing by the headmaster
- insistence of the DEO that enrolment should increase and the reform be properly implemented
- visits by local inspectors (medium to low impact).

The factor that discriminates the excellent and the very good schools is the follow-up by the deputy headmaster. The impression is a strict regime where full implementation is expected.

Received resources (worktable 33) also give a picture of many common elements that show high impact:

- provision of instructional materials from the DEO

- provision of land, labour, finance, materials and, where relevant, teachers' housing, by the Community
- the ability of the school to generate its own income.

There are two sub-factors that discriminate the excellent and the very good schools: the provision of materials by the Community and the use of APC model teaching aids.

Success experiences (worktable 34) is another factor that shows some common high to high/medium impact ratings. These are:

- professional development
- classroom management
- income generation.

Compared to other variables discussed for Ethiopia, however, we see more variation, and that most sub-factors discriminate the excellent and the very good schools from the good schools:

- expansion of buildings
- self-reliance
- consistency with goals
- school-community relations
- the organization of the school
- teacher leadership.

The excellent schools are discriminated from the very good and the good schools on the following sub-factors:

- the production of teaching-learning aids
- professionalization and the exchange of experiences.

The Ethiopian reform is a comprehensive one, success can mean many different things, and our schools are experiencing success in most aspects of the reform.

Empowerment (worktable 35) shows several common high impact factors:

- teachers decide classroom activities
- the school is authorized to generate its own income
- the deputy heads evaluate teachers
- heads and teachers together decide about school activities
- teachers are responsible for producing teaching aids
- the head evaluates teachers
- the school works around the rules.

The following factors discriminate the excellent and the very good schools from the good schools:

- the degree to which the SMC decides financial and administrative issues

- the degree to which teachers take responsibility for co-curricular activities
- the degree to which the school is responsible for physical expansion
- the degree to which the parents are involved in solving student discipline problems.

Despite of a fairly strict administrative system of policy implementation and control, school personnel in our sample schools feel empowered, and they do take responsibility for a range of important issues.

Local adaptation (worktable 36) is yet another factor that shows several common high impact sub-factors:

- flexible use of the labour education programme
- adaptations of the curriculum in the first three grades in social sciences and home economics
- use of a shift system, where appropriate.

The factors that discriminate the excellent and the very good schools from the good schools are:

- flexible production of teaching aids
- wider involvement of the community
- use of locally produced teaching-learning materials
- student contributions.

Community support (worktable 37) shows another fairly consistent picture, though with more sub-factors discriminating. Two sub-factors commonly seen as high impact are labour support and materials support from the community. The factors that discriminate the excellent and very good schools from the good schools are community financial support and participation in school administration. The excellent and very good schools show moderate impact on helping to solve discipline problems, while the good schools did not answer.

The number of factors that seem to have importance in the Ethiopian case is overwhelming. What, then, does success look like in the Ethiopian case? Or more precisely, what seem to be factors that show high impact in the excellent schools and discriminate these schools from the other schools? A successful rural primary school in our sample is different from the other schools in that:

- the headmaster plays a more active coordinating and pedagogical supportive role
- there is a higher degree of exchange of professional experiences among the teachers
- there is a wider involvement of the community.

These are factors that deal with the internal climate and the relationship with the community which is such an important component of the Ethiopian reform.

The dynamics of change in the Ethiopian reform process

How does the reform work in Ethiopia? It is a comprehensive system that combines a centralized decision-making system with local participation and a strong headmaster role. The headmaster is a person who knows what is going on in the classroom, is an instructional leader and is a link to the authority structure (e.g. the DEO) and to the community.

Political stability and commitment (1) were the basis for the Ethiopian reform process (see Figure 8.2). This led to the design of a system of reform (2), which in turn led to the division of labour (3). This was based on legal regulations (4) that provide legitimation for personnel at the national, regional, local and school levels. It distributes responsibilities, gives an important role to parents (5) (e.g. participation in the school management committee, responsibility for finances, etc.), gives a very clear supervisory responsibility to the DEO (6), a daily supervision and support role to the headmaster (7) and a chance for teachers to participate in the development (and/or adaptation) of the reform, which again was based on a moderate form of decentralization (8).

Teachers' mastery (9) is also a key factor in this reform. It is, however, dependent on a much more comprehensive network of factors. The new textbooks and materials (10), for example, would not have been delivered without strong national organizations (11). The local, school-based materials development would not have been there without the district APC model materials development (12) and training of the school SPC teacher (13). It is likely that the most critical element of staff development in the Ethiopian system is the on-going daily discussions between the staff and the headmaster, facilitated through the formal responsibilities for supervision (14) and the feedback of quarterly reports (15).

This aspect of the dynamics needs some further clarification. The Ethiopian reform, unlike the Colombian, is to a large degree built on feedback-loops. It starts in the classroom. The head and the teacher discuss progress. It is informally discussed in the school, then reported in the quarterly reports (15), which are discussed by the DEO and the headmaster (supervision (14)), and often with the entire staff, sometimes referring to governmental guidelines (14). Data from the SMC, a body where the parents play an important role, also belongs to this report. In principle these reports are fed back and up the system and form the basis for parts of the agenda in the annual education conference. Without doubt, the supervision and feedback mechanisms developed in the Ethiopian reform are an important part of the process.

This means that in Ethiopia the school and the district office are closely connected. There are several interdependencies including a support structure through the APC (12) and SPC, and the regular and on-going in-service training efforts (13) (which are often limited by the lack of resources). The core of the reform process in Ethiopia, in our view, is relationship between the school and the district.

Success experiences (16) also play an important role in the Ethiopian reform, partly as a consequence of teacher mastery (9) and a well-organized

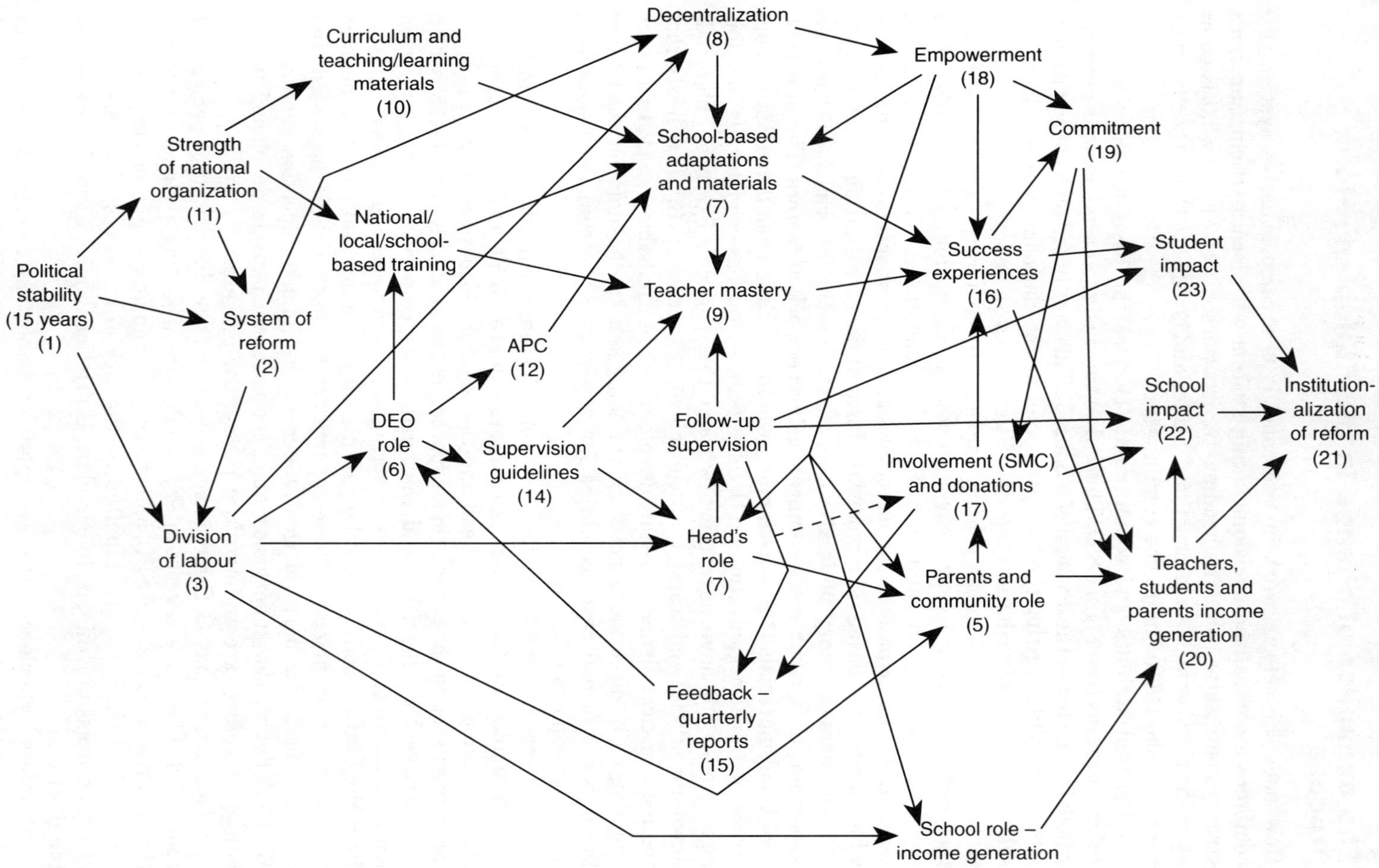

Figure 8.2 Ethiopia: the reform process.

school, and partly as a result of the involvement and contribution from the community (17), the empowerment (18) felt by the head and the teachers and the positive effects of local adaptations (7).

Gradually these early success experiences lead to more commitment (19), more involvement and an ability of the entire school and community to generate their own income (20). This is certainly important for the institutionalization of the reform (21) in a resource poor country, and it has a positive impact on the school (22) as a whole. The changes in the classrooms (experienced as teacher mastery and success) have impact on students' learning and behaviour (23).

It is through a systematic development of a system of reform, with division of labour, acceptable roles for all key players that produce empowerment and commitment, that such a tight and strict management driven system can function, and with considerable success.

BANGLADESH

Assistance (worktable 38) is a strong factor in the reform in Bangladesh. As in Ethiopia it is a role divided between the inspector and the headmaster. The inspector role in the Bangladesh case is mostly played by the AUEO, the intermediate role between the school and the district education officer (UEO). There are some common strong factors:

- Cluster training by the AUEO is an overall high to medium impact factor, and it discriminates the excellent and the very good schools from the good schools.
- Supervision by the AUEO is another overall strong factor, and it discriminates between all three groups of schools.
- Headmaster training and advice is also a strong factor (from high to medium/low impact) that discriminates between all three groups of schools.
- Staff development organized by the headmaster is a medium impact factor common to all three groups of schools.
- Supervision by the UEO is a moderately strong factor and it discriminates between all three types of schools.
- Supervision by the DPEO (from the regional office) is a medium/low impact factor across the board.
- Training abroad is commonly a low impact factor.

Several of these sub-factors are probably best discussed under the factor called supervision; however, they are mentioned here because the supervision component is seen as assistance. The general picture is of on-going training and supervision from the AUEO, supported by the head and the UEO.

The role of headmaster (worktable 39) indicates an active headmaster. There are some common trends:

- The headmaster has served long in the school and is seen as having a positive attitude towards the reform in all three categories of schools.

- The control of teachers' work is a common behaviour making teachers aware of reform intentions (discriminating factor).
- The monitoring of time (punctuality) is a medium to high impact factor, and so are reminders of rules and regulations.
- Reporting to the district office is another fairly common behaviour (high/medium impact).
- Good relations with the community is a medium to high impact factor, as is the coordination of school activities (including co-curricular activities).
- The headmaster commonly attends to resource-needs (high/medium impact).
- The most dominant behaviour, however, is follow-up work and assistance in terms of training and advice-giving on pedagogical issues.

The headmasters in the Bangladesh schools play both an administrative control function and a pedagogical or instructional leadership role.

The role of the administrator (worktable 40) indicates a few common strong sub-factors:

- The administrator has also served for a long time and is seen as having a positive attitude towards the reform.
- The control and monitoring of the implementation of the reform is a common behaviour for district inspectors in all categories of schools. The monitoring of school reports discriminates the excellent and very good schools from the good schools.
- UEO visits and the instruction of teachers are commonly seen as having a medium impact.
- The AUEO commonly delegates the coordination to the headmaster, and he or she informs the head about new developments (discriminates the excellent schools).
- The head's attempts to link the school to the community is generally fairly moderate, and seen as weakest in the excellent schools.
- The district officer sees to it that the needed materials are provided (commonly high impact factor).
- The pedagogical support role, particularly through training and supervision (the AUEO), is also shared among all three types of schools. Training discriminates moderately.
- The inspector helps to problem-solve more in the excellent schools than in the other schools.

In Bangladesh as in Ethiopia, the sample schools have a fairly active district administrator fulfilling both a policy-monitoring role and a support role, particularly through training. We also find that the better schools have a more active district administrator.

Supervision (worktable 41) confirms the supervision data noted above, namely:

- The AUEO role is strong in all categories of schools (both supervision and training), and both aspects of the role discriminate between all three categories of schools.
- The supervision of the head has varied impact, and discriminates between all three types of schools.
- The UEO supervision has medium impact across the board.

The picture that emerges is a system of management where the AUEO plays a key role, the headmaster works closely with the AUEO and follow-up, the UEO is more rarely involved and the impact is also seen as smaller.

Commitment (worktable 42) in the Bangladesh case is viewed in terms of key personnel giving priority to the reform, and the extent to which there is a 'strong team spirit. We find the following results:

- All key actors, i.e. teachers, headmasters, AUEOs, higher officials, UEOs and the communities, have all given priority to the reform in all categories of schools ranging from high impact to medium impact.
- The ratings for the AUEO, the headmaster and the UEO discriminate between all three categories of schools.
- The degree to which there is a strong team spirit also discriminates between the three categories of schools.

Received pressure (worktable 43) is another factor that is clearly felt as having impact, usually moderate impact. The commonly felt pressures are the circulars from the DPEO and the degree of political support and demands. The AUEO pressure, and to some extent the pressure from the UEO, discriminates the excellent schools from the very good and good schools.

It is interesting to note that the Bangladesh team sees problem-solving by the UEO and the AUEO as received pressure. We assume this means that the administrators intervene in local conflicts and put pressure on the parties and/or demand particular solutions. This factor discriminates between the three types of schools.

Received resources (worktable 44) is a factor that clearly discriminates the three categories of schools in general. More specifically, the following factors discriminate the excellent schools from the others:

- the construction of new buildings
- specially allotted resources from the government
- building of a new latrine and tubewell.

The delivery of teaching/learning materials discriminates between all categories of schools. New furniture is a common factor seen as having a medium impact. Other resources include help from the district and contingency grants, both of which have a relatively low impact.

Success experiences (worktable 45) are also more clearly seen in the excellent schools. These schools have, more than the other schools, success experiences in terms of increased enrolment and recruitment of more female teachers and girls. Discriminating between all three categories of schools are:

- higher achievements, fewer drop-outs and less repetition
- more punctuality among teachers
- more scholarships
- increased enrolment of poor children
- extra classrooms.

Empowerment (worktable 46) is felt only to a minor degree in a system where everything comes from above. This feeling, in fact, is felt to have a higher impact in the excellent schools than in the other schools. At the same time the excellent schools feel more strongly than other schools that teachers implement decisions, and we assume those to be decisions taken by the authorities.

The degree to which the 'project people' listen to the concerns of local people is only marginal, though it is somewhat higher in the excellent schools. The scope for modifications at the local level is seen as low to medium/low. To some extent the upazila (the district) has got more power, and this seems to influence the reform at a low to medium level.

Local adaptation (worktable 47) also indicates that the excellent schools to a larger extent than the other schools have accepted the reform as designed. These schools more than others feel that:

- all components fitted well
- there is little need for adaptation
- there is less scope for local adaptation.

There is medium to low involvement of teachers in co-curricular activities where some local initiative is expected and carried out. The role of the community in the school management committee and the parent-teacher association is also seen to have a medium impact on the reform. The role of the teachers and the headmaster is seen to have a low impact.

Community participation (worktable 48) indicates that community involvement in the reform is minimal. This part of the reform is simply not implemented. There is one exception in the excellent schools, in that the parents in all these schools show an interest in their children's education, and the impact is rated as high. The community in these schools is clearly more supportive than in the other schools (this factor discriminates between all three categories of schools). On the other hand, parents are not aware of the reform, the PTA is not functioning, and with a couple of exceptions, the SMC is not functioning either. The relationship with the parents and the community seems to have a much lower emphasis in the Bangladesh reform than in the other two cases.

The dynamics of the reform process

The Bangladesh reform effort can best be understood as a major improvement in the management of schools, particularly by introducing the following elements (numbers in brackets refer to numbers of factors in Figure 8.3):

- A new management position, the AUEO (1), that is given a selected number of schools to work with. He or she can work intensively as a combined supervisor (1B) and trainer (1C).
- An upgraded headmaster role (2) seen as the key link to the AUEO (who communicates the government policies). The head is responsible for the follow-up (2B), support and monitoring (2C) of the changes (much as in Ethiopia).
- A moderate up-grading of buildings, facilities, furniture (3) and teaching/learning resources to include free textbooks and a free teachers' guide (3B) to provide the minimum for the school to operate effectively.

The key word here is supervision (1B) which is the heart of the AUEO work. It implies the transition of government policies, the monthly training of teachers (1C), and the supervision of the work in the schools (mostly by visiting with the headmaster) (2B). The in-service training is also given by several others, including PTIs (1D). The regular follow-up by the headmaster and the on-going supervision is seen to have an impact on teachers' punctuality (15).

The AUEO is not alone. He or she is supported by the more distant UEO (4), who has a moderate impact on supervision, and he or she puts pressure (4B) on the headmaster (e.g. monthly reports). The AUEO is also supported by the authorities represented by the DPEO (5) who, usually through circulars and irregular visits, support the work of the AUEO. All in all, it is a fairly heavy management system that tries to transmit downwards the policies of the government. Overall, this implies a new management system (5B) that is seen as a career ladder for headmasters (5C), as a success experience (5D), and as strengthening institutionalization (5E).

The headmaster follows up on a daily basis, partly by providing further training, but most often through problem-solving, discussions and joint development work. These combined efforts are seen as positively related to teachers' mastery (6). Also positively related is the fact that the government is providing resources to upgrade buildings and furniture, textbooks and other necessary learning materials that have a positive impact on commitment (7).

However, there are other parts of the policy that probably have a less positive, and possibly negative impact on both teachers' mastery and the final outcomes. This is particularly related to the centralistic nature of decision-making (8) which is seen as hindering local adaptations (9), reducing teacher commitment (7) and reducing the interest of the parents to become involved (10), which may have a negative impact on the final outcomes (e.g. increased female enrolment (11)).

The strong positive factors, teachers' mastery (6), supervision (1B), regular follow-up (2B) and materials delivery (3B) contribute to improved classroom practice (12), which has a positive impact on the drop-out rate (13), retention (14) and teachers' punctuality (15). As in Ethiopia the national factors also play an important role, particularly because the reform has top priority (16). This was the basis for developing a system of reform (16B), legal regulation (16C) and a division of labour (16D), which is a condition for strengthening national institutions (17) and helped to establish the AUEO role (1), developed curriculum materials (18) and provided some decentralization (19). The political will was also important for the involvement of external donors (20), and for the provision of an adequate budget (21).

At the far right of the 'map' some factors, such as the teachers' association role, are seen as having a site-specific negative impact on the implementation of the reform, while the Hindu community is seen as a cultural component having a strong positive impact on student outcomes (site-specific). Figure 8.3 shows the network of factors that the study has identified to best explain the success of implementation in Bangladesh.

We have also tried to summarize those factors that work when the Bangladesh reform has most success (those factors that discriminate the excellent schools). The reform has most success when:

- the AUEO supervision and training role (Cluster training) is well implemented
- the headmaster and the administrator are both giving pedagogical support as well as monitoring policy implementation
- it is felt that management (head, AUEO and UEO) gives priority to the reform
- there is a strong team spirit
- there is pressure from the AUEO and both he or she and the UEO intervene in problem-solving
- needed resources for the physical structure and teaching materials are fulfilled
- success is felt in terms of student-related goals
- the teachers accept the reform as intended
- it is felt that the reform is making a good fit
- parents are interested in their children's education
- the community attitude and support is available.

These are all factors that discriminate the excellent schools (and for some factors also the very good schools). It is a very comprehensive list of factors and does mean that many schools do not meet these criteria, or only partly meet these criteria.

The three change strategies

We are now in a position to compare the reform strategies in the three countries, to see what makes them look alike, and what makes them differ. There are some important common elements:

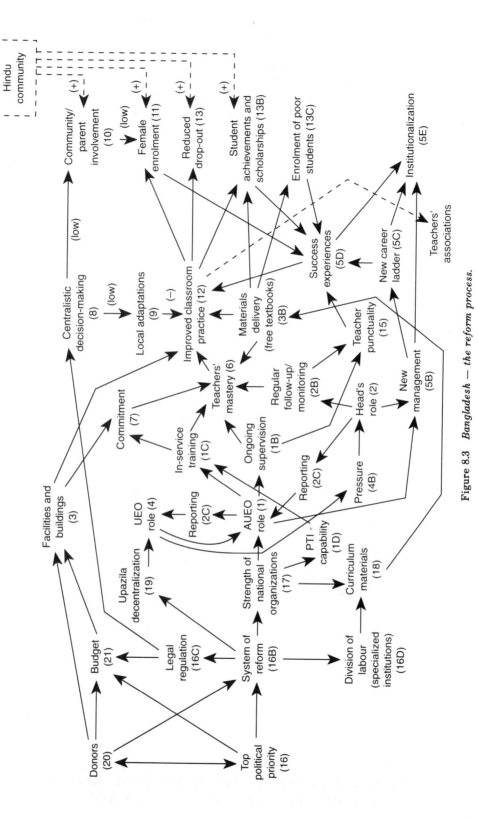

Figure 8.3 *Bangladesh — the reform process.*

1. Rural primary education has been a top political priority in all three countries over many years. This was clearly expressed in Bangladesh and Ethiopia from the outset; it has become a policy over time in Colombia, and is presently an established national policy.
2. The reforms have a base in a strong national team, or educational leaders with knowledge and skills and commitment to the cause. It was originally an independent group in Colombia (the EN resource team), and an official national team in both Ethiopia and Bangladesh. It is strong leadership sustained over many years.
3. All three reforms aim at changing classroom practice, and therefore attempt to influence teachers, students and the school as an organization.
4. All three systems have tried to reach the teacher, to change his or her attitudes, behaviour and role. Teachers' mastery is central to all three reform efforts.
5. Various forms of staff development, to include school-based in-service training, local adaptation of the curriculum and materials, pedagogical supervision as well as national training efforts (e.g. Ethiopia), are a key strategy in all three systems.
6. Assistance is a key strategy in all three reforms. Also, school-based assistance, or at least assistance as close to the school and the classroom as possible, is a common characteristic. Often assistance means in-service training; however, it is also forms of supervision, consultancies, advice-giving and problem-solving. The closer the 'advice-giver is to the school, the greater the impact.

The three reform strategies also differ considerably:

1. In terms of their degree of restructuring the entire system, and the extent to which the reform efforts took the existing structure for granted and instead tried to change the teacher and classroom practice directly:
   - The Ethiopian reform is the most comprehensive in terms of restructuring the system, changing policies, national institutions, division of labour, roles and relationships, the curriculum and the organization of schooling. As a consequence it also had a longer way to go to reach the teacher and the classroom.
   - The Colombian reform is the case with the shortest way from the reform idea to the classroom, a fairly straightforward package that relatively quickly could positively influence the daily life of students. At the same time the existing Colombian school system and its structure were left untouched, which may have consequences for dissemination and institutionalization.
   - The Bangladesh reform is closer to the Ethiopian strategy than to the Colombian strategy; however, there are differences. It does take restructuring seriously; however, this is mainly in the area of

management. In this area significant innovations are introduced that clearly have had a positive impact on rural primary schools. On the other hand, it gave less emphasis to areas like user involvement, community involvement, and even the teaching-learning process was partly neglected.

2. In terms of the degree of decentralization, the systems are clearly different. The Colombian reform effort is basically a bottom-up effort that gradually has been given national status and legitimacy. The Ethiopian reform is a centrally managed reform that has delegated certain functions down the system, and gradually given power to various personnel at the local level. The Bangladesh reform effort is the most centralistic effort, and lacks almost any degree of delegation to the school level (although it does have an aspect of decentralization to the upazila level).

3. The use of management and systematic monitoring differ in the three systems. This is partly related to the degree of centralization; however, it goes beyond this dimension of management. The Colombian system does not use management and monitoring through the hierarchy as an important element of the reform strategy. It is much more based on collegial interaction and in-service training. The costs are that some schools are not succeeding, and the solutions may be ad hoc. The Ethiopian and the Bangladesh systems use management and monitoring systematically as a communication vehicle, as pressure and as a feedback mechanism to ensure successful implementation. In-service training and collegial supervision is also important in these systems, and the central role of management, particularly through on-going monitoring, is playing an important role.

4. Linkage that enables the user to connect with the ideas, policies and norms of the innovation is common to all three systems. However, the communication links differ:

    - In Colombia the linkage is mainly the guide combined with training, more or less a self-instructional package that transmits the message. To some extent the external resource persons, through regular supervision and support, also help to connect.
    - In Ethiopia there are many strong linkages. The strongest are probably the regular quarterly reports, supervision visits and in-service training. The annual education conference also serves as a pep-talk mechanism and helps to transmit the latest ideas.
    - In Bangladesh the link is the AUEO. He or she is supported by the UEO and others, but it is through the AUEO that the messages are carried.

5. The development and use of materials is another key factor that differs in the way it is practised. In Bangladesh the materials are centrally produced, and the teacher is mainly seen as a consumer of

this material. The consequences seem to be less commitment, less local adaptation and less enthusiasm. In both Ethiopia and Colombia the teacher is assumed to actively develop materials, locally produced. The guide gives these possibilities in Colombia, while the SPC gives a similar opportunity in Ethiopia. It seems to imply that the teacher is seen as a producer, and it does seem to lead to higher commitment, success experiences and an active role.

6. The roles of parents and the community differ considerably in the three systems. In Ethiopia parents and the community play an important formal role in rural schools, participating in the school management committee, contributing land, labour and cash. Also in Colombia parents are involved, more as a consequence of the success they experience with the EN reform. Parents and community participation may be an official part of the reform in Bangladesh; however, it does not work in our sample schools. This may be a consequence of a fairly rigid centralistic system of management.

Chapter 9

Findings

INTRODUCTION

The HSI project is based on an earlier World Bank study: Adrian Verspoor's, Pathways to Change — Improving the Quality of Education in Developing Countries (Verspoor, 1989). The 'national' part of the HSI study was set up mainly to test the conclusions of the Verspoor study. We shall therefore go back to these conclusions first and test them against the findings of this study.

Secondly, the HSI study in its main area of investigation, at the local level, was set up to be exploratory in nature, testing out a number of hypotheses and 'going deep' into the nature of a number of factors (see Appendix 1, page 304). We shall look closely at the following key variables:

- assistance
- supervision
- pressure
- decentralization and delegation
- empowerment
- commitment
- local adaptation
- teaching-learning materials
- political commitment and stability.

Thirdly, we shall describe and analyse the outcomes of a successful primary school reform. Fourthly, we have attempted to study roles and functions in the system, e.g. the role of the local administrator. The study provides a rich opportunity to understand the role of the parent, the teacher, the headmaster, the local administrator and the role of the 'support-giver' in educational change. We shall look at some of the variables that explain effectiveness in these roles.

Finally, the How Schools Improve study is about success. We have analysed paths to successful implementation of educational reforms. The question we want to answer is the following: What makes for 'excellence' in rural primary schools? This chapter will sum up our findings in the study.

REVISITING VERSPOOR

The Verspoor study was a World Bank desk study, primarily building on formal World Bank and country documents, supervision reports and audit reports. It included projects in some 21 countries and covered all levels of education and was based on data from thousands of schools in most countries, but it did not go deep into actual implementation and outcomes at the school level. As such, it was a broad rather than 'close up' study. The HSI study was more focused and limited in scope (31 rural primary schools in three countries, most implementing reforms fairly successfully), and looked closely at the reasons for success, seen nationally and regionally, and at the ways schools actually operate in their local, regional and national contexts. The study went deep, with intensive interviews and observations in the field based on a structured deductive research approach.

These differences in scope and approach make it clear that we cannot assume that we are in a position to make a full test of the conclusions of the Verspoor study. But we can, on the basis of our systematic methodology, comment on the Verspoor findings, in some cases confirming them, and in addition expanding and explaining some of the factors that are studied at the local level. We shall now turn to the Verspoor conclusions (page numbers of the Verspoor study in parentheses):

1. **Significant educational change demands long-term, stable political support** (page 71). This finding is related to another conclusion, namely that **government commitment has been repeatedly and consistently identified as one of the critical conditions for successful project implementation** (page 101).

These findings are supported and confirmed by the HSI study: in Ethiopia (stable political support during the entire educational reform period from 1974 to 1990); in Bangladesh where Universal Primary Education has been a top political priority for more than ten years, and where primary education has been given additional resources in spite of severe economic problems in the country; and finally in Colombia, a case that is different from the other two. In Colombia, political support from national authorities (for the EN reform) was not automatic. In fact, it was a local group with external donor support that gained internal political support throughout the reform period. It now has stable national political support, a factor that the interviewees see as fundamental for the dissemination of the reform. (See also Table B, Chapter 6, page 176.) The importance of stable political support is also seen as legitimation at the local level, and it has a positive effect on local commitment.

2. **Successful change strategies strengthened the administrative capacity at both the centre and the periphery of the system** (page 91): Verspoor has several findings related to this main finding:

   - the improvement of support and supervision
   - strengthening policy and planning institutions
   - the development of a competent cadre of national staff
   - the development of a clear structural arrangement to coordinate and reinforce the efforts
   - adequate resources
   - a form of monitoring system, or a system that keeps managers

informed (Verspoor found that formal mechanisms for monitoring and evaluation were weak in all systems).

The HSI study has studied these factors at both the central and local level. The various components turn out differently in the three national systems, and we shall therefore deal with each one separately.

Strengthening policy and planning institutions. This is clearly the case in Ethiopia and Bangladesh, as expressed by the central informants; however, it is not a significant part of the Colombian reform. In both Ethiopia and Bangladesh it meant the creation of new central institutions (e.g. for curriculum development and textbook production), a clearer division of labour, legal regulation and what we have called 'infrastructure development' (see Table A, Chapter 6, pages 171-3). According to central informants these factors show high impact in our study, except for curriculum development; the Colombian reform has not (so far) invested in the infrastructure.

At the local informant level, it is difficult to confirm if the creation and development of these central institutions makes a difference. It is mainly the products and resources delivered that make a difference at the local level. Comparing the three countries, we find (Table D, Chapter 6, page 179):

- The administrative build-up in Ethiopia and Bangladesh results in a higher degree of received pressure as experienced by the schools.
- It does not lead to higher user involvement or higher commitment (which also corresponds to the views of central informants — see Table C, Chapter 6, page 177).

The development of a competent cadre of national staff. The Colombian EN resource team has been instrumental in the implementation of the reform throughout the entire reform period (although it did not mean capacity building of national organizations, see Table A, Chapter 6, page 171). In both Ethiopia and Bangladesh the capacity building factor is seen as highly important and instrumental for the reform (as seen nationally). Indirectly, the importance of administrative competence at the national level is confirmed by local informants (e.g. the importance of the National Education Conference in Ethiopia, or the supervision system in Bangladesh). The nature of the reform and the reform strategy in Colombia meant that the EN resource team actually worked in the field and trained a large number of teachers. Their competence was linked directly to the development of teacher mastery, a key to the reform.

Clear structural supports for coordination. This conclusion by Verspoor has not been tested in the HSI study. The closest factor is division of labour, which is rated high impact by central informants in Ethiopia and medium impact in Bangladesh, a factor that is related to decentralization (see below). It is unanswered in Colombia.

Adequate resources. In all three reforms the question of resources was central. In some cases, in particular in Ethiopia, the success of the reform led to increased enrolment, overcrowded classes and a relative decline in resources (per student).

Resources in our study meant both materials resources (e.g. instructional materials) and the total amount of resources per student.

Table D (Chapter 6, page 179) indicates that although central informants in Ethiopia and Bangladesh express the view that resource delivery has been important for the success of the reform (although declining and inadequate, as seen by several central informants both in Bangladesh and Ethiopia), the informants at the school level see received resources as inadequate. Local informants value the delivery of instructional materials (see 'resource delivery', Table C, page 177), which also corresponds with the view of central informants ('availability and quality of materials', Table D, page 179). Both groups of informants see these resources having high impact, and contributing to the linkage dimension (relating various parts of the system to each other).

The excellent schools in Colombia have a stronger materials delivery system than the other two categories of schools. The support of materials from DEO discriminate the excellent and very good schools from the good schools in Ethiopia (so does community support). The construction of new classrooms and the provision of facilities discriminate the excellent schools in Bangladesh.

We are studying three systems where the use of quality teaching-learning materials is essential for the reform, and the best schools (in Colombia and Ethiopia) show high impact as far as materials delivery is concerned. At the same time we see the problems of systems that cannot increase the allocation of resources as the success of the reforms leads to higher enrolment and higher retention.

Managers of high outcome programmes keep themselves informed. Central informants in both Ethiopia and Bangladesh value both monitoring and control and effective communication as two high impact country level factors that have contributed to the reform. Both factors are rated as medium impact in Colombia. Verspoor did not find any reform that had a built-in systematic monitoring and evaluation function. Ethiopia, in particular (and to some extent Bangladesh) has this, and it is seen as an important variable in explaining the change process in both countries (see Figures 8.2 and 8.3, Chapter 8, pp. 212 and 219). Regular follow-up and monitoring has impact on teacher mastery, improved classroom practice, reduced drop-out and retention and teacher punctuality in Bangladesh. Follow-up and quarterly reports in Ethiopia influence teacher mastery and also keep the district officer informed and more able to interact.

3. **High outcomes were achieved by programmes adopted on the basis of internally — as well as externally — driven policies** (page 43). Verspoor underlines the importance of diagnosis of key issues confronting the education sector, the development of a strategic framework, and focusing on the capacity to manage change. This capacity has to be institutionalized (page 117). What do we find in the three reforms studied?

Internally driven policies was a key factor in all three countries. In Colombia the support behind the EN project was local and fairly marginal in the first few years, growing slowly to a national commitment. In Bangladesh the internal concern for universal primary education was a matter of political priority. The new Ethiopian regime (1974) set out to fundamentally reform the education system and had a big stake in the reform process.

Indicators of internally driven policies have already been discussed (e.g. strengthening national organizations, infrastructure development, etc.). One critical factor was the development of a competent staff at the national and local level. An internally driven reform can only be realized through a competent staff, a factor that is rated as having had high impact in all three systems (see above).

One factor that is related to the internal priority to the reform is the factor we have called protection from environmental turbulence. Central informants see this as having had high impact in Bangladesh (financial security), medium impact in Colombia (insecure funding the first years), and medium/low impact in Ethiopia. In Ethiopia the national political campaigns often instructed teachers to leave their classrooms for the political cause, which was seen both centrally and locally as a hindering factor. At this level, other priorities were seen as more important than the implementation of the primary school reform.

Externally driven policies. International and national donor agencies have played an instrumental role in the initiation, development and implementation of these three reforms. In Colombia a group of local innovators got early professional and financial support from UNESCO, and later from several national and local donors and from the World Bank. In Bangladesh a series of primary school projects were financed by bilateral donors and the World Bank (about 80 per cent of the development costs), and in Ethiopia the reform efforts got support at an early stage, for example from SIDA as well as from the World Bank.

How do central informants see the external donor support? In all countries it is seen as a country level factor with high impact on the success of the reform (we do not have information from the local level informants). Our data does not give a full account of the relative impact of the internal and external forces for change. However, we find the basis for the following conclusion. The external agencies have played a significant role in formulating the ideas of the reform: in Colombia the UNESCO model (the unitary school) was the basis for the internal reform effort from 1961; however, this was modified and further developed by the EN resource team. In Bangladesh the World Bank contributed to several of the key ideas for strengthening the administrative system (e.g. the AUEO), and in Ethiopia several external donors (in particular experts from the former GDR) played an important part. Gradually, as competence grew nationally and locally, the Ethiopians were increasingly in control of their own development. Donor financial support continued to be essential throughout all phases of the reform. It is through long term sustained support that results are produced.

4. **Provide permanent and locally available in-service teacher training, and establish an effective system of supervision and support** (pages 93 and 95). These are two conclusions in the Verspoor study;

however, we will see the two conclusions in relationship to each other.

All three systems have invested in extensive in-service teacher training, and all three reform models as presented in Chapters 6 and 8 indicate that the training component is essential for the implementation of the reform as seen by both central and local informants (see 'assistance' Table A, Chapter 6, as assessed by central informants, and 'assistance' as seen by local informants in Chapter 8).

In Ethiopia the combination of the local district training and development centre (APC) and the in-school pedagogical centre (SPC) provided most of the training throughout the reform period. This aspect of the reform is seen as having high impact in the excellent and the very good schools and medium impact in the good schools, and is therefore a discriminating factor. These are the factors that are associated with greater success (e.g. excellent schools) in implementation, student impact, teacher impact, school impact and institutionalization, all of which add up to success.

The discriminating factors are also connected with the climate of the school (teachers helping each other) and the leadership of the schools (feedback from the headmaster and the local inspector). Therefore training, in the Ethiopian context, is a complex interaction of several activities, including national and locally provided courses, weekly in-school work in the pedagogical centre, teachers helping each other, and support and feedback from the headmaster (and to some extent from the local inspector). The key to successful training is the organization of the work processes in the school, and a system of staff development locally available that contributes to teacher impact and innovation in use.

In-service training is also seen as having a 'high impact' on the reform in Colombia (see worktable 16, Appendix 4, page 329). Training is mainly provided in the first year of the reform. Pedagogical supervision and coaching by EN resource persons or local inspectors does take place in the following years; however, less frequently than in the Ethiopian case. In fact the good schools only have initial training. One additional training aspect of the Colombian reform is the nature of the guide and the opportunities for local adaptation. This process gives teachers challenging tasks, which improve their mastery (see Figure 8.1, the EN reform process, Chapter 8, page 203). Training, therefore, does mean something more than courses in the Colombian case, it is the total work situation of the teacher that helps him or her to learn and develop.

In Bangladesh the training factor is hard to isolate from assistance and supervision. Most of the support is institutionalized locally in one person, the AUEO. This person, when successful, works closely with about 20 schools (usually with the headmaster), provides regular seminars, supervises, gives advice and consults with headmasters and teachers. As shown in Figure 8.3 in Chapter 8 (page 219), the AUEO role is seen as being central to the reform. Training is mainly taken care of through regular local seminars (cluster training), follow-up is conducted by the headmaster, and supervision is a combined effort of local administrators and the headmaster.

To what extent have the three systems established an effective system of supervision and support? In Bangladesh the system, as seen by both central and local informants of the sample schools, is an effective system. The AUEO role is seen as having high impact, while the role of the headmaster discriminates the schools. The excellent and the very good schools have higher impact supervision through the combination of the AUEO and the headmaster role.

The system is also effective in Ethiopia. In this case a regular quarterly reporting system strengthens the control dimension of supervision. In this system the headmaster is the key person involved in supervision, while the local administrator plays a more distant role. In Colombia the supervision and follow-up component is also seen as having high impact; however, it varies considerably from region to region. Supervision is mainly pedagogical in nature.

In all three systems supervision is mainly seen as support, although there is a control element built in (particularly in Ethiopia). The more local, or accessible, supervision is (e.g. the headmaster or a local inspector like the AUEO), the more effective it is seen to be.

5. **Encourage teacher motivation and commitment** (page 98). Verspoor argues for a teacher role where teachers are active participants rather than passive recipients, and that extrinsic rewards seldom work.

The reform effort where the teacher clearly has been delegated most responsibility, where empowerment is felt, and where commitment is high, is the Colombian programme. Here the teachers and the head decide on all important issues, which is an encouragement for teachers and builds commitment, provided they are given an opportunity for professional development and on-going support.

The Ethiopian reform also gives the teacher freedom to some extent. This system, however, is more controlled, the opportunities for local initiative are more limited, and the power is shared among many (e.g. parents, the deputy head, the head and the district office). Nevertheless, commitment in Ethiopia shows high impact in many schools, and discriminates the excellent and the very good schools from the good schools.

In Bangladesh the teachers have less opportunity to take initiative and adapt the reform. Although there is a general positive attitude of giving priority to the reform, it is less clear what the actual commitment of teachers is, which again is related to improved performance and outcomes.

Our data tends to support the Verspoor finding. More empowerment through delegation, combined with staff development and support, produces higher commitment among teachers.

6. **Commitment is built and maintained through local participation (e.g. parents), external agency support and demonstrated success** (page 106). Verspoor argues that 'communication of program objectives and achievements to parents in several instances helped broaden the base of support for the project in the community'.

Community participation is seen as a high impact factor in both Ethiopia and Colombia, and a missing component in Bangladesh. In Ethiopia in particular

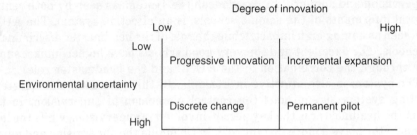

Figure 9.1 *Institutionalization process.*

parents play an important role, both through their involvement in the school management committee and as contributors in financial and labour terms. Without this central role of parents, it is unlikely that several of the schools would have made it this far, and it is seen as essential for institutionalization. The headmaster plays an important role in facilitating cooperation with the community, and in particular with the parents.

In Colombia parents got involved after having seen the first results of the EN programme. The success experience helped parents to see the importance and to get involved.

In Bangladesh parents have had only a very limited role in the reform. There is also limited scope for local participation, adaptation and development. But again in Bangladesh, where parents showed an interest in their children's education and community support was positive, success was more likely (worktable 48, page 345).

From these data it seems clear that parent and community involvement may be instrumental to implementation and institutionalization. However, it is possible to implement the reform without parent involvement. The question in Bangladesh is whether the country will be able to sustain the reform without active parent and local community involvement.

The role of the external donor agencies has been commented on above. It may well be that in the Bangladesh case the external support to some extent has compensated for the lack of local community support. We do not, however, have data that directly confirm this statement. However, external donor support does seem to contribute to commitment in Bangladesh and it seems to have an indirect impact on commitment in Ethiopia.

7. **The national implementation strategy** (pages 47 to 53): Verspoor developed an analytical model to analyse the national reform strategy. He grouped four implementation strategies within the matrix shown in Figure 9.1.

Verspoor explains the matrix in the following way. The upper boxes of the matrix represent scenarios that allow for the implementation, over a number of years, of major change programmes with ambitious educational and coverage objectives. The combination of variables in the lower boxes permits only the implementation of programmes with modest change objectives or the limited implementation of ambitious programmes. The implication of the matrix is that implementing major educational change requires a reasonable degree of environmental stability. Environmental uncertainty — economic upheavals and political turbulence — virtually prevents the implementation of ambitious change programmes and makes the adoption of more modest goals inevitable. But environmental uncertainty does not preclude successful implementation, provided it is taken into account in the selection of the objectives and the implementation strategy of the programme. For example, the assurance of substantial external financing over a long period could insulate a programme from short-term internal economic shocks, and thus reduce the risks associated with environmental uncertainty.

As shown, the four implementation strategies that emerge from this matrix are:

(i) Progressive innovation, a strategy that is designed to implement in a large geographic area (a country, state or province) a number of successive changes, each rather modest in itself, which, when taken together, result in considerable change over time; the long-term objective is comprehensive and large-scale reform.

(ii) Incremental expansion, a strategy geared toward the implementation of ambitious educational goals in a gradually increasing number of schools; the long-term objective again is comprehensive and large-scale change.

(iii) Discrete change, the traditional project approach which implements the change programme in a limited number of schools without clearly specified generalization objectives.

(iv) Permanent pilot, programmes that aspire to national coverage and show promising results in the pilot phase, but do not manage to mobilize enough support and/or resources to embark on nationwide application.

We have had some difficulty establishing criteria for both environmental uncertainty and degree of innovation. Most of these reforms are highly complex, have a number of dimensions (see definition of reforms, Chapters 3 to 5), and it is not an easy task to judge to what extent an innovation is low or high in a given context. Similarly, we have found it difficult to establish the degree of environmental uncertainty. In all the three countries under study, there have been major reasons for instability over the past three years. Bangladesh has had several dramatic floods, with severe impact on national budgets. Ethiopia has lived through a damaging civil war, and has recently changed its government, and Colombia has experienced violence (e.g. as a consequence of the drug war). It is possible to say that this means high environmental uncertainty in these countries. However, this external turbulence does not seem to have had any significant impact on the stability of the educational system. One may argue that Ethiopia would have had more resources to cope with increasing enrolment had the war not taken so much of the resources; however, such an argument is rather speculative. As far as the sample schools are concerned, their development has

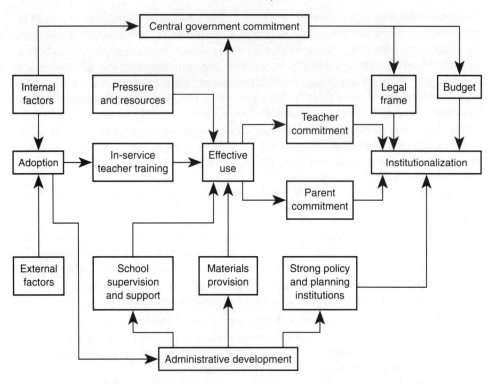

Figure 9.2 *The institutionalization process.*

taken place in a relatively stable environment. External turbulence has not had any significant impact on the stability of the daily work in the schools.

We have defined the implementation strategy for each country. First permanent pilot and then incremental expansion for Colombia, progressive innovation for Bangladesh, and nationwide from the start in Ethiopia. In the Ethiopian case the innovation is clearly high in terms of scope and complexity, and probably medium as far as teacher change is concerned. The political and economic environments (for schools) have been fairly stable. The Ethiopians decided to go nationwide from start (although it was some time before the various components were in place). On the basis of the HSI study, we cannot judge if the given strategy was optimal for the country, or if another strategy would have been more appropriate.

  8. **The institutionalization of the reform** (page 122). Verspoor presents a model illustrating factors that may contribute to the 'institutionalization process' (page 122).

We shall compare this model (Figure 9.2) with our models from the three countries presented in Chapter 8. The government role is seen as both commitment that leads to a legal frame and a budget, and as administrative development that leads to strong policy and planning institutions, supervision and support and materials provision. As already discussed, all three country reform programmes enjoy government commitment (although in Colombia this came fairly late in the process), and in Ethiopia and Bangladesh administrative development has been a key factor in the reform. This component is to a large extent missing in Colombia (until recently), resulting in some fear that the massification of the programme may lead to a watered-down effect, resulting in less control, lower quality and lower impact.

Pressure and resources have been applied in both Ethiopia and Bangladesh and are seen to have a positive impact on effective use (e.g. AUEO in Bangladesh and quarterly reports in Ethiopia). Resources also have (a more indirect) impact on effective use in Colombia. Legal frame and budget have played a role in all three reforms; however, their impact on institutionalization is unclear. The budget is seen as inadequate (Ethiopia and Bangladesh) and also in Colombia the cut-back to training is seen as a threat to the reform. An adequate budget, therefore, is clearly a condition for successful institutionalization.

The HSI study does not clearly distinguish between implementation of the reform in our sample schools and the institutionalization of the reform. In most schools studied, the change process had been going on for between five and 15 years, and — except for Colombia — the reforms were national from the beginning. There was no doubt that the reforms would be, or were indeed already, institutionalized. The term itself is taken from another change process tradition, describing a sequence of events from planning to development (often with testing, trial and errors), implementation, dissemination and institutionalization. In the HSI schools an implemented programme is assumed to stay. There is not yet another competing innovation coming along. The reform will gradually find its form, and a series of governmental decisions, among others, help or hinder institutionalization.

With this cautionary note in mind, we cannot directly prove that central government commitment and and administrative commitment lead to institutionatization. However, it is very likely that they do. That the government is serious, stays with the reform for up to 15 years and constantly supports it, is simply a condition for schools to be involved in the first place (see discussion of 'central factors' below).

User commitment, defined by Verspoor as parent commitment and teacher commitment, is also seen as leading to institutionalization. Teacher commitment in Ethiopia leads to local income generation, often with teachers in a key role, a condition for institutionalization. In Colombia teacher commitment has a more indirect (but positive) effect on institutionalization, while this factor is less clear in Bangladesh.

Parent commitment is clearly a factor that has an effect on finances and helps institutionalization in Ethiopia and Colombia. In Bangladesh the centralistic decision-making process leads to the absence of parent participation, and it has a negative impact on the recruitment of girls. We do not know the impact on institutionalization. However, it is likely that the effect is not positive.

Effective use of the innovation, in Verspoor's study, is determined by four factors:

- supervision and support
- materials provision
- in-service teacher training
- Pressure and resources.

The HSI study confirms that all four factors in all three countries are determinants of effective use (called improved classroom instruction). Beyond these four factors, this study finds the following determinants of effective use:

- responsive local adaptation
- community and parent involvement.

Both factors contribute positively to outcomes in Ethiopia and Colombia, and the lack of local adaptation and community involvement has a negative impact on classroom changes in Bangladesh.

WHAT ARE THE OUTCOMES OF THE REFORMS?

A full discussion of outcomes is given in Chapter 7. This section summarizes the outcomes that characterize successful reforms in all the three countries.

Implementation The classrooms have changed in all three systems, though the nature of the changes differ. In Colombia the very nature of the teaching-learning process has changed towards more individualized instruction and group work. In Ethiopia new curricula, new materials and the use of radio education changes the daily instructional process, and in Bangladesh newly constructed classrooms and free textbooks have to some extent improved daily instruction.

In-service training, on a regular basis (at least in Ethiopia and Bangladesh), has given the teacher additional support; and materials support, often locally produced and/or adapted, has been achieved in Ethiopia and Colombia.

Student impact Student attitudes and behaviour have been positively influenced in all three systems. Student leadership in Colombia, more regular attendance in Ethiopia (medium/high impact), and participation in co-curricular activities are examples of a more active and involved student. The excellent and very good schools in all three countries have improved achievement scores (examination results), while the enrolment rate is going up in Ethiopia (high/medium impact) and Bangladesh. The impact on the repetition rate and drop-out rate is modest (and is a discriminating factor in Bangladesh).

Teacher impact Teacher motivation shows high to medium impact and discriminates the excellent and very good schools from the good schools. Also teacher classroom behaviour shows high to medium impact in all three countries (and is a discriminating factor in Colombia and Ethiopia), as does teacher personal behaviour (this is a discriminating factor in Bangladesh, while data from Colombia is missing).

School outcomes The improvement of the physical facilities shows from high to medium impact in all three systems. It is commonly high impact in Colombia and Ethiopia and a discriminating factor in Bangladesh. School-community relations also shows high to medium impact and it appears as a discriminating factor in all three countries.

Institutionalization The reforms studied have been practised for many years. All three systems have to a large extent routinized key elements of the reform, at a high impact level in Colombia and Ethiopia, and at high to medium level in Bangladesh. What outcomes discriminate between the excellent, the very good and the good schools in all three countries? The following factors do:

- student achievement or cognitive gains
- teacher motivation and attitudes
- teacher knowledge (implied factor in Colombia)
- teacher mastery
- school community relations.

These are outcomes that are more frequently observed in the excellent schools than in the very good schools and the good schools.

THE KEY FACTORS — CLOSE UP

In this study we have focused on determinants of educational change, singled out factors that seem to have an impact, and attempted to understand how these factors work in a given local and country context (see Chapter 8). Our task here is to understand what these factors look like when they are effectively contributing to successful outcomes, defined as the sum of outcomes, implementation, impact and institutionalization. Later in this chapter we shall summarize our findings as they relate to specific outcomes (e.g. student impact). The key factors are the same as those discussed in Chapter 8, and those that in the HSI study are key to explaining success (sum of outcomes). The basis for this analysis are the worktables (Appendix 4), as well as the maps of factors illustrated in Figure 8.1 in Chapter 8 (page 203).

The nature of assistance

In nearly all cases assistance is defined as in-service teacher training, and often local training. It is a key determinant for teacher mastery in all three systems. Teacher mastery is a key variable to understand improved classroom practice in all three countries. In-service training discriminates the excellent and very Good schools from the good schools in Ethiopia and Bangladesh, and is a common high impact factor in Colombia.

Assistance works best when it is concrete (e.g. work with the student guide in Colombia); when it is locally available (e.g. the SPC in each school in Ethiopia); when it is regular and on-going (e.g. the cluster training in Bangladesh); when it is linked to practice (e.g. the follow-up function of the headmaster in Bangladesh); when teachers can actually practise new behaviour (e.g. the development of teaching-learning aids in the SPC in Ethiopia); and when it is supported by a climate of cooperation among teachers, and between the headmaster and the teachers. In-service training also may lead to a higher level of school-based adaptations and materials development (Ethiopia and Colombia), and it may lead to higher commitment (Bangladesh).

The nature of supervision

Supervision is another key element in a successful change strategy. The function is usually shared between the headmaster and local inspectors. Supervision is most effective when it has a pedagogical function (all three countries); when it is seen as help (defined as such by both parties); when it is timely and relevant (related to practice and locally available); and when it is practised in an atmosphere of trust. Supervision is a commonly high impact factor in Colombia and Ethiopia and it discriminates the excellent and the very good schools from the good schools in Bangladesh.

We find that successful schools in Colombia receive more on-going pedagogical support through external supervision, and generally have a stronger and more pedagogically supportive and committed headmaster than less successful schools. A more active coordinating and pedagogical support role by the headmaster is also associated with success in Ethiopia, and in Bangladesh an active supervision and training role by the AUEO, as well as a headmaster who gives pedagogical support and monitoring, is associated with the most successful schools. Without doubt, therefore, a combined internal and external supervision function is associated with success.

The nature of pressure

The nature of pressure is different in the three systems. In Colombia it is defined as pedagogical requirements, or a pressure to 'do it right'. It could almost be defined as a pressure for professionalization. In Bangladesh the reporting and control function played partly by the headmaster, and partly by the AUEO, exerts real pressure to perform. The very presence of the AUEO is indeed pressure. In Ethiopia the pressure is possibly felt even more clearly, particularly through the quarterly reports and the combined work of the headmaster and the supervisor. Pressure in the form of controlling teachers' work (by the headmaster and the local inspector) is a commonly high impact factor in Bangladesh and Ethiopia, and to some extent in Colombia.

It is unclear where the line is drawn between on-going supervision and support on the one hand, and pressure on the other. The very nature of a caring, supportive, ever present headmaster may well be experienced as as much of a pressure as a more distant inspector who comes on irregular visits to monitor (and mostly sees the headmaster, as is the case with the inspectors in Ethiopia and the UEO in Bangladesh). The most effective pressure is related to practice. It deals with the goals and requirements of instruction (e.g. the supervision in Colombia), it is close to implementation (e.g. the AUEO in Bangladesh), it has real data to work with, and it is seen as relevant (e.g. the reporting system in Ethiopia). It sets standards, keeps the school occupied with goal-directed work and is on-going.

The nature of decentralization and delegation

The HSI study gives examples of real decentralization and delegation, empowerment, opportunities for teacher-involvement and commitment to the reform, responsive local adaptation and shared decision-making. We see these factors as a consequence of real decentralization.

Empowerment in Colombia means that teachers and the headmaster decide all important things (an attitude strongly felt in the excellent and very good schools), and teachers in the successful schools are committed, take responsibility and make responsive local adaptations. Empowerment in Ethiopia means that the local people (including teachers and parents) take real responsibility, based on a careful division of labour (that means real delegation) and decision-making among parents, teachers and management. It leads to commitment and local adaptations. In addition, it leads to parents and teachers taking more responsibility for school finances, and it leads to success experiences. Empowerment is a commonly high impact factor in Ethiopia.

Empowerment is felt only to a marginal degree in the sample schools in Bangladesh, a probable consequence of a fairly centralistic system that, so far, has not resulted in real delegation. The critical variable, therefore, is decentralization and real delegation at the institutional level. This is happening in both Colombia and Ethiopia.

Commitment is possible without empowerment. In Colombia commitment is a result of delegation and empowerment. It means a positive attitude to the EN reform among teachers and heads, it leads to the head taking responsibility for follow-up (except for the good schools) and it is a contributing factor to teacher mastery. In Ethiopia, where positive attitudes among teachers and heads is a commonly high impact factor and behaviour change discriminates the excellent and very good schools, we find that commitment is partly based on empowerment and partly on success experiences (partly due to technical mastery and partly due to contributions from the community). Commitment among heads, and to a lesser degree among teachers, in Bangladesh shows high/medium impact. There are two factors leading to this commitment, namely the on-going cluster training and the construction of new buildings, classrooms and facilities. Bangladesh is the clearest example that commitment is possible without empowerment.

Local adaptation is a consequence of empowerment in Colombia, and it is a commonly high impact factor (e.g. adaptation of the guide). In Ethiopia this is also true; however, we find that there is a direct relationship between decentralization (and delegation within the school) and school-based adaptation of materials (through the APC and SPC systems). In other words, although empowerment is important, a well organized, decentralized model that clarifies the space of manoeuvre for the teachers (as well as parents and the head) leads to local adaptation, probably because it meets a clear and expressed need in the school and the community (e.g. modification of labour education). On the other hand, in Bangladesh, where decentralization is weak, we find very few, if any, local adaptations.

Decentralization in Ethiopia implies a new system of decision-making,

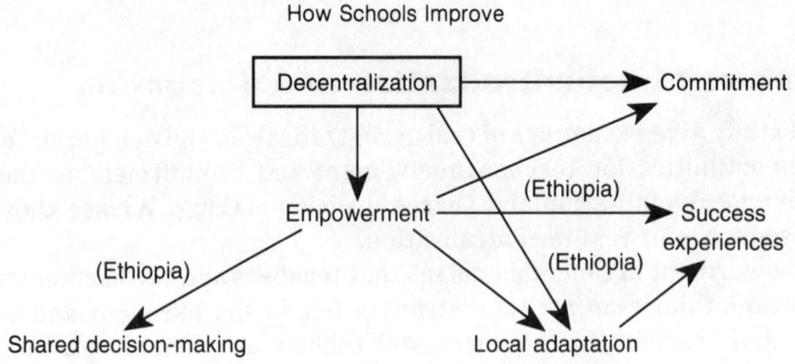

How Schools Improve

Figure 9.3

where parents for example have an active role in the school management committee (e.g. taking decisions concerning school finance), where the deputy head is responsible for supervision, and where teachers collectively take many important decisions. This shared decision-making system leads to a new role (e.g. for parents, the head, etc.) which has a number of practical consequences (e.g. parent donations and work with discipline problems etc.) which again are related to either teacher mastery (e.g. head follow-up) or to success experiences (e.g. parent donations). The schools in Colombia are very small (often only the head and one teacher), and they already take most important decisions. Parent involvement here is a consequence of proven success in the classroom, and not a matter of a legal role in the school (only indirectly connected with decentralization).

In Bangladesh decentralization has taken place to the upazila level (to include the AUEO). If we study the effects at this level (AUEO), we see real indications of both empowerment, commitment and local adaptation. Although it does not happen to the same degree at the school level, it illustrates again the importance of decentralization and delegation. The relationship between these factors is presented in Figure 9.3 (for Ethiopia and Colombia only).

The role of teaching-learning materials

All three countries have invested in curriculum development and new teaching-learning materials. In fact it is one of the most important dimensions in the EN reform in Colombia, and contributes to teacher mastery (e.g. the teacher's manual and student guides). It is a determinant of teacher mastery in Ethiopia as well (e.g. the production at the APC and SPC), and it is one of several components for the improvement of classroom practice in Bangladesh. The delivery of teaching-learning materials shows a medium to high impact in Colombia for the excellent and very good schools, high impact in Ethiopia and it discriminates all three categories of schools in Bangladesh.

That materials lead to teacher mastery, and not just to an improved classroom situation as in Bangladesh, is related to the nature of the materials development process. In both Colombia and Ethiopia, the adaptation and further development of central materials is a key aspect of the reform. It is on-going and school-based. It happens in cooperation with other teachers (and sometimes with the head or supervisor). It is, in many ways, how the teacher 'translates' the curriculum into his or her own context, and for his or her students.

Teachers involved in this process learn a lot. They familiarize themselves with the concepts and ideas of the curriculum. They need to find concrete and practical ways of translating these ideas into materials for children. They discover their own strengths and weaknesses in cooperation with others, and they know whom to ask when they need help. This leads to better materials, to teacher mastery (Colombia and Ethiopia), and to success experiences (Ethiopia and Colombia indirectly).

Success experience

This is a commonly high impact factor in Colombia, and is interpreted as seeing changes in children, in terms of cognitive and socio-emotional gains as well as several other student behavioural changes. Acceptance from the community (in various forms) also contributes to a feeling of success. The Ethiopian schools experience success more related to the changes in the school as a whole, and in particular its ability to generate its own income, the production of local teaching learning aids and the organization of the school (commonly high impact factors). The excellent and very good schools show higher impact on several factors than the good schools, including classroom management, technical mastery, school-community relationships and satisfaction with consistency of goals.

Success experiences in Bangladesh are mainly associated with increased enrolment, improved achievement and increase in scholarships. Teacher punctuality is also seen as a success factor. The factors discriminate among all three categories of schools.

Community support

Community support is a commonly high impact factor in Colombia and Ethiopia, and a discriminating factor (in terms of parents' interest in their child's education) in Bangladesh. In Colombia parents and the community were convinced about the EN programme, they actually experienced a difference in their children, and that led to involvement and support. In Ethiopia the community support has both a participatory role (e.g. in the school committee) and a support role (e.g. donations). It is a result of empowerment, legal regulation (giving legitimacy for a new parent role) and the active work of the headmaster with the community. In Bangladesh parents do not have a role in the school; however, their attitudes toward their children's schooling discriminate the excellent schools from the other schools.

Political commitment and stability[1]

Ethiopia and Bangladesh have both experienced political commitment to universal primary education and to the reform effort, and this support has been stable and sustained over many years and development periods (Bangladesh). The EN reform in Colombia, as discussed above, has a different

---

[1] The information here is taken from Chapter 6 (data from central informants).

How Schools Improve

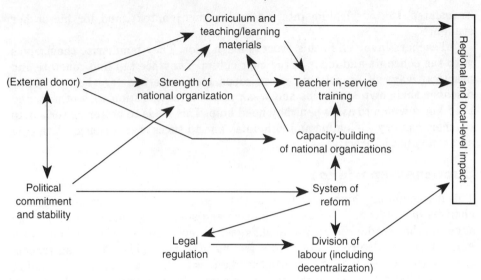

Figure 9.4 *National-level factors (Ethiopia and Bangladesh)*.

history. The achievement of national recognition and central political and financial support (which it has gained over the past five years) was central to the EN strategy.

In Ethiopia and Bangladesh this on-going commitment led to the development of a system of reform that encompassed *legal regulation* and a division of labour, including decentralization (which had a positive effect at the local level (Ethiopia). The system of reform also led to capacity building of national organizations which, together with political commitment, led to strong national organizations. These aspects were also supported actively by external donors. Both the capacity building factor and the strength of national organizations helped produce new curricula and teaching/learning materials, as well as teacher in-service training. Both have been important for the implementation of the reform. Figure 9.4 illustrates the relationships between these national factors (for Ethiopia and Bangladesh).

The assumed relationships between these national factors in Ethiopia and Bangladesh are based on central level interviews only. It is not always clear from these interviews how these factors are related, although they have all played an important role at the central level, according to central informants (see Chapter 6). We are, however, less certain about these relationships compared to the local level factors, because most of the build-up of the central activities took place many years ago (while what happened in the school is often quite recent), and the interview format gave less opportunity to probe the relationships.

The question raised above is whether these major infrastructure-developments have had an impact on the institutionalization of the reform. The chances are that they have. The system has built up a capacity which is institutionalized, not only through established institutions, but through a legal framework and a concept of division of labour. Again, our case studies cannot prove such a relationship, but the likelihood that it has an impact on institutionalization is very real. It can best be understood when comparing Ethiopia and Bangladesh with Colombia. The EN reform (in Colombia) has successfully been implemented in the sample schools. At this stage, however, as the reform gets national attention, there are real fears that control, quality and impact may decline. The reason is that the in-service component may be reduced, or even cut in half. In Colombia, with thousands of very small schools spread around in the rural areas, an infrastructure that can serve schools at all levels of competence in all corners of the country is a great challenge. As the massification of the EN programme starts, the need for a system of reform becomes clear. In other words, the implementation of the reform in some schools does not guarantee the dissemination of the reform to others, or the sustained support and institutionalization of the reform in the country as a whole.

System linkages

In all three countries, the following factors can be seen to play a significant role 'linking' national reform policies with local implementation:

1. Assistance, in terms of in-service training, is a very strong linkage factor in all three countries. Through on-going and intense local in-service training that reaches all teachers, policies can be explained, intentions clarified, technical matters understood and new skills exercised.

2. Commitment, in terms of transmitting enthusiasm and motivation from central leaders to local leaders and school people, works through personal contacts in Colombia (with the EN leaders). It is seen as high motivation on the part of central and local administrators in Ethiopia and Bangladesh.

3. Administrative role, in terms of supervision and support to do it right, is a strong linkage factor in Ethiopia and Bangladesh, though somewhat weaker in Colombia. Both Bangladesh and Ethiopia have developed a highly qualified educational administration and are using this resource to ensure policy implementation. The administrative role in Colombia is mainly in the form of pedagogical support.

4. Pressure, in terms of supervision and control, is clearest in Ethiopia and Bangladesh, and weakest in Colombia. In Ethiopia the quarterly reports are a strong pressure and linkage factor, in Bangladesh the AUEO role functions in much the same way.

What we see is that the reform travels with people, not on paper! It is through contacts and communication among key people at all levels of the system that the reform intentions are translated into practice.

The determinants of success

How are the factors described linked to the various forms of outcome? We have already described the inter-relationships of factors that describe implementation outcomes (e.g. in-service training, teacher mastery, etc.) What factors can best explain the reform impact on students, teachers and the school, as well as institutionalization? We are using the maps of factors, showing the dynamics of the change process, in Chapter 8 as the basis for our conclusions:

- **Student impact** defined as changes in student learning and behaviour has one common strong determinant in all three countries: improved classroom practice. In Bangladesh and Ethiopia regular follow-up and monitoring is also a strong determinant.

- **Teacher impact** in terms of teacher mastery and teacher behaviour (e.g. punctuality, cleanliness, etc.) have three common strong determinants in all three countries:
  − headmaster follow-up and control
  − regular supervision
  − regular, on-going in-service training.

- **Materials** and **local adaptation of materials** play an important role in Ethiopia and Colombia, while **teacher commitment** is a strong determinant in Colombia and Bangladesh (on teacher mastery and behaviour).

- **School impact** means quite different things in different schools, ranging from improved instruction, new curriculum and improved materials, reorganization of the school and the involvement of the community, to new roles and relationships and a different organizational climate. No single factor contributes to all these outcome measures.

  We could ask the question somewhat differently: What is it now that makes the school different from how it was then? In Colombia it is clearly the organization of the classroom itself, methods of teaching, the use of better materials and the involvement of parents. The determinants of teacher mastery were discussed above. The determinant of community involvement is success experience, the fact that parents see a difference in their children.

  The answer for school impact in Ethiopia is somewhat more complex, but changes in the classroom and in methods of instruction are also important here. Possibly even more important are changes in the organization, in the roles and relationships (e.g. between the headmaster and the teachers, and in the relationship between the school and the community), and in the role of management.

  In Bangladesh, enrolment increases, new instructional materials, improved teaching, an active head, an acceptance of supervision, better school discipline and a better school environment are important indicators of school impact.

The determinants of classroom changes have been discussed in part above. In Colombia the changes are determined partly by new and adapted materials, and changes in the classroom organization (that are implied using the new guide). Key to success in Colombia is teacher mastery and success experiences that help to get parents and the community interested and involved. All these factors are commonly high impact factors.

In Ethiopia a well organized school (which includes a well functioning classroom according to the new curriculum) is determined by teacher mastery (discriminating factor), development of local teaching-learning materials (discriminating factor), and the follow-up and supervision role of the headmaster (discriminating factor).

In Bangladesh improved classroom practice is also determined by technical mastery (discriminating factor), regular follow-up and monitoring by the headmaster (discriminating factor) and the delivery of materials (discriminating factor). In both Ethiopia and Bangladesh improved classroom practice discriminates the excellent and the very good schools from the good schools.

- **Institutionalization** of the reform may also mean different things in the three systems. However, the following common elements are seen as having a high impact in all three systems:

  — routinization of the programme, e.g. implementing the curriculum (Ethiopia) and implementing the teaching-learning process right (Colombia)

  — assistance and supervision available as a regular service (all three reforms)

  — community support, e.g. financial support, participation in the school management committee (Ethiopia)

  — teaching-learning materials and resources available as promised.

In Colombia stability and institutionalization is positively influenced by improved student learning, improved classroom instruction, community commitment and donations and innovations in teacher training. The last factor is a long-term effect on the country's teacher training system as a consequence of the EN in-service, training programme. On the other hand, the massification of the EN programme may reduce its control quality, which may have a negative effect on institutionalization.

Much the same factors seem to work in Ethiopia, namely the effects of student impact, school impact and the role of the community (as well as teachers and students) in generating income. In other words a proven programme, well implemented in the school with secured, on-going local financial support, will secure institutionalization. There may be parts of the programme that are dependent on central political support and may be discontinued (e.g.

labour education). In other words, not only local factors but also country factors may influence institutionalization in the long term.

The best guarantee for the routinization of the reform in Bangladesh is the continuation of the new administrative system (e.g. the AUEO role and the head role) that provides on-going supervision and training, combined with on-going delivery of materials and other necessary resources. This is dependent on continuous support from the centre. A factor that threatens institutionalization in Bangladesh is the low degree of decentralization and community involvement.

ROLES AND FUNCTIONS

This section summarizes what we have learned about successful roles in the reform process. Our question is the following: what characterizes roles that productively contribute to reform implementation?

The teacher role

What helps the teacher to 'do it right'? We have seen that in-service training, relevant and locally available, is important. Teacher performance is also influenced by successs experiences (Ethiopia and Colombia), which is related to an active role as a developer (e.g. in making locally adapted materials), to the experience that others care (e.g. donations from parents (Ethiopia)) and to empowerment (Colombia and Ethiopia). Teachers in the excellent and very good schools enjoy more active, pedagogically motivated supervision, better and more regular in-service training, more sharing among colleagues (Ethiopia) and more interested parents. Teacher performance, in other words, is not determined by one factor alone (e.g. in-service training). His or her performance is the result of a complex interplay of factors in the school and the immediate environment.

How do teachers contribute to success? We have looked at what teachers in the most successful schools do, and that discriminates these schools. Teachers in the best schools have motivation for the work. They are regular and punctual, able to use new methods and work with the new curriculum and materials, they are more knowledgable (Ethiopia and Bangladesh), and they are able to motivate students (Ethiopia). They work better with the community (Colombia and Ethiopia), and they work more and better together (e.g. interchange of experiences, Colombia and Ethiopia).

The role of parents

Parents in both Ethiopia and Colombia play an active role in the schools. Parent participation in Bangladesh is very rare, but there is evidence of parents expressing interest in their children's schooling in the excellent schools. Our data show that parent commitment has a positive effect on the classroom and on success experiences. It helps to provide needed resources for the school, to deal with discipline problems (Ethiopia), to recruit more girls (when it functions in Bangladesh), to manage the schools (parents in the SMC in Ethiopia), and it helps to institutionalize the reform (Colombia and Ethiopia).

It is necessary to work for community involvement. In Colombia five of 12 communities changed from negative to positive as they experienced the EN programme. It is sometimes difficult to get parents involved in school affairs in the first place (Ethiopia), however, giving them a real decision-making role is critical to their participation. Even in Bangladesh, where parent participation is rare, in the excellent schools that have worked to get parents involved, parents' interest in their children's education is high, and these communities are more positive to the reform efforts than other communities.

The role of the headmaster

The role of the headmaster shows clear and consistent common traits in both the excellent and the very good schools in this study. The headmaster is committed and stable in his or her position (all countries), having been in the same school for many years, and having been responsible for introducing many of the reform elements.

The headmaster is seen as active and coordinating (particularly in the excellent schools). He or she coordinates, follows up, communicates with the community, gives advice, and assists. He or she cares for teachers and ensures that they 'do it right'. The pedagogical function is the predominant one, although in both Ethiopia and Bangladesh the administrative functions also appear to be important. The head in these two countries also looks after policy implementation, by performing a more formal monitoring and control role, and by reporting regularly to the district office. Knowing the small size of the Colombian schools, this function may be performed much more informally than in the two other countries.

A headmaster in the most successful schools in the rural primary schools is an active, supportive, pedagogical and policy oriented leader, who also communicates well with the community and the district office.

The role of the district education officer

This role is somewhat different in the three countries. In Colombia it may be the district inspector or an EN resource person at a regional resource centre. In Ethiopia it is the inspector from the awraja office (local district), and in Bangladesh it may be the AUEO, the UEO (local upazila office) or even the DPEO (at the regional education office). What is common to these roles is that they play the external supervisory role, and it is this role we shall summarize in this section.

One function is common to all three systems: the external supervisor provides pedagogical advice, though he or she uses different methods. In Colombia, the supervisor gives training in the beginning and advice during school visits later. In Ethiopia and Bangladesh the on-going training function is common, combined with supervisory visits. Supervisors in Ethiopia and Bangladesh share other functions as well. Supervisors in the excellent and very good schools are more active, they follow up, control and are concerned with policy implementation. Also the use of guidelines (the UEO in Bangladesh) is common. In Colombia, however, the administrator is present mainly as a pedagogical problem-solver and supervisor. He or she is also, to some extent, controlling and attends to resource-questions.

The external supervisory role is difficult to perform. In some cases it is also too seldom and irregular to make much difference to teachers. Often the inspector works only with the headmaster on administrative affairs (may happen in Ethiopia). Supervisors in the most successful schools combine the pedagogical and the administrative functions, they stay close to the schools, and work often through in-service training programmes.

The role of the government

We are studying three quite different countries, and three reform efforts where the governments have played different roles. We cannot judge from the HSI study what the appropriate, or most successful role of governments in educational reform would be. What we can do is to point out behaviour and strategies seen as useful by our informants.

What is seen as very helpful is for the government to be committed over time. This gives security and legitimation for local innovators, and secures stable funding and needed services. Although the government came in late in the EN reform, it was this central commitment and adoption of the programme that the EN resource team was looking for, and succeeded in getting.

A competent national leadership is seen as essential for the reform effort. It helps bridge the gap between central planners and local implementers (it is easier to communicate), it builds trust and it produces high quality ideas, programmes and products (through the strength of national organizations). A well thought through division of labour is essential for successful change. This implies a fairly radical decentralization of responsibilities and tasks to lower levels of the system, to include the single school (Ethiopia and Colombia). A well planned decentralization (with the necessary back-up services) helps develop empowerment at the local, district and school level, which is instrumental to further commitment and use of the innovation.

Securing the necessary professional and physical resources is an obvious expectation of the government. This can best be done by creating professional organizations to deal with the curricula, textbooks and other teaching-learning materials, the required training programmes, etc. It is a consequence of a well thought out division of labour, infrastructure development and capacity building at the national level. Regular and reliable delivery of materials is one of the most important factors in local implementation, as is a supply of basic resources to deal with daily operations (and the often increasing enrolment, which is a consequence of successful reforms).

Closeness to implementation is another aspect of the governmental role, which is a key to success. In Bangladesh this was done through the construction of a new role, the AUEO, which is an important link between the field and the government. In Colombia the EN resource team served this role in the first few years, and in Ethiopia the district office with the APC-SPC linkage served much the same function, combined with supervision and quarterly reports. Closeness to implementation serves two purposes: communication with the field that helps resolve a number of conflicts and problems; and feedback to the central level that gives central decision makers real data to work on as they plan further development of the reform.

The role of external donors

We have not studied the role of external donors explicitly; however, the reform history of the three systems give us some insights into this role as well. In fact, external donors have played an instrumental role in all three reforms. In Colombia UNESCO gave legitimation to the first attempts to develop a unitary school programme and both national and international donors gave substantial funding to the development of the reform in subsequent years. In fact, the external donors replaced national funding for several years.

In Bangladesh external donors pay about 80 per cent of the costs of the reform, and have had a significant input into the ideas of the reform as well. In Colombia UNESCO played a significant role giving legitimation to the EN project at an early stage, and several external donors have since provided significant resources. In Ethiopia, external assistance from the former GDR, Swedish Development Aid (SIDA) and several other external donors, has played an active role during much of the reform period, with the World Bank as the main donor.

Most of the comments on the role of external donors have been positive. Our interviewees at the central level benefitted from the work of the donors, as did the schools. The situation described by Verspoor, reform adoption being a 'meeting point' between internal and external needs (factors), seems to be a good description of what has happened in the three countries. We do not know what these needs were. We have not studied the dynamics of the interaction between the government (or initiation group) and the external donors. We do not know what the priorities were and how the outcomes reflect the priorities of the parties. What we do know is that both parties played an active role, pushed for their interests, and that the programme was adopted and implemented. On the basis of this study we can say no more; however, we do think that this process deserves considerable attention and should be the focus of other studies.

WHAT MAKES SUCCESS?

What characterizes the excellent and the very good schools? We have already seen that they differ in several respects in terms of their outcomes (see Chapter 7). In this section we shall summarize what characterizes them in terms of the factors studied, as compared to the good schools:

- The in-service training process is well implemented, regular, relevant and practical.
- The school works actively on the adaptation of the curriculum and the production of local teaching-learning materials (except Bangladesh).
- The needed resources (buildings, classrooms, etc.) are available.

- The headmaster is motivated, plays a more active, coordination and supportive role, is an instructional leader, works closely with teachers, encourages teachers and shares responsibilities.
- There is a team spirit in the school, teachers cooperate, student attitude towards the reform is positive and teachers help each other with instructional problems.
- Supervision is regular, shared between the supervisor and the headmaster (though not in Colombia), and appears as a combination of pressure and support.
- The school experiences more success, more positive students, 'changes in children' (Colombia), teacher cooperation, professional exchanges and extra resources (e.g. from the community).
- The school gets more support from the community: parents are more interested in the schooling of their children and the community gives material support and financial support (Ethiopia).

There are other country specific factors that discriminate these schools, including empowerment (Ethiopia), local adaptation of materials (Ethiopia) and pressure (Bangladesh).

The change strategies

In this section we shall go back to Figures 8.1, 8.2 and 8.3 in Chapter 8 which show the dynamics of the reform process, and summarize our findings of how success is achieved. How can the government, local authorities, schools and communities work together so that successful implementation and institutionalization are achieved?

We are now in a position to compare the reform strategies in the three countries, to see how they are alike, and how they differ. There are some important common elements:

1. Rural primary education has been a top political priority, sustained over many years. This was clearly expressed in Bangladesh and Ethiopia from the outset, it has become a policy over time in Colombia, and is presently an established national policy.
2. The reforms have a base, in a strong national team, or educational leaders with knowledge, skills and commitment to the cause. It was originally an independent group in Colombia (the EN resource team) and an official national team in both Ethiopia and Bangladesh. The strong leadership has been sustained over many years.
3. All three reforms aim at changing classroom practice, and therefore attempt to influence teachers, students and the school as an organization.
4. All three systems have tried to reach the teacher, to change his or her attitudes, behaviour and role. Teacher mastery is central to all three reform efforts.

5. Various forms of staff development, including school-based in-service training, local adaptation of the curriculum and materials, pedagogical supervision and national training efforts (e.g. Ethiopia) are a key strategy in all three systems.
6. *Assistance* is a key strategy in all three reforms. Also, school-based assistance, or at least assistance as close to the school and the classroom as possible, is a common characteristic. Often assistance means in-service training, however, it is also forms of supervision, consultancies, advice-giving and problem-solving. The closer the advice-giver is to the school, the greater the impact.

The three reform strategies also differ considerably:

1. In terms of their degree of restructuring the entire system, and to the extent that the reform efforts took the existing structure for granted and tried instead to change the teacher and classroom practice directly:

    - The Ethiopian reform is the most comprehensive in terms of restructuring the system, changing policies, national institutions, division of labour, roles and relationships, the curriculum and the organization of schooling. As a consequence it also had a longer way to go to reach the teacher and the classroom.
    - The Colombian reform is the case with the shortest way from the reform idea to the classroom. It was a fairly straightforward package that could have a positive influence on the daily life of students in a relatively short period of time. At the same time the existing Colombian school system and its structure was left untouched. This may have consequences for dissemination and institutionalization.
    - The Bangladesh reform is closer to the Ethiopian strategy than to the Colombian strategy, but different to both. It does take restructuring seriously, however, mainly in the area of management. In this area significant innovations are introduced that have clearly had a positive impact on rural primary schools. On the other hand, it gave less emphasis to areas like user involvement, community involvement, and even the teaching-learning process was partly neglected.

2. In terms of the degree of decentralization, the systems are clearly different. The Colombian reform effort is basically a bottom-up effort that has gradually been given national status and legitimacy. The Ethiopian reform is a centrally managed reform that has delegated certain functions down the system and gradually given power to various people at the local level. The Bangladesh reform effort is the most centralistic effort, and lacks almost any degree of delegation to the school level (although it does have an aspect of decentralization to the upazila level).

3. The use of management and systematic monitoring differs in the three systems. This is partly related to the degree of centralization; however, it goes beyond this dimension of management. The Colombian system does not use management and monitoring through the hierarchy as an important element of the reform strategy. It is much more based on collegial interaction and in-service training. The costs are that some schools are not succeeding, and the solutions may be ad hoc. The Ethiopian and the Bangladesh systems use management and monitoring systematically as a communication vehicle, as pressure and as a feedback mechanism to ensure successful implementation. In-service training and collegial supervision is also important in these systems, and the central role of management, particularly through on-going monitoring, is playing an important role.

4. Linkage that enables the user to connect with the ideas, policies and norms of the innovation, is common to all three systems; however the communication link differs:

- In Colombia the linkage is mainly the guide combined with training, a more or less self-instructional package that transmits the message. To some extent the external resource persons, through regular supervision and support, also help to connect.

- In Ethiopia, there are many strong linkages. The strongest are probably the regular quarterly reports combined with supervision visits and in-service training. The annual education conference also serves as a 'pep-talk'-mechanism and helps to transmit the latest ideas.

- In Bangladesh the link is the AUEO. He or she is supported by the UEO and others, but clearly it is through the AUEO that the messages are carried. Monthly school reporting has also contributed to establishing a link between the managers and the school.

5. The development and use of materials is another key factor that differs in the way it is practised. In Bangladesh the materials are centrally produced, and the teacher is mainly seen as a consumer of this material. The consequences seem to be less commitment, less local adaptation and less enthusiasm. In both Ethiopia and Colombia the teacher is assumed to actively develop materials, locally produced. The guide gives these possibilities in Colombia, while the SPC gives a similar opportunity in Ethiopia. It implies that the teacher is a producer, and does seem to lead to higher commitment, success experiences and an active role.

6. The roles of parents and the community differ considerably in the three systems. In Ethiopia parents and the community play an important formal role in rural schools, participating in the school management committee, contributing land, labour and cash. In

Colombia parents are involved more as a consequence of the success they experience with the EN reform. Parents' and community participation may be an official part of the reform in Bangladesh; however, it does not work in the sample schools. There is some evidence that where parents show an interest in their children's schooling it has a positive impact on outcomes; however, the general impression is that 'all comes from above'. The image is a teacher who does a good job doing what he or she is told, a teacher being a high morale bureaucrat rather than an empowered professional. The Bangladesh reform is a centralized system that hasn't built enough local capacity; however, where we find small signs of local commitment, adaptation, etc., it works.

What have we learned?

Before the HSI study and other ground-breaking studies many people assumed certain things about the reform. That reforms should be incremental and gradual rather than wide-ranging; that tight inspection and control are essential for success; that the issue is designing a reform and its materials so well that it can be implemented faithfully and well with minimal training and assistance — in other words that teachers are consumers of new reform ideas; that success mainly depends on the quality of the reform ideas; that schools in general are resistant to reforms; that either 'top-down' or 'bottom-up' strategies work — depending on what educational context is referred to. All these 'obvious truths' have been shown to be false, both in this study as it relates to developing countries, and in other recent studies in industrialized countries.

What we have found in the HSI study about effective reform strategies can be summarized in the following way:

1. **Educational reform is a local process.** The school is the centre of change, not the ministry or the district administration. Schools determine the degree of success, they can block implementation, enfeeble it or bring it to effective life. For schools to improve the quality of their programmes effectively, they need to play an active and creative role.

2. **Central support is vital.** The issue for the central ministry is learning to support local schools in their efforts. In other words, how to make demands on support, encourage, empower, enable and build a strong local school. More responsibilities to the individual school presupposes a strong support structure from the system at large, one that must be built around the real needs of schools in development. For the central level it implies that a system of reform and a division of labour is needed to effectively support the local level.

3. **Effective system linkages are essential.** The strategy in complex systems is to identify effective linkages, non-bureaucratic in nature, between the national, district and local levels. For communication

within the system to be effective, local empowerment is needed, usually as a consequence of more decentralization. A clear administrative role that combines pressure and support and secures the delivery of needed resources is also required.

4. **The reform process is a learning process**. The process is evolutionary and developmental in nature. It cannot be blueprinted ahead of time. The key to success is to get good data from all parts of the system on a continuous basis, studied and worked on at the school/district level, and subsequently at the central level. This implies a competent supervision and monitoring system.

5. **Think systemic and big**. A vision of reform that affects school life substantially will have more effect than a cautious, incremental approach. Any major reforms in complex systems need to build structures and capabilities at all levels. Ad hoc solutions will not work in the long run, only institution-building based on sustained commitment works.

6. **Focus on classroom practice**. The clue is to focus on the dynamics of the classroom and the individual school, since this dynamic to a large extent determines implementation success. It is essential that the supporting materials are of good quality, whether nationally developed and locally adapted, or locally built from the start.

7. **See teachers as learners**. Good materials and facilities are a necessary but insufficient condition. Teacher mastery is crucial for impact on students, and that can best be developed through a systematic local learning process that includes in-service training, supervision and coaching in a collegial atmosphere.

8. **Commitment is essential at all levels**. It is crucial at the central level for sustained effort and the maintenance of needed support structures. It is also essential at the district and school level; however, it cannot be transmitted directly to schools. Commitment at the school level results from empowered successful action, personal mastery that starts with good assistance and develops from practice. In effect, local empowerment builds emotional as well as administrative and problem-solving capacity.

9. **Both local and central initiatives work**. An innovative idea that starts locally (Colombia), nationally (Ethiopia) or with external donors (Bangladesh) can succeed, if programmes meet the criteria of national commitment, local capacity building and linkage, in a configuration that makes sense for the particular country.

10. **Parent and community participation contribute to success**. Parent and community participation lead to commitment and contribute to outcomes, and are essential for the development and maintenance of primary schools in rural areas. Effective participation includes a real role for parents in school decision-making.

These basic findings, seen at a national and local level, echo what has been found in the earlier Verspoor study as well as in major studies of national reform efforts in the industrialized countries (Dalin, 1973; Berman and McLaughlin, 1977; Crandall *et al.*, 1982) and in-depth studies of smaller-scaled innovations (Huberman and Miles, 1984; Louis and Miles, 1990; Fullan, 1992; Dalin and Rolff, 1992). Thus we believe they are generic and quite fundamental.

REFERENCES

Berman, P. and McLaughlin, M.W. (1977) *Federal Programs Supporting Educational Change*. Vol. IV: *The Findings in Review*. Santa Monica, CA: Rand Corporation.

Crandall, D.P., *et al.* (1982) *People, Policies and Practices: Examining the Chain of School Improvement*. Volume I: Setting the stage for a study of school improvement; Volume II: Portraits of the changes, the players and the contexts; Volume III: Models of change; Volume IV: Innovation up close: A field study in twelve school settings; Volume V: Dissemination for school improvement: an analysis of nine federal education programs; Volume VI: Dissemination at the National Institute of Education: contending ideas about research, practice and the federal role; Volume VII: Configuration of federal and state dissemination activities; Volume VIII: The infrastructure of innovation: the case of the national diffusion network; Volume IX: Implications for action; Volume X: Executive Summary. Andover, MA: The Network Inc. Contract #E30-78-0527, US Department of Education.

Dalin, P. (1973) *Case Studies of Educational Innovation. Volume IV: Strategies for Educational Innovation*. CERI (OEC).

Dalin, P. and Rolff, H.-G. (1992) *Changing the School Culture*. London: Cassell.

Elmore, R.F. (1979-80) Backward mapping: implementation, research and policy decisions. *Political Sciences Quarterly*, 94, 601-16.

Fullan, M.G. and Stiegelbauer, S. (1992) *The New Meaning of Educational Change*. New York: Teachers College Press.

Huberman, A.M. and Miles, M.B. (1984) *Innovation up Close. How School Improvement Works*. New York: Plenum.

Louis, K.S. and Miles, M.B. (1990) *Improving the Urban High School: What Works and Why*. New York: Teachers College Press.

Verspoor, A.M. (1989) *Pathways to Change: Improving the Quality of Education in Developing Countries*. Washington, D.C.: World Bank Discussion Paper 53.

Chapter 10

Implications

This final chapter in the HSI study presents what we see as the implications of the study. These are discussed at the school level, the local level and the country level for each of the three countries involved in the study. We shall not repeat the recommendations made at the end of each of Chapters 3 to 5; however, we shall highlight some issues in each country that have been made clearer by the cross-country study (Chapters 6 to 9).

The HSI study provides us with a rich experience base for looking at the more generic issues related to educational reforms in lesser developed countries (LDCs). A major part of this chapter will deal with generic recommendations for LDCs. We shall take up issues from the cross case findings (Chapters 6 to 9), provide illustrations and discuss the implications of the findings.

In a final section we shall present and discuss recommendations to donors, based on the same set of findings. Donors have played an active role in the three reforms studied. Moreover, several of the ideas that were supported in these reforms have support from many donors. The question is: what can and should donors do to facilitate successful outcomes of educational reform?

Implications: Colombia

A total of six recommendations are given by the research team and summarized in Chapter 3, page 64. These recommendations are taken into account and the implications discussed in relation to the major issues now confronting the EN reform process. We see the major dilemma in the EN reform to be the dissemination process. The reform was built up around a highly motivated and committed core group of local resource persons, well supported by donors. The EN project has successfully gained national status.

The continuing question is whether the rapid dissemination foreseen can secure the necessary quality, so important to secure classroom changes. At this stage of the development we recommend the following:

1. Continue to build on the notion of a high degree of delegation to the individual school. It mobilizes energy, empowerment and commitment, and is an important 'added value' to the reform.

2. Invest in a nationwide training of trainers programme, using the most successful teachers and headmasters, who have effectively used the EN model. This expanded core of trainers should be supported by the existing EN team, thereby gaining legitimacy and expanding the support base for the EN reform.

3. Continue to invest in full scale in-service training of new teachers, using the micro-centres as a place where peer-learning can take place, well supported by the new generation of trainers (see above).
4. Strengthen and expand the supervision capacity, to enable coaching of new users and the further development of old users. The importance is in follow-up and using the strength of local and national networks.
5. Provide training for the regional and local administrators who will have a supervisory responsibility for the EN programme. As the EN programme becomes institutionalized, it is essential that the administrators are positive and knowledgeable enough to perform their role.
6. Invest in formative evaluation, by training teachers to use evaluation techniques to monitor parent and community attitudes, and to assess the disputed components of the reform (e.g. the promotion component). For the reform to be effective it needs to develop, by carefully listening to the communities and learning from practice.
7. Add resources. We believe that the EN programme does require additional resources, just to maintain it. It would, in our opinion, be in the interest of both the government and the donors, to guarantee that the EN reform is given the resources needed, and thereby a real chance, as it now has become a national reform.

Implications: Ethiopia

The Ethiopian research team presented a total of 17 recommendations at the end of Chapter 4, pages 117 to 119. We have taken these recommendations into account and suggested some overall strategies to deal with the major issues now facing the reform. The country is undergoing major changes, and a new government has been in position since 1990. Over and above this change is the major resource scarcity that is part of daily life for most Ethiopians. We recommend the following:

1. Political support and stability have been essential for the Ethiopian primary education reform. It is essential for the many people working in the system to re-establish the contract with the central government. This may include re-negotiations of some of the more political aspects of the reform, e.g. labour education, aspects that from the view of some users were only partly accepted under the old regime.
2. The new culture of management, in particular the new way of organizing the school and the definition of roles (e.g. the parent, the headmaster, etc.) is a cornerstone of the reform. We strongly recommend that the government maintains and further strengthens the established management system. One aspect needs particular attention: the role of the district administrator, which is often seen

as having only a modest impact, and on administrative matters only. The Bangladesh model of the AUEO or a similar one, where the administrator is close to implementation, is recommended.

3. Teacher mastery is also a key determinant of success in the Ethiopian reform. Well organized and high quality local in-service training is seen as critical for teacher mastery, as is the follow-up role and presence of the headmaster. We recommend strengthening both components:

    (a) The in-service component should be more regular, combined with the annual conferences, directly linked to the production of teaching-learning aids, and teachers should be coached in the classrooms to ensure the effective use of the materials. This could be secured by peer supervision or follow-up by the deputy head or the headmaster.

    (b) The training of headmasters should become a regular component of the system. The HSI study provides us with a fairly clear picture of what the most successful headmasters actually do (see Chapter 9). Based on these findings, both initial and in-service training of heads should take place.

4. The role of parents and the community is a core element of the Ethiopian reform. However, it is not always effective, particularly in providing local finances or getting parents actively involved in the SMC. Nevertheless, excellent and very good schools do demonstrate success in providing extra money and in active school management participation. This kind of community and parent participation has a positive impact on the institutionalization of the reform. It is probably a necessary component for this comprehensive reform to survive, given the limited resources at the national level. We recommend the following:

    (a) The system of community involvement should be further developed to a more formal stage where the local community gradually takes over the responsibility for certain school operations and maintenance, and rules are set for a local 'tax' that could build on the existing practice.

    (b) The local education officer should provide further training for parents and local representatives to work more actively with school policy and practice. The goal is to stabilize and further develop the parent and community role, and make participation real in all schools.

5. The Ethiopian reform sees examples of local adaptation (e.g. curriculum in the social studies grades 1 to 3); however, the norm has been that teachers have adopted a reform that was initiated, planned and developed by the central authorities. Gradually, the benefits of delegation and local adaptation have become clearer. We recommend that the government uses the local organizations more

actively in the further development of primary education, to include parents, community representatives, teachers and administrators, and allow for more regional variation based on the needs expressed by the local people.

6. Teaching-learning materials play an important role in Ethiopia for teacher mastery and for a well organized school. The textbook-pupil ratio is much better in the excellent schools than in the other schools. The provision of textbooks and other materials should be strengthened, to include a stronger APC-SPC component with adequate training of the materials' coordinators.

Implications: Bangladesh

The Bangladesh team makes some 15 recommendations at the end of the country chapter (Chapter 5, pages 147 to 150). Again, we do not intend to repeat the proposals from the research team, but will instead look at the findings and discuss what we see as the implications of these findings. It is clear from our analysis that even in our sample of successful schools, we find only medium success, with the exception of the four excellent schools. The general finding is that when the various elements are properly implemented, the reform works! (e.g. in excellent schools). It is therefore a question of strengthening key factors to enable the reform to work more generally:

1. Strengthen local involvement. The weakest part of the Bangladesh reform is local involvement, in particular the involvement of parents and the community, but also the active involvement of teachers in the reform. Where the reform has succeeded in this respect, it is with the involvement of the headmaster and the AUEO. The local administrative system is fully involved. Our data indicate that in the excellent schools parents show a greater interest in the education of their children, and there is higher support from the community, higher teacher motivation, and better teacher-community relations (worktable 48). We make the following recommendations:

    (a) A higher degree of decentralization to the school/community level is critical for higher involvement of local personnel. This will probably lead to empowerment, higher commitment, more local adaptations and improved practice. We therefore recommend that in the next phases of the reform a comprehensive plan for decentralization is worked out and implemented.

    (b) Community involvement should also imply access to more local resources for the primary school (much in line with the Ethiopian case). The existing structure of PTA and the SMC should be strengthened by giving more power to these bodies, by offering training and support to parents and community members in school affairs, and by institutionalizing regular meetings between the inspector and the community representatives.

2. Add resources and rewards. Adequate physical facilities and free

textbooks and teachers' guides have clearly played an important role in the reform, and in terms of facilities the excellent schools have some advantages over the other schools. These schools also have a closer and more regular interaction with the inspector system, and it may be that this two-way communication is the reason for added facilities. Nevertheless, added resources is clearly seen as a reward, and it produces commitment ('someone really cares'). We recommend the following:

(a) Continue to provide free textbooks and teacher guides, which clearly have an impact on student achievement and the enrolment of poor students, as well as having a positive impact on teacher mastery and classroom practice.

(b) Provide more scholarships for girls. The problem of girls' poor attendance is probably wider than a mere economic issue (e.g. better school-parent communication); nevertheless, a scholarship incentive seems to be very appropriate.

(c) Map needed resources. There is a need for the improvement of facilities; however, the needs vary considerably. Some needs might be met by government or donor resources, others by local donations. A mapping of needs and a plan for implementation is needed.

3. Strengthen the supervisory system. In this respect the Bangladesh system does have many advantages. It stays close to implementation, it is regular, it combines supervision with training and it links the system through monthly reporting. We also observe, however, that the best schools have closer communication and more supervision than the weaker schools. For supervision to be effective, it needs to combine support with pressure. The supervisory system is there to enable the schools to reach the maximum level of outcomes. It looks after the standards of the system. The weaker schools get less supervision and attention than the best schools. We recommend that the AUEO and the UEO spend more time with the weaker schools. Since our sample schools are successful, it probably means that the supervisory system in general terms needs to be strengthened to play a significant role.

4. Build capacity. Again this is an area where our sample schools can demonstrate implementation success. Most of the training, however, has been directed towards the classroom teacher. Each school has at least one visit per month by the AUEO, who conducts training during this visit. Also the PTIs and other training institutions are involved in various ways. We recommend the following:

(a) The government should consider the general level of teacher qualifications. These should include subject knowledge, as well as pedagogical training. Our data indicate that a general improvement is needed.

(b) A training programme should be developed for further training of the headmasters and the AUEOs on a regular basis. Their jobs are very practice-oriented and they deliver a considerable amount of training per month. (The AUEO may give as many as 25 training seminars per month!) This system will eventually be ineffective, and a programme for further training of the trainers is essential.

(c) Make cluster training more responsive. There is a tendency for the cluster training to become standard courses, and to take local needs into account to a lesser degree. This can be overcome by using the headmaster and the AUEO in a different capacity, by observing instruction, by listening to teachers and parents, and thereby getting inputs for a more relevant training programme.

(d) The total training resource for staff in primary education needs to be effectively used to provide high quality training to all staff. A better linkage between the cluster and external training institutions (e.g. PTI) is recommended.

5. Manage the local environment. In some of the weaker schools, teachers' unions have negatively influenced the implementation of the reform. In other schools (e.g. some of the excellent schools), Hindu communities have positively influenced the reform. We see it as a central role of the administration, in this case the headmaster and the AUEO, to work with teachers' unions as well as with the community, to listen to their demands, and to win their support. As part of the training of the managers, we would recommend including work with unions and communities, approaches to conflict resolution, problem-solving and communication.

IMPLICATIONS FOR PRIMARY EDUCATION REFORMS IN LDCs

In this section we use the experiences and findings from the HSI study, and examine the implications in relation to educational reform in lesser developed countries (LDCs), in particular as it is related to primary education in rural areas. The conclusions are based on the cross-country analysis made in Chapters 6 to 9, and the reader is referred to these chapters for a more detailed review of the findings.

What is the image of an excellent rural primary school?

We have used a fairly comprehensive definition of excellence, namely a school that:

1. Implements all needed components of a reform (e.g. in-service training) in an effective way.
2. Can show high impact in terms of student, teacher and school outcomes.
3. Has routinized new practices, procedures and roles so that the reform has become part of everyday life.

Using this broad definition, we find that all 31 schools in our sample of successful schools have much in common; however, the excellent schools, compared to less effective schools, have certain characteristics:

- The school gets the needed resources, from the government and district, as well as from the community.
- The school has a positive climate and the head, teachers, students and parents have a positive attitude and commitment toward the reform.
- The school works actively on the use and adaptation of the new curriculum and produces its own local materials.
- The headmaster is motivated, plays an active coordination and supportive role, is an instructional leader, works closely with teachers, encourages teachers and shares responsibilities with them (and in Ethiopia also with parents).
- Teacher mastery is a key to success; in-service training is relevant, practice oriented and locally available.
- Supervision is regular, shared between the inspector and the headmaster, and appears as a combination of pressure and support.
- The school experiences more success; more positive students, changes in children, and teacher cooperation. Success experiences enhance impact further.

If this is the image of the excellent school, how do we get there? We discuss four major findings that show the way, and examine implications.

Decentralization and delegation of responsibilities

In the excellent schools, the teachers and the headmaster (as well as parents) feel more empowered and more committed and they work more actively to adapt the new curriculum and materials to their needs. At the same time they work more closely with the supervisor and feel pressure to 'do it right'. Teachers also participate in well-designed and well-implemented in-service training. In other words, to delegate responsibilities to the school does not mean to leave the school alone! What are the implications of this finding?

1. A more systematic decentralization and delegation of responsibilities is an effective strategy to release human energy and make a centrally designed reform more relevant to the users. We recommend that primary school reform efforts look carefully at the costs and benefits of decentralization and provide the support necessary for decentralization to succeed.
2. Decentralization alone does not make sense. It is when a systematic decentralization process is combined with a clear government role in setting standards, providing materials, support, training and supervision, that decentralization works. Decentralization is not a decision, it is a learning process over years. We recommend that the

government carefully monitors the process towards decentralization and strengthens the weaker parts of its plan.
3. Delegation of responsibilities is both a challenge and an opportunity for the school. Delegation does not automatically lead to empowerment and commitment. An active, supportive and determined headmaster, active use of the opportunities of staff development, use and adaptation of materials to meet with local needs, and a cooperative climate are elements of the local institution building process that is needed for decentralization to make sense. Institution building is a complex process and needs to be supported by staff development (including leadership training for the headteacher and his or her team). We recommend that the local district office carefully supervises the school and provides necessary support to enable the school to take full advantage of decentralization.

School-community relations

Another important finding in the HSI study is the important role of the community in primary school reforms. Effective school-community cooperation contributes to student outcomes, school impact and institutionalization. It may help to generate local resources, establish good relations with parents, and involve parents and community representatives in the management of the school. What are the implications of this finding?

1. To be effective, primary schools need to build regular communication channels with parents, invite parents to take responsible roles in the school and thereby make it easier for them to discuss the needs of their children in relationship to schooling. We recommend that the school establishes regular procedures, adapted to the norms of the community, to help all parents to express their concerns, and to invite parents to contribute to solutions for the problems and issues.
2. To be able to cope with the economic challenges facing primary education, new resources must be found. Local communities can contribute significantly to the financing of school expansion, labour, facilities and materials. We recommend that a new norm for the financing of primary education be developed, to include a regular local community contribution to the school (e.g. Ethiopia). The system must be designed taking local norms and interests into account.
3. To get parents fully involved, training opportunities should be provided to help parents take the responsibilities implied in a new, more involved parent role. Also the headmaster and the teachers need to modify their roles to involve parents more in school affairs. We recommend joint training sessions moderated by the local education office.

School-district relations

The district education office is playing an important role in the reform efforts, particularly in Ethiopia and Bangladesh, but also in a different form, in Colombia. First, it is usually this office that guarantees resources and delivers the necessary materials to schools; it plays an important resource function. It also plays a key supervisory function. It represents the government, and also the goals, the guidelines and the standards of the reform, and it is responsible for monitoring the reform process. It is seen as an office that provides services and assistance to the schools, in particular in-service training and assistance. Finally, in a formal sense, it links the school with the central government. We see the following implications of our findings about the role of the district office:

1. It needs to combine pressure and support. In a sense, it needs to play a leadership role, insisting on performance and standards, and at the same time carefully listening to the users and being prepared to offer assistance. This often leads to a problem-solving style, and skills in consulting, communicating and problem-solving effectively with the users are critical. A training programme in effective consulting is recommended.

2. The inspector role is a very difficult role. Many inspectors tend to concentrate on the more formal administrative supervisory tasks, and they are not seen as very helpful in the instructional process. Although the headteacher is an important client, his or her role is closely related to instructional leadership. The inspector, therefore, needs to be qualified to assist the school in the key production process — instruction. Training in instructional leadership for inspectors is recommended.

3. For inspectors to be effective they have to stay close to implementation, to visit the school regularly, to be open and able to listen, and able to work with the head and teachers to resolve problems. It is a major change in the traditional inspector role. Training for this role and on-going coaching is essential. It is also recommended that a system like the AUEO in Bangladesh is tested in several countries.

4. Schools have traditionally not taken the inspector too seriously. After all, he or she comes to the school very seldom, usually talks to the headmaster and does not seem to be too concerned about the details of the classrooms. The new and effective inspector role places demands on the school. Teachers and heads need to be open about strengths and weaknesses, communicating this in a constructive manner, and jointly finding strategies for coping with the challenges. Many schools are not ready for an open dialogue. We recommend that organizational development strategies and skills be part of a headmaster training programme (see recommendation number 3 for

Ethiopia, number 4 for Bangladesh, and number 3 under 'Decentralization' above.)

The role of the government

The HSI study shows the importance of government priorities and sustained support over many years, for a reform to become institutionalized. A national effort is needed, a legal system that secures the institutional framework and the needed resources, and the development of an infrastructure with a division of labour that helps deal with the needed components (e.g. construction of buildings, production of school furniture, in-service training, curriculum development, materials production, etc.). The government has a very central role, even in a very decentralized system. We find the following implications:

1. Educational reforms take a generation to institutionalize. It is therefore imperative that a nation is able to mobilize political support across political party-lines for a reform effort, and gives it top priority. Changes in governments would then be of less concern than if the reform had only one-party support, or were based on a vulnerable political base. Universal primary education, and the support of an effective primary school system in the rural areas should be a top priority for most LDCs. We recommend that the government mobilizes a broad political support base and sets long term goals for the reform.

2. The government has to be as concerned with the process of reform as with the content of reform. To cope with the process, it must consider and build a system of reform that restructures and further develops the necessary institutions to deal with the challenges of reform. To support the government in this effort, experts on the management of change, organizational development and staff development can be used.

3. The government needs to be qualified or competent to develop, implement and institutionalize the reform. A core national staff, highly qualified in both the process and the content of the reform, is a necessary resource which also helps to communicate the intentions of the government throughout the system. A competent staff will also be attentive to and able to pick up the reactions to government intentions at an early stage. We recommend that the core group also has members from important local areas, involves all important interest groups, is provided with a high level, first class training programme, and is supported and coached by experts over several years.

4. The government needs to be concerned about institution building to develop the capabilities of a range of institutions that can deal with

the various and special needs of any reform effort. Of particular importance is an agency qualified in curriculum development, agencies (or publishers) capable of producing high quality textbooks and other teaching-learning materials, a teacher training system that is up-dated and qualified to train teachers in practice, and research and evaluation agencies that can deal with the more analytical tasks of the reform. Even more important are the relationships and communication between these institutions. We recommend that the government recruits experts in systems and organizational development, supports and monitors the system and uses formative evaluation as a base for modifications and restructuring.

5. The government needs to be known as a reliable producer and distributor of materials and to provide the necessary resources for the reform. Reliable mapping of local needs (e.g. facilities), negotiations with the community about financing and provision of needed resources is part of a trustworthy governmental role. We recommend that the government maximizes the possibilities for local resource generation, that the governmental support level takes the local resources into account, and that the support is based on real needs (rather than a standard support level).

6. The government needs to be represented in the field, and to stay close to implementation. This can best be done by qualified district officers, well trained and supported. The government needs to secure not only the in-service training of teachers, but staff development for all staff, including the administrators of the system.

The reform of rural primary education is a complex process of improving thousands of small school units in a countryside which is often only accessible by travelling on foot, in a system dominated by resource scarcity and traditional methods, often with teachers inadequately prepared and an administrative system without the tools and means to make a difference. Piecemeal reforms in such a complex and hardly accessible system are doomed to fail. Only comprehensive efforts that combine critical components in a system of reform have a chance of succeeding. The HSI study helps us to understand that reform strategies matter. We know more about 'what works', and we know it can be put into practice.

THE ROLE OF DONORS

Donors have played a critical role in all the three reforms studied: in the initiation of the reforms, in the financing of particular components, in research and evaluation of progress, and in large scale financing of implementation. Without donor support it is very unlikely that any one of the three reforms would have been as successful.

What can donors best do to support successful implementation of rural primary school reforms?

Implications

1. Donors play a political role. The very presence of a large donor, with its initiatives and reactions, is often seen and understood as a coalition with the government. Donors should be clear about their political role, what causes and interest groups they support, and about negotiating their own role. Above all, they must understand clearly that sustained and stable support over many years is a necessary condition for playing a successful role.

2. Donors, who have the advantage of working with several governments, should be seen as experts on strategies for educational reform. They should be concerned about the government's understanding of its own role, its short and long term perspectives, its plans for institution building, legal and contractual issues, staff development, and curriculum and materials development, to mention but a few central issues. Donors should offer their expertise about how reforms are successfully implemented by assisting governments in designing a reform plan. Donors should be less concerned with the content of the reform (e.g. should it build on self-instructional materials), than with the conditions for the plan to be implemented and institutionalized.

3. The complex dynamics of any large-scale reform plan need careful monitoring and formative evaluation. Donors should offer help to governments, providing expertise and training for the formative evaluation of specific components of the reform, as well as the formative evaluation of the total reform process (e.g. the HSI study). To understand what happens in the process, expertise in qualitative methods (like the methods used in HSI) is needed.

4. Large-scale and fairly innovative reforms demand extra resources that are hard to find in today's government budgets. Donor contributions are, therefore, both necessary and highly appreciated. Donors also legitimize and give an opportunity to try innovations. Our recommendation is that donors be selective as they finance reforms, giving room for development work, testing new ideas and rewarding success.

5. The danger is that a reform may be too dependent on donor support, which is a potential threat to institutionalization. One strategy is to gradually reduce the total amount of funding. Another strategy is to shift financing from given critical components early on (e.g. curriculum development), to reduce or discontinue this support, and to shift to other components that are more critical at later stages (e.g. training of parents). A third strategy is to assist the government in generating new resources for the institutionalization of the reform, e.g. by developing a local community base for funding certain parts of the maintenance of the reform. Donors can also help governments consider supports for eventual institutionalization very

early, during design and first implementation of the reform. Prior studies have shown that this is essential.

6. Support capacity building (e.g. teacher in-service training, headmaster training, training for administrators, local support structure, etc.). Whatever the reform is about, a competent staff at all levels (also in the ministry) is essential for success. How much project-related training (PRT) a donor should invest in, compared to a sector-investment (e.g. strengthening pre-service teacher education), is clearly a dilemma. HSI has documented the value of a local-based, practical, instructionally-oriented in-service training programme that lasts over several years. Up-front, short introductory courses have little effect. Investing in sustained in-service training, as suggested, could also mean the active involvement of teacher training institutions, and the spin-off effect to the pre-service programme might be part of the design (in other words, PRT does not exclude an impact on the sub-sector, in this case the teacher training system).

7. Support structural changes. A national reform effort is so complex that it will not have much chance of succeeding without a comprehensive reform of the institutions involved at all levels of the system, to include the ministry, national agencies (e.g. curriculum development boards), regional and local agencies. In this infrastructure development, changes in roles and responsibilities may well occur. The HSI study strongly advises governments to decentralize responsibilities under given conditions. We see an important role for donors in securing the necessary support for the decentralization process (see above).

8. Support research on the change process. The HSI study is fairly unique as an international study of change processes in rural primary schools. Its systematic qualitative approach has provided close-up, integrated information on the change process at local, regional and national levels that is inaccessible through traditional quantitative methods. In our opinion each LDC needs to get a better understanding of what works in its own country. We believe donors can play an instrumental role in this process, and we suggest the following steps:

   (a) Provide training for researchers in qualitative methods. This can be done using the experiences from HSI, and the first programme could be designed regionally, building on the existing HSI teams.
   (b) Finance new studies focusing on reforms of high national importance. The studies could be used for research capacity-building in the countries, and the studies themselves should be linked to policy makers at the central level, and to decision-makers at the local level.

(c) Network national research teams to build a forum for qualitative researchers. This forum could then serve as an important resource for donors and governments with a need to understand the dynamics of change in one or several of their funded projects. We advise donors to use more systematic qualitative research in their evaluation of reforms, and to use well-trained regional or national researchers. Therefore the need for a network and a forum.

COLOMBIA
Cross-site display 1 School outcome: implementation, impact and institutionalization

	Emilio Rocha	Cedros	El Camino	El Frutal	Patio Bonito
Implementation	**High/medium** High mastery and commitment in spite of partial delay in training and delays in receiving materials. Demo school	**High** High mastery and commitment. Complete training and materials on time. Reinforced by assistance givers. First grade teacher not trained well	**High** High mastery and commitment by teachers. Training and materials on time. Continuing pedagogical support by supervisor. Demo school	**High** High mastery and commitment. Complete training using regional strategy, phased distribution of guides. Support of local institutions	**High/medium** Good mastery and high commitment. Training on time but teachers view it as very academic. Materials/help from local groups
Student impact	**High** Teachers see cognitive and social gains. Lower drop-out, repetition and absence, but dependence on guides and poor orthography	**High** High socio-emotional gains, cognitive development stable. Lower absence, but drop-outs same because of mobility. Negative bossy children show lack of discipline and don't worry about exams	**High/medium** High socio-emotional creativity. Repetition and drop-out same. Problems in writing. Teachers feel students will have problems in high school	**High/medium** High socio-emotional, language and motivation. No absence or repetition, drop-out same. Student leaders but some delay in advancing	**Medium** More socio-emotional development but teachers feel guides don't reinforce knowledge. Absence lower. Teachers feel children write and spell worse
Teacher impact	**High** Very motivated in spite of incomplete training of one teacher. Learned to work with local materials and with community. Interchange of experience at microcentres	**High** Greater knowledge and skills to plan, teach and work with community	**High** Very interested in the school, children, and community. Have improved interactions with students. Teacher trainers present in EN programme. Teachers more creative	**High** More concern for students' learning, greater motivation. More organized, work with local materials. Interact with community, exchange ideas with teachers in microcentres	**High/medium** More pedagogical knowledge and ability to work with groups. Positive attitudes but headteacher critical of guides, flexible promotion, and evaluation

Implications

La Unión	Los Olivos	El Zipa	El Puerto	La Mina	El General	Santa María
High/medium Complete training through regional strategy. Teachers have mastery but not full commitment. Support of local institutions	**High/medium** Complete training received three times. Materials on time. Headteacher highly competent. Teacher transferred so head has four classes, teacher first grade	**High/medium** High mastery and commitment in spite of incomplete training, materials received late and of poor quality. Conflicts with non-parents in community	**Medium** Training incomplete for one teacher. Lack of commitment by this teacher. All teachers have mastered Escuela Nueva. Materials on time. New teachers trained by headteacher	**Medium** Complete training and mastery but no commitment to Escuela Nueva. Materials on time but not always used.	**Medium/low** Complete training but headteacher doesn't understand guides. Teacher has some mastery. Teacher committed but headteacher not. Community support but few materials	**Medium/low** No mastery, lack of commitment by teacher and headteacher. Internal conflicts. School in poor condition. Short training without follow-up
High Profound knowledge related to region. Creative analytic, motivated, leaders. Better writing and reading	**Medium** Only socio-emotional gains. Motivated leaders are creative and responsible	**Medium** Some gains in cognitive but lessened by malnutrition. High socio-emotional gains. Poor orthography	**Medium** Socio-emotional and cognitive gains average. Increased creativity but students lazy and passive about learning	**Medium** Little cognitive gain. High socio-emotional, creative critical, analytical gains. Motivated in school and community	**High/medium** Some gains but don't understand concepts in guides. High socio-emotional gains. Leaders motivated, responsible and independent	**Medium/low** Some cognitive gain, no socio-emotional. Higher drop-outs and repetition
Medium Better organization, better relations with students, learned to use local resources. One teacher uses EN sporadically, teachers want to change schools	**High** Better communication with students. Better use of materials. More knowledge, more creative in designing materials	**High** Highly motivated in spite of incomplete training of one teacher	**Medium** Greater ability to organize and plan work. Know how to work with groups and give individual attention. Not successful in winning community acceptance	**Medium/low** Little interest in the school, want to be moved to urban school. High rotation of teachers. Learned new reading/writing method and group work. Headteacher can't manage children	**Medium** Teacher better at planning, shows more attention to children, uses local resources, visits other schools, encourages parents	**Low** Some knowledge about local culture. Little commitment, lack of motivation, indifferent to abolishment of EN

COLOMBIA
Cross-site display 1 (cont)

	Emilio Rocha	Cedros	El Camino	El Frutal	Patio Bonito
School impact	**High** Integration with community, good relations among staff, student gov. working, little capacity for internal change	**High** Improved physical structure, relations with community good	**High** More resources, improved physical plant, good community relations, support from local administrator: school with EN in district	**High** Improved physical plant, better organization, more resources, community integrated, teachers work together	**High/medium** No consensus about enrolment and drop-outs: some staff say higher, others lower
Institutionalization	**High** EN routinized in school. Teachers have given on-job training to new teachers. Resources promised as result of 'universalization'	**High** EN routinized in school. Teachers have given on-job training to new teachers. Resources promised as result of 'universalization'	**High** Programme is routine within school. Local administrators support it and provide assistance and facilitate resources. Open preschool every 2 years	**High** Programme is routine and has support of local administrators. Permanent preschool programme. Resources available through 'universalization'	**High/medium** Programme is routinized but without flexible promotion. EN has support of local administrators and government, but teachers have been threatened by local political elements

Cross-site display 2 Key factors explaining implementation and impact

	Emilio Rocha	Cedros	El Camino	El Frutal	Patio Bonito	La Unión
Guides/self learning	**High/medium** Available in sufficient numbers. Deteriorated by extensive use.	**High** Enough in good shape. Used and 'Children learn faster'	**High** Sufficient and are used with confidence by students	**High** In use in sufficient numbers	**High** In use in sufficient numbers and in good condition	**High** In use in sufficient numbers and in good condition
Involvement with community	**High** Children and parents participate in activities in the school	**High** Children observed to be concerned about the community	**High** Know more about community, participate in interchanges with other schools	**High/medium** Parents help students with work, children do community studies	**High** Interested in community, have interchanges with other schools	No data
Group work peer teaching	**High** Observed to work in groups and individually, consistent with flexible promotion	**High** Observed to work in groups and individually	**High** Observed to work in groups, and to help each other	**High** Do both group and individual work	**Medium** Observed teacher-centred classes, but dynamic	**High** Observed to work both in groups and individually

Implications

La Unión	Los Olivos	El Zipa	El Puerto	La Mina	El General	Santa María
High Integration with community, some repetition and drop-out with migration, better physical plant	**High/medium** Lower absence, drop-out same because of migration. More resources but school functions with poor physical plant and few resources	**Medium** Cordial relations among teachers. Little credibility for EN in community, enrolment down. Demo school but could lose	**Medium/low** More resources and better physical plant. Lower enrolment because parents don't agree with EN. Absences for malaria	**High** New physical plant. Support by community. No repetition	**Medium** Better physical plant, low absence, low repetition except first grade, lower enrolment	**Low** Poor relations with community and between teachers. Feel sense of worthlessness about their work and feel other teachers see them as incompetent
High Programme routinized. Community and local administrator support. Resources committed through 'universalization'	**High** Programme is routinized in school. Support of community and local administrators. Resources available through 'universalization'	**High** EN part of routine of school. Support of assistance givers. Resources committed through 'universalization'	**High** EN routinized. Local assistance group. Receive help from núcleo. Resources through 'universalization'	**High** High support by community and local authorities as well as central and regional. Resources promised through 'universalization'	**Medium/low** Routine in teacher's classroom, nothing in headteacher's. Supervisor doesn't visit school. Political threats. Resources through 'universalization'	**Low** Only use some EN elements. Little assistance. No follow-up. Community has asked that either teachers or EN be replaced

Los Olivos	El Zipa	El Puerto	La Mina	El General	Santa María
High Are present in sufficient numbers in good shape and are used	**High** Have guides in sufficient number but deteriorated	**High** Guides in use are sufficient in number and in good condition.	**High** Use the guides with direction from teachers. Insufficient number owing to increased enrolment	**High** Sufficient number used routinely. Students use without problem	**Medium** Students have enough guides and use them constantly but without direction by teachers
No data	**No data**	**High** Students carry out activities for village and community	**High** Students know more about community, and are interested	**High** Parents give talks, children discuss national news and local problems	**High** Students interested in local problems. Sent letter on water

La Unión	Los Olivos	El Zipa	El Puerto	La Mina	El General	Santa María
High Observed to work in groups and individually	**High** Observed to work in groups with children helping each other	**High** Both group and individual work, help each other	**High** Observed group work and students helping each other	**Medium** Teacher encourages groups, headteacher does nothing	**Medium/low** Neither teacher encouraged group work	

Cross-site display 2 (cont)

	Emilio Rocha	Cedros	El Camino	El Frutal	Patio Bonito	La Unión
Active learning	**High** Ask questions, solve problems, do musical activities but writing poor	**High** Observed active, dynamic class	**High** Observed active class. Like investigation, writing problems	**High** Children observed to ask questions, use materials actively	**High** Dynamic, active, ask and answer questions, but poor writing	**High** Look for answers in and out of classroom; use local resources
Learning corners/ local materials	**High** In use with lots of materials	**High** Use of corners with local materials in good shape	**High/medium** Observed in use, with materials in fair shape	**High/medium** Corners present and observed in use, but lack of materials	**High** Well organized and clean. Observed in use	**Medium** Corners have few materials. Being redone
Flexible promotion	**High** Various levels in each grade of each class	**Medium** Extensive effort by teachers, but parents didn't accept	**High** In use — one child finishing year at mid-year	**High/medium** In use teachers feel positive towards children who go fast but some go very slow	**Low** Not used because teachers feel it takes away from personal initiative	**High** Observed children working at different levels in same grade
Rural content	**High** Teacher adapted guides to include folklore and music	**High** In use and teachers feel it has helped general knowledge of culture	**High** In use & teachers feel it helps understanding but want more memorization	**High/medium** Teach agriculture. Parents say 'EN to keep children in rural area'	**Medium** Doing new guides as feel old ones don't reinforce concepts	**High** Teachers say more profound knowledge because working with local materials
Student government	**High** In use. Helped students be assertive and independent	**High** In use, students less timid more social	**High** Very active. Students organize selves if teacher gone	**High** In use. Community helped organize. Teachers feel children more assertive	**High** In use. Leads to leadership, cooperation but also bossiness	**Medium** In use. Teachers see students more responsible, social
Library	**High** Well developed. Observed in use	**High** One hour/day for library. Observed in use	**High** Own room, library committee. Observed in use	**High** Observed in use, but teachers feel it lacks books, ask from community	**High/medium** Observed in use, but small with few books	**Medium** Library in own room but not observed in use
Self-evaluation	No data	**Low** Teacher don't see as important. Give own tests	No data	No data	No data	No data

Implications

Los Olivos	El Zipa	El Puerto	La Mina	El General	Santa María
High Observed to ask questions, be critical, active participation	**High/medium** Learn by experience, especially natural science, but malnutrition present	**High** Observed to ask questions. School has activities in and out of classroom	**High/medium** Observed to look for solutions. Headteacher gives lecture classes	**High** Observed to be active, question, searching (T)	**Medium/low** Headteacher doesn't help — lectures or individual work with guides
Medium Have corners but deteriorated with poor furniture. Being redone	**High** Complete with local materials. Observed in use	**High** All corners with students working with local materials	**High** All corners with local materials. Observed in use	**High/medium** Little material but what exists in good shape and used	**Low** Corners present but filled with trash (deteriorated materials) not used
High Using without problems. Student observed to finish fifth at mid-year	**Medium** Partially flexible schedule but students go at same rate	**High** More than one group per grade. Work with different subjects and units	**Medium/low** Only one group per grade. Headteacher says this is because children don't like to work alone	**Medium** Flexible during year but all finish together so some slowed down	**Low** No promotion, students allowed to stay in same grade for years
High Have adapted materials	**High** One day/week do activities related to agriculture	**High** Use local materials and guides adapted to Pacific Coast	**High** Use guides adapted to Pacific Coast	**High** Use local materials in handicraft, adapted guides	**Low** Nothing in classrooms related to local environment
High In use. More verbal ability, responsibility, active students	**High** In use. Teachers feel students leaders, less timid	**High** Observed in use. Students had class when teacher absent	**Medium/low** Exists, but not observed in use. Headteacher says it encourages students to talk	**High** Observed. Responsible work by selves if teacher absent	**Medium/low** Exists but not observed in use. Teachers say students lack respect
Medium Not observed in use. Furniture too small	**High** Observed in use	**High** In own room, observed in use	**Medium** Exists but not used during study visits	**Medium** Not observed in use. Small furniture	**Medium/low** Library in first grade class, not observed in use
No data	**No data**	**Medium** Teacher says students passive, do minimum to pass	**No data**	**No data**	**Low** Head and teachers say students conformists and mediocre

Cross-site display 2 (cont)

	Emilio Rocha	Cedros	El Camino	El Frutal	Patio Bonito	La Unión
Relations with teachers	**High** Observed students confident in interactions with teachers	**High** Well developed relations observed	**High** Good relations observed	**High** EN has made students lose fear of teachers	**High** Teachers see more confidence in students' interactions	**High** Observed to interact easily

Cross-site display 3 Key factors explaining institutionalization

	Emilio Rocha	Cedros	El Camino	El Frutal	Patio Bonito
Assistance	**Medium** Training late. Headteacher trained new teachers. Support positive after training. Support from microcentres	**High** Trained by CEP at start, first school. Teachers help each other in microcentres	**High** All training at start, first school. Support initiator of EN, on-going help but less	**High** All training at start by EN personnel, on-going follow-up, but more at initiation	**High/medium** Training at start, seen as academic and materials poor; support in microcentres
Administrative role	**High/medium** Headteachers both support work with community, train new teachers. Regional coordinator same — materials training, Supint. neutral	**High** Regional coordinator explained EN to teacher and community. Núcleo director administered aide after 3 yrs-plan de fomento	**High** Regional coordinator and supervisor helped in first yrs. Now less on-going support. Superintendent opposed until training	**High** Headteacher in school 10 years; supports EN. Núcleo director and supervisor give technical support. RC provides tools. No direct contact	**High** Headteacher at school 4 years. Adapt guides; motivation; RC supports núcleo director and supervisor. On-going aid
Supervision	**Medium** Became a defender of EN after training	**High** Regular visits for pedagogical input and help teachers correct problems	**High** Support and follow up	**High** Supervisor started EN. Regular technical and administrative assistance. Now visits less	**High** Supervisor visits school brings materials, gives pedagogical assistance
Commitment	**High** EN seen as positive change for students and community. Local administrators now all positive	**High** Teachers and local administrators positive. High mastery but conflict with first grade teachers	**High** Teacher committed and dynamic. Asked to be trained in 1979. Teachers at school 14 years	**High** Head and teachers committed. Teachers don't want change	**High** Head teacher dynamic. Teachers think EN helps children adapt. Supervisor & núcleo director defenders

Implications

Los Olivos	El Zipa	El Puerto	La Mina	El General	Santa María
High Warm relationship observed	**High** Children not afraid of teachers	**High** Observed to interact in friendly way	**High** Teachers see students as 'friends of teacher'	**High** Close 'motherly' relationship	**Medium/low** Head and teachers feel are good but no active interchange

La Unión	Los Olivos	El Zipa	El Puerto	La Mina	El General	Santa María
High All training at start by CEP, on-going follow-up, support of microcentres	**High** Training at start by CEP, on-going support by director of núcleo as 'Demo school'	**Medium** All training at start. New teachers trained by superintendent and teachers. Superintendent indifferent	**High/medium** All training at start by regional personnel. New teacher received one session then trained by headteacher on job. Microcentres	**High** All training at start by central and regional personnel. On-going follow-up.	**Medium/low** Training two years before EN, materials late, headteacher doesn't support. More training in 1987	**Low** Training at start by local trainers, help in first year but none after.
High Headteacher at school 11 years, teacher 10 years, supervisor 9 years and brought EN to area. Núcleo director — administers support. Headteacher worked with community	**High** Regional coordinator and núcleo director started EN in Dept. Committed RC sends trainers, materials, visits	**High/Medium** Regional coordinator supports and supervisor gives on-going technical and administrative assistance. Superintendent unfamiliar with EN, indifferent	**High** Support by national director and Regional coordinator. On-going help by núcleo director. Headteacher and teacher 10 and 9 years in school respectively	**Medium** Supervisor supported school which was named for her. New supervisor and núcleo director give on-going aid but turnover in teachers	**Low** Headteacher at school 18 years, ready to retire, doesn't support EN. Núcleo director microcentres, regional coordinator training, supervisor pro EN but never been to school	**Medium** Supervisor and superintendent helped in first year. Since change in supervisor no one has visited school
High Initiated EN in area; gives ongoing technical and administrative support	**High/medium** Supervisor gave pedagogical aid but hasn't visited in a year and didn't mention school	**High** On-going, high quality support. Continued after change of supervisor in 1987	**High** At start on all levels. Now from núcleo director. Few visits, aid in microcentres	**High** Supervisors highly qualified and give continuous aid	**Low** Supervisor doesn't go to school because of increased work. Sees teachers only at microcentres	**Low** Only in first year, no follow-up after superintendent and supervisor changed
Medium Headteacher and teachers support EN but would accept change. Want to change sites (not EN)	**High** Highly motivated, see EN as 'our programme'	**High** EN 'our own'. Would use aspects if abolished	**High/medium** Headteacher committed, teacher uses EN, but not sure is best method	**Medium/low** Use programme and like, but head and teachers want to move to urban area	**Medium/low** Headteacher doesn't support; teacher positive. Local administrator positive but passive	**Medium/low** Headteacher not interested in EN; teacher not motivated

Cross-site display 3 *(cont)*

	Emilio Rocha	Cedros	El Camino	El Frutal	Patio Bonito
Pressure	**High** Regional coordinator continually pushed implementation	**High** Regional coordinator & núcleo director insisted teachers use EN	**High** Visits by local administrator insisting on EN. Follow-up	**High** Supervisor works with teachers so 'everything perfect'	**High** Feedback of supervisor motivates teachers. Núcleo director and supervisor helping on new guides
Received resources	**Medium** Some guides 2 years late. Head got donations for repairs	**High** Well endowed EN materials provided at start. Local support	**High** Received guides and Library in first year. Help from parents, local groups	**High/medium** Guides for two classes, and materials in first year. Now guides but few materials	**High** Received guides in first year. Later local help to fix school
Success experiences	**High** In 2 yrs teachers saw change in cognitive and socio-emotional behaviours. Demo school	**High** Teachers know work rated high by supervisors from feedback	**High** Demo school, visited by other teachers and parents. Teachers train others	**High** Head saw changes in 2 years, teacher in 1 month. Community accepted flexible promotion. Started preschool	**High** At 2 years projects with community and changes in children. Evaluation of student government. New guides
Empowerment	**High** Head and teachers decide important things almost always	**High** EN programme has given teachers responsibility for running school	**High** Teachers feel they have power to make decisions about school and EN programme	**Medium** Head doesn't feel has authority, decisions from above	**High** Head has authority, eliminated flexible promotion, developed new guides
Local adaptation	**High** Extensive, use of parents for materials	**High** Had to make for EN to be appropriate for rural area	**High** Adapted guides, created student government committees. Making changes to guides in microcentres	**High** Extensive changes in EN	**High** Teachers specialize, no flexible promotion. Added evaluations. School level activities

Implications

La Unión	Los Olivos	El Zipa	El Puerto	La Mina	El General	Santa María
High On-going support of supervisor pushed for implementation	**High** Regional coordinator & núcleo director pushed implementation and quality. Demo school	**High** Local administrator pushed EN model in school	**High** Local administrator pushed EN and insists on use	**High** Central and regional directors pushed, but lost interest with supervisor change. Local administrator still pushes	**Medium/low** Teacher knows EN depends on her but feels alone. Teacher pushes head	**Low** At first supervisor pushes, but after change nothing, but use EN
High/medium Guides in first year. On-going training, corners poor	**Low** Community poor. Some help from local groups. Guides late	**Medium** Received materials and guides but now deteriorated. Desks inadequate	**High** Received guides and library at start. Resources from local groups, new building	**High/medium** Materials in first year but now few guides. Local help in building school	**Medium** Materials arrived but incomplete. Help from local groups	**Low** Lack materials for EN. Teachers got local help for restaurant
High At 2 years won community support when parents saw positive changes in children	**High** At 1 year positive changes in children, more positive community. Became Demo school	**High** Demo school, this motivated teachers	**High** At 3 years head saw changes in children, this improved community relations	**N.A.** New teachers. EN was established when arrived, nothing in their 3 years at school	**Medium** In 1 year teacher saw changes in children and community. Parents given talks at school	**Medium/low** More social students but also more irresponsible
High Staff feel allowed to make decisions on school and EN	**High** Head & teachers feel they have authority to make decisions, revise norms	**High** At start combined EN and traditional method, gave sense could make decisions	**High** EN allows them to make changes when necessary	**Medium** Head feels can't make decisions but that implementation still good. Teacher feels can make programme decisions	**Medium** Teacher has adapted programme but doesn't feel can adapt guides	**Low** Head and teachers indifferent, just go along, don't make decisions
High Adapted guides, use local materials to make instructional aids	**High** Except for adaptations in guides have seen no need	**High** Adapted guides No flexible promotion to avoid problems with community	**High** Adapted Andean guides, Head participated	**High** Using guides for coastal region designed by group of teachers	**High** Teacher has developed guide for remedial work, dropped flexible promotion	**High** Adapted guides to local environment

Cross-site display 3 (cont)

	Emilio Rocha	Cedros	El Camino	El Frutal	Patio Bonito
Community support	**High** Head sold EN to community — active participation despite poor economic conditions	**High** From start good relations despite out migration	**High** At first unions opposed, said less teacher jobs, after talks positive	**High** Community at first rejected flexible promotion and students' assignments, but after meetings supported	**High** Community positive, involved in school activities, head encourages

Implications

La Unión	Los Olivos	El Zipa	El Puerto	La Mina	El General	Santa María
High At first little support, after seeing changes in students, positive	**High** Head and teacher active in community, help although poor, especially after seeing results	**Medium/low** Only parents support, rest of community and local agencies oppose, high drop-outs	**Medium** High community expectations. After first year reacted negatively to results	**High** Built school, requested EN, highly positive	**High/medium** In spite of complaints about head, community helps programme	**Low** Parents reject EN, take children from school

ETHIOPIA
Cross-site display 1 School outcome: implementation, impact and institutionalization

	Gedeo I	Tegulet I	Tegulet III	Gedeo II
Implementation	**High** High teacher technical mastery; commitment, cooperation; good classroom and school management; outstanding community support. DEO supplies instructional materials, though there is little resource. DEO organizes in-service training and education conferences	**High** Good teachers and high technical mastery; commitment, interest, motivation and classroom management. Good provision of materials from DEO and strong community support. DEO organizes in-service training and education conferences	**High/medium** Good teachers' technical mastery of classroom management; good division of labour; participation in co-curricular activities; strong community support. DEO supplies instructional materials and organizes in-service training and workshops	**High/medium** Improved teachers' technical mastery. High participation in co-curricular activities, co-operation; very good community support and participation. DEO supplies textbooks and other teaching materials; provides in-service training and conferences
Student impact	**High** Improved national examination results and promotion rate; decreasing drop-out rate; regular classroom attendance, good attitude towards labour education activities, good knowledge of environment, nutrition and sports	**High** Good national examination results; change in superstitious beliefs; high regard for manual labour, cleanliness and education; decreasing drop-out and repetition rates	**High/medium** Good achievement in national exams; improved attendance; high interest for education; knowledgable and skilled in producing teaching aids; participation in labour education; high hopes in education; good involvement in social life	**Medium** Medium national exam results and classroom tests; good attitude towards labour education and learning; high drop-out and repetition rates
Teacher impact	**High** High use of locally produced teaching aids; show good efforts to improve teaching, e.g. effective academic competition; very good teacher-teacher co-operation and teacher-headmaster cooperation	**High** Improved knowledge and skills to use teaching aids, plan, teach, document and motivate students; high interest in education and good personal cleanliness; experience exchange	**High/medium** Good mastery of subject matters, classroom management and productive work help understand student needs and motivation; good teacher-teacher cooperation	**High/medium** Good in classroom management and leading co-curricular activities; co-operative with one another; good attitude towards their profession; minimal use of teaching aids

Implications

Tegulet II	Chilalo I	Gedeo III	Chilalo II	Chilalo III
High/medium Satisfactory technical mastery of classroom management with average use of teaching aids. Teachers use continuous assessment technique; good community support. DEO supplies instructional materials, organizes in-service programme and workshops	**High/medium** Good teachers' technical mastery of classroom management, interest and commitment; strong community support. DEO supports the school in various forms and provides in-service training	**Medium** Improved teachers' technical mastery. Effective participation in co-curricular activities; average community support. DEO supplies textbooks and materials, though inadequate; provides in-service training	**Medium** Improved teachers' technical mastery; medium community support. DEO supplies textbooks and other teaching materials; provides in-service training	**Medium** Medium teachers' engagement in school activities; good community financial, material and labour support. DEO supplies textbooks and other instructional materials
High/medium Good national exam and classroom test results; good respect for teachers; good attitude for learning; decreased drop-out rate and absenteeism; good attitude towards sports, labour education; care for school property (except in grades 1 to 3)	**Medium** Good effort in poetry writing; satisfactory national exam result; average motivation for schooling though high enrolment and low repetition rates	**Medium** Satisfactory national exam results; moderate performance in classroom tests; low participation in co-curricular and labour education activities	**Medium** Decreasing national exam results; low repetition rate in classroom tests; low motivation; engaged in trade activities; however, high attendance rate	**Medium/low** Poor academic performance; good behaviour; low motivation for learning though high attendance and low repetition rates
High/medium Good mastery of subject matters and classroom management; good co-operation and commitment; high involvement in school activities, literacy and community service	**High/medium** Good academic and pedagogical knowledge and handling of problematic students; teachers have positive attitude towards their work and cooperate with each other	**Medium** Good classroom management; better assessement skills; exercise group plan and teaching; low use of teaching aids	**Medium** Good in classroom management; co-operative with headmaster and each other; positive attitude towards school activities	**Medium** Good subject matter knowledge; moderate pedagogical knowledge; good participation in co-curricular activities

ETHIOPIA
Cross-site display 1 *(cont)*

	Gedeo I	*Tegulet I*	*Tegulet III*	*Gedeo II*
School impact	**High** High organization — SMC, departments, library etc; effective school-community relations; active co-curricular and labour education activities; increased school income and improved physical structure; good school beautification	**High** Improved school facilities; increased school income; change undesired traditional beliefs and other malpractices	**High** Good school environment; healthy working staff relations; increased enrolment; improved physical structure; exemplary school-community relations	**High** Good organization; increasing enrolment; generates adequate internal income; improved physical facilities; exemplary community financial, material and labour support; good school beautification
Institutionalization	**High** All change components — the curriculum, labour education radio programme, etc., have become daily routines; teachers get good support from headmaster, SPC coordinator, department heads and other teachers; good community financial, material and labour support. DEO supplies textbooks and other instructional materials	**High** All change components are in practice; good community financial, and material support; new teachers get orientation; DEO persuades parents to increase enrolment. DEO supplies textbooks and other instructional materials. Good documentation and record keeping	**High** All change components are in practice; strong communities financial material and labour support. DEO supplies textbooks and other instructional materials. New teachers oriented	**High/medium** All change components are in practice; very strong community support. New teachers get orientation. Headmaster plays key role in school life

Cross-site display 2A Key factors explaining success — implementation, impact and institutionalization

	Gedeo I	*Tegulet I*	*Tegulet III*	*Gedeo II*
Assistance	**High/medium** In-service training for untrained teachers; annual education conference and workshops; teachers help each other in departments and SPCs; feedback from inspector visits	**High/medium** In-service training for untrained teachers; annual education conference and workshops; teachers help each other in departments and in SPCs; inspectors and APC give advice.	**High/medium** In-service training for untrained teachers; annual education conference and workshops; teachers help each other in SPCs, headmaster and APC give advice	**High/medium** In-service training for teachers by phase; teachers participate in in-service programme; DEO organizes conference and workshops; teachers help each other and exchange experiences

Implications

Tegulet II	Chilalo I	Gedeo III	Chilalo II	Chilalo III
High/medium Good school environment; healthy working relations; active co-curricular activities; improved physical facilities; very good school-community relations	**High** Beautified school compound; high income; good school-community relations; improved physical structure; provided accommodation for teachers; school beautification; care for school property	**Medium** Increased enrolment; good school organization; high teacher-teacher headmaster-teacher cooperation; generate adequate internal income; low community financial support; School cannot absorb additional applicants	**Medium** Increased enrolment; good organization, improved physical facilities; poor headmaster-teacher relations; average internal income generation, medium community financial, material and labour support	**Medium** Good school organization; high internal income generation; moderate community support and involvement.
High/medium All change components are in practice; good community support. DEO supplies textbooks and other instructional materials. Assistance to new teachers	**High** All change components are in practice; strong headmaster and SMC support; good community financial material and labour support. New teachers get orientation. DEO supplies textbooks and other instructional materials	**Medium** All the reform components are in practice. DEO organizes in-service programme and workshops. Community support the school with materials and labour; however, teachers have low motivation. Little assistance to new teachers	**Medium** All the reform components are in practice; medium community material, financial and labour support. DEO organizes in-service programmes and workshops	**Medium** All reform components are practiced to some degree; community provides materials and labour. Inspectors organize seminars and headmaster orients new staff members

Tegulet II	Chilalo I	Gedeo III	Chilalo II	Chilalo III
High/medium In-service training for untrained teachers; annual education conference and workshops; teachers help each other in SPCs; Inspectors and APC give advice	**High/medium** In-service training for untrained teachers; annual education conference and workshops; teachers help each other in departments and SPCs; teachers teach each other; feedback from inspectors	**Medium** DEO organizes conferences and workshops which few teachers attend	**Medium** DEO organizes in-service courses, seminars and workshops; teachers exchange views in departments and the SPC	**Medium** DEO organizes annual education conferences, workshops; headmaster gives advice to teachers

Cross-site display 2A *(cont)*

	Gedeo I	Tegulet I	Tegulet III	Gedeo II
Administrative role	**High/medium** Headmaster facilitates, coordinates and evaluates school activities and works closely with teacher and community. DEO provides school guidelines	**High** Headmaster coordinates school activities, orients teachers works closely with SMC. DEO helped the school to get land, supervises school progress, sends guidelines and communicates with local officials on school affairs	**High/medium** Headmaster coordinates and leads school activities. DEO supervises the school and supports it by mobilizing the community and sending guidelines	**High/medium** Headmaster facilitates and evaluates school activities, encourages teachers, coordinates community input. DEO sends guidelines
Commitment	**High/medium** Headmaster, teachers, students and DEO staff like the changes. Headmaster and teachers spend most of their free time working in the school	**High** Headmaster, teachers and students spend their spare time doing school work. DEO responds to the school's request immediately	**High/medium** Headmaster, teachers and students like changes and work on school activities in their spare hours with dedication	**High** Headmaster, teachers and students like the changes though there was a problem at the beginning. SMC, teachers and headmaster work closely during and after school hours
Pressure	**High/medium** Strict directives, sending quarterly progress reports and follow-up of headmaster and inspectors pushed teachers to implement changes	**High/medium** Quarterly progress reports, inspectors' visit and headmaster follow-up contributed to implementation of the changes	**High/medium** DEO insisted school increased enrolment and implemented the changes. Headmaster insists and evaluates teachers' work	**High/medium** Strict guidelines, follow-up of headmaster and department heads pushed implementation of changes
Received resources	**High/medium** Instructional materials and tools from DEO. Finance, materials and labour from community. School generates internal income	**High/medium** Instructional materials and tools from DEO. Community provides finance, materials, labour and lodging for teachers. School generates own income	**High/medium** DEO provides instructional materials. Community gave land, materials and finance. School generates its own income	**High** DEO sends textbooks and other instructional materials. Community provides financial, material and labour support. School generates own income
Success experiences	**High** Great progress in physical expansion, self reliant. Consistent with its achievements. There is satisfaction with its progress. Improved school-community relations	**High/medium** Good professional development. Exchange of knowledge through planned activities and collaborative efforts. Improved school-community relations	**High/medium** Satisfactory school self training. Improved classroom management. Teachers lead and get involved in different school activities. Improved school-community relations	**High/medium** School is well organized, physically expanded, and generates adequate internal income. Improved school-community relations

Implications

Tegulet II	Chilalo I	Gedeo III	Chilalo II	Chilalo III
High/medium Headmaster coordinates the SMC. DEO reorganized school and discusses and finds solutions to the school problems, sends guidelines	**High/medium** Headmaster supervises classrooms, checks lesson plans, coordinates and leads school activities. Inspectors visit the school and give guidelines	**High/medium** Headmaster with deputy facilitates and supervises all activities. Inspectors give advice on administration matters. DEO sends guidelines	**High/medium** Headmaster coordinates and evaluates all activities in the school and shares in responsibilities with teachers. DEO sends guidelines	**High/medium** Inspectors and APC coordinators supervise the school. Headmaster shares responsibility with teachers. DEO sends guidelines
Medium Teachers and headmaster like the changes and spend their spare time doing school work	**High/medium** Headmaster, teachers, students and SMC like changes. Headmaster works after school hours. DEO rewarded the headmaster for his efforts	**Medium** Teachers work with interest in co-curricular activities. Headmaster spends a lot of his spare hours working in school	**Medium** Teachers and students have a positive feeling towards the school activities	**High/medium** Teachers and headmaster give priorities to co-curricular activities and show positive attitude to the changes
High/medium Inspectors evaluate school work. DEO encouraged community to collaborate with the school and care for school property	**High/medium** Strict orders and guidelines, inspectors visits and headmaster's close follow-up pushed implementation of the changes	**High/medium** Circulars from DEO and sending quarterly progress pushed teachers to implement the changes	**Medium** DEO, headmaster and department heads pressed teachers to implement the changes	**Medium** Strict guidelines, inspector's supervision and headmaster follow-up
High/medium APC provide model teaching aids. DEO supplies tools and instructional materials. Community provides finance, materials, labour and free houses for teachers. School generates own income	**High/medium** Instructional materials and tools from DEO. Community supplies finance, labour and lodging for teachers. School generates own income	**Medium** DEO supplies textbooks and other teaching materials. Community provides finance and labour. School generates own income	**Medium** DEO supplies textbooks and other teaching materials. Community provides finance and labour. School generates own income	**Medium** DEO supplies textbooks and other teaching materials and model teaching aids. Community provides finance and free labour. School generates own income
High/medium Improved pedagogical knowledge. Good classroom management and experience exchange. Improved school-community relations	**High/medium** Good organization and classroom management; showed physical expansion. Improved school-community relations	**Medium** Generates its own income. Teachers are satisfied with what they have achieved	**Medium** Produces own teaching aids and generates its own income	**Medium** Teachers' pedagogical ability improved. School generates its own income

Cross-site display 2A *(cont)*

	Gedeo I	Tegulet I	Tegulet III	Gedeo II
Empowerment	**High** SMC makes major financial and administrative decisions. Teachers decide what they do in the classroom. School is authorized to generate its own income. Department heads evaluate teachers	**High** SMC makes major financial and administrative decisions. Classroom activities are decided by teachers. School is authorized to generate its own income. Department heads evaluate teachers	**High** School is responsible for physical expansion, income generation, production of teaching aids and administrative decisions. Department heads evaluate teachers	**High** Headmaster and teachers plan and decide school activities. Financial issues are settled by SMC. Department heads evaluate teachers
Local adaptation	**High** Flexible labour education programme and teaching aid production. Wider involvement of community. Use of shift system. Use of locally prepared teaching materials	**High** Flexible labour education programme and teaching aid preparation. Supressing aetheistic views in political education. Use of locally prepared teaching materials	**High** Handicraft lessons are adapted to local religious holidays. Flexible labour education programme and teaching aid production. Use of locally prepared teaching materials	**High** Teachers prepare contents of grades 1–3 social science and home economics course. Flexible labour education programme and collection of students' school contribution. Wider involvement of community
Community support	**High** Strong community financial, material and labour support. Participation in school administration; follow up drop-outs.	**High** Strong community financial, material and labour support. Assist in accommodating teachers	**High** Strong community financial, material and labour support. High participation in school administrative affairs	**High** Strong community financial, material and labour support. High participation in school administrative affairs
Organizational context	**High** New education proclamation and organizational set-up created conducive atmosphere	**High** New education proclamation and organizational set-up created conducive atmosphere	**High** New education proclamation and organizational set-up created conducive atmosphere	**High** New education proclamation and organizational set-up created conducive atmosphere

Implications

Tegulet II	Chilalo I	Gedeo III	Chilalo II	Chilalo III
High/medium School works around rules; SMC decides on administrative and financial matters	**High** SMC makes financial and administrative decisions. Teachers feel responsible for co-curricular activities. School is authorized to generate its own income. Department heads evaluate teachers	**Medium** Headmaster and teachers plan and decide school activities. Department heads evaluate teachers. SMC not fully excercising its power	**Medium** Headmaster assigns teachers to coordinate different duties and co-curricular activities. Department heads evaluate teachers. SMC not fully excercising its power	**Medium** SMC is empowered to make administrative financial decisions. Parents' committee is in charge of students' disciplinary problems
High Flexible labour education. Student contribution. Adapted social science and home economics curriculum	**High** Flexible labour education programme and teaching aid preparation. Adapted social science and home economics curriculum for grades 1 to 3. Use of shift system	**High/medium** Teachers prepare contents of grades 1 to 3 social science and home economics courses. Flexible labour education programme	**High/medium** Teachers prepare contents of grades 1 to 3 social science and home economics courses. Shift system	**High/medium** Participation of students in labour education is determined based on their age group. Contents of grades 1 to 3 social science and home economics courses prepared by teachers
High Strong community financial and labour support. Assists in accommodating teachers	**High** Strong community financial, material and labour support. Helps in solving disciplinary problems	**High/medium** Moderate financial support; high material and labour support. Average participation in school administrative affairs	**High/medium** Moderate provision of financial and material support; high provision of labour services	**High/medium** High financial and material support and moderate labour services. Average participation in school administrative affairs.
High New education proclamation and organizational set-up created conducive atmosphere	**High** New education proclamation and organizational set-up created conducive atmosphere	**High** New education proclamation and organizational set-up created conducive atmosphere	**High** New education proclamation and organizational set-up created conducive atmosphere	**High** New education proclamation and organizational set-up created conducive atmosphere

BANGLADESH
Cross-site display 1 School outcome: implementation, impact and institutionalization

	Hasnahena	Champa	Aparajita	Palash	Chameli
Implementation	**High** New classroom, free textbooks and teachers' guides, block teaching, cluster training, female teachers, supervision by AUEO	**High** New school building, latrine constructed, free textbooks, teaching aids supplied, school furniture supplied. A few new teachers inducted, regular cluster training provided, curriculum orientation training given to all teachers. Supervision strengthened by AUEO	**High** New semi pacca building, furniture, textbooks/guides, cluster training, regular supervision, co-curricular activities	**High/medium** New classroom, supervision by AUEO, free textbooks, teachers' guides, cluster training, female teachers	**High** New school building, latrine constructed. Furniture supplied, free textbooks, teachers' guides, teaching aids supplied. Some new teachers inducted, regular supervision geared up by AUEO, curriculum orientation training provided. Cluster training provided regularly
Student impact	**High** More students are getting scholarships and can read and do sums; high attendance rate; failures and repetition reduced, active participation	**High** Students' performance improved; students getting more scholarships; student attendance increased and regular; student attitude towards school positive; student habits improved. As they are free, some students do not take care of textbooks. Students creative in making handicraft works	**Medium** Higher achievement; more scholarships; wider attitude; increased interest in co-curricular activities, high enrolment, retention and attendance. Students are cleaner and more regular in attendance.	**High** More students getting scholarships and can read and do sums; attendance and success rate high; repeat rate and failures declined; fewer students leave at meal time	**High** Student performance increased; more students getting scholarships. Attendance increased; drop-out and repeater's rate reduced. Student attitude towards school improved; student habits improved
Teacher impact	**High** Use teaching method prescribed by cluster training leaflets. Teachers more interested; active teaching; punctual and regular; teachers' association making grouping among teachers	**Medium** Teachers' capabilities increased; teachers' attitude towards school positive; teachers' attendance regular but less functional. Girls' enrolment increased; latrine helped girls' enrolment	**High** Increased knowledge; improved teaching methods; positive attitude towards teaching profession. More job satisfaction; cordial relations with students and community; less corporal punishment	**Medium** Show interest in reform; teaching good. More punctual, teachers' association making groupings	**Medium** Community sympathetic towards school. Liberal promotion system increased number of students resulting in class management difficulties; children from other areas enrolled in this school

Implications

Ulatchandal	Rangan	Padma	Shapla	Jaba
Medium New classroom (1), instructional material, training of teachers, female teachers, supervision by AUEO, teaching methods implemented	**High** One new classroom, furniture, textbooks, teaching guides, cluster training, co-curricular equipment, child survey, improved supervision	**Medium** Classroom constructed and furniture supplied, textbooks and teachers' guides available, female teachers added, impressive supervision, cluster training introduced, technical mastery satisfactory. Community participation generally satisfactory	**Medium** Physical facilities (one new classroom), learning materials, training file for cluster training, teacher training supervision by AUEO, new teaching materials	**Medium** Physical facilities and pedagogic reforms implemented satisfactorily. Technical mastery including curriculum reforms largely achieved, cluster training. Teachers interested in acquiring better techniques and applying them in practice, AUEO support. Changes brought in elements of planning, preparation, application and internal evaluation of class lessons by teachers
High/medium Students achievement increased. Attendance (60%) and students' behaviour improved.	**Medium** High enrolment, high attendance, high retention, physically sound. More scholarships; increased interest for higher education	**Medium** Student achievement level and behaviour improved; participation in talent exams in large numbers; more participation in co-curricular activities; attendance 80%	**Medium** Student achievement better; attendance 50–60%; students are active in classroom. Student behaviour better, peer group relations better	**Medium/low** New curriculum and teachers' technical mastery succeeded in increasing knowledge; discipline improved; attitudes better; attendance rate higher and repeat rates decreased
Medium Better trained; pupil attendance increased; teachers' knowledge increased using lesson plan and teachers' guide. Healthy attitude and co-operation among teachers enhanced	**High** Improved knowledge, skills, attitude and methods; regular and punctual attendance; high job satisfaction	**High/medium** Larger participation of primary age children including girls in particular; community support enhanced; improved teaching; reduced drop-out and repeater rate (30%); healthy attitudes and better co-operation among teachers	**High/medium** Teachers follow lesson plan and teachers' guide; attendance of teachers better; teachers' knowledge increased	**Medium/low** Larger size of the school; better organized and equipped with better teaching stock; support from local key people; improved skill and helpful attitudes

BANGLADESH
Cross-site display 1 *(cont)*

	Hasnahena	*Champa*	*Aparajita*	*Palash*	*Chameli*
School impact	**High** More students, fewer classrooms; more regular reporting and better teaching. Teachers talk to parents; betelnut garden for income. Reward teachers, for raising enrolment, high headteacher initiative	**Medium** Community co-operation towards school; community extends help, cash and kind to school. Number of children increased in class I and II resulting in unmanageable class; children from other school areas enrolled in this school	**High** One of the best schools; staffing system and school discipline improved; improved environment and community interest	**High/medium** Regular reporting; close supervision; better teaching; high headteacher initiative	**Medium** Community co-operation towards school. Liberal promotion has increased number of children resulting in class management difficulties. Children from other schools enrolled in this school.
Institutionalization	**High** Teaching improved due to cluster training becoming part of routine	**Medium** Supply of textbooks, teachers' guides, cluster training continued; activity-based teaching continued; SMC and PTA continued; new teacher appointment not regular; supply of teaching aids not regular	**Medium** Regular punctual attendance of teachers and students; cluster training; regular supervision; efficient methods; child-survey	**High/medium** Cluster training, free textbooks and guide have become part of routine	**Medium** Supply of textbooks, cluster training, activity-based classroom teaching continued; SMA and PTA continued; promotion system continued; new teacher appointment not regular; supply of teaching aids not regular

Cross-site display 2 Key factors explaining implementation and impact

	Hasnahena	*Champa*	*Aparajita*	*Palash*	*Chameli*
Assistance	**High** AUEO organizes cluster training once a month. Headteacher organizes staff development class every Thursday.	**High** Curriculum orientation for teachers; regular monthly cluster training for teachers. New school building, furniture, teachers' guide, equipment, tubewell, latrine, sports equipment	**High** Orientation of personnel at different levels; cluster training for headteacher at school; premises based on need. Supervision and support with emphasis on pedagogy, capacity building and built-in-ness; this assistance proved effective.	**High** Cluster training by AUEO; supervision by AUEO and UEO advice, guidance, encouragement; guidance by headteacher individually and in groups	**High** AUEO provides cluster training once a month; more class supervision

Implications

Ulatchandal	Rangan	Padma	Shapla	Jaba
Medium Enrolment increased; better physical and learning facilities, PTA and SMC meets as required; community participation and support better	**Medium** Accomm. scope for fulfilling natural calls, overcrowded classes I and II.	**High/medium** Larger participation of primary-age children, including girls in particular; community support enhanced	**Medium** Enrolment rate increased; teachers' attendance improved; community participation not better	**Medium/low** Larger size of school; better organized and equipped with better teaching stock; support from local key people
High/medium Cluster training; use of teachers' guide; regular reporting; supply of textbooks free of costs; AUEO visit	**Medium** Cluster training; frequent supervision; co-curricular activities; improved teaching; child-survey	**Medium** Reform bundle except the physical facilities are part of the routine and expected to continue. Training and textbooks supply to continue.	**Medium** Cluster training; teachers are using lesson plan (follow teachers' guide); supply of textbooks; visit of AUEO	**Medium** Training and re-training of teachers routinized; new nucleus created (AUEOs) for regular supervision; community support likely to continue and assistance for physical facilities, though inadequate, will hopefully continue

Ulatchandal	Rangan	Padma	Shapla	Jaba
High Government support for better service terms of teachers, co-operation and assistance come from the community; supply of free textbooks; extensive and intensive teacher training (including cluster training) introduction	**High** Curriculum orientation training and regular, monthly cluster training for teachers. New school building, furniture, latrine and tubewell	**High/medium** Addition of one classroom; continuous cluster training; orientation on new curriculum	**High/medium** Addition of one classroom, supply of free textbooks, teachers' guide; cluster training; orientation on new curriculum	**Medium** Assistance came in many ways and from various quarters: government education of local information persons and community for implementation of the reform 'bundle'

Cross-site display 2 *(cont)*

	Hasnahena	Champa	Aparajita	Palash	Chameli
Administrative role	**High** AUEO observe classroom teaching and give instruction. Headteacher planted betelnut trees for extra income and extended school building out of that money	**High/medium** Regular and daily classroom visits by headteacher; making contact with community; advice and encouragement to teachers by headteacher. Occasional visit to school and encouragement to school people assisted school people to implement programme; explanation of government policy to school people and community by DPEO and AUEO	**High** Headteacher and AUEO aware of association with reform programme; delegated authority to teachers; checked on classroom activity; provided help. Supply of materials and maintenance linked with community and higher authority. Stability and pressure involved. Demanded supervision support; other administrators provided support as needed by them.	**Medium** Pressure by AUEO and UEO; headteacher active.	**High** AUEO provide cluster training once a month; more class supervision
Supervision support	**High** Supervises 21 schools per month; organizes cluster training in the school once a month	**High** Intensive supervision rendering advice; help teachers to prepare timetable; cumulative record form by AUEO	**High** Classroom works continuously and there is regular supervision by AUEO, UPEO, DPEO and other concerned officers; supervision; headteacher also supervises class occasionally (FAC); checking teachers' work, helping them and guiding in adaptive changes	**Medium** Supervised by AUEO and occasionally by UEO	**High** AUEO provides cluster training once a month; more close supervision
Commitment	**High** Headteacher introduced small award for class who enrolled highest number of students	**High** Headteacher and teachers have strong commitment to teaching and school has strong team spirit	**High** Teachers, headteachers, local administrators, including community and higher officials at all levels committed to implementing reform; they have positive feelings	**Medium** Teachers, AUEO, UEO gave priority to changes; they wanted continuation of the reform	**High/medium** Headteacher took initiative to implement reform. UEO, AUEO gave pressure to work better

Implications

Ulatchandal	Rangan	Padma	Shapla	Jaba
High DDCC and Parishad support; monitors progress and problems monthly. Upazila education parishad gives management support	**High/medium** Regular and daily class visits by headteacher making contact with community. Occasional visit to school gave encouragement to school people; insist on implementation of programme; explanation of government policy to school people and community by DPEO and AUEO	**High** Frequent supervision by AUEO	**High/medium** Frequent supervision by AUEO	**Medium** DEO and visiting section officer helped with suggestions and instruction as well as rapid administrative action; DDCC and parishad also extended help in the programme success
Medium Cluster training carried out regularly; supervision visits frequent with introduction of a new supervisory cadre	**High** Headteacher and AUEO supervise intensively class activities and school	**High** Creation of supervisory post, i.e. appointment of AUEO for about 20 schools	**High** Creation of additional post of AUEO	**Medium** UEO and in part AUEO gave supervision and guidance; upazila parishad sometimes provided local financial support
Medium Government commitment high to achieve UPE by year 2000. This has induced district administration as well to pay surprise visit to school	**High/medium** Headteachers and teachers have strong commitment to teaching and school has strong team spirit	**Medium** Government commitment for UPE; local commitment; community participation	**High** Government commitment for UPE; local commitment is low (i.e. community)	**High** Government commitment for success of UPE programme induced local level administrative machinery. However commitment of headteacher and his colleagues played key role

Cross-site display 2 *(cont)*

	Hasnahena	Champa	Aparajita	Palash	Chameli
Received pressure	**Medium** Received pressure from UEO, AUEO, DPEO did not give any pressure	**High** DPEO, AUEO exerts pressure maintaining programme strongly	**High** Political awareness constant obligation for universal education; commitment of officials etc. put pressure on all concerned with execution and implementation of the reforms; the project had full and stable political support during this period	**High/medium** By headteacher, by AUEO, by UEO, by DPEO through circular	**Medium** DPEO gave pressure to some extent; UEO, AUEO solve problems faced by headteachers and teachers
Received resources	**High** Lists of schools' requirements drawn up; UEO, AUEO provided resources allotted by government	**High** Contingency grant; black boards; teaching aids; furniture; three new male teachers and one female teacher	**High** UPE (IDA) project and national project received full financial support from the World Bank and Government of Bangladesh; they provide inputs shown in 'bundle' and necessary services	**High** Textbooks; teachers' guides; construction of new building; new furniture; tubewell; latrine; financial help from upazila	**High/medium** List of school requirements was sought; UEO, AUEO provided whatever was given by government. Sometimes resources did not reach school in time
Success experiences	**High** Extensive building; large number of students, female teachers and girl students; teachers more punctual; more scholarships; fewer failures and more passes	**Low** Enrolment increased; success of the programme encourages teachers	**High** Increased enrolment of students, particularly of girls and poor students; decreased repetition, drop-out and wastage seen as success which led to intensive efforts; level of student achievement improved greatly	**Medium** Achievement of more scholarships; trying to increase enrolment	**High** More students, classrooms and teachers; more punctual; more scholarships
Empowerment engagement	**Low** Everything came from above, project people listened to concerns of local people	No data	**Medium/low** Programme tailor-made at central level to serve all areas uniformly yet scope for some modification at school to some extent.	**Medium** Teachers and headteacher try out the change in their school. No involvement in decision to making	**Medium** Decisions taken by the directorate and ministry; project people listened to the concerns of local people

Implications

Ulatchandal	Rangan	Padma	Shapla	Jaba
Medium Pressure for proper and timely execution are put by education officer at the level of DDCC; Zila Parishad also put pressure	**Medium** DPEO, AUEO exert pressure to implement and maintain the programme.	**Medium** From UEO and DPEO	**Medium** From UEO and DPEO	**Medium** Pressure exerters are the DPEO, UEO offices and DDCC as well as the zila parishad for implementation success
Medium Resources for the project from the government in Dhaka	**High** Contingency grant Tk. 30/- teachers' guide; school furniture; teaching aids, one male teacher one female teacher	**Medium** National (i.e. from UPE, IDA) support for project	**Medium** National (i.e. from UPE, IDA) support for project	**Medium** Resource control and allocation for teachers' salary and contingency expenses made annually. Development fund spent by various agencies directly. Resource control felt
Medium Noticeable success experience gained during later years of project implementation	**Low** Enrolment increased and more scholarships encouraged teachers as sources of the programme	**High/medium** Tradition for good academic performance of students	**Medium** Tradition for good achievement of students	**Medium** Yes, later years (or second phase) of programme saw better implementation of targets. In initial years experienced a lot more seminars/workshops and training etc.
Medium Decentralized management of the primary education at the upazila (sub-district) level a helpful process	No data	**Medium** Decentralized administration introduced for primary education	**Medium** Decentralized adminstration system for primary education	**Low** Experience gained induced decentralized management at the upazila level. To make more functional, resources are requested to be allocated at the local level

Cross-site display 2 *(cont)*

	Hasnahena	Champa	Aparajita	Palash	Chameli
Local adaptation of programme	**High** All components fitted well in school routine	**Low** Little scope for local adaptation in any component of programme	**Medium/low** Headteacher, teachers have scope for making some adaptation of methods and materials to suit the local situation	**Low** Little scope for local adaptation	**High/medium** All components fitted well with the school routine. They did not change anything
Community support, parent support	**Medium** Parents eager for children's education; PTA not functioning; parents unaware of reform	**High/medium** Rich parents gave help in cash and kind when schools needed it	**Medium** Support of parents and community	No data	**Medium** Parents show interest in children's education; PTA is not functioning
Other	**High** Hindu parents eager for their children's education				

Cross-site display 3 Key factors explaining institutionalization

Hasnahena	Champa	Aparajita	Palash	Chameli
High AUEO organizes cluster training every month. Long stay of headteacher. Headteacher trains staff in development class every Thursday	**High** Cluster training; co-operation by community; supply of materials by government	**High** Orientation of personnel at different levels; cluster training for headteacher and teachers at school premises based on need assessment with scope for local revision; continuous supervision; support with emphasis on pedagogy, capacity-building and built-in-ness; this assistance proved effective	**High/Medium** Addition of classroom; supply of free textbooks; continuous cluster training; orientation on new curriculum	**High** Government's high priority and commitment for UPE; better service terms for the school teachers; extensive physical facilities and free textbooks for all; continuous teacher training

Implications

Ulatchandal	Rangan	Padma	Shapla	Jaba
Medium Achieved to a degree. Community involvement through SMC and PTA made the programme generally popular; observation of annual education week helped popularity	**Low** Little scope for local adaptation	**High/medium** Teachers were found active in organizing co-curricular activities	**Medium/low** Teachers were not interested in organizing co-curricular activities	**Medium** Programme such as education week observed annually and activity of SMC and PTA helpful for popular participation and programme mobilization.
Low Teachers' association at times deters overall interest of teachers by holding back administrative decisions (negative)	**High/medium** Formation of SMC and PTA around interest of community; community helped cash and kind when needed	No data	No data	No data
High Hindu community show interest in children's education Ex-headmaster initiative very high				

Ulatchandal	Rangan	Padma	Shapla	Jaba
High/medium Addition of one classroom; supply of free textbooks and teachers' guides; cluster training; orientation on new curriculum	**High** Cluster training; supply of materials by government; co-operation by the community	**Medium** AUEO imparts cluster training; AUEO supervision of school occasionally; union parishad game; latrine; one teacher was sent to Philipines for training on impact	**Medium** Cluster training and supervision by AUEO; occasional supervision by AUEO; encouragement and guidance from headteacher	**Medium** Assistance of local influential people and community support; assistance and support received from the education officials

Cross-site display 3 *(cont)*

	Hasnahena	Champa	Aparajita	Palash	Chameli
Administrative role	**High** AUEO and headteacher observe classroom teaching and give instructions to teachers; headteacher generated a source of income through betelnut garden	**High** DPEOs occasionally visit; AUEOs give regular advice; strong permatism. Headmaster has strong rapport with teachers and community	**High** Headmaster and AUEO were aware of and associated with reform programmes; delegated authority to teachers; checked up on classroom activity; provided help; supplied materials; maintained linkage with the community and higher authorities; stability and pressure involved; facilitated monitoring regularly; demanded supervision support; other administration provided support when needed by them	**High/medium** AUEO and UEO visit school and organize cluster training; distribute textbooks	**High/medium** Local level administration and managerial support; monitoring and motivation
Supervision support	**High** Supervises 21 schools per month; AUEO a new recruit who provides cluster training once a month; more responsiblity to the local office.	**High** DPEO's occasional and AUEO's regular supervision; headmaster's strong instruction and managerial supervision of school activities	**High** School and its classroom work continuously supervised by AUEO, UEO, DPEO and other official supervision; headteacher also supervised classes (FAC), checked teachers' work, helped, guided	**High/medium** By AUEO	**High** Creation of a nucleus of supervisory officials and monthly cluster training
Commitment	**Medium** Headmaster introduced award for class teacher who enrolled highest number of students	**Medium** Headmaster and teachers' devotion to school; teachers' regular attendance, punctuality and team spirit	**High** Teachers, headmaster, local administrators, community, other officials and leaders at all levels were committed to implementing reforms; they have positive feelings for all components	**High/medium** Government commitment; commitment of AUEO and teachers	**High** Government gives high priority and commitment to UPE

Implications

Ulatchandal	Rangan	Padma	Shapla	Jaba
High/medium AUEO and UEO visit school and organize cluster training; distribute textbooks	**High** DPEOs occasional and AUEO's regular advice and strong supervision. Headmaster has strong rapport with teachers and community	**Medium** UEO puts pressure; headteacher's role democratic and supportive.	**Medium** AUEO observes school and classroom teaching; UEO puts pressure to implement changes; Headteacher guides and puts pressure to implement changes	**Medium** Active participation in the process of reform bundle by the local level education officials; monitoring support from the administration; political representation of the area
High/Medium By AUEO	**High** DPEO's occasional and AUEO's regular supervision and training; headmaster's strong instruction and managerial supervision of school activities	**Medium** Supervision by AUEO once a month; supervision by UEO occasionally	**Medium** AUEO supervised the school eight times per year; UEO supervises twice	**Medium** AUEOs supervised as their prime responsibility and gave training monthly
High/medium Government commitment; commitment of teachers	**Medium** AUEO, headmaster and teachers' devotion. Teachers' regular attendance, punctuality and team spirit	**Medium** Positive feeling of teachers and headteacher towards changes; they give priority to changes.	**Medium** Teachers, headteacher, AUEO committed to implementing changes and gave priority; they had positive attitude towards cluster training; all wanted continuation of the changes	**High** Key commitment came from headteacher and colleagues; government support and commitment induced the reform.

Cross-site display 3 *(cont)*

	Hasnahena	Champa	Aparajita	Palash	Chameli
Received pressure	**Medium** Received pressure from UEO, AUEO; DPEO did not give any pressure	**Medium** Recurrent pressure and strong persuasion from AUEO; occasional pressure from DEO; continuous supervision from headmaster	**High** Political awareness, constitutional obligation for universal education, commitment of all officials etc. put pressure on all for implementation of the reforms; the project had full and stable political support	**Medium** From local level supervision, i.e. AUEO	**Medium** From local level supervising staff, i.e. AUEO
Received resources	**High** Lists of schools' requirements were drawn up; UEO, AUEO provided resources; extension of building; tubewell; toilet; free textbooks; teaching guides	**High** Received regular monthly contingency grant; school building, latrines, tubewell, equipment, textbooks from government. Money and materials help from community.	**High** UPE (IDA) project and national project received full financial support from the World Bank and the Government of Bangladesh; they provided the inputs as shown in the bundle and provided necessary services	**Low** For petty repair from community	**Medium** Yes, but not adequate (wastage not accounted for)
Success experiences	**High** Extended building; large number of students, female teachers and girl students; teachers more punctual; more scholarships; fewer failures and more passes	No data	**High** Increase in enrolment of students, particularly girls and poor students; decrease in repetition, drop-out and wastage were seen as success which led to intensified efforts; level of student achievement improved greatly	**Medium** Students' past achievement	**Medium/low** Enthusiasm noticeable among teachers and community leaders
Empowerment engagement	**Medium** Everything came from above; project people listened to concerns of local people	**Low** No scope for local adaptation	**Medium/low** Programme tailor-made and uniform; but scope for school and classroom level modification allowed	**Medium** Decentralized administrative system	**Low** Mobilization at the local level productive
Local adaptation	**High** All components fitted well in school routine; all reform inputs are termed as basic needs of school by all	**Medium** Parents offered cash money and material help as support	**Medium** Headmaster and teachers have scope for making some adaptation of methods and materials to suit the local situation	**High/medium** Teachers found active; regular reporting on enrolment (attendance, drop-out, repeaters etc.)	**Low** To a degree, yes

Implications

Ulatchandal	Rangan	Padma	Shapla	Jaba
High Headteacher gives pressure; AUEO gives pressure; DPEO gives pressure through circulars	**Medium** Pressure from the local level education and administrative officials	**High/medium** AUEO gives pressure, UEO occasionally gives pressure; DPEO gives pressure through circulars; headteacher gives pressure	**Medium** Pressure from AUEO, UEO, DPEO and from DDCC and zila parishad.	**No data**
Low For petty repair from community	**High/medium** Received contingency grant regularly. Textbooks; materials; equipment	**High** Textbooks, teachers' guides; new schoolhouse; new furniture; new teaching aids; latrine; tubewell	**High** Textbooks, teachers' guides; new school building; new furniture, tubewell; latrine; financial help from upazila parishad	**Medium** Yes; inadequate but not insignificant
Medium/low Students' past achievement	**No data**	**Medium** Increased enrolment; reduced drop-out; more scholarships; increased interest of children and parents	**Medium** Achievement of scholarship; increased enrolment; reduction in drop-out	**Medium** Moderate support for on-going process of reform
Medium Decentralized administrative system	**Low** No scope for adaptation	**No data**	**No data**	**Low** Experience dictated decision of local level decentralized management
Medium Teachers seen to be active; regular reporting on enrolment	**Medium** Offered help, cash and support in kind	**No data**	**No data**	**Medium** Functioning of SMC and PTA; observance of annual education week

Cross-site display 3 *(cont)*

	Hasnahena	Champa	Aparajita	Palash	Chameli
Owner parent supports	**Medium** Parents are eager for children's education; PTA is not functioning; parents unaware of reform	**High** Very strong hopes for the continuation of cluster training; regular monthly supervision and headmaster gives strong instruction and managerial supervision; teachers' attendance regular; supply of free textbooks	**Medium** Support by parents and community	No data	**Medium/low** Parent support positive (but not up to expectations yet)
Other hopes for continuation	**Medium** Teachers, headteacher, UEO and AUEO hope free meal, sports goods and gardening plots together with reform inputs will improve school	**Medium** Long stay of some headteachers	**High** Already accepted for continuation nationally. In this school it will be continued	**Medium** Addition of classroom; furniture; more training strengthening supervisory staff	**Medium/low** Headmaster hopeful of continuation; local officials have reservations
Other personnel stability	**Medium** Personnel are more or less stable	No data	**Medium** At higher levels personnel may change, but at school level stable	**Medium** Appointment of new teachers	**Medium** Administrative and management structure is likely to continue
Other political stability	**Medium** Political support came as a law – universal primary education	No data	**High** Political stability at local level assured; instability at higher level will have few effects at school level	No data	**Medium** Doubtful; unrest may continue for some time; administrative set-up will continue to function irrespective of political instability as UPE is a constant obligation.
Others	No data	No data	**High** Central political support; strong national organization; comprehensive staff development programme; carefully monitored, efficient administrative arrangement from central local levels	No data	No data

Implications

Ulatchandal	Rangan	Padma	Shapla	Jaba
No data	**High** Very strong hopes for cluster training; Regular supervision and contingency grant; teachers' attendance regular	**No data**	**No data**	**No data**
Medium Addition of classroom; one more teacher; more furniture	**High** Long stay for teachers and headmaster	**No data**	**No data**	**Medium** Hopeful that adequate furniture will be available for the continuation of the programme
Medium Appointment of new teachers	**No data**	**No data**	**No data**	**No data**
No data	**No data**	**No data**	**No data**	**No data**
No data	**No data**	**No data**	**No data**	**No data**

Appendix 1

Research Questions

The major research questions of the study are as follows:

1. What are the outcomes of successful strategies for the implementation of educational change, seen in terms of quality of implementation, institutionalization and student outcomes, as well as in terms of unexpected outcomes?

2. What do successful strategies look like, both at the macro (country) level and the micro (local school) level?

3. What determines successful strategies? Determinants may include administrative capacity development, teacher training and commitment-building efforts, among others.

4. How are successful strategies linked at the macro and micro levels?

These major questions, with associated sub-questions, are organized below in terms of the two major sub-studies of the project, the country-level and school-level studies.

COUNTRY-LEVEL SUB-STUDY (CSS)

This sub-study is brief, and mostly confirmatory, aiming to see whether the previous desk case study of the programme was accurate, and to revise its conclusions where needed. There are some exploratory questions as well, which are marked with an (E) below.

1. What are the outcomes of successful strategies for the implementation of educational change, as perceived at the country level? How closely do these outcomes resemble those found in the previous desk case study?
   (a) Quality of implementation (specific indicators to come).
   (b) Institutionalization/sustainability (specific indicators to come).
   (c) Student outcomes (specific indicators to come).
   (d) Quality and capacity of institutions at system level.
   (e) Unanticipated outcomes (these may be positive or negative, and may be political, economic, social, cultural, etc. as well as educational). (E)

2. What do successful strategies for the implementation of educational change look like? Is the description of the strategy in the prior desk case study reasonably accurate? Attention should be given to:

(a) The change itself: what was to be implemented at national, regional and local levels?

(b) Chronology and sequence of events.

(c) General nature of the strategy.

(d) How resources were allocated.

(e) How the strategy was planned and adapted during implementation.

(f) The role of environmental factors (social, political, economic, cultural and physical).

3. What determines successful strategies? In particular, to what degree were the following factors present, and did they lead to programme success? Are these factors reasonably like those found in the desk case study?

(a) Strength of national organizations.

(b) Building of commitment (national, regional and local).

(c) Matching of strategy to environmental stability/turbulence and the degree of innovation involved.

(d) Coordinated division of labour among specialized agencies.

(e) Development of needed infrastructure for administration, supervision and assistance (institution-building).

(f) Devolution of decision-making to regional and local levels.

(g) Closeness to implementation (careful monitoring).

(h) Responsive adaptation (learning from experience).

(i) Budget and legal decision-making to support institutionalization, (moving from project status to routine status).

(j) Other specific determinants unique to the country that appeared in the desk case study.

4. How are successful strategies at the macro level linked to local school implementation? (E)

(a) Linkages that occur as intended.

(b) Unintended linkages.

(c) Instances of success where no clear linkage existed.

All of the factors listed above under question 3 above will be examined, as well as unintended linkages.

SCHOOL-LEVEL SUB-STUDY (SSS)

This sub-study is more extensive, and mostly exploratory, since little is known about how local-level implementation proceeds. Some confirmatory questions are proposed, drawn from the prior desk case studies, and from studies of change in developed countries, and these are marked with a (C).

1. What are the outcomes of successful strategies for the implementation of educational change, as they occur at the school level?

    1.1 Quality of implementation

    1.11 technical mastery of the innovation or practice
    1.12 quality of materials
    1.13 teacher engagement, interest
    1.14 teacher performance
    1.15 compatibility with other classroom methods, content, etc. (if 'part-innovation' is looked at)
    1.16 extent or widespreadness of use among teachers (%).

    1.2 Institutionalization of the programme

    1.21 'built-in-ness' (used regularly/routinely)
    1.22 consolidation at the classroom level (regular, routine use)
    1.23 likelihood of continuation.

    1.3 Student outcomes (use whatever assessments on judgement are routinely made, plus observations)

    1.31 cognitive (knowledge, information)
    1.32 behaviour (skills, actions)
    1.33 social-emotional (affect, self-esteem, etc).

    1.4 Unanticipated outcomes

    1.41 positive second-order changes (increased capacity, transfer of skills to new areas, etc.)
    1.42 negative changes of any sort
    1.43 changes in the school which appear unconnected to the programme, but occurred during the same period.

    1.5 Prognosis for the future

    1.51 scenario for future use of the programme
    1.52 anticipated hopes, needs
    1.53 school's capacity for further change.

2. What do successful strategies for the implementation of educational change look like at the school level?

    2.1 How do school people (teachers, headmasters, nearby supervisors or assistance-givers) perceive or evaluate the change or innovation involved in the programme under study?

    2.11 how they construe it, what it means to them
    2.12 what they think it's 'for'
    2.13 what do they see as the important elements of the reform **to them?**

    2.2 What is the 'fit' between the programme and the needs/priorities of school people?

    2.21 what the programme does for people

Research Questions

  2.22 'centrality': how important the programme is for people
  2.23 how programme is affected by staff characteristics (background, age, experience, pedagogical views)
  2.24 how the programme connects with needs, or current instructional practices in the school
  2.25 main motives or incentives to start and use the programme (e.g. professionalization, pressure, problem-solving, career advancement, etc.).

 2.3 How do school people describe the process of implementation?
  2.31 how programme was initiated
  2.32 aspects or events which were most salient
  2.33 what helped
  2.34 what hindered
  2.35 how programme was redesigned, altered, adapted
  2.36 how successful they consider implementation to be
  2.37 whether attention was given to 'building in' the programme.

3. What *determines* successful strategies of implementation at the school level? (This will be approached through comparing schools with varying amounts of success.)

 3.1 Which contextual factors affect the degree of success? These may have been important at various times: adoption or start, implementation, institutionalization.
  3.11 general cultural, demographic, political, economic factors as they play out locally
  3.12 local community support (C)
  3.13 student characteristics
  3.14 environmental turbulence/instability (C).

 3.2 Which local factors affect the degree of success? These may occur at the school level (headmaster), or at the level of local school clusters or networks (specialists, supervisors). The aim is to see how these help or hinder.
  3.21 organizational context issues
   (a) personal networks among staff (or among headmasters in an area)
   (b) past experience with innovation
   (c) resources
   (d) climate, norms
   (e) existing routines, prior practice
   (f) other
  3.22 administrative capacity (C)
   (a) stability over time
   (b) presence or involvement (includes attentiveness, knowledgeability, advocacy, buffering/protection, stable commitment etc.)

(c) facilitation (includes rapid authorization, relaxing of usual routines when needed, delegating authority, making needed organizational changes, providing resources (material, technical, time), etc.)
(d) monitoring, regulating (includes getting data on programme, coordination, adjusting as needed)
(e) demandingness (includes pressure for implementation, maintaining a sustained level of change, insisting on effort, etc.)
(f) supervision and support (C) (includes real-time, on-going help for teachers as they work with the programme, trouble-shooting, etc.)

3.23 assistance (C) (includes formal training, consultation, technical assistance)

(a) continuity (sustained throughout implementation)
(b) local availability (source may be peers, headmaster, local centre)
(c) need-responsiveness (tailored to actual needs)
(d) pedagogical emphasis (not just administrative)
(e) professional capacity-building emphasis (goes beyond the immediate programme)
(f) consequences for teacher mastery of the change

3.24 success experiences with the change (C)

(a) practice mastery
(b) results with students

3.25 commitment (C) (note also resistance)

(a) how it occurred at various levels (teachers, parents, headmaster, local specialists, supervisors)
(b) when it occurred during the stages of the programme (early, middle, late, etc.)

3.26 community pressure and support.

4. How are successful strategies at the local school level linked to or influenced by macro-level strategies of implementation? The aim is to discover the linkages between country-level strategies and what occurs locally. These linkages can be traced by 'following down' national initiatives to the local level, and by 'looking up' from the local school to see what the influences have been. Attention should focus on: (a) linkages that occur as intended; (b) unintended linkages; and (c) instances of success where no clear linkage existed. Types of possible linkage include:

4.1 received pressure (C)
4.2 received resources
4.3 assistance (C)

4.4 supervision/support (C)
4.5 administrative competence (C)
4.6 empowerment, engagement (C)
4.7 local adaptation of the change (C)
4.8 others (to be discovered).

Linkages can be looked at as either absent, loose, or tight.

Appendix 2

Local-level Study

INTERVIEW GUIDE: TEACHERS

[INTRODUCE YOURSELF] Let me tell you what I'm doing here. I'm here to look at the changes that have gone on in your school over the past ten years or so. Some of these changes may have started at the national level, in the ministry, sometimes with help from outside the country. I want to find out what these changes look like inside the school and the classrooms. That's what really matters. I want to know how the changes actually work, and why they are successful or not. That will be useful in helping other schools change.

I would like to talk with you for an hour and a half or so today, and perhaps visit your classroom. Then I'll come back again for another talk in a few weeks.

What you tell me is confidential. I will not repeat it to other people. I will write a report, but it will not identify you, or the name of the school. The report will come back to the school, and be circulated for advice and correction to be sure it is accurate.

Here is a one-page written explanation of the study that you can keep.

Do you have any questions about this?
[NOTE THEM HERE AND GIVE ANSWERS]

(NOTE TEACHER'S NAME HERE)

Q.1(a) How long have you been teaching here? [YEAR STARTED _____]
What subjects or grade levels?

Q.1(b) What did you do before you taught here?

Q.1(c) What are your academic qualifications?

Q.1(d) How did you happen to come to this school? When was that?

   Probes: Events or determinants that led teacher here
   Reasons given by the teacher himself for coming

Q.2(a) Now I'd like to know something about this school and how it has changed over the past _____ years, since you came here. [DATE OF REFORM START, OR DATE TEACHER CAME HERE, IF LATER.] You've probably seen some changes. How is it different now from the way it was then?

| How things were done THEN | How things are done NOW | How do you feel about these changes? (+, −, why*) |

Q.2(b) I understand that there might have also been some other changes coming from the ministry, though you haven't mentioned them. In particular, I'm thinking of (SHOW CARD 2(b)):

ELEMENTS OF REFORM	START DATE IF KNOWN	FEELINGS (+, −, why)
_____		
_____		
_____		

Have you heard about them? Did these changes happen in your school? (IF YES) When did they start? What do you remember the most about them? How do you feel about them overall?

Probes: Are they sensible or misguided? Connected to priorities in the school or not central to the school?

The aim is to have got from the headmaster a reasonable 'bundle' of changes that look like this:

1. They have some overlap with the district administrator bundle.
2. They go together, can be seen as linked.
3. They started about the same time, at least two to three years ago.
4. They are reasonably salient to the respondent. [CHECK TO BE SURE OF THIS]

Using the headmaster bundle will make for a great deal more comparability of information.

Remember that it is OK to take just one change if that looks salient. But it will usually be a bundle.

Q.2(c) And what did you actually do differently in your work as a result of these changes? [PROBE FOR +, − AND WHY]

I need a little history of how all these changes happened, as much as you can tell me. First, let's go back to _____, when some of these changes were just getting started [OR .. when you first got here.]
Here are the ones I'd like to talk about. [READ FROM ABOVE, GIVE THE CHANGES A NAME, WHICH WILL BE USED REPEATEDLY IN FOLLOWING QUESTIONS.]

Q.3(a) Do you remember what was going on in the school then?

Probes: What year ... what staff ... mix of students ... performance of students ... curriculum and didactic materials ... main problems or

---

*Aim is to find how respondent feels about the changes — positively and/or negatively. Are changes seen as good or bad? Important to find out why — what the change means to the person. BE ALERT TO CHANGES WHICH STEM FROM NATIONAL REFORMS WHICH ARE SUPPORTED BY THE WORLD BANK.

concerns being confronted in the school ... material conditions of work in the school (equipment, materials).

Q.3(b) Were there things going on outside the school at that time — things in the nation or the community that influenced life at the school for teachers or students?

Probes: Issues in the community ... economic situation in the region ... national or regional politics which were playing out locally ... issues having to do with health and welfare of children.

Q.3(c) At first, did it make good sense to spend time at the school on this kind of change?

Probes: Priority or not? ... connected to needs of the school or not? ... likely to have positive effects or to complicated existing problems ... (if workable:) how colleagues felt about this.

Q.3(d) How did (NAME OF CHANGES) get started in this school? Who did something? Was there somebody who pushed for them or started first? What did s/he do?

Q.3(e) Did that make it easier to get started in the school? How?

Q.3(f) Did the actions of these people actually make it harder to get (NAME OF CHANGES) introduced into the school in any way? How?

Q.3(g) Then do you remember a little later on, when you and other people were beginning to use (NAME OF CHANGES)? How was it going then? Difficult or easy?

Q.4 You've told me some of the history. Who else in the school could tell me more about it? Maybe someone who would have a different idea about how (NAME OF CHANGES) went.

Q.5(a) Now I'd like to ask you some more detailed questions about these changes and how they were carried out. Could we go back again to the time when you first heard about (NAME OF CHANGES)? [Bring informant back to the year, the class, or other salient event in the life of the school.]
Back then at the beginning, how important was it to you personally that (NAME OF CHANGES) got started in the school? Did it matter a lot? Or didn't you care? Or did you have doubts about it?

Q.5(b) And how about the other teachers you know best? Was it important to them?

Q.5(c) And what about _____ [GIVE NAMES OF KEY ADMINISTRATORS: headmaster, inspector, etc.] How much did it matter to them?

Probe: How they know this; indices on which judgment is being based.

Q.6 I'd like to spend a little more time on this. Here's a list of possible reasons for getting involved with changes in schools. (GIVE CARD 6) Which ones of them were important to you, back then?

Local-level Study

Reasons for getting involved	Not an important reason		Somewhat important reason		Very important reason
	1	2	3	4	5
1. I had no choice; it came down through the system.	1	2	3	4	5
2. It was something I thought we really needed here.	1	2	3	4	5
3. It was a chance for me to get some training, to learn something.	1	2	3	4	5
4. It looked promising; it was worth a try.	1	2	3	4	5
5. It was something new and interesting.	1	2	3	4	5
6. I would benefit financially.	1	2	3	4	5
7. I had already worked on similar changes.	1	2	3	4	5
8. Other people liked it, and that influenced me.	1	2	3	4	5
9. It would give the school more resources.	1	2	3	4	5
10. I thought it might help me get a different job, here or somewhere else.	1	2	3	4	5
11. I thought I would get something else out of it. (What? _____)	1	2	3	4	5

Any other reasons that you got involved?

You said that numbers _____ were very important. Can you say a little more about that?

Q.7(a) When changes like these come to a school, they may or may not 'fit' with the local situation. Thinking back to the way (NAME OF CHANGES) looked at the beginning, was it a good 'fit' or 'match' to the way you like to work, or have to work, in the school?

Q.7(b) Let's talk in more detail about what you just said and about how well (NAME OF CHANGES) fit things in this school. Here's a card (GIVE CARD 7b) with a list of things. How good was the fit between (NAME OF CHANGES) and each of these?

Fit (good, OK but some problems, poor)

1. My students (their background, abilities, motivations, etc.).
2. The rest of the curriculum.
3. The kinds of methods and materials I work with best.
4. The time and energy I have for doing something new.
5. The methods and materials other teachers feel comfortable with.
6. Daily organization in the school (schedule, grouping, etc.).
7. Other demands made on us by administrators (headmaster, supervisor, inspector, etc).
8. What parents would like.
9. What community officials would like.
10. Others:

Good. Let's talk about the ones where you said the fit was poor or had some problems.

Q.7(c) What kind of problems were there?

Q.7(d) Could you tell me how, or if, the problems were solved? First, did you or other people change (NAME OF CHANGES) in any way to make them fit better?

Q.7(e) And second, did you or other people change anything in the school — for example, the school organization, curriculum, administrative demands, etc. — to make the fit better?

Q.7(f) And were there any other changes made in (NAME OF CHANGES), even though the fit might have been pretty good? What were they?

Q.8 About how often do you use (NAME OF CHANGES)? All day, some of every day, a few times a week, or less? And how do you like it?
[MAY HAVE TO ASK ABOUT DIFFERENT PARTS OF THE BUNDLE]

Q.9(a) Once more, let's go back to the time when you first started using (NAME OF CHANGES). I'm interested in how you learned to use it, and what kind of help you got. How did it go, the first few months?

Probes: Feelings + and − (good/bad, like/dislike) ... reactions of students ... generally easy or difficult to use ... parts that seemed ready, parts that didn't work well ... reactions of colleagues ... how big a change it seemed, and why.

Q.9(b) Did you feel you had been adequately prepared or trained?
IF YES: What was done? How was it helpful?

IF NO: In which respects, and why not?

Q.9(c) Have you had any help later on, as you were using (NAME OF CHANGES)? What do you remember getting?

[DISPLAYS 7A, 7B, 7C]

Q.10(a) I'd like to go into the question of help or assistance in more detail. Here's a list of people who might have given you help at the beginning, or along the way. (GIVE CARD 10a) I'd like to ask for each what kind of help they gave, when they did it, and how it helped you — what you could do better as a result. Of course, sometimes 'help' isn't really helpful, and I need to know that too.

	Kind of help	How much/when (early/late)	If helpful, how; if not, how not
Trainer or programme specialist			
Specialist teacher			
Fellow teacher in the school			
Fellow teacher outside the school			
Headmaster			
Supervisor or inspector			
District or regional administrator (WHICH?)			
Other:			

(Check if things were *not* done that is seen as useful)

IF FIRST INTERVIEW IS STOPPING HERE:

It looks like our time is up. OK, then I'll visit your class at _____ .

I'd like to see how (NAME OF CHANGES) works in action in the classroom, so we can talk about it more concretely. Could I do that with you soon? I'd also like to see some of the materials you use with (NAME OF CHANGES). And some of the things students have done with it — their products. Would that be possible?

Many thanks for your time and your willingness to help me understand what things are like in this school. I enjoyed talking with you.

Anything else on your mind that we haven't talked about?

To researcher: See list of possible intervention strategies ('Kind of help') (Manual). If appropriate, use it (Card 10b) as probes.

PRIOR TO SECOND INTERVIEW:

- Review interview/observation notes, and put the data in the displays.
- Get more familiar with the changes as implemented locally, through reviewing observation notes and documents.
- Note leads, questions and gaps to be covered in the second sitting.
- Prepare a list of 'plausible outcomes' that the reform might be expected to accomplish:
  — at the school level
  — at the student level
  — at the individual teacher level.

  This list will be used with Q.13(a) and Q.16 as things to be probed for.
- Prepare a sumary of the 'NOW' answers to Q.2(a) for use with Q.15(b).

[SECOND INTERVIEW STARTS HERE]

Nice to see you again. As before, I have a lot of questions that will take us about two hours.

Q.11(a) I've seen you working with (NAME OF CHANGES) once or twice now. For example, I saw you when _____ . Was that session typical — the way it usually works?

[ADD IN ANY OTHER OPEN-ENDED QUESTIONS ON YOUR MIND ABOUT THE OBSERVATION]

Q.11(b) I have the impression that you feel reasonably comfortable doing (NAME OF CHANGES). [IF NOT THE CASE, GIVE ACCURATE IMPRESSION] Is that so?

Q.11(c) Are there any parts of (NAME OF CHANGES) you don't yet feel you've fully mastered, that you're not fully comfortable with, not getting you the results you want? (IF YES) Which parts?

Q.11(d) Would you say you'd feel comfortable if another teacher who was learning to use (NAME OF CHANGES) came here for a week to learn from you by watching what you do? Could you tell me more about why you feel that way? [IF NECESSARY GO BACK TO Q.9(a), 9(b), 9(c), 10 TO FILL IN, THEN RETURN TO Q.12(a).]

Q.12(a) Here's a curious question. I'll ask it in the form of a game, but the idea behind it is an important one for me. Suppose — of course, there's no reason why this would actually happen — that someone told you that, as of next year, (NAME OF CHANGES) would be taken out, discontinued, how would you feel? [Look for disappointed, neutral, relieved, etc.]. Tell me some more about that.

Q.12(b) How about your colleagues here and in other schools using (NAME OF CHANGES)? How do you think they would react? Why is that?

Q.12(c) And how about some of the key administrators we've talked about, like the headmaster and administrators outside the school? How would they react if (NAME OF CHANGES) were discontinued? Why?

Q.13(a) Let's talk about students for a while. I've just been asking about (NAME OF CHANGE), and about a list of other changes. Looking at ALL these changes, what do you think they've done for students?

Probes: Ask for specific indicators

[Probe also for any other changes on your prepared list of 'plausible outcomes' that have not been mentioned]

Q.13(b) Do you know of any data, such as test scores, students' work products, written evaluations, repeater and drop-out rates, that shows what has happened to students? What's available?

How could I see those data?

Q.13(c) Did these changes do anything for students that you didn't expect, something that was surprising? What?

Q.13(d) Sometimes changes are not always good. Do you think that maybe students are actually worse off in some way because of these changes? Which ones? Can you give me some examples of changes you think are not good and tell me why?

How students worse off	Which changes did this	Specific indicators

Q.14 I'm also interested in what these changes have done for you as a teacher (positively and negatively). Are you different as a teacher in some ways?

Probes	Specific indicators or examples
Substantive knowledge	
Pedagogical knowledge	
Skills in teaching	
Skills in planning your work	
Attitudes towards work in the school	
Ideas about students' learning or motivation	
Skills in working with other teachers	
Skills in developing materials for class	
Others:	

[Probe also for any other changes on your prepared list of 'plausible outcomes' that have not been mentioned]

Q.15(a) Here are some questions about the future. Suppose that I came back a year or two from now. Would I still find (NAME OF CHANGE) in your own classroom? Why is that?

Q.15(b) Back when we first started talking together, you told me how the school was in _____ [YEAR], and how it is now. [GO BACK TO NOTES for Q.2(a) AND MAKE A SUMMARY OF THE MAIN FEATURES OF 'NOW']

What do you think will probably happen over next two or three years? Will things stay the same or change? How will they do that?

Q.15(c) And what do you *hope* will happen? What would you like to seen changed in the school over the next three to four years?

Probe: Which changes does teacher think should be made for school to meet needs of children in the community.

Q.15(d) What does the school need if you are to get what you hope for? What will it take to make those changes real?

Probes: Specific examples of what will be needed

Resources

Training

On-going assistance

Leadership

Commitment

Others:

Q.15(e) As you look ahead, are there some things that give you cause for worry? (IF YES) What are they?

Q.16(a) Now we're coming to the last part. We've been talking about changes in the school, and how they happened. Now I want to ask *why* they happened.

There have been many studies in other countries of how changes come to a school, and why they work successfully. There is a long list of factors that explain why changes succeed. What we don't know is whether these factors matter in _____ [COUNTRY NAME].

I'd like you to think over your experience with the changes we have been talking about, both (NAME OF CHANGE) and the other ones. I will give you cards with a list of factors, and ask you what happened for each one, and whether you think it made a difference in this school. It might have helped, or made things harder. [GIVE CARD 16a]

This first list is about what key administrators outside the school did. I mean the local supervisor or inspector, district or regional officials. For each one of these people, I want to know what happened, and whether it helped make the changes easier or made things harder.

[DISPLAY 7D]

| Factor | Is this a good description of what happened? (yes ... somewhat ... no) | Did it help, or make things harder? How much? |

Key administrators
outside the school

Q.16(b) Did your own headmaster do any of these things? Which ones? Were they helpful, or did they make things harder?

Probe: Card 16a

Q.17 Here's another list of factors. It's about what you and other teachers did. (GIVE CARD 17)

| Factor | Is this a good description of what happened? (yes ... somewhat ... no) | Did it help, or make things harder? How much? |

We teachers in the school

Q.18 Here's the last list. It's about the assistance you got when you were working with the changes. (GIVE CARD 18)

| Factor | Is this a good description of what happened? (yes ... somewhat ... no) | Did it help, or make things harder? How much? |

The assistance we got

Q.19 We've talked about a lot of things in these interviews. Are there things we haven't touched on that you think are important?

Q.20 Are there people who could tell me more about some of these questions that I should talk to?

ENDING COMMENTS

Many thanks for your time and your willingness to help me understand what things are like in this school. I enjoyed our talks.

What you've told me won't be repeated to others, and your name and the name of the school won't be in the report. The report will come back to the school to be checked for its accuracy.

Any last questions?

Appendix 3

Country-level Factors Accounting for Success of the Programme

Factor*	Illustrative indicators	Impact†
	(list and mark: pos = +, neg. = −)	(H,M,L,)
Strength of national organizations	E.g. ministry maintains close control over supervisors through clear rules and frequent regional contact	H
Capacity building of national organizations		
Building of commitment		
Strategic matching	E.g. because programme was ambitious and far-reaching, early decision was made to proceed incrementally (5% of schools in year 1, then 10% more in year 2)	H
Legal regulation		
Decision-making		
Pressure for good implementation		
Curriculum development		
Division of labour		
Infrastructure development		
Availability and quality of materials		
Resource allocation		
Resource delivery		
Closeness to implementation		
Effective communication		
Responsive adaptation		
User involvement		
Protection from environmental turbulence		

* See Appendix 6 for operational definitions.
† These ratings only done towards end of analysis, after all data complete and display filled in.

Country-level Factors

Factor*	Illustrative indicators	Impact†
Decisions supporting institutionalization		
Assistance		
Monitoring and control		
Other:		

Appendix 4

Worktables

Key to worktables

HI – High impact

HMI – High/medium impact

MI – Medium impact

MLI – Medium/low impact

LI – Low impact

NA – Not answered

A blank space indicates that the information was not clearly documented.

Worktable 1 Colombia, implementation (school ordering as in CSD 1)

Factor	Schools											
	Excellent			Very good							Good	
	1	2	3	4	5	6	7	8	9	10	11	12
Teachers' technical mastery	HI	HI	HI	HI	MI	MI	HI	HI	HI	HI	MI	LI
Teachers' commitment	HI	HI	HI	HI	HI	MI	MI	HI	MI	MI	MI	LI
Materials delivery	MI	HI	HI	HI			HI	LI	HI	MI	LI	
Training delivery	MI	HI	HI	HI	MI	HI	HI	MI	MI	HI	HI	LI
Assistance		HI	HI									
Head's competence	HI	HI	HI					HI			LI	
Support of local institution				HI	MI	HI						

Worktables

Worktable 2 Colombia, student impact

	Schools											
	Excellent			Very good							Good	
Factor	1	2	3	4	5	6	7	8	9	10	11	12
Cognitive gains	HI	HI	HI	HI	MI	HI	HI	LI	MI	LI	MI	MI
Socio-emotional gains	HI	HI	HI	HI	MI	HI	HI	HI	HI	HI	HI	LI
Drop-out rate	HI	MI	MI	MI								LI
Repetition rate	HI		MI	HI								LI
Attendance	HI	HI		HI	HMI							
Dependence on guide	MI					HI						
Orthography	LI		LI		LI	HMI		LI				
Discipline		LI										
Creativity analytical			HI			HI	HI		HI	HI		
Motivation					HI		HI	HMI	MI		HI	HI
Student leadership	HI	HI	HI	MI	MI	HI	HI	HI	HI	HI	HI	LI

Worktable 3 Colombia, teacher impact

	Schools											
	Excellent			Very good							Good	
Factor	1	2	3	4	5	6	7	8	9	10	11	12
Teachers' motivation	HI	HI	HI	HI	HI	HI	HI	HI	HMI	LI	MI	LI
Work with local materials	HI				HI		HMI	HMI			MI	
Work with community	HI	HI	HI	HI					LI		MI	MI
Interchange of experiences	HI				HI							
Ability to work with groups			MI			HMI			HI	MI		
Interaction with students			HI	HI		HMI	HMI				MI	

Worktable 4 Colombia, school impact

	Schools											
	Excellent			Very good							Good	
Factor	1	2	3	4	5	6	7	8	9	10	11	12
School-community relations	HI	HI	HI	HI		HI		LI	LI	HI		LI
Staff relations/co-operation	HI			HI				HI				LI
Student government	HI	HI	HI	MI	MI	HI	HI	HI	HI	HI	HMI	LI
Physical structure		HI	HI	HI		HI			HI	HI	HI	
Resources			HI	HI			HI		HI			
Demo-school	HI		HI					HI				

Worktable 5 Colombia, institutionalization

	Schools											
	Excellent			Very good							Good	
Factor	1	2	3	4	5	6	7	8	9	10	11	12
EN routinized	HI	HI	HI	HI	MI	HI	HI	HI	HI	HI	MI	MI
Teachers orient new teachers	HI	HI							HI			
Resources promised	HI	HI								HI		
Local administrative support			HI	HI		HI	HI					LI
Resources committed			HI	HI		HI	HI	HI	HI		HI	
Open pre-school			HI	HI								
Community support	HI	HI	HI	MI	HI	HI	HI	MI	HI	HI	MLI	LI
Assistance givers								HI	HI	HI		

Worktable 6 Ethiopia, implementation (school-ordering as in CSD 1)

	Schools								
	Excellent		Very good				Good		
Factor	1	2	3	4	5	6	7	8	9
Teachers' technical mastery	HI	HI	MI	MI	MI	MI	MI	MI	MI
Commitment/cooperation	HI	HI	HMI	HI	MI	MI	MI	MI	MI
Classroom management	HI	HI	HMI	HMI	HMI	MI	MI	MI	MI
School management	HI	HI	MI	HI	MI	MI	MI	MI	MI
Community support	HI	HI	HI	HI	MI	HI	MI	MI	MI
DEO support material	HI	HI	HI	HI	HI	MI	HI	MI	MI
DEO support training	HMI	HMI	HMI	HMI	HMI	HMI	HMI	HMI	MI
Use of teachers' aids	HI	HI	MI	MI	MI	MI	MI	MI	MI
Use of assessment techniques	MI	MI	MI	MI	MI	MI	MI	MI	MI
Co-curricular activities	HI	MI	MI	HI	MI	LI	HI	LI	MI
Division of labour	HI	HI	HMI	HI	HMI	HMI	MI	MI	MLI
Use of new curriculum	HI	HI	HI	HI	HI	HI	HI	HI	HI
Radio programme	HI	HI	HI	HI	HI	HI	HI	HI	HI
Labour education	HI	HI	HI	HI	HMI	HMI	HMI	HMI	HMI
SPC	HI	HMI	HI	MI	HMI	MI	MI	MI	MI

Worktables

Worktable 7 Ethiopia, student impact

Factor	Schools								
	Excellent		Very good				Good		
	1	2	3	4	5	6	7	8	9
Examination results	HI	HI	HI	MI	HMI	MI	MI	LI	MI
Promotion rate	HI	HMI	HI	MI	HI	MI	MI	MI	MI
Drop-out rate	LI	LI	MLI	MI	LI	LI	MLI	MLI	MLI
Regular attendance	HI	HMI	MI	MI	HI	MI	HI	MI	MI
Attitude towards labour education	HI	HI	HI	HI	HI	MI	LI	LI	LI
Attitude towards schooling	HI	HI	HI	HI	HI	MI	HI	MI	MI
Repetition rate	LI	LI	LI	MI	LI	HI	MI	HI	MI
Enrolment	MI	MI	MI	HI	HI	HI	HI	HI	HI

Worktable 8 Ethiopia, teacher impact

Factor	Schools								
	Excellent		Very good				Good		
	1	2	3	4	5	6	7	8	9
Use of local teaching-learning aids	HI	HI	MI	MI	MI	MI	LI	MLI	MLI
Teaching-learning process/class management	HI	HI	HMI	HMI	HMI	HMI	HMI	MI	MI
Teacher–teacher cooperation	HI	HI	HI	HMI	HMI	HI	MI	HI	MI
Teacher–headmaster cooperation	HI	HI	HMI	HI	HMI	HMI	MI	MI	MI
Participation in academic competition	HI	HI	HI	HMI	HI	HI	HI	NA	NA
Ability to motivate students	HI	HI	HMI	MI	HI	MLI	MI	LI	LI
Interest in labour education	HI	HI	HMI	HI	HI	MI	LI	MLI	MLI
Personal cleanliness	HI	HI	HI	HI	HI	HI	HI	HI	HI
Mastery of subject matter	HI	HI	HMI	MI	HMI	HMI	HMI	MI	MI
Commitment	HI	HI	HMI	HI	MI	HMI	MI	MI	MI
Involvement	HI	HI	HMI	HI	HI	HMI	MI	HI	HMI

Worktable 9 Ethiopia, school impact

	Schools								
	Excellent		Very good				Good		
Factor	1	2	3	4	5	6	7	8	9
Organizational changes	HI	HI	MI	HI	HI	HI	HI	HI	HI
SMC	HI	MI	HI	HI	MI	HI	MI	MI	MI
School divided into several subject departments	HI	HI	HI	HI	HI	HI	HI	HI	HI
Library	HI	HI	MI	HI	MI	MI	MI	HI	MI
School-community relations	HI	MI	HI	HI	HI	HI	MI	MI	MI
Labour education	HI	HI	HI	HI	HI	HI	MI	MI	MI
Co-curricular activity	HI	HI	HI	MI	HI	MI	MI	MI	MI
School income	HI	HI	HI	HI	HI	HI	HI	MI	HI
Physical structure	HI	HI	HI	HI	HI	HI	HI	HI	HI
School beautification	HI	HI	HI	HI	HI	HI	MI	MI	MI
School climate	HI	HI	HI	HI	HI	MI	HI	NA	MI
Enrolment	MI	MI	HI	HI	HI	HI	HI	HI	HI

Worktable 10 Ethiopia, institutionalization

	Schools								
	Excellent		Very good				Good		
Factor	1	2	3	4	5	6	7	8	9
All change components	HI	HI	HI	HI	HI	HI	HI	HI	HMI
Curriculum changes	HI	HI	HI	HI	HI	HI	HI	HI	HI
– Labour education	HI	HI	HI	HI	HI	HI	MI	MI	MI
– Radio programmes	HI	HI	HI	HI	HI	HI	HI	HI	HI
– Documentation	HMI	HI	HMI	HMI	MI	MI		MI	
– SMC support	HI	HMI	HI	HI	HMI	HI	HMI	HMI	HMI
– Head support	HI	HI	HI	HI	HI	HI	HMI	HMI	HI
– SPC coordination	HI	HI	HI	HMI	HI	MI	MI	MI	MI
Community support	HI	HMI	HI	HI	HI	HI	HI	HMI	MI
– Financial	HI	HI	HI	HI	HI	HI	HMI	HMI	HMI
– Materials	HI	HI	HI	HI	HI	HI	HI	HMI	HI
– Labour	HI	HI	HI	HI	HI	HI	HI	HMI	HI
Orientation of new teachers	HI	HI	HI	HI	HI	HI			HI
DEO support	HI	HI	HMI	HMI	HI	HMI	HMI	HMI	HMI
– Textbooks delivery	HI	HI	HI	HI	HI	HI	HI	HMI	HMI
– Instructional materials	HI	HI	HI	HI	HI	HI	HI	HMI	HMI
– Training	HMI	HMI	HMI	HMI	HMI	HMI	HMI	HMI	HMI

Worktables

Worktable 11 Bangladesh, implementation (school-ordering as in CSD 1)

Factor	Schools									
	Excellent				Very good			Good		
	1	2	3	4	5	6	7	8	9	10
New classroom/facilities	HI	HI	HI	HI	HI	MI	MLI	MI	MI	MI
Free textbooks/guides	HI	HI	HI	HI	HI	HI	HI	HMI	HI	HMI
Block teaching	HI	NA	MI	HI	NA	NA	MI	LI	NA	LI
Female teachers	HI	HI	MLI	HI	MI	HMI	MLI	MI	MI	MLI
AUEO supervision	HI	HI	HMI	HI	HI	HMI	MI	HMI	HMI	HMI
Community involvement	HMI	HMI	MLI	MI	LI	MI	MLI	MLI	MLI	MLI
Co-curricular activity	MI	MI	MI	MI	MI	MI	MI	LI	MI	LI
Head/teacher motivation	HI	HMI	HMI	HI	MI	HI	HMI	HI	HMI	HI
New teachers	LI	MI	LI	LI	MI	MI	LI	MLI	MLI	MLI
Curriculum training	HI	HI	MI	HI	HI	HMI	MI	MI	HMI	MI
Teachers' technical mastery	MI	HI	MI	MI	MI	MI	MI	MLI	MI	MLI
Repair/maintenance	NA	NA	HMI	NA	NA	MI	MI	NA	LI	NA
Support of local institution	LI	HI	MI	LI	LI	MI	MI	MI	NA	MI
Child survey	HMI	NA	HMI	MI	NA	HMI	MI	LI	HMI	LI

Worktable 12 Bangladesh, student impact

Factor	Schools									
	Excellent				Very good			Good		
	1	2	3	4	5	6	7	8	9	10
Student achievement and scholarship awards	HI	HI	HMI	HI	HI	HMI	HMI	HMI	MLI	HMI
Reading	HI	HI	HMI	HI	HI	HMI	MI	MI	MI	MI
Arithmetic	HI	HI	HMI	HI	HI	HMI	MI	MI	MI	MI
Attendance	HI	HMI	HMI	HI	HMI	MI	HMI	HMI	MI	MI
Repetition rate	HI	HMI	MI	HI	HMI	MI	MI	MLI	MI	MLI
Active participation	HI	MI	MLI	MI	MI	HMI	MLI	MLI	MI	MLI
Student behaviour	HMI	HI	HMI	HMI	HI	MI	MI	MLI	MI	MLI
Motivation/attitude	MI	HI	HMI	MI	HMI	MI	MI	MLI	MI	LI
Co-curricular interest	MI	MI	MI	MI	MI	HMI	MI	MLI	MI	MLI
Enrolment	HI	HI	HI	HI	HI	HI	HI	MI	MLI	MI
Retention	HI	HMI	HMI	HI	HMI	MI	HMI	MI	MI	MI
Student cleanliness	MI	MI	HMI	MI	MI	MI	MI	MLI	MI	MLI
Student creativity	NA	MI	MI	NA	MI	MI	MI	LI	MLI	LI
Interest in higher education	HI	MI	MI	HMI	MI	NA	MI	NA	NA	NA
Participation in talent competition	HI	HMI	MI	MI	HMI	MI	MI	HMI	MLI	MLI

Worktable 13 Bangladesh, teacher impact

Factor	Schools									
	Excellent				Very good			Good		
	1	2	3	4	5	6	7	8	9	10
Use of described methodology	HI	HI	MI	HMI	HI	HMI	MI	HMI	MI	MI
Teachers' motivation	HI	HI	HI	HI	HMI	MI	MI	MI	MI	MI
Use of active teaching	HMI	HMI	MI	HMI	HMI	HMI	MI	MI	MI	LI
Teachers' punctuality	HI	HI	HMI	HI	HMI	HMI	HMI	HMI	MI	HMI
Teachers' association activity	LI	MI	LI	LI	MI	MI	MI	MI	MI	MI
Pedagogical knowledge	HI	HMI	HMI	HI	HMI	HMI	MI	MI	MI	MLI
Subject matter knowledge	HMI	HMI	HMI	HMI	HMI	HMI	MI	MLI	HMI	MLI
Planning skills	MI	HMI	MI	MI	MI	MI	MI	MLI	MI	LI
Job satisfaction	NA	HMI	HMI	NA	MI	MI	HMI	MI	MI	MLI
Relations with students		MI	MI	MI	MI	MI	MI	MI	MI	MLI
Relations with community	MI	MI	MI	MI	MI	MI	MI	MI	MLI	MI
Teacher–teacher relations	MI	MI	MI	MI	LI	MI	MI	MI	MI	MLI

Worktable 14 Bangladesh, school impact

Factor	Schools									
	Excellent				Very good			Good		
	1	2	3	4	5	6	7	8	9	10
More students (enrolled)	HI	HI	HI	HI	HI	HI	HMI	HMI	MI	HMI
Regular sporting	HI	HI	HI	HI	MI	HMI	HMI	MI	HMI	MI
Improved teaching	HI	HMI	HMI	HMI	HMI	MI	MI	MI	MI	MI
Teacher-parent and community relations	HI	HMI	MI	MI	MI	MI	MI	MI	MLI	MLI
Teachers' attendance	HI	HMI	HI	HI	LI	MI	MI	MI	MI	MLI
Active head	HI	MI	HI	HI	HMI	HMI	HMI	HMI	MI	MI
Teachers' collaboration	HI	MI	MI	HMI	MI	MI	MI	MI	MI	MI
Teachers accept supervision	HI	MI	HI	HI	MI	HMI	HMI	MI	HMI	MI
Instructional materials	HI	HMI	HMI	HI	HMI	HMI	MI	HMI	HMI	HMI
Female teachers recruit girls	LI	MI	MI	LI	MLI	HMI	MLI	MI	MI	MI
Enrolment (girls)	HI	HI	MI	HMI	HMI	MI	MI	MLI	MI	MLI
Physical facilities	HI	HMI	HI	HMI	MI	HMI	MI	MLI	MI	MLI
School discipline	HI	HI	HI	HI	HMI	MI	MI	HMI	MI	MI
School environment	HI	HI	HI	HMI	HMI	MI	MI	HMI	MI	MLI
PTA and SMC	LI	MI	MI	LI	MI	LI	MI	HI	LI	MLI

Worktable 15 Bangladesh, institutionalization

Factor	Schools									
	Excellent				Very good			Good		
	1	2	3	4	5	6	7	8	9	10
Cluster training	HI	HI	HI	HI	HI	HMI	HI	HMI	MI	MI
Teaching-learning process	HI	MI	HMI	HI	MI	HMI	MI	MI	MI	MLI
Key people support	HI	MI	HMI	HI	MI	MI	HMI	MI	MI	MI
Community resources	HI	MI	MI	HI	MLI	MI	MI	MI	MI	MI
Built-in main features	HI	MI	HI	HI	MI	NA	MI	MLI	NA	MLI
Punctuality	HI	HI	HMI	HMI	HI	MI	MI	MI	MI	MI
Regular supervision	HI	HI	HI	HMI	HMI	MI	MI	MLI	MI	MLI
Child survey	HI	NA	HI	HI	NA	HMI	MI	HMI	MI	HMI
Materials support	HMI	MI	HMI	HMI	MI	MI	MI	HMI	MI	HMI
SMC and PTA	LI	HI	MI	LI	MI	MI	MI	MLI	MI	MLI
Appointment of new teachers	NIL	LI	MI	MI	LI	MLI	LI	MLI	MLI	MLI
Co-curricular activities	HMI	MI	MI	MI	MI	MLI	MI	MLI	MLI	MLI
Promotion system	HI	MI	MI	MI	MI	MI	MI	LI	MI	LI
Regular reporting	HI	HI	HI	HMI	HI	HMI	HMI	MI	HMI	MI
Continuous assistance	MI	MI	NA	MI	MI	MI	MI	MI	MI	MI

Worktable 16 Colombia, assistance

Factor	Schools											
	Excellent			Very good							Good	
	1	2	3	4	5	6	7	8	9	10	11	12
Training at start		HI	HI	HI	MI	HI	HI	HI	HI	HI		HI
Training delivery late	HI											
Head trains new teachers	HI								HI			
Supervisors train new teachers								HI				
Training two years early										HI		
Supervisor positive after training	HI											
Support from micro-centres	HI	HI			HI	HI			HI			
On-going supervision			HI	HI		HI	HI			HI		
Demo school						HI						
Supervision in early phase of implementation										HI		HI
Materials late delivery										HI		
Supervisor/head indifferent								HI		HI		

Worktable 17 Colombia, role of headmaster

	Schools											
	Excellent			Very good							Good	
Factor	1	2	3	4	5	6	7	8	9	10	11	12
1. Stability/commitment												
– years served		HI	HI	HMI	HI	HI			HI		HI	HI
– positive attitude/commitment		HI	HI		HI			HI	HI		MI	MI
2. Policy implementation/continuation												
– 'paperwork'	HI											
– teachers committed/push each other		HI	HI					HI			HI	
– evaluated EN					HI			HI				
3. Co-ordinate/facilitate												
– co-ordinate school activities		HI			HI	HI		HI				
– problem-solving meetings		HI										
– headmaster and teachers work together					HI	HI			HI			
– represents school	HI				HI						MI	
4. Attitude to resources												
– looked for community help					HI							
– provided resources								HI				
5. Pedagogical support												
– trained new teachers	HI	HI							HI			
– follow-up/give help/assist	HI	HI	HI	HI	HI			HI				
– assist teachers to work with mothers		HI										
– teachers help each other		HI			HI							
– Sought help from núcleo director				HI	HI							
– design new guide				HI								

Worktable 18 Colombia, role of administrator

	Schools											
	Excellent			Very good							Good	
Factor	1	2	3	4	5	6	7	8	9	10	11	12
1. Stability/commitment												
– years served		HI	HI	HI		HI			HI	MI	HI	MLI
– positive attitude/ commitment		HI		HI	MLI	HI		MI	HI	HI	HI	MLI
2. Policy implementation/control												
– school visit	MLI					HI		HI				
– check, monitor implement		HI	HI			HI				HI		
– Push, give direction			HI									
3. Co-ordinate/facilitate												
– talks with community		HI										
4. Attitude to resources												
– provides materials		HI			HI	HI				HI		
– Supports maintenance									HI			
5. Pedagogical support												
– provides training		HI		HI		HI			HI		HI	
– supervisory visits		HI	HI	HI		HI			HI	HI	HI	
– helped schools/problem solve		HI	HI	HI		HI				HI	HI	
– encourages evaluation					HI							
– supports adaptations					HI							

Worktable 19 Colombia, supervision

	Schools											
	Excellent			Very good							Good	
Factor	1	2	3	4	5	6	7	8	9	10	11	12
Supervisor became a defender of EN after training	HI											
Regular on-going visits with pedagogical input			HI		HI	HI	HI	HI	HI	HI		HI
Support and follow-up			HI									
Regular administrative assistance					HI	HI						
Núcleo director visits, aid in micro-centres									HI	HI		

Worktable 20 Colombia, commitment

Factor	Schools Excellent 1	2	3	Very good 4	5	6	7	8	9	10	Good 11	12
EN seen as positive change (ownership)	HI				HI		HI	HI	MI	HI		
Local administrator attitudes	HI	HI										
Teachers' attitude	HI	HI	HI	HI	HI	HI	HI	HI	MI	MI	HI	LI
Stability of teachers' group			HI									
Head attitude	HI	HI	HI	HI		HI	HI	HI	HI	HI	LI	LI
Supervisor attitude					HI						LI	
Núcleo director attitude					HI							
Headmasters/teachers want to move (but not leave EN)						HI						

Worktable 21 Colombia, received pressure

Factor	Schools Excellent 1	2	3	Very good 4	5	6	7	8	9	10	Good 11	12
Regional coordinator continues to push implementation	HI	HI					HI					
Núcleo director insisted teachers use EN		HI					HI					
Visit by local administrators insisting on EN, follow-up		HI						HI	HI	HI		
Supervisors work with teachers/good feedback				HI	HI	HI						MI
Núcleo director helps new guide					HI							
Demo school								HI				
Central and regional directives pushed										MI		
Teacher pushes head										HI		

Worktable 22 Colombia, received resources

Factor	Schools Excellent 1	2	3	Very good 4	5	6	7	8	9	10	Good 11	12
Guides delivery (1) = first year	MI	HI (1)	HI (1)	MI (1)	MI (1)	MI	MI (1)	HI (1)	MI (1)			LI
EN material quality/delivery (1) = first year		HI (1)	HI	MI				MI	HI	MI	MI	LI
Head got donations for repair	HI	HI	HI		HI		MI		HI	HI	HI	HI
Community support	HI											

Worktables

Worktable 23 Colombia, success experiences

Factor	Schools Excellent 1	2	3	Very good 4	5	6	7	8	9	10	Good 11	12
Changes in cognitive development	HI	HI		HI	HI	HI	HI	MI	HI		HI	
Changes in socio-emotions	HI	HI	HI	HI	HI	HI	HI	HI	HI	HI	HI	MI
Demo school	HI		HI				HI	HI				
Supervisors' feedback positive		HI										
Teachers train others			HI									
Visits by other teachers and parents			HI									
Community accept flexible presentation				HI								
Started pre-school				HI								
Projects with community					HI							
Student government					HI							
New guides					HI							
Community acceptance						HI	HI		HI		HI	

Worktable 24 Colombia, empowerment

Factor	Schools Excellent 1	2	3	Very good 4	5	6	7	8	9	10	Good 11	12
Teachers and head decide all important things	HI	HI	HI				HI	HI	HI	HI	MI	LI
Decisions from above				HI								
Head has authority						HI				HI		
Head developed new guide						HI						

Worktable 25 Colombia, local adaptation

Factor	Schools Excellent 1	2	3	Very good 4	5	6	7	8	9	10	Good 11	12
Extensive help from parents for materials						HI						
Adjust EN for rural area												
Adapted guide	HI	HI	HI				HI	HI	HI	HI	HI	HI
Created student government committee		HI										
Extensive changes in EN				HI								
Flexible promotion changes						HI			HI		HI	
Teachers specialize						HI						
Evaluations added						HI						
School level activities						HI						

Worktable 26 Colombia, community support

	Schools											
	Excellent			*Very good*							*Good*	
Factor	1	2	3	4	5	6	7	8	9	10	11	12
Active participation	HI	HI	HI	HI						HI		
Good relations		HI			HI		HI					
Community changed from negative to positive attitude			HI	HI		HI	HI			HI		
Only parents support								HI				
Community reacted negatively to results									HI		HI	HI

Worktable 27 Ethiopia, assistance

	Schools								
	Excellent		*Very good*				*Good*		
Factor	1	2	3	4	5	6	7	8	9
In-service teachers' training	HI	HI	HI	HI	HI	HI	MLI	MLI	MLI
Annual education conference	HI	HI	HI	HI	HI	HI	MI	MLI	HI
Teachers help each other and teach each other	HI	HI	HI	HI	HI	HI	LI	HI	LI
Teachers work in SPC	HI	HI	HI	MLI	HI	HI	LI	HI	LI
Feedback from inspector/headmaster	HI	HI	HI	LI	HI	HI	LI	LI	HI
DEO conference/workshop	HI	HI	MI	HI	MI	MI	HI	HI	HI

Worktables

Worktable 28 Ethiopia, role of headmaster

Factor	Schools								
	Excellent		Very good				Good		
	1	2	3	4	5	6	7	8	9
1. Stability/commitment									
– years served (>5 years = HI)	HI	HI	MI	HI	HI	HI	HI	HI	HI
– positive attitude to reform	NA	HI	HI	HI	NA	NA	NA	NA	NA
2. Policy implementation/control									
– control teachers' work	HI	MI	HI	HI	NA	HI	HI	HI	HI
– instructs teachers/sets rules/regular pressure for reform policy implementation	NA	HI	MI	NA	MI	NA	NA	MI	NA
– reports to district office	NA	NA	HI	NA	NA	HI	NA	NA	HI
3. Co-ordination/facilitation									
– co-ordination of school activity	MI	HI	HI	HI	HI	NA	NA	NA	NA
– chair meetings	HI	HI	NA	NA	NA	NA	NA	HI	HI
– initiate reforms/changes	MI	MI	NA	NA	HI	NA	NA	NA	NA
– represented the school externally	NA	NA	HI	HI	NA	NA	HI	HI	HI
4. Attention to resources									
– attention to texts and teaching-learning materials	HI	HI	HI	HI	HI	NA	HI	HI	HI
– Attention to budget	NA	MI	NA	NA	HI	NA	NA	NA	NA
5. Pedagogical support									
– give suggestions/help/advice	HI	HI	NA	HI	NA	HI	HI	HI	NA
– rewards teachers	HI	NA	NA	HI	NA	NA	NA	NA	NA
– follow-up	HI	NA	NA	NA	HI	NA	HI	NA	NA

Worktable 29 Ethiopia, role of administrator

Factor	Schools								
	Excellent		Very good				Good		
	1	2	3	4	5	6	7	8	9
1. Stability/commitment									
– years served (>5 years = HI)	HI	MI	NA	HI	NA	HI	HI	HI	HI
– positive attitude/commitment/defended programme	NA	HI	HI	NA	HI	HI	NA	HI	NA
2. Policy implementation/control									
– yearly school visit	HI	NA	HI	HI	NA	NA	HI	NA	HI
– study school's quarterly report	HI	HI	NA	HI	NA	NA	NA	NA	HI
– push, give direction/rules/regulations	NA	HI	HI	NA	HI	NA	HI	HI	HI
– check, monitor implementation carefully	NA	HI	HI	NA	HI	HI	NA	HI	NA
3. Co-ordinate/facilitate									
– revised school administration	NA	HI	HI	NA	HI	NA	HI	NA	NA
– send guides, materials	NA	HI	HI	NA	NA	NA	NA	NA	NA
– helped school work around rules	NA	HI	HI	NA	HI	NA	NA	NA	NA
– helped exchange experiences	NA	HI	HI	NA	NA	NA	NA	NA	NA
– worked with community	NA	NA	HI	NA	NA	NA	NA	HI	HI
– gave schools more autonomy	NA	HI	HI	NA	HI	NA	NA	NA	NA
4. Attention to resources									
– quota books/materials delivery	HI	HI	HI	HI	HI	NA	NA	HI	NA
– resources/permission to build more classrooms	NA	NA	HI	NA	NA	NA	NA	NA	NA
5. Pedagogical support									
– local training/conferences	HI	HI	HI	NA	HI	HI	NA	NA	NA
– encouraged/assisted teachers	NA	HI	HI	NA	NA	NA	NA	NA	NA
– supervision visits	NA	HI	HI	NA	HI	HI	NA	HI	NA
– helped schools/encouraged	NA	HI	HI	NA	HI	NA	HI	NA	HI
– organize yearly conference	NA	NA	NA	HI	NA	NA	HI	NA	NA

Worktables

Worktable 30 Ethiopia, supervision

Factor	Schools								
	Excellent		Very good				Good		
	1	2	3	4	5	6	7	8	9
Head facilitates/coordinates	HI	HI	HI	HI	HMI	HI	HI	HI	MLI
Head evaluates teachers' activity	HI	HI	HMI	HI	HMI	HI	HI	HI	MLI
Head works closely with teachers	HI	HI	HI	HI	HI	HI	MI	HMI	MLI
Head works with SMC	HI	HI	HI	HI	HI	HI	MI	MI	MI
Head encourages teachers	HI	HI	HI	HI	HI	HI	MI	MI	MI
Head checks lesson plans	HI	HI	HI	HI	HI	HI	HMI	HMI	MI
Head shares responsibility with teachers	HI	HI	HI	HI	HI	HI	MI	HI	MI
DEO provides school guidelines	HI	HI	HI	HI	HI	HI	HI	HI	HI
DEO helped school get land		HI							
DEO supervises school progress	MLI	HI	HI	MLI	MLI	HI	MLI	MLI	HI
DEO communicates with local officials about school		HI	HI						
DEO reorganizes school and problem solves	MLI	HMI	LI	LI	HI	LI	LI	LI	LI
DEO advises administration	MLI	MI	LI	LI	MI	LI	HI	LI	LI

Worktable 31 Ethiopia, commitment

Factor	Schools								
	Excellent		Very good				Good		
	1	2	3	4	5	6	7	8	9
Students like changes	HI	HI	HI	HI	HI	HI	MI	MI	MI
Teachers like changes	HI	HI	HI	HI	HI	HI	HI	HI	HI
Head likes changes	HI	HI	HI	HI	HI	HI	HI	HI	HI
Teachers spend free time at school	HI	HI	HI	HI	HI	HI	MI	MLI	MLI
Head spends free time at school	HI	HI	HI	HI	HI	HI	HMI	HMI	HMI
Students spend free time at school	MI	HI	HI	MI	HMI	MI	MLI	MLI	MLI
DEO responds quickly to requests	MI	HI	MI	MI	MI	MI	MI	MI	MI
SMC, teachers and head work closely together	HI	HI	HI	HI	HI	HI	MI	MI	MI
DEO rewarded head						HI			
SMC like changes	HMI	HMI	HMI	HMI	HMI	HMI	MI	MI	MI

Worktable 32 Ethiopia, received pressure

	Schools								
	Excellent		Very good				Good		
Factor	1	2	3	4	5	6	7	8	9
Strict directiveness	HI	HI	HI	HI	HI	HI	HI	HI	HI
Quarterly progress report	HI	HI	HI	HI	HI	HI	HI	HI	HI
Head follow-up/evaluated/pushed teachers	HI	HI	HI	HI	HI	HI	HI	HI	HI
Inspectors visited, pushed teachers	MI	MI	MI	MI	MI	MI	MI	MI	MI
Inspectors evaluated teachers' work	LI	LI	LI	LI	LI	LI	LI	LI	LI
DEO asked community to support school		HI			HI				
Department heads follow-up	HI	HI	HI	HI	HI	HI	HI	MI	MI
DEO insistent (enrolment increase) and implementation of reform)	HI	HI	HI	HI	HI	HI	HI	HI	HI

Worktable 33 Ethiopia, received resources

	Schools								
	Excellent		Very good				Good		
Factor	1	2	3	4	5	6	7	8	9
DEO instructional materials	HI	HI	HI	HI	HI	HI	HI	HI	HI
Community:									
– land	HI	HI	HI	HI	HI	HI	HI	HI	HI
– finance	HI	HI	HI	HI	HI	HI	MI	HI	HI
– labour	HI	HI	HI	HI	HI	HI	HI	HI	MLI
– lodging for teachers		HI	HI	HMI	HI	HI			HI
– materials	HI	HI	HI	HI	HI	HI	HI	MI	MI
School income generation	HI	HI	HI	HI	HI	HI	HI	HI	HI
APC model teaching aids	MI	HMI	HMI	LI	HI	MI	LI	LI	HI

Worktables

Worktable 34 Ethiopia, success experiences

Factor	Schools								
	Excellent		Very good				Good		
	1	2	3	4	5	6	7	8	9
Progress physical expansion	HI	HI	HI	HI	HI	HI	MI	MI	MI
Self-reliance	HI	HI	HI	HI	HI	HI	MI	MI	MI
Consistency with goals (satisfaction)	HI	HI	HI	HI	HI	HI	MI	MI	MI
School/community relations	HI	HI	HI	HI	HI	HI	MI	MI	MI
Professional development	HMI	HMI	HMI	MI	HMI	HMI	MI	MI	MI
Exchange of experiences	HI	HI	HI	HMI	HI	HMI	MI	MI	MI
Classroom management	HI	HI	HI	HMI	HMI	HI	HI	MI	MI
Well organized school	HI	HI	HMI	HI	HI	HI	MI	MI	HI
Income generation	HI	HI	HI	HI	HI	HI	HI	HI	HI
Teachers' leadership	HI	HI	HI	HI	HI	HI	MI	MI	MI
Produce own aids	HI	HI	HI	MI	HI	HMI	HMI	HI	MI

Worktable 35 Ethiopia, empowerment

Factor	Schools								
	Excellent		Very good				Good		
	1	2	3	4	5	6	7	8	9
SMC make financial and administrative decisions	HI	HI	HI	HI	HI	HI	MI	MI	HI
Teachers decide classroom activities	HI	HI	HI	HI	HI	HI	HI	HI	HI
School authorized to generate own income	HI	HI	HI	HI	HI	HI	HI	HI	HI
Department heads supervise (evaluate teachers)	HI	HI	HI	HI	HI	HI	HI	HI	HI
School works around rules	HMI	HMI	HMI	HMI	HI	HMI	HMI	HMI	HMI
Head and teachers decide school activities	HI	HI	HI	HI	HI	HI	HI	HI	HI
Teachers responsible for co-curriculum activities	HI	HI	HI	HI	HI	HI	MI	MI	MI
School responsible for physical expansion	HI	HI	HI	HI	HI	HI	MI	MI	MI
Teachers responsible for production of teaching aids	HI	HI	HI	HI	HI	HI	HI	HI	HI
Head evaluates teachers	HI	HI	HI	HI	HI	HI	HI	HI	HI
Parents conduct students' discipline	HMI	HMI	HI	HI	HMI	HMI	MI	MI	MI

Worktable 36 Ethiopia, local adaptation

	Schools								
	Excellent		Very good				Good		
Factor	1	2	3	4	5	6	7	8	9
Flexible labour education programme	HI	HI	HI	HI	HI	HI	HI	HI	HI
Flexible teaching aids production	HI	HI	HI	HI	HI	HI	MI	MI	MI
Wider involvement of community	HI	HMI	HI	HMI	HMI	HMI	MI	MI	MI
Shift system	HI			HI		HI	HI	HI	HI
Use of locally prepared teaching materials	HI	HI	HI	HI	HI	HI	MI	MI	MI
Supress aetheistic views in political education		HI							
Student contribution	HI	HI	HI	HI	HI	HI	HMI	HMI	HMI
Social science curriculum adaptation	HI	HI	HI	HI	HI	HI	HI	HI	HI
Home economics curriculum adaptation	HI	HI	HI	HI	HI	HI	HI	HI	HI

Worktable 37 Ethiopia, community support

	Schools								
	Excellent		Very good				Good		
Factor	1	2	3	4	5	6	7	8	9
Financial support	HI	HI	HI	HI	HI	HI	MI	MI	HI
Material suppport	HI	HI	HI	HI	HI	HI	HI	MI	HI
Labour support	HI	HI	HI	HI	HI	HI	HI	HI	MI
Participation in school administration	HI	HMI	HI	HI	HMI	HMI	MI	MI	MI
Follow-up drop-outs	HI			MI					
Accommodation of teachers	MI	HI	HI	MI	HI				
Help with disciplinary problems	MI	MI	MI	MI	MI	MI			

Worktable 38 Bangladesh, assistance

	Schools									
	Excellent				Very good			Good		
Factor	1	2	3	4	5	6	7	8	9	10
AUEO organize cluster training monthly	HI	HI	HI	HI	HI	MI	HI	MI	MI	MI
Head organizes staff development weekly	HI	MI	HMI	LI	MI	NA	MI	MI	NA	MLI
Supervision by AUEO	HI	HI	HI	HI	HI	MI	HMI	MI	MLI	MI
Supervision by UEO	HI	MI	HMI	HI	MI	MI	MI	MLI	MLI	MLI
Training abroad	NA	LI	HMI	LI	MLI	LI	LI	NA	LI	NA
Head training/advice	HI	HI	MI	HI	HI	MLI	MI	MLI	MLI	LI
Supervision DPEO (+support/facilitation)	MI	MLI	MI	LI	MLI	MI	MI	MLI	MLI	LI

Worktable 39 Bangladesh, role of headmaster

Factor	Schools									
	Excellent				Very good			Good		
	1	2	3	4	5	6	7	8	9	10
1. Stability/commitment										
– years served	HI	HI	HI	HI	HI	HMI	HI	HMI	HMI	HMI
– positive attitude	HI	HI	HI	HI	HMI	HMI	HI	HMI	HMI	HMI
2. Policy implementation/control										
– control teachers' work	HI	HMI	HI	HI	HMI	MI	HMI	MI	MI	MI
– make teachers aware	HI	HMI	HI	HMI	HMI	MI	HMI	HMI	MI	MI
– monitor punctual attendance	HI	HMI	HMI	HMI	HMI	MI	HMI	MI	MI	MLI
– instructs teachers/rules/regulates	HMI	MI	HMI	HMI	MI	MI	MI	MI	MI	MLI
3. Co-ordinate/facilitate										
– co-curricular activities	HMI	MI	HMI	HMI	MI	MI	MI	MI	NA	NA
– assigned duties	MI	MI	MI	MI	MLI	MLI	MI	MI	MLI	MLI
– good relations with community and SMC	HMI	HMI	MI	HMI	HI	MI	MI	MI	MI	MI
– reports to district office	HI	HMI	HMI	HI	HMI	MI	HMI	MI	HMI	MI
– co-ordinates school activities	HI	HMI	HMI	HMI	MI	MI	HMI	MI	HMI	MI
4. Attention to resources										
– texts and teaching-learning materials	HMI	HMI	HMI	HMI	HMI	HMI	HMI	HMI	HMI	MI
– got extra resources	HI	LI	MLI	LI	MI	MI	LI	LI	LI	LI
5. Pedagogical support										
– train teachers	HI	HMI	HI	HI	MI	MI	HMI	MI	MI	MI
– follow-up/give help/assistance	HI	HMI	HI	HI	MI	MI	HMI	MI	MI	MI
– help to adapt to local conditions	MI	MI	MI	MI	MLI	MLI	MI	MLI	MI	MI
– motivate teachers/discuss vital issues	HMI	MI	HMI	HMI	MI	MI	HMI	MLI	MI	MI
– conduct child survey	HI	NA	HI	HI	NA	NA	HI	NA	NA	NA

Worktable 40 Bangladesh, role of administrator

	Schools									
	Excellent				Very good			Good		
Factor	1	2	3	4	5	6	7	8	9	10
1. Stability/commitment										
– years served	HI	HI	HI	HI	HI	HMI	HMI	HMI	HMI	HMI
– attendance/commitment	HMI	HMI	HMI	HMI	HMI	HMI	HMI	MI	MI	MI
2. Policy implementation/control										
– control, monitor, implement	HMI	HMI	MI	MI	MI	MI	MI	MI	MI	MI
– school reports	HI	HI	HMI	HI	HMI	MI	HMI	MI	MI	MI
– instruct teachers	HMI	MI	HMI	MI	MI	MI	MI	MI	MI	MI
– UEO visits	HI	HMI	HI	HMI	MI	HMI	HMI	MI	MI	MLI
– push co-curricular activities	MLI	MI	MI	MLI	MI	MI	MI	MI	MI	LI
3. Co-ordinate/facilitate										
– delegated to head	HMI	MI	MI	HMI	MI	MI	MI	MI	MI	MLI
– informed head	HMI	HMI	HMI	HMI	HMI	MI	MI	MI	MI	MI
– linkage with community	LI	MI	MI	LI	HMI	MI	MI	MI	MI	MLI
– linkage with authorities	MI	MI	MI	MI	MI	MLI	MI	MLI	MLI	MI
4. Attention to resources										
– provided material	HI	HMI	HI	HI	HMI	HMI	HI	MI	HMI	MI
– provided local funds	NA	MLI	NA	NA	MLI	MLI	NA	NA	MLI	MLI
5. Pedagogical support										
– provided training	HI	HMI	HI	HMI	HMI	MI	HMI	MI	MI	MI
– supervision	HMI	HMI	HMI	MI	HMI	MI	MI	MI	MI	MI
– helped school/problem solve	MI	MI	MI	MI	MI	MLI	MI	MLI	MLI	MLI
– helped local adaptation	MLI	MLI	MLI	MLI	MLI	MLI	MLI	MLI	MLI	MLI
6. Others										
– contact with unions	MI	NA	NA	MI	NA	LI	NA	HMI	NA	MI

Worktable 41 Bangladesh, supervision

	Schools									
	Excellent				Very good			Good		
Factor	1	2	3	4	5	6	7	8	9	10
AUEO supervise school once per month	HI	HI	HI	HI	HI	MI	HI	MI	MLI	MLI
AUEO organize cluster training once per month	HI	HI	HI	HI	HI	MI	HI	MI	MLI	MLI
UEO supervision	HMI	MI	MI	MI	MI	MI	MI	MLI	MLI	LI
Head supervises class occasionally/regularly	HI	HI	HMI	HI	HI	MI	MI	LI	MI	LI

Worktables

Worktable 42 Bangladesh, commitment

Factor	Schools									
	Excellent				Very good			Good		
	1	2	3	4	5	6	7	8	9	10
Teachers gave priority to change	HI	HMI	HMI	MI	HMI	MI	HMI	MI	MI	MI
AUEO gave priority to change	HI	HI	HI	MI	HI	HMI	HI	MI	MI	MI
Head gave priority to change	HI	HI	HI	HI	HI	MI	HMI	HMI	MI	HMI
Higher official gave priority to change	MI	MI	MI	MI	MI	MI	MI	MI	MI	MI
Community gave priority to change	MI	MI	MI	MI	MI	LI	MI	MI	LI	HMI
UEO gave priority to change	HI	HI	HMI	HI	HI	MI	HMI	MI	MI	MI
Strong team spirit	HI	HI	HMI	HMI	HMI	MI	MI	MI	MI	MI

Worktable 43 Bangladesh, received pressure

Factor	Schools									
	Excellent				Very good			Good		
	1	2	3	4	5	6	7	8	9	10
UEO pressure	HI	MI	HMI	HI	MI	MI	HMI	MI	MI	MI
AUEO pressure	HI	HI	HI	HMI	HI	MI	HMI	MI	MI	MI
DPEO pressure (circular)	LI	HMI	MI	LI	HMI	MI	HMI	MI	MI	MI
Political support	HI	MI	MI	HI	MI	MI	MI	MLI	MI	MLI
UEO solves problems	HI	HMI	MI	HI	HMI	MLI	MI	MLI	MLI	MLI
AUEO solves problems	HI	HI	HMI	HMI	HI	MI	HMI	MLI	MI	MLI
Zila parishad put pressure	NA	NA	LI	NA	NA	NA	LI	MI	NA	MI

Worktable 44 Bangladesh, received resources

Factor	Schools									
	Excellent				Very good			Good		
	1	2	3	4	5	6	7	8	9	10
New building	HI	HI	HI	HI	HI	MI	MI	MLI	MI	MLI
New furniture	MLI	HMI	HMI	MLI	HMI	MI	HMI	MLI	MI	MLI
Government alloted resources	HI	HI	MI	HI	HI	MI	MI	HMI	MI	HMI
Latrine	HI	HI	HI	HI	HI	MI	MI	MI	MI	MI
Tubewell	HI	HI	HI	HI	HI	MI	HI	MLI	MI	LI
Teaching materials	HI	HI	HI	HI	HI	HMI	HMI	MI	MI	MI
Upazila financial help	NA	MI	HMI	NA	MI	NA	HMI	MLI	NA	MLI
Contingency grant	NA	MLI	MI	NA	MLI	NA	MI	LI	NA	LI

Worktable 45 Bangladesh, success experiences

Factor	Schools									
	Excellent				Very good			Good		
	1	2	3	4	5	6	7	8	9	10
Enrolment increase	HI	HI	HI	HI	HI	HMI	HMI	HMI	MI	HMI
Female teachers and girls	HI	HI	HI	HI	HMI	MI	MI	MI	MI	MI
Punctuality	HI	HI	HI	HI	HMI	MI	HI	MI	MI	MI
Scholarships	HI	HMI	HMI	HMI	HMI	MI	HMI	MLI	MLI	MLI
Achievements (and drop-out/repetition)	HI	HI	HI	HI	HMI	MI	MI	MLI	MI	MLI
Enrolment of poor children	HI	HMI	HMI	HI	HMI	MI	MI	MLI	MLI	MLI
Extra classrooms	HMI	MI	HI	MLI	MI	MI	MI	MI	MLI	MLI

Worktable 46 Bangladesh, empowerment

Factor	Schools									
	Excellent				Very good			Good		
	1	2	3	4	5	6	7	8	9	10
Everything came from above	HI	HI	HI	HI	HI	MI	HMI	MI	MI	MI
Project people listen to concerns of local people	HI	LI	MLI	HI	LI	MLI	MLI	MLI	MLI	MLI
Teachers implement decisions	HI	HI	HI	HI	HI	MI	MI	MI	MI	MLI
Scope for some modification school/local level	LI	MI	MLI	LI	MI	MLI	MLI	MLI	MLI	LI
Upazila responsible for pedagogical education	MI	LI	MI	MI	LI	MI	MI	HI	MI	MLI

Worktable 47 Bangladesh, local adaptation

Factor	Schools									
	Excellent				Very good			Good		
	1	2	3	4	5	6	7	8	9	10
All components fitted well	HI	HI	MI	HI	HI	MI	MI	MI	MI	MI
Less scope	HI	MI	HI	HI	MI	MI	MI	MLI	MLI	MLI
Little need	HI	MI	HI	HI	MI	MI	HMI	MI	LI	MI
Heads and teachers slight modifications	MI	MLI	MLI	LI	LI	LI	MLI	MLI	LI	MLI
Community involved in SMC/PTA	MI	MI	MI	MI	MI	MI	MI	MI	MI	MLI
Teachers involved in co-curricular activities	HMI	HMI	LI	HMI	HMI	MLI	LI	MLI	MLI	LI

Worktable 48 Bangladesh, community support

Factor	Schools									
	Excellent				Very good			Good		
	1	2	3	4	5	6	7	8	9	10
Parents interested in child's education	HI	HI	HI	HI	MI	MI	HMI	MI	MI	MI
Parents' awareness about reform	LI	LI	LI	LI	LI	LI	LI	LI	LI	LI
PTA functioning	LI	LI	LI	LI	LI	LI	LI	LI	LI	LI
SMC functioning	LI	LI	LI	LI	HI	MLI	MI	MLI	MLI	MLI
Community attitude and support	HI	HMI	MI	HI	HMI	LI	MI	MLI	LI	MLI
Rich parents give donations	LI	MLI	LI	LI	MI	NA	LI	LI	NA	LI
Attitude to teachers' association	MI	MLI	LI	LI	MLI	MI	LI	MLI	MI	MLI

Appendix 5

Summary of Factors Accounting for Success of Local Implementation*

Factor	Illustrative indicators	Impact (H,M,L)
Assistance		
Administrative role	(The indicators provide a summary of the factor as it is played out locally. If the factor can be traced to a country-level initiative, mark it with (C); others are assumed to be locally generated.)	
Commitment		
Received pressure		
Received resources		
Success experiences		
Empowerment, engagement	E.g. training sessions encouraged teachers to use community as resource (CAA)	H
Local adaptation of the programme		
Community support		
Other:		

*This is an analytical summary, done very late in the analysis.

Appendix 6

Operational Definitions

19 July 1989

TO: HSI research teams and coaches

RE: The displays

This memorandum explains the approach to specific displays, with emphasis on clear definitions of the concepts in rows and columns. It's important for the team to discuss the memo, and be clear about exactly how the displays will be filled out. Otherwise you will not be able to make clear analyses, and they may not be comparable from school to school.

Display 1: Key events before and during the educational change programme, and their consequences

Chronology: for an example of how a chronology might look, see the enclosed sample.

Period: these are times or stages of the project.

Before	The time before the actual project planning began at the national level.
Planning	When work is done to design the project.
Early implementation	When plans are carried out into practice, up to and including the first year's use of the project in the classroom.
Later implementation	All subsequent project work (at national, regional and school level).

Key events: These are specific occurrences, focused and limited in time, which you feel had an important impact on the programme's planning and implementation. See the examples. Do not use general 'conditions' or states of affairs, such as 'Minister is dissatisfied with progress', but be specific, naming important events: 'Minister calls meeting of regional officers and expresses irritation with progress.' Put the date of the event (month, year); keep events in sequence.

Consequences: indicate what happened in programme implementation as a result of the key event. If not clear to you, put DK (don't know).

Display 2A: Country-level success factors

Factors: these are the heart of the display. They are the factors that may affect the success of implementation, and explain why it succeeded as well as it did. Please note the definitions carefully, and discuss if not clear. In most cases we are describing the positive side of the factor. The factor may well be negative or weak in your case, and should be explained as such in the display.

Strength of national organizations	Capacity of the regular educational system (national, regional, district) to get things done, carry out action. Basic question is: how good is the system at really managing the change? Can include good policy-making, goal-setting, planning, support for implementation in schools, monitoring, control, administration, coordination, logistics. National organizations includes both the operating agencies such as the ministry and regional or district offices, and specialized policy and planning groups working on such things as curriculum, materials, examinations, teacher training, etc. (NOTE: The regional and/or district structure varies from country to country: 'regional' or 'district' refers to whatever administrative units come between the local school and the ministry.)
Capacity building of national organizations	Efforts to make national organizations stronger, more effective. Can include: changing structure, improving systems for communication and information, improving competency of staff, adding more funds for human resources.
Building of commitment	Efforts to increase positive attitude towards the programme, and 'ownership' of it at national, regional/district and local level (school people and parents). Commitment means that the programme has a strong priority in the minds of people. There may also be efforts to increase commitment of external agencies (such as World Bank or other lenders).
Strategic matching	The degree to which the general strategy for implementation fits the turbulence of the environment and the innovativeness of the programme. Adriaan Verspoor's study of World Bank-funded projects (Verspoor, 1989) indicates the following relationships:

Operational Definitions

1. If the environment is very turbulent (unstable, many crises and problems), the best-matched strategy is usually discrete changes, where a few limited projects are tried, but not on a nation-wide basis. More ambitious strategies are poorly matched and will probably fail, or just be implemented in a few schools.
2. If the environment is fairly stable, not turbulent, and the programme is not so innovative for the country (a more modest change), then a good strategy is progressive innovation, where a series of specific changes (such as textbooks, teaching methods, new specific curricula, etc.) are tried, one after the other, in all schools. It's a 'piece by piece' approach.
3. If the environment is stable, but the programme is more innovative and ambitious (a big change), then the best-matched strategy is incremental expansion, where the entire programme is tried first in some pilot schools, then a second wave, then another, until all schools are covered. It's a 'more and more schools' approach. For this factor, you should note briefly the amount of turbulence and the programme's innovativeness, then describe the general strategy (discrete change, progressive innovation, or incremental expansion) and comment on whether the match is good or poor.

Legal regulation	Laws or ministry rules that control some aspects of implementation.
Decision-making	The degree to which decisions about implementation are made centrally, at the national level, or devolved to the regional/district or school level.
Pressure for good implementation	National or district/regional emphasis on 'doing it right', implementing the programme carefully and well.
Curriculum development	Changes in the subject matter, or addition of new subject matter, originating at the national level.
Division of labour	Agreement at the national level that different agencies will be responsible for different aspects of implementation (e.g. curriculum, materials, examinations, training), and careful coordination among these agencies.

Infrastructure development	Building or strengthening the system at the regional and local levels to improve implementation (e.g. better administration, supervision, training, assistance, logistics, delivery of materials, etc.). It is like capacity-building, but at district/regional and local rather than national level.
Availability and quality of materials	Degree to which new materials for classroom use (text-books, guides, workbooks, etc.) are well developed and sound, and are actually delivered to schools for use.
Resource allocation	Decisions are made about the money and human resources needed for implementation at district/regional and school level. (Describe what is supposed to happen.)
Resource delivery	Region/districts and schools actually get or don't get the funds and people needed. (Describe what actually happened.)
Closeness to implementation	The people who are steering the programme at the national level have a good feel for what local programme problems are like. (E.g. they visit schools regularly, meet with those giving assistance, district/regional people, etc.) They understand the reality of implementation.
Effective communication	Degree to which information travels easily from national to regional and local level, and from local to district/regional and national.
Responsive adaptation	Programme planners and managers learn from experience; they adjust and redesign the programme based on how well it's going, what the problems are. The adaptations made preserve the core or essential spirit of the programme.
User involvement	The people closest to the actual implementation of the programme (usually teachers and administrators, sometimes parents or district/regional administrators or support staff) are active participants, trying out the programme, revising it, making suggestions for improvement. They are not passive or withdrawn, but empowered to manage implementation.
Protection from turbulence	Actions taken by headmasters, district/regional or environmental national staff to protect or

Operational Definitions

	safeguard the programme from unstable conditions arising outside the school (such as political changes, loss of key advocates, criticism, natural disasters).
Decisions supporting institutionalization	Decisions made at national level that will aid the stable continuation of the programme. May include new laws or regulations, regular funding, regular training mechanisms, a permanent management set-up for the programme, etc.
Assistance	Assistance refers to in-service help (usually for teachers, but also headmasters) that is continuous, easily available locally, and responsive to the specific needs teachers and headmasters have in carrying out the programme. It includes supervision, coaching and pedagogical support as well as formal training.
Monitoring and control	Methods for getting honest and realistic information about the programme's progress, and for taking action based on the information to improve implementation. May be present at district/regional and/or at national level.
Other	Add any other key national factors that were important in affecting the success of implementation.

Illustrative indicators: here put specific examples of the factor, such as those shown in the display. If the factor is basically positive (for example, a well-developed monitoring and control system), put a + mark. If it is weak (for example, ministry people have little or no idea of what is going on at the school level), put a − mark.

Impact: these ratings (high, medium, low) should be made only after all the data are in, and the display is filled out. Use the + and − marks as an aid to your judgement. High means the factor is strong, positive, good. Low means it is absent, weak or even negative. Medium is in between.

Display 2B: Linkage between country, district and school levels

How linkage is done: see the directions for entering information. Remember that in this, as in most other displays, you will be entering information that is marked by its source (H for headmaster, T for teacher, S for support person, etc.) Linkage means methods, procedures, mechanisms through which national, regional (or district) and local schools are tied together, coordinated (as contrasted with operating independently or alone). Think of each factor, and examine your data to see if there are definitely no linkages, weak linkages or strong ones. Distinguish linkages from national to regional/district, and from national or regional/district to local. Describe the linkage. Use DK when you have no information. Do not strain to find a linkage for every factor, just note the ones that are clearly present (whether weak or strong), or absent.

Consequences: indicate any effects of strong, weak or absent linkage that you have seen in the data. For example, under 'Local (or responsive) adaptation', you might have noted some strong linkages (curriculum experts visit the schools, talk with parents, try out pilot curriculum changes and revise them before making them firm). The consequences might be that parents and teachers feel the new curriculum materials are practical and relevant to the needs of children.

Researcher comments/explanations: here make any added comments based on your own judgement. In the example, you might say:

'This seems to be done only in a few rural schools, however' or

'The actual changes are pretty minor' or

'Maybe this works because the personality of the science curriculum expert is so easy and friendly.'

Display 2C: Outcome at the system level

Illustrative indicators: these are different types of outcome that may have occurred in the national educational system (not school-level changes, which are in display 3).

Demand for schooling	Pressure (national, regional) to increase schooling capacity, reach more children, keep more of them in school.
Capacity of central	Same as 'Strength of national organizations' in institutions (display 2A).
Capacity of support	Ability of the assistance-giving system to deliver the training, consultation, assistance and help that local schools need. Have support institutions been expanded? Has quality of service improved?
New roles and relations between central, regional and local institutions	Essentially the linkages described in display 2B. This is more of a summary description; were new roles and relationships created, and how strong do they look? Will they last? Are they determined by new legislation or regulations? Are key roles defined?
Changes in innovation strategy	Has the general strategy described in display 2A shifted or changed over time? Are the authorities approaching new reforms in a different way than before?
Changes in funding level	Have the financial resources for this programme decreased, stayed the same or increased? How much

Operational Definitions

	of these funds comes from the national budget, how much from external donor agencies such as the World Bank or other aid programmes?
Interest from external donors	Has the wish of external donor agencies to support additional improvement programmes increased, stayed the same or decreased?

Outcomes: enter specific examples showing how the indicator has changed because of the programme.

Impact: after the examples are entered, make a general judgement whether the outcomes noted represent a high, medium or low amount of outcome at the system level.

Display 3: School-level changes as seen locally

Aspect: these are things about the school that may have changed from 'then' to 'now'. (Be sure the date of 'then' is clearly established.)

Methods in the classroom	How teaching proceeds (lecturing, workbooks, projects, small group work, demonstrations, rote recitation, dictating the textbook, etc.).
Curriculum	The actual subject matter to be covered.
Student abilities, motivations	Students' intelligence, learning speed, prior preparation, interest in school, eagerness to learn.
Materials, texts, equipment	Books, texts, guides, cassettes, radios, lab equipment, paper, chalkboards, etc.: whatever is needed for direct classroom use.
Way school is organized, regulations	Rules, procedures, organizational set-up, grouping of students and teachers, how decisions are made and by whom, time schedule, etc.
Teacher innovation	This aspect refers to teachers' attitudes and practice in relation to new ideas: are they accepting, resistant, committed? Do they try many things, a few, or none? Do they invent new things, or rely on ideas from outside the school?
New staff	New teacher or other staff members who have come to the school.
Role of headmaster	What the headmaster does (stays in his office, visits classrooms, advises teachers, talks with parents, makes the schedule, teaches his own classes, leads meetings, etc.)

Role of supervisor	What the regional or district supervisor does (visits the school every month, talks with headmaster, explains new rules, leads training sessions, discusses the budget, etc.)
Parent, local community leader role	What parents and community leader do (come to evening meetings with teachers, help build new school facilities, raise extra money for the school, help in school as teacher aides, work in school garden, offer jobs to students, etc.).
School goals, priorities	What the school hopes to accomplish with students (improve science learning, teach skills that are relevant to the community, encourage outstanding students to attend university, increase student initiative and self-reliance, etc.). May also include enrolment, drop-out and repetition goals (see below).
What school accomplishes with students	What the school actually does accomplish with students (like items above).
Enrolment, drop-out, repetition	What school actually accomplishes in terms of numbers of students attending (girls, boys, or both); the percentage of students who stay in school (until a given age); percentage of students who repeat a given grade.

Now: refers to any of the aspects as they occur at present (this school year) in the school.

Then: refers to the same aspects as they occurred at a pre-specified 'then' time, established during the course of previous interviews with central and perhaps regional people. 'Then' is usually the time just before the programme was implemented at the school.

Meanings: whether people like the 'then to now' change or not, what it means to them personally, how they think about it, what difference it makes to them in their daily work.

Display 4: The change process at the local level

Aspect of the situation: this refers roughly to the stages or sequence of the change process.

Initiation of reform and changes: what happened when the programme first came to the school, people first heard about it and began trying to use it.

Early implementation: the first school year or so when the programme was being used or carried out.

Operational Definitions

Redesign or adaptation of changes: alterations in the programme that were made to make it easier, better, more effective, simpler, stronger, etc.

Later implementation: the second and following school years when the programme was being carried out.

Continuation or 'building in' the changes: decisions and actions that made the programme more stable, more 'built in', more likely to continue as a regular part of the school. Might include: having a regular budget for the programme, regular training for new teachers, a changed schedule, new rules or procedures, a programme coordinator or responsible group, etc.

Description: a brief outline of what was happening during this aspect of the situation. What the problems were, what people felt good about.

What was done: a specific description of what someone did at that time. See example.

How it helped: what the action or intervention did that was positive, helpful, good, effective.

How it hindered: what the action did that was negative, not helpful, bad, ineffective.

Display 5A: The changes as implemented (as seen at school, district, and regional level)

Note that this is a summary table, pooling results from the local, regional and central levels, done very late in the study.

Programme version aspects: see explanation at bottom of display. Basically, the aspects are different pieces or parts of a 'bundle' of changes, which taken together add up to the programme. The 'aspect' column just names the aspect (for example, 'teacher training' or 'regional centre' or 'school garden' or 'science experiments).

As intended: give a brief description of what the specific aspect was supposed to look like when carried out. 'Teacher training sessions every month, with local committee managing them', or 'Students and parents plant and harvest garden, selling the crops to make money for the school'.

Fit programme and school: a brief description of how well the programme (as originally planned) fitted with the usual way of doing things, or with people's priorities, motives and hopes. For example: 'Training sessions conflicted with fact that many teachers had second jobs', or 'In most communities, the garden used the skills parents had, and was cultivated outside of regular school hours, thus not competing with classroom work, or 'The new method of encouraging student inquiry was a poor fit to the usual practice of teacher lecturing or dictating material to be copied.')

Changes and adaptations (including deletion): any alterations made in this aspect of the programme during the course of implementation (to make it easier, better, simpler, stronger, a better fit, etc.)

Final version: how the aspect looked after the adaptation had occurred (what its current description is).

Display 5B: Degree of success in implementation

Criterion: these are criteria by which the success of implementation can be judged.

Delivery of inputs	Did the intended resources actually arrive at the school? Could include: school buildings, new classrooms, textbooks or other materials, added teachers, added supervision, funds, equipment, new training sessions, etc.
Technical mastery	Did teachers learn to use the programme skilfully and easily; did they know how to do what was required? Did they feel competent in their use of the programme? Did they know how to do it right?
Teacher engagement, interest	Were teachers excited and involved as they used the programme? Was their energy and motivation high?
Teacher performance, productivity	Did teachers do a consistently good job with the programme, day in and day out? (They might have technical mastery, as above, but not carry out the programme regularly and well.)
Compatibility with other classroom routines and content	Was the programme finally a good 'fit' with other classroom procedures, or other classroom content? Or was it still in conflict, poorly fitting with the part of the teacher's work that was not the programme?
Extent or widespreadness of use	What proportion of teachers who could have used the programme were actually using it? (E.g. three of the four high school science teachers were using the science experiments; all of the grade 1 and 2 teachers were using the early reading programme; 20 per cent of the elementary teachers used the radio lessons.)

Illustrative indicators of success: show the degree of success by citing specific examples for each criterion. Look at the data (which will be marked T, H, A, S or O to show the source) and form a general judgement of how well this criterion was met (high, medium or low).

Display 6: Outcomes and institutionalization at the local level

This display is done near the end of data collection, and answers the question: 'What effects did the change programme have in this school?' On the first page, these are the different types of outcome that might be seen.

Student outcomes

Student knowledge — Information, ideas, content (as measured by exams, tests, etc.)

Student behaviour, skills — What students can actually do (accurate computation, read for comprehension, write a letter, repair a car, swim, type, etc.)

Student feeling, attitudes, motivations — What students feel (e.g. liking school, more interest in science, more wish to attend university, wanting to stay in the community rather than leaving for the city, more self-confidence, etc.).

Attendance, repeat rates — What percentage of enrolled students actually come to school? What percentage of students are required to repeat each grade?

Negative student changes — Any changes that are seen as undesirable or bad in some way, by more than one person or role. For example several teachers think students are harder to control now; headmaster and support staff say teachers are lazier than before; headmaster and a teacher agree that parents are more critical and don't help as much.

Teacher outcomes

Teacher knowledge — Information or ideas, about curriculum, teaching methods, the new programme, etc.

Teacher skill — What the teacher can actually do (use project groups, manage learning centres, carry out classroom discussion, maintain discipline, participate actively in decision-making with colleagues, etc.).

Teacher attitudes — What teachers feel (e.g. excitement about innovation, boredom, sense of cohesiveness with other faculty, wish to continue in teaching, liking for students, etc.).

Teacher negative — Any changes in teachers seen as undesirable or bad by more than one person or group (e.g. increased rate of new teachers quitting the job; discouragement of several vocational teachers; polarization of faculty into pro and con groups, etc.).

School outcomes

School-level positive changes (specific) — Changes in the school's organization, rules, procedures, or working relationships (e.g. teachers feeling much more warm and collaborative with each other; better decision-making; feeling that 'we are a good school'; meetings of grade-level groups; improved method of working with parents to discuss their child's progress, etc.).

School-level capacity for further change — Changes in the school that have strengthened its ability to carry out new innovative projects (e.g. a school council of several teachers, the headmaster and some parents to steer new projects; an arrangement where experienced teachers help new teachers; a small fund for mini-projects that teachers would like to try; a copying machine; a room with new materials where teachers can meet and talk, etc.).

School-level negative changes — Changes in the school's organization, relationships, rules, etc. that more than one person or group agrees are bad, undesirable, etc. (e.g. we are more overloaded than before; there are too many meetings, the school council thinks they are an 'elite'; the headmaster no longer asks our opinion on anything).

Outcomes, illustrative indicators: put specific examples to show what has occurred for the particular outcome. If an indicator has occurred that is apparently unconnected with the programme, put it in brackets [...]

Impact: make a judgement of high, medium or low outcome after the data are entered.

Institutionalization

These are various signs that the programme has become built-in and is likely to continue as a routine part of the school's life.

Classroom consolidation — The programme is carried out routinely as a regular part of the teachers' classroom work; it does not stand out as something novel or special any more.

Likely consolidation — There is general agreement from many different people and roles that the programme will keep on being used at the school.

Support of key people — The funds, equipment, materials, people needed for the programme are guaranteed for the immediate or longer future.

Built-in-ness to procedures, roles — The key aspects of the programme are not special any more, but embedded or built into the school

Operational Definitions

	structure's ordinary set-up. They are part of the regular routines.
Assistance for new teachers	Any new teachers coming to the school are automatically trained to use the programme.

Institutionalization, illustrative indicators: enter specific descriptions that show how the indicator was present (or not). (E.g. nearly everyone agrees that the school garden will continue every year; the district supervisor has often said at meetings that he favours the science labs; there is now a regular budget for the maths workbooks for fifth and sixth grades; we have regular meetings of the science teachers about the environment project; the school can expect at least 30 days a year of training help from the local assistance centre, etc.)

Impact: judge as high, medium or low after the data are entered.

Display 7A: Sources, types and effects of assistance

Source: these are different roles or groups that might provide assistance to people at the school, such as teachers, the headmaster, other staff.

Specialist	Expert or staff person who works in a particular area, such as reading, science, testing, administration, etc. Usually based in central office or region.
Regional assister	Someone based in regional or district office whose general job it is to provide schools with help, usually on a broad (not specialized) range of problems.
Supervisor	The immediate authority over the headmaster. May be called inspector or administrator. Based in a regional or district office.
Headmaster	The person designated as school leader or principal. May or may not teach classes as well.
Other teachers	Colleagues within the same school.

Description: enter type of assistance given (see list of categories), and indicate when and where it was given.

CON:	Control. Assister exerts pressure to make receiver do something.
TTR:	Training/teaching. Assister transmits information or develops skill in receiver through structured situation (workshop, etc.).
SOL:	Solution-giving. Assister provides answers, advice, solutions to receiver problems.
RES:	Resource-adding. Assister provides materials, money, time or other needed resources.
ADV:	Advocacy. Assister actively represents the interests of receiver to others, such as administrators, supervisors, parents, headmaster, etc.
FAC:	Facilitation. Assister helps receiver to achieve goals, giving at-the-elbow help with the process.

INQ: Inquiry. Assister collects data from receiver or implementation situation, feeds it back to help next steps.

SUP: Support. Assister provides encouragement, reinforcement, emotional support.

Problems/needs: describe the problems, difficulties or issues that led to a need for assistance. Who needed assistance, and why?

Consequences: explain what the assistance did for teachers and/or the headmaster; how they changed, what they could do better, etc.

Display 7B: How assistance affected implementation

Factor: these are characteristics of assistance which affect its success.

Continuity	The assistance was sustained throughout implementation, not just concentrated at the beginning.
Quality (people and materials)	The assistance was well and carefully carried out; the assister did a competent job. Any associated materials were well developed.
Local availability	The assistance was given at the school, or nearby. People did not have to travel far to get it.
Need-responsiveness	The assistance was tailored to what people's needs and problems were; it was not standard or uniform.
Pedagogical emphasis	The assistance gave teachers direct help on classroom use of the programme.
Capacity-building emphasis	The assistance helped the school do its own assistance in the future (for example, by training teachers or headmaster to train their own teachers).
Built into routines	Future assistance is a normal and expected part of the school's work; regular times, places and funds are set aside for it.

Degree present: Rate the factor as high, medium or low, explain with a phrase.

Effect on commitment: what did the assistance do to increase or decrease people's positive feeling about the programme, their ownership, the priority they give to the programme? Mark the effect with a + or a − to show whether the assistance helped or hindered commitment.

Effect on mastery: what did the assistance do to help or hinder people's skill in carrying out the programme in the classroom easily and well? How did it increase or decrease their competence, their ability to 'do it right'?

Effect on implementation: in general, what did the assistance do to help or hinder the effective carrying out of the programme at the school and classroom level?

Display 7C: Role of headmaster and local administrators

Aspect: this refers to types of behaviour the headmaster or administrator might carry out. All are associated with success of implementation.

Stability	Remaining in the same job during the course of implementation.
Presence, involvement	Being active, visible, taking an important part in the implementation of the programme.
Facilitation	Doing whatever was necessary to support and help teachers as they carried out the programme.
Monitoring, regulating	Paying careful attention to what was happening in the programme (e.g. through visits, discussions, observation, meetings) and taking any corrective action needed.
Demandingness	Putting pressure on teachers to 'do it right', setting standards for good performance and holding people to them.
Supervision and support	Advice, consultation, assistance, coaching or other help given by administrator to headmaster or teachers, and by headmaster to teachers.
Other	Any other behaviour of headmaster or local administrator you thought was affecting implementation.

Headmaster (what he/she did or didn't do): give a brief description of typical behaviour (e.g. visited every classroom at least once a week, usually for a half hour). If headmaster's typical behaviour omits one of the factors, describe and explain (e.g. never seems to push teachers, lets them do the programme any way they want).

Consequences: describe the typical effects of the headmaster's behaviour using, if possible, the types of outcomes seen in Displays 5B and 6 (e.g. this seemed to increase teachers' interest in the programme; the visits improved teacher understanding of the programme since headmaster often discussed it with teachers; teacher mastery did not improve).

Local administrator (what he/she did or didn't do): brief description, done in same way as for headmaster.

Consequences: typical effects described as above (note that effects may be on the headmaster, or on teachers).

Display 7D: Summary of factors accounting for success of local implementation

As noted (Appendix 5, p. 346), this display should be done very late in the analysis; it summarizes a great deal of data.

Factor: these are a series of possible factors that might lead to success in implementing the programme at the local level. Note that most of them are in principle major types of 'linkage' between country-level and local-level efforts. As with other factors, they may be present in a positive way, be weak, absent or even negative.

Assistance	In-service help for teachers and headmasters (includes training, supervision, support, advice, coaching, etc.).
Administrative role	Typical behaviour of headmaster and local administrator (includes stability, presence, facilitation, monitoring/regulating, demandingness, supervision and support).
Commitment	Positive feelings toward the programme, ownership, priority given to it.
Received pressure	Feelings on part of headmaster and teachers that they are expected by important others to 'do it right'.
Received resources	Funds, equipment, materials and people that actually arrived at the school to help implement the programme.
Success experiences	Short-term results of the programme that worked and gave people a positive feeling. Success experiences can occur through practice mastery or through seeing good results with students.
Empowerment, engagement	People's sense that they were actively involved in decisions about carrying out the programme — trying it out, revising it, improving it.
Local adaptation of the programme	Revisions or changes in the programme that make it easier, stronger, a better fit, simpler, more effective, while keeping the basic spirit of the programme.
Community support	Positive, encouraging attitudes of parents and community leaders toward the programme.
Other	Any other factors that were important causes of good local implementation, such as student characteristics, environment turbulence, the history of the school, etc.

Illustrative indicators: give a brief summary of the factor, as it occurred in the local setting (e.g. the headmaster was very active in helping teachers with the programme, gave much support and expected a high standard of teaching, but the local administrator was somewhat lax and rarely came to the school). If you think the description can be traced to a national initiative, mark it with C (for country). In this example, C might be given if the headmaster had gone to a very successful nationally-initiated training session on the programme.

Operational Definitions

Impact: after the summary description is entered, make a judgement of high, medium or low for the factor.

Display 8: Prospects for the future, at the local level

Source: the people whose responses are being reported. NOTE: you should still insert H, T, A, S, etc. to show where the data came from. For example, the headmaster might tell you that teachers think the programme will continue. That should go in the 'Teachers' row, but be marked with an H.

Teachers	Anyone teaching in the school, whether or not they are using the programme.
Headmaster	This school's headmaster.
Local administrator, inspector, supervisor	The immediate person over the headmaster in the formal authority structure; the person who has most responsibility for seeing that the school functions correctly.
Assistance-giver	The person or persons outside the school who have given most direct help, training, advice, consultation, coaching, etc. to the school.
Parents	Parents of students in this school.

What will happen: a brief description of what people are predicting for the next two to three years: whether the programme will continue, how it may change, what else will happen at the school. (E.g. more teachers will be using the programme; we will still do the science experiments, but fewer of them; we will have fewer students repeating grades; the school will have two new classrooms.)

Hopes for the future: what people wish to have happen, regardless of prediction. (E.g. several teachers want to have better maths materials; headmaster wants to have more girls attend school; parents want the school to teach more practical things.)

Worries: what people are worried or concerned about when they think of the immediate future. (E.g. several senior teachers are thinking of leaving for another job; the new examinations will put a lot of pressure on us; the local administrator still does not give enough help; the maths workbooks are wearing out and we may not get enough new ones.)

What is needed to reach hopes: what the school should have (money or people, assistance, materials, stronger leadership, commitment, etc.) if the hopes are to be realized. (Sometimes this will mean dealing with the worries.)

Bibliography

Ahmadullah, A.K., *et al.* (1984) Institute of Social Welfare and Research, University of Dhaka. Newly constructed physical facilities and enrolment of children in primary schools (case study of three schools).

Akhter, S. (1987) Institute of Education and Research, University of Dhaka. A study report on evaluation of the academic aspects of the cluster training programme. Volume 1: Summary of findings, conclusions and recommendations. UNDP-UNESCO illustrative study.

Akhter, S. *et al.* (1984) Institute of Education and Research, University of Dhaka. A study on the role of the assistant upazila education officers in academic supervision of the primary schools under UPE (IDA) project.

Alauddin, K. (1985) National Academy for Primary Education, Mymensingh. An illustrative study on the utilization of the learning materials under UPE (IDA) project (1980-1985), Bangladesh.

A tracer study of 100 assistant female teachers appointed under the UPE project. (1984) Draft report, BANBEIS in cooperation with UNESCO. Dhaka: Ministry of Education.

Balaghatullah, M. (1984) Human Resources Division, BIDS, Dhaka. Study report on supply and utilization of textbooks under the UPE (IDA) project.

Berman, P. and McLaughlin, M.W. (1977) *Federal Programs Supporting Educational Change. Volume IV: The Findings in Review.* Santa Monica, CA: Rand Corporation.

Case study on supply, distribution and utilization of school furniture for UPE (IDA), project primary schools. (1984) The Foundation for Research on Educational Planning and Development (FREPD), Bangladesh in cooperation with UPE, Dhaka.

Central Statistics Authority (1986) *Ethiopia Statistical Abstract*. Addis Ababa.

Central Statistics Authority (1990) *Facts and Figures*. Addis Ababa.

Curriculum Department (1976) *Grade 5 Geography Textbooks*. Addis Ababa.

Curriculum Department (1986) *The Evaluative Research of the General Education System in Ethiopia*. Addis Ababa.

Crandall, D. *et al. People, Policies and Practice: Examining the Chain of School Improvement* (Vols 1-10). Andover, MA: The Network.

Dalin, P. (1973) *Case Studies of Educational Innovation. Vol. IV: Strategies for Educational Innovation*. Paris: CERI/OECD.

Bibliography

Dalin, P. (1978) *Limits to Educational Change*. London: Macmillan.

Dalin, P. and Rolff, H.-G. (1993) *Changing the School Culture*. London: Cassell.

Department of Educational Mass Media (1987) *Evaluation of Primary School Radio Programmes*. Addis Ababa.

EMPDA (1989) *Textbook Publishing and Printing in Ethiopia*. Addis Ababa.

ERGESE Report (1986) Volumes I to IV.

Fullan, M.G. and Stiegelbauer, S. (1991) *The New Meaning of Educational Change*. New York: Teachers College Press.

Haque, S. (1990) For and on behalf of the National Task Force, Dhaka. *Wastage in Education*.

Haque, S., et al. (1987) UNDP/UNESCO Project BGD/85/018, Dhaka. Reform of primary teacher training in Bangladesh, final report and recommendations, Part 1, Study on teacher effectiveness.

Huberman, A.M. and Miles, M.B. (1984) *Innovation up Close: How School Improvements Work*. New York: Plenum Press.

Huq, M.N., Chowdhury, S.A. and Karim, M.R. (1984) National Institute of Educational Administration, Extension and Research (NIEAER), Dhanmondi, Dhaka. Illustrative study: UPE (IDA) project, training of ATEOs as primary school supervisors.

Ko-Chih and Chinapah (1985) *Universalization of Primary Education and Literacy*. Addis Ababa.

Last, G.C. (1960) *A Geography of Ethiopia for Senior Secondary Schools*. Addis Ababa: Ministry of Education.

Latif, A.H. (1991) IER, Dhaka University, IIEP, UNESCO. A case study on Bangladesh rural advancement committees' facilitation assistance programme on education.

Lockheed, M.E., Verspoor, A.M., et al. (1991) *Improving Primary Education in Developing Countries*, Washington, D.C: Oxford University Press.

Louis, K.S. and Miles, M.B. (1990) *Improving the Urban High School: What Works and Why*. New York: Teachers College Press.

Miah, A., et al. (1984) Institute of Social Welfare and Research, Dhaka University. Situation of female enrolment and dropout in primary schools (a case study of three schools).

Miles, M.B. and Huberman, A.M. (1984) *Qualitative Data Analysis: A Sourcebook of New Methods*. Beverly Hills, CA: Sage.

Ministry of Education (1972) *Education Challenge to the Nation: Report of the Section Review*. Addis Ababa.

Ministry of Education (1979) WPE *Programme of Education*. Addis Ababa.

Ministry of Education (1979) *The New Ethiopian Educational Directives*. Addis Ababa.

Ministry of Education (1979-1989) *The Ethiopian National Literacy Campaign Retrospect and Prospects*. Addis Ababa.

Ministry of Education (1984) *Basic Information on Education in Ethiopia*. Addis Ababa.

Ministry of Education (1984) *Education in Socialist Ethiopia*. Addis Ababa.

Ministry of Education (1985) *Basic Education Statistics*. Addis Ababa.

Ministry of Education (1988) *Joint Annual Education Sector Review*. Addis Ababa.

Nigussie H. (1990) *Assessment of In-Service Training Provision for Educational Managers by the Management and Training Service of the Ministry of Education 1981-1989*. Addis Ababa.

Qadir, S.A. (1984) Division of Human Resources, BIDS. UPE in Bangladesh — An enquiry into the issues of enrolment, dropout and repetition.

Rahman, S. (1986) IER, Dhaka University, July 1986: Reform of Primary Teacher Training Programme in Bangladesh. Supportive Illustrative study 1 of 4 Profile of Primary School Teachers.

Rahman, S. (1990) Institute of Education and Research in cooperation with UNICEF, Dhaka. A Study on Recurrent Cluster Training Programme.

Rosser (1989) *Awraja Pedagogical Centres*. Addis Ababa.

Sjøstrøm, R. (1986) *A Pilot Study of Effects of Primary Schooling in a Rural Community of Ethiopia*. SIDA.

Study on Non-formal Education — Final Report. (1988) Universal Primary Education Project, Prokaushali Sangsad Limited, Dhaka, Bangladesh & UNESCO.

Synopses of Three Research Studies on Primary Education, Non-formal Education, Technical/Vocational Education (S. Haque and M.A. Jinnah, eds). (1990) The Foundation for Research on Educational Planning and Development (FREPD) in cooperation with the Ford Foundation.

Tesfa Yesus Mehari (1989) *Rapid Population Growth and Its Impact on Socio-Economic Development in Ethiopia*. Addis Ababa, pp. 11-15.

Verspoor, A.M. (1989) *Pathways to Change: Improving the Quality of Education in Developing Countries*, World Bank Discussion Paper 53. Washington, D.C.

Index

Page numbers in **bold** type refer to figures; page numbers in *italic* type refer to tables; page numbers followed by 'D' refer to displays, e.g. 78D. For brevity, subheadings refer to the country in question, not the name of the reform programme.

Academy of Fundamental Education (now NAPE), Bangladesh 124
achievement xi, 101, 104, 116, 196
adaptation
  local, *see* local adaptation
  responsive 85, 88D, 157, 163, 350
administration 5, 72
  Bangladesh 136, 137, *137*
  Colombia 48, 49–50
administrative role 224–5, 362
  Bangladesh 138, 144, 169, 292–3D, 298–9D
  Colombia 59, 159, 160, 174, 200–1, 274–5D
  Ethiopia 93D, 94–5, 111, 164, 174, 207, 284–5D
  linkage factor 159, 164, 169, 241
administrator role 36, 361
  Bangladesh 170, 214, 342
  Colombia 201, 255, 331
  Ethiopia 206–7, 336
ADPEO (assistant district primary education officer), Bangladesh 126
agricultural calendar 49
alliances, Colombia 160
analysis methods 182–4
Antioquia University (Colombia) 51
Aparajita school, Bangladesh 141, 288–303D
APC (awraja pedagogical centre), Ethiopia 77, 83, 115, 118, 162, 166
assistance xiii, xv, 197, 220, 249, 359–60

Bangladesh 137–8, 168, 169, 290–1D, 340
  and implementation success 142, 144, 146, 213
  Colombia 58–9, 157, 158–9, 200, 274–5D, 329
  definition 351, 362
  Ethiopia 86, 88D, 92–4, 93D, 110, 334
    cross-site display 282–3D
    as linkage factor 164
    success factor 206
    Tegulet I school 26–7, 28
  as linkage factor 158–9, 164, 169, 178, *179*, 241
  nature of 235–6
  see also teacher mastery; teacher training, in-service
AUEO (assistant upazila education officer), Bangladesh 130, 134, 136, 147, 259
  and linkage 137–8, 169
  role of 125, 129, 134, 138, 170, 228–9
  and success 213, 214–15
  success factor 36, 168, 174–5, 213, 214–15, 217

Bangladesh
  central-level change 126
  cross-site displays 288–303D
  recommendations and implications 257–9
  reform comparison 220–2

worktables 327-9, 340-5
see also Universal Primary Education (UPE) project (Bangladesh)
behaviour, student, see student impact
Boyacá (Colombia) 53

capacity building 27, 81, 147, 258-9, 266, 348
CAPEC (Colombia) 51
case writing and analysis 11
Cedros school, Colombia 61, 268-78D
central capacity 352
central factors xii-xiii
central institutions 89-90, 225
central support xvii, 55-6, 57, 165, 251
Chameli school, Bangladesh 141, 288-303D
Champa school, Bangladesh 141, 288-303D
change process 354-6
Chilalo I, II and III schools, Ethiopia 97, 98, 99, 103-8, 104, 107, 110-12, 114, 280-7D
classroom changes 195, 243, 248, 252
  Bangladesh xi, 217-18, 243
  Ethiopia 102, 105, 243
classroom practice xiii, xiv, xviii
  methods 353
cluster training
  Bangladesh 124-5, 127, 134, 140, 168, 170, 259
    Hasnahena school 35, 36, 37, 38
    success factor 146-7, 148, 174-5, 213
co-curricular activities 20, 25, 189, 192, 216
coaching and training 11
Colbert, C.V. 47-8
Colombia 268-78D, 322-4, 329-34
  education system 43-5
  recommendations and implications 254-5
  reform comparison 220-2
  see also Escuela Nueva (EN) programme (Colombia)

commitment xviii, 5, 142, 143, 229-30, 237, 252
  Bangladesh 138, 143, 144, 147, 169, 215, 343
    cross-site display 292-3D, 298-9D
    government 128, 133-4, 135, 138
  Colombia 59-60, 156, 159, 201-2, 204, 332
    cross-site display 274-5D
  definition 362
  Ethiopia 28, 93D, 95, 111, 114-15, 337
    cross-site display 284-5D
    linkage factor 164
    success factor 208, 211, 213
  government xi-xii, 128, 133-5, 138, 224, 246
  linkage factor 159, 164, 169, 241
  political 239-41
  success factor 201-2, 204, 208, 211, 213, 215
commitment building 56, 81, 179, 179, 348
communication
  effective 85, 88D, 166, 226, 350
  links, see linkage
community leader role 354
community support 36, 197, 222, 239, 362
  Bangladesh 121, 124, 125, 143, 189, 216, 251, 257
    cross-site display 296-7D
    inadequate 169
    and success 149
    worktable 345
  Colombia 17, 47-8, 49, 61, 63, 187, 251
    cross-site display 270-1D, 278-9D
    implementation factor 60
    lack 65
    linkage factor 159
    success factor 202, 204
    worktable 334
  Ethiopia 21, 23, 96, 106, 108, 113
    cross-site display 286-7D
    financial 99, 99-100, 102, 103
    school involvement 72, 103, 115, 250, 256

success factor 210
worktable 340
findings 229-30, 245, 252
reform strategy difference 250-1
role of xvi, xviii, xix
success factor xiii, 202, 204, 210
Compulsory Primary Education Acts,
 Bangladesh, (1917-27 & 1990) 126,
 128
control 351
 Bangladesh 126, 168, 170, 214
 Ethiopia 86-7, 88D, 165-6
country-level study (CSS) 6-7, 304-5
country-level success factors 6, 87-8D,
 157-8, 162, 167, 168, 320-1
 Bangladesh 34-7, 167-70, *173*, 174-5
 Colombia 54-6, 157-8, *171*, 174, 202,
 204, 206
 definitions 348-51
 Ethiopia 87-8D, 162, *172*, 174,
 209-10
croquis (school map) 49
cross-school analysis 148-9, 195, 197,
 198
 Ethiopia 96-114, *97*, *98*
cross-site displays 268-79D, 280-7D,
 288-303D
CSTCs (community skill training
 centres), Ethiopia 77
cultural factors 101, 145
Cundinamarca (Colombia) 53
curriculum 353
 Bangladesh 124, 125
 Colombia 48, 49-50, 156
 Ethiopia xi, 70, 71, 76, 91
curriculum development 176, 349
 Bangladesh 129, 134, 168
 Colombia 157, 176
 Ethiopia 82-3, 85-6, 87D

data 10, 181
decentralization xiii, xv, xviii-xix, 78,
 221, 246
 Bangladesh 169, 257
 Colombia 204
 Ethiopia 164-5, 166

implications of findings 260-1
 nature of 237-8, 238
 reform strategy difference 249
 see also APC; delegation; SPC
decision-making 157-8, 168, 349
 Bangladesh 129, 168, 217
 Colombia 157-8
 Ethiopia 80, 82, 86, 87D, 88D
definitions, operational 347-63
delegation xiii, xviii-xix, 237-8, 260-1
 Colombia 204, 254
 see also decentralization
DEO (awraja/district education office),
 Ethiopia 78, 83, 85, *99*, 103, 106-13,
 107
 inspection role 117, 207
displays, Ethiopia 78-80D, 87-8D,
 93D, 94D
district administrator 26, 27-8, 36,
 255-6
district education office 262-3
 see also DEO
district education officer 207, 245-6
 see also DPEO; UEO
district-school relations xix
division of labour 83, 87D, 113, 211,
 240, 349
donor support 227, 230, 247, 266,
 353
 Bangladesh 31, 122, 127, 128, 129,
 130-1
 Colombia 52, 54, 56-7, 64, 157
 Ethiopia 76, 91
 role xix-xx, 264-7
DPEO (district primary education
 officer), Bangladesh 37, 126, 129,
 130, 217
drop-outs 15, 21, 24, 104, 130, 354

economic security, Colombia 156
Education Commission (1882),
 Bangladesh 126
Education Sector Review (Ministry of
 Education 1972), Ethiopia 73
education systems 43-4, 68-9, 72-4,
 121, 121-2

Educational Policy for Colombia (1982-6) 55
El Camino school, Colombia 59, 268-78D
El Frutal school, Colombia 268-78D
El General school, Colombia 58, 59, 62, 64, 268-79D
El Puerto school, Colombia 268-79D
El Zipa school, Colombia 61, 268-79D
Emilio Rocha school, Colombia 14-18, 59, 268-78D
EMPDA, *see* Ministry of Education, Ethiopia
empowerment xiii, 159, 164, 237
  Bangladesh 216, 344
  Colombia 159, 202, 206, 276-7D, 333
  Ethiopia 112, 164, 209-10, 286-7D, 339
  success factor 202, 206, 209-10, 216
empowerment/engagement 95, 159, *179*, 179, 362
  Bangladesh 144-5, 294-5D, 300-1D
enrolment 44, 45, 123-4, 130-1, 354
  Ethiopia 68-9, 71, 72-3, 89, 188
entry strategies 184-5, *185*
environmental turbulence 157, 227, 231-2, 350-1
  Ethiopia 86, 88D, 163
ERGESE (Evaluative Research of the General Education System in Ethiopia) 78, 83
Escuela Nueva (EN) programme (Colombia) ix, 8, 15-16, 43-65
  administration 57
  change process explanation 200-6
  components 48
  country context 43-5
  description 47-50
  development 155-6
  Emilio Rocha school 14-17
  history 50-4
  implementation elements 49-50
  implications 64-5
  incremental expansion 56
  lessons from 12 cases 57-64
  link to local sites 204-5
  methodology characteristics 48-9
  objectives 47-8
  origin 45-7
  process dynamics 202-6, 203
  rural content 62, 272-3D
  success factors 54-6, 205
  summary 159-60
  Towards a New School manual 46-7, 52
Ethiopia ix
  cross-site displays 280-7D
  education system 68-9
  follow-up and monitoring 226
  proclamations 77
  recommendations and implications 255-7
  reform comparison 220-2
  slogans 74-5, 161
  worktables 324-6, 334-40
  see also NDR; primary education reform programme (Ethiopia)
evaluation 72, 130
  self-evaluation 62
excellent schools 259-60
  Bangladesh 139-40, 141, 142-3
  Colombia 57-8
  Ethiopia 98-103, *99*, 208
expenditure *84*, 84, 122, 233
external agencies, *see* donor support

feedback mechanisms, Ethiopia 211
females
  students 37, 71, 258
  teachers 71, 125, 131
finance 352-3
  Bangladesh 127, 129
  Colombia 56-7, 64, 157
  Ethiopia 23-4, 90-1
  see also donor support; expenditure
findings xi-xii, xvii-xviii, 223-53
flexible promotion, Colombia 61-2, 64, 65, 272-3D
follow-up 48, 157, 160, 163
formal education 43-5, 68, 73, 121
funding, *see* finance

Gedeo I, II and III schools, Ethiopia 97, *98*, *99*, 99–112, *104*, *107*, *114*, 118, 280-7D
German Democratic Republic (GDR) 76, 227
girls' participation, *see* females
good schools 57, 58, 64, 106–8, 140–3
government
  Colombia 50, 62, 187
  role of xix, 232–3, 246–7, 263–4
  school 50
  student 62, 272-3D
  see also commitment, government
group work, Colombia 61, 270-1D
guides 61
  student 50, 56, 61, 202, 204, 270-1D
  teacher 37, 61, 131, 191, 258

Hasnahena government primary school, Bangladesh 29–40, 141, 288-303D
headmaster role 114–15, 245, 353, 361
  Bangladesh 142–3, 148, 217, 258–9, 341
    commitment 142, 143
    Hasnahena 34, 34–6, 39
    and implementation 142–3, 147
    success factor 147, 213–14, 217
  Colombia 59, 64, 65, 200–1, 204, 330
  Ethiopia 26, 27–8, 110, 111, 113, 256
    planning ability 116
    success factor 206, 207–8, 211
    worktable 335
higher education, Colombia 44–5, *45*
'How Schools Improve' study (HSI) ix–xvi, xvii–xviii, 5–13, 11

IDA support, Bangladesh 31, 122, 127, 129, 130–1
illiteracy, Colombia *45*, 45
impact
  Bangladesh 142–3, 146–50, 194
  Colombia 60–3, 187
  Ethiopia 97, *98*, 98, 101, 104–8, *109*, 190
    accounting factors 110–14, *114*
  see also school impact; student impact; teacher impact
IMPACT (instructional management by parents, community and teachers), Bangladesh 127
implementation xi, *4*, 4–5, 147, 234
  Bangladesh 38, 128–9, 139–50, 288-9D, 327
  closeness to 88D, 157, 163, 168, 350
  Colombia 58–60, 322
  in cross-country analysis 195–6, 268-9D
  Ethiopia 22–4, 88–92, 96–110, 324
    accounting factors 110–14, *114*
    cross-school analysis 96–114, *97*, *98*, 280-1D
  and Verspoor study 230, 230–2
implementation success 356
  Bangladesh 139–42, 144, 146, 149, 213, 214
  country-level factors 133–7, 167–8, 348–51
  excellent schools 139–40, 141, 146, 194
  from national viewpoint 128–37
  good schools 140–1, 141, 146
  seen locally 191–2, 194
  seen nationally 128–33
  very good schools 140, 141, 146
  Colombia 60, 156, 157–8, 186, 187
  Ethiopia 97, *98*, 161, 161–4
    excellent schools 99–101, *109*
    good schools 106–7, *109*
    seen locally 188, 191
    seen nationally 88–92
    very good schools 103–4, *109*
  factors 170–80, *171-3*, 320–1, 346, 361–3
  as outcome 181–2, 185–94
implications xviii–xx
IMTEC x, 9, 12
in-service training, *see* teacher training, in-service
income generation, Ethiopia 90–1, 100, 106–8, 116, 118
infrastructure development 225, 240–1, 350

371

Bangladesh 135, 136
Ethiopia 83, 87D, 165
initial situation, schools 184–5
innovation 161, 233–4
  strategy 90, 352
input–output model, Bangladesh 123
inputs, Bangladesh 32–3, 123, *123*
inspection
  Bangladesh 126, 168
  Ethiopia 87, 117
inspectors 21, 26, 27, 110, 262–3
institution building 263–4
institutionalization xi, 5, 197–8, 358–9
  Bangladesh 132, 168, 244, 288–303D, 329
    cross-site display 290–1D
    Hasnahena school 38
    key factors 142–3, 146–50, 168
    as locally seen outcome 193, 194
  Colombia 54–6, 63–5, 157–8, 243, 324
    cross-site display 270–1D
    as locally seen outcome 187, 188
  decisions supporting 157–8, 168, 351
  Ethiopia 92, 117, 162, 197, 213, 243–4
    accounting factors 110–14
    cross-site display 282–3D
    excellent schools 102–3, *110*
    good schools 108, *110*
    as locally seen outcome 25–6, 189–90, 191
    ratings *98*, 98, *114*
    schools distribution *97*
    Tegulet I school 25–6
    very good schools 105–6, *110*
    worktable 326
  and infrastructure developments 240–1
  at local level 357–9
  as outcome 25–6, 182, 187–91, 193, 194
  success determinants 243–4
  summary 235
  and Verspoor study 232, 232–4
  see also routinization
Instituto Superior de Educación Rural (ISER), Pamplona 46, 51

instrumentation 10
intermediate education, Colombia 44

Jaba school, Bangladesh 141, 288–303D
junior secondary education, Ethiopia 69

key events 347

La Mina school, Colombia 60, 268–79D
La Unión school, Colombia 61, 268–79D
labour education, in Ethiopia 71–2, 91–2, 101, 112
  Tegulet I school 20, 22, 23, 24, 25
LDCs (lesser developed countries), reform implications 259–67
learning, active, Colombia 61, 272–3D
learning corners, Colombia 49, 61, 272–3D
legal regulations 82, 87D, 135, 211, 240, 349
liberal promotion policy, Bangladesh 125, 130
libraries
  Colombia 49, 53, 62, 272–3D
  Ethiopia 20, 189
linkage xii, xvi, xvii, 221, 250
  Bangladesh xvi, 147, 168–9, 221, 250
  from national level 137–9, 169
  Colombia xvi, 57, 158–9, 221, 250
  definition 179, 351–2
  essential 251–2
  Ethiopia xvi, 92–6, 93–4D, 164, 221, 250
linkage factors 165, 175, *177*, 241
  Bangladesh 169, 178–80, *179*
  Colombia 158–9, 177–8, 178–80, *179*
  Ethiopia 164, 178–80, *179*
literacy 19, 26, 30, 89, 120
local adaptation 237, 362
  Bangladesh 145, 169, 216, 296–7D, 300–1D, 344

Colombia   60, 159, 202, 276-7D, 333
Ethiopia   95-6, 112-13, 116, 166, 256-7, 340
　cross-site display   286-7D
　linkage factor   165
　success factor   210
linkage factor   159, 165, 178-9, *179*
success factor   202, 210, 216, 242
local level   363
　changes   32-4, 125
local-level study, interview guide   310-19
Los Olivos school, Colombia   61, 268-79D

macro-factors   175-6, *176*
madrasah education system, Bangladesh   121-2
management   xv-xvi, 221, 250
　Bangladesh   124
　Ethiopia   255-6
materials, *see* teacher-learning materials
methodology   x-xi, 10-12
middle education, Colombia   44
Ministry of Education
　Bangladesh   122, 126
　　Directorate of Primary Education (DPE)   126-30, 132, 133, 168, 170
　　National Curriculum and Textbook Board (NCTB)   127-30, 134, 168-9
　Colombia   64
　　Experimental Pilot Centres division   157, 158
　Ethiopia   70, 75, 90, 115
　　conferences   90, 115, 117-18, 166
　　Curriculum and Supervision Department (later Institute for Curriculum Development and Educational Research)   71, 75
　　Education Mass Media Service (EMMS)   75, 80
　　Educational Materials Production and Distribution Agency (EMPDA)   71, 75, 83, 85, 87

'Ethiopia First' seminars   74
　Institute for Curriculum Development and Research (ICDR)   80, 82, 83, 85, 87
　management and training services courses   *81*, 81
　Office of the National Committee for Central Planning (ONCCP)   76
　policy committee   80
　proclamations   86, 96
　Schools' Construction and Maintenance Services (SCMS)   75-6
Mogollón, Professor Oscar   46, 51, 51-2, 53
monitoring   xv-xvi, 221, 226, 250, 351
　Bangladesh   147, 168, 170, 214
　Colombia   50
　Ethiopia   72, 96-7, 88D, 162
motivation
　student, *see* student impact
　teacher   195
'multiplier' agents   53-4, 55

NAPE (National Academy of Primary Education), Bangladesh   127, 129, 132, 134
national coordination, Colombia   55
National Curriculum Development Centre (NCDC), Bangladesh   127, 128
national objectives, Ethiopia   165
national organizations
　Bangladesh   132, 167
　Ethiopia   80-1, 87D, 162
　strength of   87D, 162, 167, 348
national team   xiv, 55, 220, 225, 248, 263
national-level factors   240, 240
NDR (National Democratic Revolution) Programme, Ethiopia   67-8
　Programme   70
　Ten-Year Perspective Plan   70
negative factors, Bangladesh   133, 144, 145, 149
non-formal education, Ethiopia   73
Norte de Santander (Colombia)   53, 54

Norwegian Ministry for Development Cooperation x, 12

organizational context, Ethiopia 113-14, 286-7D
outcomes xi, 181-2, 194-8, 234-5
 Bangladesh 32, 38, 130, 133, 191-4
 Colombia 56-7, 186-8
 country-level 6
 Ethiopia 89-92, 188-91
 local-level 181-98, 353-4, 357-9
 system-level 56-7, 89-92, 130, 352-3
 see also implementation; implementation success; institutionalization; school impact; student impact; teacher impact

Padma school, Bangladesh 141, 288-303D
Palash school, Bangladesh 141, 288-303D
parent-teacher associations (PTAs), Bangladesh 37, 125, 127, 129, 131, 135, 216
parental role xvi, xviii, xix, 222, 354
 Bangladesh 132, 145, 149, 230, 250-1
 cross-site display 296-7D, 302-3D
 Colombia 16, 159, 230, 251
 Ethiopia 230, 250, 256
 findings 233, 244-5, 252
parents' committees, Ethiopia 77, 99
parishad, Bangladesh 139
participation rate, *see* enrolment
Patio Bonito school, Colombia 268-78D
peer teaching, Colombia 270-1D
personal networks 28, 160
physical facilities 197
 Bangladesh 123-4, 124, 129, 131, 133, 135
 Hasnahena school 31-2, 32
 and implementation success 148-9
'Plan de Fomento de la Educación Rural', Colombia 54, 55

planning, Ethiopia 72, 115
policies 226-7
political education, Ethiopia 19, 20, 23, 24-5, 27
political priorities 167, 220, 248
political stability 239-41
 Bangladesh 302-3D
 Colombia 156
 Ethiopia 162, 165, 211, 255
political support 224, 255, 263
polytechnic education system, Ethiopia 76-7, 82-3
pre-school education 43, *44*, 68
pressure xiii, 236
 Colombia 276-7D
 Ethiopia 111, 284-5D
 for good implementation 178, *179*, 241, 349
  Bangladesh 168
  Ethiopia 82, 87D, 162
 received 362
  Bangladesh 138-9, 145, 148, 169, 215, 343
   cross-site display 294-5D, 300-1D
  Colombia 159, 202, 206, 332
  Ethiopia 87D, 95, 164, 208, 338
  linkage factor 159, 164, 169, 178, *179*
  success factor 87D, 202, 206, 208, 215
primary education
 Colombia 43-4, 45, 50-1
 Ethiopia 68-9, 70-1
 rural xiv
primary education reform programme (Ethiopia) 8, 66-119, 108
 change dynamics 211-13, 212
 country context 66-8
 development 161
 implementation 77-8, 79D, 80D
  success factors 207-8
  success seen nationally 88-92
 key events/consequences 78-80D
 major components 71-2, 88-9
 planning phase 75-7, 79D
 post-revolution efforts and

achievements 70-1
recommendations 117-19, 255-7
schools distribution 97
success factors, country-level 87-8D, 162, *172*, 174, 209-10
summary 165-7
Tegulet I school 22-9
primary training institutes (PTIs), Bangladesh 124
private education, Colombia 44-5, *45*
professionalization, Colombia 157, 160
project management, Ethiopia 72
PRT (project-related training) 266
Bangladesh 127, 167, 168
psychomotor skills 101, 104
public education, Colombia 44-5, *45*
pupil-teacher ratio, Ethiopia 69

quality control committee, Ethiopia 76
Qudrat-e-Khuda commission, Bangladesh 133

radio support, Ethiopia 19, 20, 24, 72, 75
Rangan school, Bangladesh 141, 288-303D
reform bundle, Bangladesh 31, 32, 123, 124, 141, 146
reform strategies xiv-xvi, xvii-xviii, 5-6, 7, 251-3
common elements xiv-xv, 248-9
comparison 218-22, 219-22
differences xv-xvi, 249-51
refresher courses, Ethiopia 117
regional coordinators, Colombia 53, 55, 57, 59
regional education offices, Ethiopia 85
repetition 45, *46*, 91, 354
report, international 11-12
research questions x, 5-6, 10, 304-9
country-level study (CSS) 304-5
school-level study (SSS) 305-9
resources 225-6, 233, 258
Bangladesh 139, 142, 257-8
Colombia 56, 255

Ethiopia 102, 106, 111-12, 163
resources allocation 176, 350
Bangladesh 135-6
Ethiopia *84*, 84, 87D
resources delivery 178, *179*, 226, 350
Bangladesh 135-6
Colombia 157
Ethiopia 84, 87D
resources received 178, *179*, 362
Bangladesh 145, 169, 215, 294-5D, 300-1D, 343
Colombia 159, 202, 276-7D, 332
Ethiopia 95, 207, 208-9, 284-5D, 338
success factor 202, 207, 208-9, 215
routinization xi, 187, 197, 235

Santa Mariá school, Colombia 58-65, 268-79D
Sargent Report (1944), Bangladesh 126
school administration committees, Ethiopia 77
school building and expansion, Ethiopia 72, 76, 113
school impact xi, 7, 197, 242-3, 358
Bangladesh 131-2, 139, 242-3, 328
cross-site display 290-1D
Hasnahena school 38
as locally seen outcome 193, 194
very good schools 140
Colombia 187, 188, 242-3, 270-1D, 323
Ethiopia 92, 101, 105, 107-8, 109-10D, 242-3
cross-site display 282-3D
as locally seen outcome 189, 191
Tegulet I school 25
worktable 326
as outcome 182, 187-9, 191, 193, 194
summary 234-5
School Management Committees (SMCs)
Bangladesh 125, 127, 129, 131, 135, 149, 216
Ethiopia 25, 99, 115-16
school organization, definition 353
school outcomes, *see* school impact
school-community relations xix, 261

school–district relations xix, 262-3
school-level changes xiii, 353-4
  Bangladesh 31-2, 123-5
school-level study (SSS) 7, 305-9
schooling demand 89, 352
secondary education, Colombia 44
self-evaluation, Colombia 62-3, 65, 272-3D
self-monitoring, Colombia 50
self-reliance, Ethiopia 117
senior secondary education, Ethiopia 69
Shapla school, Bangladesh 141, 288-303D
SIDA (Swedish International Development Agency) 91, 227
social studies, Ethiopia 22
SPC (school pedagogical centre), Ethiopia 77, 83, 100, 115, 118
  Tegulet I school 20, 22
special education, Ethiopia 69
staff, new 353
staff development xv, 72, 163, 213, 220, 249
starting conditions 184
strategic matching 81-2, 87D, 158, 163-4, 167-8, 348-9
student abilities/motivation 353
student impact xi, 196, 234, 242
  Bangladesh 130-1, 192, 194, 288-9D, 327
    Hasnahena school 38
    very good schools 140
  Colombia 61, 186, 187, 268-9D, 323
  Ethiopia 91, 101, 104, 107, 116
    cross-site display 280-1D
    as locally seen outcome 188, 191
    Tegulet I school 24-5
    worktable 325
  as outcome 182, 186, 187, 192, 194, 357
student knowledge, *see* student impact
student outcomes, *see* student impact
student-teacher relations, Colombia 63
success xiv, 8-9, 242-4, 247-53
  Bangladesh 34-7, 39, 213, 214-15

Colombia 57-64, 155-60, 205
Ethiopia 26-8, 161-7
factors 7, 34-7, 39
  Bangladesh 36, 146-7, 148, 213-18
  Colombia 200-6, 242-3
  Ethiopia 80-8, 162, 206-13, 229, 242-4
  see also community support; excellent schools; implementation success; local adaptation; resources received; supervision; very good schools
success experiences xiii, 239, 362
  Bangladesh 139, 145, 149, 215-16, 344
  cross-site display 294-5D, 300-1D
  Colombia 159, 204, 276-7D, 333
  Ethiopia 95, 112, 209, 211-13, 284-5D, 339
superior education, Colombia 44-5
supervision xiii, 228-9, 236, 245-6
  Bangladesh 140-1, 144, 168, 229, 258
    by AUEO 134
    and implementation success 147
    ineffectiveness 169
    success factor 213, 214-15, 217
    support 292-3D, 298-9D
    worktable 342
  Colombia 255, 274-5D, 331
    success factor 201, 204, 206
  Ethiopia 207, 337
    success factor 201, 204, 206, 207, 213, 214-15, 217
supervisor role 354
support 229
  capacity 352
  system, Ethiopia 166, 174
sustainability 102, 108, 132
system
  linkages 241
  management 162
  restructuring xv, 220, 249
system-level outcomes, *see* outcomes

teacher impact xi, 195, 196-7, 242, 357
  Bangladesh 131, 192, 194, 288-9D, 328

Hasnahena school 38
  Colombia 63, 186-7, 268-9D, 323
  Ethiopia 91, 101, 104-5, 107, 183,
    189, 191
    cross-site display 280-1D
    Tegulet I school 25
    worktable 183, 325
  findings on 229
  as outcome 182, 186-7, 189, 191,
    192, 194
  summary 234
teacher mastery xiii, xiv, xviii, 195,
    220, 248
  Bangladesh 195
  Colombia 186, 195, 204
  Ethiopia 26, 100, 103-4, 107, 195,
    211, 256
  findings 235, 252
  role of 238-9
  success factor 204, 211
  see also teacher-learning materials
teacher motivation, *see* teacher impact
teacher outcomes, *see* teacher impact
teacher role 174, 244
teacher training 195, 197
  Bangladesh 124, 149-50, 195, 228,
    259
  Colombia 57, 156, 186, 228, 254-5
  Ethiopia 77, 86, 115, 116, 117, 166
  in-service xiii, 5, 228
    Bangladesh 125, 127, 129
    Colombia 48, 52, 53-4, 55, 158,
      204, 255
    Ethiopia 91, 106, 110, 195, 206,
      228, 256
  see also cluster training; PRT
    (project-related training)
teacher-learning materials 157, 162,
    174, 226, 353
  availability 83, 87D, 157, 162, 195-6,
    350
  Bangladesh 124, 124
  Colombia 52-3, 157, 159, 174,
    272-3D
  delivery 167, 186, 215, 226, 264
  development and use 221-2, 250
  Ethiopia 23-4, 162, 257

  as linkage factor 159, 177
  role of 238-9
  as school-level factor xiii
  success determinant 242
  use and development xvi
teacher-learning methodology, Ethiopia
    71
teacher-learning process
  Bangladesh 33, 37, 38, 125, 148
  Colombia xi
  Ethiopia 19
teacher-pupil ratio, Ethiopia 84
teacher-student dynamics 18
teachers 258
  Bangladesh 37, 131, 140, 149
    quality 124, 124, 146-7
  Colombia 60-3, 186, 274-5D
  commitment 186, 229, 233, 242
  Ethiopia 21, 91-2, 114-15
  innovation 353
  motivation, *see* teacher impact
  see also females
teaching quality, Hasnahena school
    33
technical education, Ethiopia 69
Tegulet I, II, and III schools, Ethiopia
    18-29, *97*, *98*, *99*, 99, 101-5, *104*,
    110-18, *114*, 280-7D
textbook-pupil ratio, Ethiopia 106, 118
textbooks, free, Bangladesh xi, 36, 124,
    131-2, 135-6, 148, 258
training, *see* teacher training
tuition fees, Ethiopia 68
turbulence, *see* environmental
    turbulence
two-shift system, Ethiopia 112, 118

UEO (upazila education officer),
    Bangladesh 36, 37, 130, 169
  and success 213, 214-15, 217
Ulatchandal school, Bangladesh 141,
    288-303D
UNESCO 45-6, 50-1, 54, 227
unitary schools, Colombia 45-6, 50-2,
    54, 155

Universal Primary Education (UPE)
    project (Bangladesh) ix-x, 8,
        30-40, 120-51, 169-70
    change description 122-6, 123-6
    change story 126-7
    country context 120-2
    development 167
    Hasnahena school 30-40
    objectives 30-1
    priority for 167
    process dynamics 217-18, 219
    reform comparison 220-2
    success factors 213-18
        country-level 133-7, 167-70, *173*,
            174-5
'Universalization of Primary Education'
    Plan, Colombia 54, 56
upazila (sub-district) primary education
    committees, Bangladesh 122
USAID (US Agency for International
    Development) 52, 155
user commitment, findings on 233

user involvement 85-6, 88D, 157, 163
    as linkage factor 178-9, *179*

Verspoor study (1989) 3-5, 8, 102,
    223-4
    conclusions 224-5, 226, 227-8, 229,
        230, 232
very good schools
    Bangladesh 140, 141, 142, 143
    Colombia 57, 58
    Ethiopia *99*, 103-6, 208
vocational education, Ethiopia 69

wastage, Ethiopia 89, *90*
weak factors 163-4, 191-2
World Bank ix-x, 3, 12, 54, 56, 127, 227
    HSI selection criteria 8
WPE (Workers' Party of Ethiopia) 67,
    70